THEORIES OF
SEXUAL OFFENDING

WILEY SERIES IN
FORENSIC CLINICAL PSYCHOLOGY

Edited by

Clive R. Hollin
Clinical Division of Psychiatry, University of Leicester, UK
and

Mary McMurran
School of Psychology, Cardiff University, UK

COGNITIVE BEHAVIOURAL TREATMENT OF SEXUAL OFFENDERS
William L. Marshall, Dana Anderson and Yolanda M. Fernandez

VIOLENCE, CRIME AND MENTALLY DISORDERED OFFENDERS:
Concepts and Methods for Effective Treatment and Prevention
Sheilagh Hodgins and Rudiger Müller-Isberner (*Editors*)

OFFENDER REHABILITATION IN PRACTICE:
Implementing and Evaluating Effective Programs
Gary A. Bernfeld, David P. Farrington and Alan W. Leschied (*Editors*)

MOTIVATING OFFENDERS TO CHANGE:
A Guide to Enhancing Engagement in Therapy
Mary McMurran (*Editor*)

THE PSYCHOLOGY OF GROUP AGGRESSION
Arnold P. Goldstein

OFFENDER REHABILITATION AND TREATMENT:
Effective Programmes and Policies to Reduce Re-offending
James McGuire (*Editor*)

OFFENDERS WITH DEVELOPMENTAL DISABILITIES
William R. Lindsay, John L. Taylor and Peter Sturmey (*Editors*)

NEW PERSPECTIVES ON AGGRESSION REPLACEMENT TRAINING:
Practice, Research and Application
Arnold P. Goldstein, Rune Nensén, Bengt Daleflod and Mikael Kalt (*Editors*)

SOCIAL PROBLEM SOLVING AND OFFENDING:
Evidence, Evaluation and Evolution
Mary McMurran and James McGuire (*Editors*)

SEXUAL OFFENDER TREATMENT:
Controversial Issues
William L. Marshall, Yolanda M. Fernandez, Liam E. Marshall
and Geris A. Serran (*Editors*)

THEORIES OF SEXUAL OFFENDING
Tony Ward, Anthony Beech and Devon Polaschek

THEORIES OF SEXUAL OFFENDING

Tony Ward
School of Psychology, Victoria University of Wellington, Wellington, New Zealand

Devon L. L. Polaschek
School of Psychology, Victoria University of Wellington, Wellington, New Zealand

Anthony R. Beech
School of Psychology, University of Birmingham, Edgbaston, Birmingham, UK

John Wiley & Sons, Ltd

Other Wiley Editorial Offices

John Wiley & Sons Inc., 111 River Street, Hoboken, NJ 07030, USA

Jossey-Bass, 989 Market Street, San Francisco, CA 94103-1741, USA

Wiley–VCH Verlag GmbH, Boschstr. 12, D-69469 Weinheim, Germany

John Wiley & Sons Australia Ltd, 42 McDougall Street, Milton, Queensland 4064, Australia

John Wiley & Sons (Asia) Pte Ltd, 2 Clementi Loop #02-01, Jin Xing Distripark, Singapore 129809

John Wiley & Sons Canada Ltd, 22 Worcester Road, Etobicoke, Ontario, Canada M9W 1L1

Wiley also publishes its books in a variety of electronic formats. Some content that appears in print may not be
available in electronic books.

Library of Congress Cataloging-in-Publication Data

Ward, Tony.
Theories of sexual offending/by Tony Ward, Devon L. L. Polaschek, and Anthony R. Beech.
    p. cm.—(Wiley series in forensic clinical psychology)
  Includes bibliographical references and index.
  ISBN-13 978-0-471-49167-5 (cloth: alk. paper)–978-0-470-09481-5 (pbk. : alk.)
  ISBN-10 0-471-49167-5 (cloth: alk. paper)–0-470-09481-8 (pbk. : alk. paper)
  1. Sex offenders—Psychology. 2. Sex offenders—Mental health. 3. Sex offenders—Rehabilitation.
  I. Polaschek, Devon L. L.   II. Busch, Anthony R.   III. Title.   IV. Series.
  RC560.S47W37 2005
  616.85'83—dc22   2005010208

British Library Cataloguing in Publication Data

A catalogue record for this book is available from the British Library

ISBN-13   978-0-471-49167-5 (hbk) 978-0-470-09481-5 (pbk)
ISBN-10   0-471-49167-5 (hbk)   0-470-09481-8 (pbk)

Typeset in 10/12pt Palatino by Thomson Press (India) Limited, New Delhi

CONTENTS

ABOUT THE AUTHORS

Tony Ward, PhD, DipClinPsyc, is a clinical psychologist by training and has been working in the clinical and forensic field since 1987. He was formerly Director of the Kia Marama Sexual Offenders' Unit at Rolleston Prison in New Zealand, and has taught both clinical and forensic psychology at Victoria, Canterbury, and Melbourne Universities. He is currently the Director of Clinical Training at Victoria University of Wellington. Professor Ward's research interests fall into five main areas: rehabilitation models and issues; cognition and sex offenders; the problem behaviour process in offenders; the implications of naturalism for theory construction and clinical practice; and assessment and case formulation in clinical psychology. He has published over 110 research articles, chapters and books. These include *Remaking Relapse Prevention*, with D. R. Laws and S. M. Hudson (Sage, 2000) and the *Sourcebook of Treatment Programs for Sexual Offenders*, with W. L. Marshall, Y. A. Fernandez, and S. M. Hudson (Plenum, 1998). Email: Tony. Ward@vuw.ac.nz.

Devon Polaschek, PhD, DipClinPsyc, is a senior lecturer in criminal justice psychology at Victoria University of Wellington, New Zealand, and former Director of Clinical Training. Her research interests include (a) offence processes of rapists and violent offenders, (b) cognition in and cognitive-experimental research with violent and sexual offenders, and (c) offender rehabilitation theory and evaluation. She is also a research consultant to the Violence Prevention Unit at Rimutaka Prison, near Wellington. Email: Devon.Polaschek@vuw.ac.nz.

Anthony Beech, DPhil, BSc, is professor in criminological psychology in the School of Psychology at the University of Birmingham and a Fellow of the British Psychological Society. Over the last 10 years he has been the lead researcher of the STEP (Sex Offender Treatment Evaluation Project) team. Here he has been involved in treatment evaluation and the development of systems to look at treatment need and treatment change in sex offenders. This work is regarded as having a major influence on assessment and treatment in the UK. He has written widely on the topics of assessment and treatment of sexual offenders, and other related subjects. Email: a.r.beech@bham.ac.uk.

SERIES EDITORS' PREFACE

ABOUT THE SERIES

At the time of writing it is clear that we live in a time, certainly in the UK and other parts of Europe, if perhaps less so in other areas of the world, when there is renewed enthusiasm for constructive approaches to working with offenders to prevent crime. What do we mean by this statement and what basis do we have for making it?

First, by 'constructive approaches to working with offenders' we mean bringing the use of effective methods and techniques of behaviour change into work with offenders. Indeed, this view might pass as a definition of forensic clinical psychology. Thus, our focus is the application of theory and research in order to develop practice aimed at bringing about a change in the offender's functioning. The word *constructive* is important and can be set against approaches to behaviour change that seek to operate by destructive means. Such destructive approaches are typically based on the principles of deterrence and punishment, seeking to suppress the offender's actions through fear and intimidation. A constructive approach, on the other hand, seeks to bring about changes in an offender's functioning that will produce, say, enhanced possibilities of employment, greater levels of self-control, better family functioning, or increased awareness of the pain of victims.

A constructive approach faces the criticism of being a 'soft' response to the damage caused by offenders, neither inflicting pain and punishment nor delivering retribution. This point raises a serious question for those involved in working with offenders. Should advocates of constructive approaches oppose retribution as a goal of the criminal justice system as a process that is incompatible with treatment and rehabilitation? Alternatively, should constructive work with offenders take place within a system given to retribution? We believe that this issue merits serious debate.

However, to return to our starting point, history shows that criminal justice systems are littered with many attempts at constructive work with offenders, not all of which have been successful. In raising the spectre of success, the second part of our opening sentence now merits attention: that is, 'constructive approaches to working with offenders *to prevent crime*'. In order to achieve the goal of preventing crime, interventions must focus on the right targets for behaviour change. In addressing this crucial point, Andrews and Bonta (1994) have formulated the *need principle*:

> Many offenders, especially high-risk offenders, have a variety of needs. They need places to live and work and/or they need to stop taking drugs. Some have poor self-esteem, chronic headaches or cavities in their teeth. These are all 'needs'. The need principle draws our attention to the distinction between *criminogenic* and *noncriminogenic* needs. Criminogenic needs are a subset of an offender's risk level. They are dynamic attributes of an offender that, when changed, are associated with changes in the probability of recidivism. Non-criminogenic needs are also dynamic and changeable, but these changes are not necessarily associated with the probability of recidivism. (p. 176)

Thus, successful work with offenders can be judged in terms of bringing about change in noncriminogenic need *or* in terms of bringing about change in criminogenic need. While the former is important and, indeed, may be a necessary precursor to offence-focused work, it is changing criminogenic need that, we argue, should be the touchstone in working with offenders.

While, as noted above, the history of work with offenders is not replete with success, the research base developed since the early 1990s, particularly the meta-analyses (e.g. Lösel, 1995), now strongly supports the position that effective work with offenders to prevent further offending is possible. The parameters of such evidence-based practice have become well established and widely disseminated under the banner of 'What Works' (McGuire, 1995).

It is important to state that we are not advocating that there is only one approach to preventing crime. Clearly there are many approaches, with different theoretical underpinnings, that can be applied. Nonetheless, a tangible momentum has grown in the wake of the 'What Works' movement as academics, practitioners and policy makers seek to capitalise on the possibilities that this research raises for preventing crime. The task now facing many service agencies lies in turning the research into effective practice.

Our aim in developing this Series in Forensic Clinical Psychology is to produce texts that review research and draw on clinical expertise to advance effective work with offenders. We are both committed to the ideal of evidence-based practice and we will encourage contributors to the Series to follow this approach. Thus, the books published in the Series will not be practice manuals or 'cook-books': they will offer readers authoritative and critical information through which forensic clinical practice can develop. We are both enthusiastic about the contribution to effective practice that this Series can make and look forward to continuing to develop it in the years to come.

ABOUT THIS BOOK

In the current enthusiasm for offending behaviour programmes, much is made of the need for such programmes to be cognitive-behavioural in orientation. However, in reading the academic literature, across disciplines, it is evident that there is a distinct level of conceptual confusion about exactly what is meant by the term 'cognitive-behavioural'. For example, Kendall (2004) makes the comment 'Cognitive behaviouralism essentially regards offending behaviour to be a consequence of distorted or deficit thinking' (p. 73). This is a very selective view of a cognitive-behavioural perspective, which is, in fact, a complex theoretical position (Bandura, 1977, 1986). As one of us has commented previously, a cognitive-behavioural position 'Suggests that a person be seen as a complex interplay of biological, private, and motor behaviours. The term *private* refers to activities within the skin, such as cognition and emotion. A person does not exist in a vacuum. The functioning of the human system is related to previous events including, for example, biological insult, type of upbringing, level of education, and so forth. Current functioning is related to the available reinforcement and punishment in the environment. . . . Cognition is not afforded an autonomous, independent role as in some cognitive theories; rather it is viewed as an integral, if covert, aspect of human behaviour having a reciprocal relationship to overt behaviour' (Hollin, 1990, pp. 16–17). In other words, the application of a cognitive-behavioural perspective would typically see offending behaviour as a form of social behaviour, shaped and maintained by the social environment in which the person lives their life. Certainly, cognition would be a part of this understanding, but not afforded the primacy given by Kendall. Further, as cognitive-behavioural theory is a theory based in learning, those working with an understanding of this perspective see behaviour as a product of an interaction between the person and their environment rather than in pathological terms as suggested by words such as 'deficit'. Indeed, the invocation of pathology whenever a psychological theory is mentioned within the context of offending is simply not to understand that most psychological theories, including cognitive-behavioural, are concerned with normal, rather than abnormal, human behaviour (Hollin, 2002).

The reduction of complex theories, of any persuasion, to sound-bite proportions may make them easy to criticise in an academic piece and, indeed, this might all be brushed off as an irrelevancy or of minor importance in the busy world of practice. However, we would argue that a lack of theoretical understanding or sophistication is a highly undesirable state of affairs in engendering good practice. We take this position for several reasons. First, if practitioners are to use theory to inform their work, then a full appreciation of the basic premises of a theory, alongside its subtleties and nuances, is not only desirable but essential. A practitioner with limited comprehension of theory can have little or no depth to their understanding of the procedures they are undertaking with their clients. Second, a practitioner with no theoretical sophistication will be much more likely to adopt a 'cook-book' approach to practice, rather than a flexible approach that is based on a sophisticated, theoretically informed, formulation of the issues at hand. Third, theories shift and change over time as knowledge grows and, accordingly, trends in practice shift and change. A theoretically aware practitioner will be aware of such shifts in theory and see the logic in developing their practice. Fourth, as theory, research and practice are often bound together, practitioners with an appreciation of theory may well be likely both to use and to contribute to research.

In this book we see the principles regarding theory outlined above being brought sharply into focus and centred on the topic of sex offenders. The primacy of theory in informing both practice and research is implicit throughout this book; the critical role of theory in understanding sex offending is made absolutely explicit. Yet further, a strength of this book is to be seen in the rigour by which theories are tested and evaluated. The careful evaluation of theory is one important route that leads to effective practice. It is with the importance of theory uppermost in our thoughts that we are pleased to welcome this book to the Wiley Series.

Clive Hollin and Mary McMurran

REFERENCES

Andrews, D. A. & Bonta, J. (1994). *The psychology of criminal conduct*. Cincinnati, OH: Anderson.

Bandura, A. (1977). *Social learning theory*. Englewood Cliffs, NJ: Prentice Hall.

Bandura, A. (1986). *Social foundations of thought and action: A social-cognitive theory*. Englewood Cliffs, NJ: Prentice Hall.

Hollin, C. R. (1990). *Cognitive-behavioral interventions with young offenders*. Elmsford, NY: Pergamon Press.

Hollin, C. R. (2002). Criminological psychology. In M. Maguire, R. Morgan & R. Reiner (Eds), *The Oxford handbook of criminology* (3rd edn). Oxford: Oxford University Press.

Kendall, K. (2004). *Dangerous thinking: A critical history of correctional cognitive behaviouralism*. In G. Mair (Ed.), *What matters in probation*. Cullompton: Willan.

Lösel, F. (1995). Increasing consensus in the evaluation of offender rehabilitation? *Psychology, Crime, and Law*, 2, 19–39.

McGuire, J. (Ed.) (1995). *What works: reducing reoffending*. Chichester: John Wiley & Sons.

ACKNOWLEDGEMENTS

Tony Ward first signed a contract with Wiley UK for this book over six years ago. In the intervening years the project has been postponed a number of times and was even on the verge of abandonment a year or so ago. It was really only the encouragement and support of Professor Clive Hollin and Dr Mary McMurran, the series editors, and Vivien Ward, Wiley Psychology Editor, that has enabled us to persevere and to complete the book. We would like to thank them for their patience and belief in the value of the project.

Tony Ward would like to thank the following people for their intellectual companionship, support, practical help, and contribution to his thinking about theories and sexual offending over the last 20 years or so: Richard Laws, Bill Marshall, Claire Stewart, Steve Hudson, Brian Haig, Richard Siegert, Mayumi Purvis, Tom Keenan, Astrid Birgdin, Robin Jones, Mark Brown, Grant Devilly, Lynne Eccleston, Karl Hanson, David Thornton, Ruth Mann, Hilary Eldridge, Steve Webster, James Bickley, Dawn Fisher, Shadd Maruna, Devon Polaschek, Tony Beech, Marie Connolly, Fran Vertue, Joseph Lee, Chris Drake, Pamela Nathan, Patrick Tidmarsh, Garth Fletcher, Nicola Panapa, and Jo Thakker. He would particularly like to thank Mayumi Purvis for her major contribution to Chapter 11 while working as a research assistant. In this role, Mayumi reviewed and summarised the major feminist approaches to the explanation of child sexual abuse. Her wonderful eye for detail and thorough descriptions of the different perspectives proved to be invaluable in the writing of Chapter 11, thank you!

Devon Polaschek would like to thank the following friends and colleagues for supporting her, intentionally or otherwise, in developing the ideas that came to fruition in this book: Sue Calvert, Theresa Gannon, Steve Hudson, Lucy King, Jim Vess, Tony Ward, Carolyn Wilshire, and Nick Wilson.

Tony Beech is privileged to have the intellectual companionship of a number of those in the field of sexual offending research and treatment both in the UK and overseas. Apologies to those he has missed out, but the people that immediately spring to mind in terms of his thinking, in regard to this book, are (in the UK): of course the original STEP team: Dawn Fisher, Richard Beckett, Ann Scott Fordham, plus Bobbie Print, Roger Kennington, Tony Morrison, James Bickley, Don Grubin, Ruth Mann, Steve Webster, and Hilary Eldridge. Internationally he has been fortunate to benefit from both the intellectual companionship and encouragement of particularly Tony Ward, David Thornton, Richard Laws, Bill

Marshall, Karl Hanson, Jean Proulx, Ray Knight and many others associated with ATSA, thank you all.

He would also like to thank the following for the preparation of particular chapters of this book: Michael Sheath for his insightful observations of the clinical usefulness of the risk model presented in Chapter 13; Ian Mitchell for providing the detail about the neurobiology of attachment in Chapter 12; James Bickley for his work that has provided some of the material in Chapter 17 and many other aspects of this work; Ruth Mann for some of the ideas that appear in Chapter 19; his wife Dawn Fisher for many hours of proof-reading, spotting his many missing words and typos, plus providing useful insights in the area, and having to put up with him and his many hours hunched over a word processor, and Helen Brown for sorting out the references.

The authors would like to thank the following people and publishers for permission to reprint and include material from a number of sources: Sage Publications for Figure 5.1, Aetiological pathways emerging from a base of vulnerability, reprinted from M. Connolly (2004) Developmental trajectories and sexual offending, *Qualitative Social Work*, 3, 39–59; Elsevier for Figure 13.1, An aetiological model of risk, reprinted from A. R. Beech and T. Ward (2004) The integration of etiology and risk in sexual offenders: a theoretical framework, *Aggression and Violent Behavior*, 10, 31–63; and Taylor & Francis for Figure 15.4, Descriptive model of rape, reprinted from D. Polaschek and S. Hudson (2004), Pathways to rape: preliminary examination of patterns in the offence processes of rapists and their rehabilitation implications, *Journal of Sexual Aggression*, 10, 7–20.

A final expression of gratitude goes to Dr Theresa (Tag) Gannon. Tag read through the whole book, line by line, making numerous excellent suggestions for improving the writing style and clarifying the lines of argument. We are forever in her debt. Thank you Tag!

PART I
INTRODUCTION

Chapter 1

THEORY CONSTRUCTION, DEVELOPMENT AND EVALUATION

Why would a man want to sexually molest a prepubescent child? Does such behaviour reflect entrenched sexual preferences for children or rather a misguided attempt to seek intimacy? Does the predisposition to seek sex with children reside in psychological characteristics found in only a small number of males or are all men capable of such abusive actions? Why would a man in a stable intimate adult relationship want to have a sexual relationship with a teenage girl? It is hard to see how his needs would effectively be met in such an unequal relationship, and yet it does happen. How is it possible for someone to become sexually aroused to a child who is neither physically mature nor sexually motivated? In this case, the cues that normally elicit sexual arousal in adults are missing and yet some men do report feeling extremely aroused by prepubescent children. Finally, how is it possible for a male to force sex upon a woman when she is clearly unwilling and distressed or when she is drunk, unconscious, asleep or otherwise unable to respond? And importantly, how do such individuals reconcile the woman's obvious distress with the view that she was a willing partner?

The answers to these questions have significant practical implications for clinicians and policy makers. Understanding why child molestation or rape occurs, and how it develops and changes over time, is of the utmost importance in helping us reduce the frequency of this serious social problem. The assessment of sexual offenders is designed to detect those characteristics that have predisposed them to engage in sexually abusive actions, and to this end, therapists invest time and resources into the development of sound psychometric instruments and valid assessment procedures. Thus, we rely on obtaining a clear description of the clinical phenomena associated with an offender's actions, for example, problems with managing and controlling negative emotional states, the presence of thoughts and attitudes that legitimise or excuse sexual abuse, and difficulties establishing and maintaining close intimate relationships with other adults.

Identifying clinical phenomena associated with an individual's offence gives valuable insight into the specific causes or aetiological factors that lie behind his abusive behaviour, and helps in the design of intervention programmes to stop him from reoffending. Treatment programmes for sexual offenders are typically based on theoretical assumptions concerning the psychological, biological and socio-cultural mechanisms (i.e. causes) that result in child molestation and rape. There are always clinical theories underlying the selection of the modules contained in treatment manuals. For example, the inclusion of relapse prevention strategies in most state-of-the-art intervention programmes for sexual offenders follows from the belief that relapse is a sequential process influenced by different cognitive, affective and contextual factors (Marshall, 1999). In addition, attempts to equip individuals with enhanced intimacy skills is based on the assumption that their acquisition will lead to improved relationships with adults, therefore reducing the desire to seek sexual contact with children (Marshall, 1999).

The above comments point to the necessity of engaging in aetiological thinking when treating sexual offenders, or at the very least, endorsing the causal assumptions built into treatment manuals used by therapists. There is no way of avoiding dependence on theory and therefore it is desirable to be explicit about the aetiological assumptions underpinning our practice. Formulation-based approaches assume that in order to treat sexual offenders effectively, therapists need to develop a comprehensive understanding of their psychological vulnerabilities and problems (Ward, Vertue & Haig, 1999). The result of this process is a conceptual model representing the client's various problems, the hypothesised underlying causes and their interrelationships. In essence, this clinical theory specifies how the symptoms or problems are generated by psychological mechanisms, for example, dysfunctional core beliefs or behavioural deficits. This process requires us to be theoretically literate.

In order to benefit fully from reading this book, it is necessary to acquire at least a basic understanding of certain ideas in the philosophy of science. Therefore in the remainder of the chapter we will discuss the following concepts: scientific realism, the nature and levels of theory, scientific models, what constitutes an explanation, the role of methodology in science, the process of theory knitting, and criteria for theory evaluation.

THE NATURE OF SCIENCE

There are a number of influential philosophies of science, each with its own perspective on the nature of explanation, theories, models, causality, laws of nature and the concept of truth (Newton-Smith, 2002). These include empiricism, instrumentalism, logical positivism, realism, conventionalism, and numerous variations of these views of science. In this book, we adopt a critical realist view of science. That is, we believe that our best theories converge on the way the world really is and that this knowledge provides a fundamental knowledge base for the construction and implementation of technology, and therefore our efforts to intervene and control the world. According to Psillos (1999) scientific realism has three core theses: metaphysical (a claim about the nature of reality), semantic (the relationship between scientific terms and the world) and epistemological (the kind of knowledge obtained).

According to the metaphysical thesis, the world has a distinct and mind-independent structure. This means human beings do not literally create their own realities and therefore should endeavour to construct and test theories that help them to elucidate the structure of the world. The world exists independently of individuals' wants, wishes, beliefs and attitudes, and therefore the successful implementation of a cherished life plan or personal project requires them to know how it works, at least to some degree. This understanding of the natural and social aspects of life enables human beings to seek and achieve things that are important to them and to reduce or avoid harmful conditions and events. In the case of sexual offending, this means developing an understanding of the psychological, biological, social and cultural processes and structures that result in sexual abuse.

The semantic thesis of scientific realism states that successful theories accurately describe this world and refer to *real* entities and processes. From this perspective, it is a mistake to view theoretical claims about attachment style, cognitive distortions or self-regulatory style as simply convenient fictions that enable us to work with offenders. According to scientific realism such terms genuinely refer to aspects of offenders' psychological make-up; they point to vulnerability factors and social conditions that result in abuse.

The epistemological thesis states that theories that are well developed and predictively successful are likely to be (approximately) true and as such give us knowledge of reality. The notion of approximate truth means we are able to claim that not only do theories refer to aspects of the world, but that the processes and structures posited by successful theories really do exist. To extend the example outlined above, if attachment explanations of sexual offenders' intimacy problems are well supported by the evidence, then we can be confident that such individuals do in fact have insecure attachment styles and distorted internal working models of relationships (Marshall, Anderson & Fernandez, 1999a). The notion of approximate truth is important because it reminds us that while theories may give a partial picture of certain aspects of life, they still need to be fleshed out and refined in some respects.

The version of realism we take in this book is a modest one, and we accept that even our best theories may only be partially true (Kitcher, 2001). In addition, it is possible that for any given scientific problem there could be more than one way of solving it. Any solution to a scientific problem will always reflect human values and interests (see below), and given that these can legitimately vary, different groups often favour different answers.

Of course, it could be argued that the different solutions to scientific problems collectively constitute the global or overall solution. In other words, there is really only one solution. While this may be strictly true, it fails to capture what happens during scientific progress due to differences in values and interests. Individuals frequently focus on different aspects of a problem and therefore their explanatory efforts are concentrated on that particular aspect, with other ways of approaching and researching the problem being deemed to be of little or no interest. For example, evolutionary psychologists and criminologists may both want to solve the problem of crime and develop good aetiological theories that explain why human beings consistently hurt each other and break the law. Evolutionary psychologists set out to discover the distal selection pressures bearing on this issue and to identify the particular adaptations that enabled human beings to counter threats to themselves and their kin. The next explanatory step is to consider what proximal psychological mechanisms generate violent behaviour in contemporary humans and to trace their development through the human life cycle. The critical point is that biological considerations will constrain any acceptable theoretical work and focus attention on a subset of possible mechanisms and processes. In contrast, criminologists may not accept that human beings have an inherited human nature at all and seek to explain violent behaviour in terms of macro-level structures and processes such as gender construction, unemployment and socialisation. What constitutes a good theory will be viewed quite differently and it is possible, perhaps even inevitable, that criminologists and evolutionary psychologists will think their opponents have got hold of the wrong end of the stick, and regard each others' explanatory efforts as at best irrelevant and at worst, dangerously confused.

According to scientific realism, we know the world in terms of our theories. Human beings construct representations of the mechanisms and structures that lie beneath the surface of life and create phenomena. In turn, we act upon the basis of these representations and change the world in accordance with our interests and needs (Kitcher, 2001). Therefore, knowledge leads to the construction of the institutions and physical and psychological conditions governing individuals' lives. The fact that our interests constrain what counts as (valuable) knowledge, means that human values (as evident in needs and interests) guide the application of scientific knowledge and methods to the everyday world. If these representations are accurate, our interests will be promoted and needs met, but failure to get it right can result in devastation and misery. There is truth in the claim that we construct our world, but only in the sense that scientific knowledge underpins actions that modify the world, the consequences of which may prove to be beneficial or harmful.

So, scientists attempt to detect and then to explain the occurrence of phenomena by developing scientific theories. These explanations describe the causal mechanisms and processes causing phenomena, enabling predictions to be made concerning their future occurrence. The valuable thing about scientific knowledge is that it can lead directly to the development of technologies that enable individuals to intervene in the world and achieve important goals. For example, understanding how infections develop and impact on the body has resulted in the invention of powerful drugs, better sanitation and hygiene practices, and ultimately, improved physical health.

Scientific theories of human behaviour set out to achieve two fundamental goals: explanation and prediction (Siegert, McPherson & Dean, in press). A theory explains phenomena, why they exist, and why they possess certain properties. An explanation is basically the application of a theory in order to help understand certain phenomena. It tells a causal story concerning why and how specific events happen and why people behave the way they do. For example, the intimacy deficit model claims that child molesters seek children as intimate partners because they are unable to meet their emotional needs with adults (Finkelhor, 1984). Explanation is *backward* looking; it helps us understand why a particular outcome happened. By way of contrast, prediction is *forward* looking and is concerned with the precise forecasting of outcomes within a system (Siegert et al., in press). For example, a researcher might predict that an offender with a dismissive attachment style is more likely than individuals with other attachment styles to behave aggressively toward his victim.

THE NATURE OF THEORY AND SCIENTIFIC METHOD

It is now time to consider in more depth just what a theory is and its relationship to scientific laws and models. In a nutshell, a theory is any description of an unobserved aspect of the world and may consist of a collection of interrelated laws or a systematic set of ideas (Kukla, 2001). Laws are true universal propositions referring to all time and space, that express causal or necessary relationships among properties. They are discovered by science. An example of a scientific law is 'All pieces of copper expand when heated'. An example of a possible law in forensic psychology is 'All child molesters have sexual preferences for children'. This is not in fact a law because it is only true for a certain subset of child molesters (Marshall et al., 1999a). It should perhaps be qualified in some way and rephrased as a probable law that only applies to those child molesters with certain characteristics (as yet to be determined!) Theoretical terms refer to entities and processes that are unobservable (e.g. intelligence, character traits) while observation terms denote processes that can be directly observed (e.g. test scores, behaviour).

The terms 'models' and 'theories' are often used interchangeably; however, it is useful to distinguish them from one another. One major use of the term 'model' refers to the utilisation of scientific metaphors or analogies in the development of scientific theory. In this sense an analogy is derived from a source and applied to a target domain. The assumption is that there is some degree of similarity of structure between the model and its referent. A good example of a model is the depiction of the heart as a pump. In this model it is assumed that certain relationships between the components of a pump and its overall functioning also hold for the heart. Just as the major function of a pump is to compress and push air into some object so the heart functions to push blood around the body. Other examples of scientific models based on analogies include the atom being compared to a solar system, the mind being likened to a computer (mind as software and brain as hardware; the hydraulic model of mind), and seeing children as lay scientists (Gopnik, 1996). Models function to help simplify and focus research and if successful may be fleshed out into a mature scientific theory. For example, the claim that the heart is a pump enabled researchers to develop comprehensive theories of the circulation system and also to acquire knowledge about functional and dysfunctional physical systems, leading to the development of effective medical treatments. Models can be conceptual or physical (e.g. Watson and Crick's physical model of DNA: Newton-Smith, 2002).

It is useful to see science from a methodological perspective rather than simply in terms of specific theories and knowledge (Hooker, 1987). Method provides scientists with a *plan of inquiry*, which can guide the search for empirical phenomena, and the subsequent construction of satisfactory explanatory theories. The normative force of methodology (the fact that it prescribes how researchers should proceed) depends partially on the fact that it recommends methods that have worked in the past, that is, that have led to successful problem solving. Typically, science proceeds as follows: constrained by a developing problem and relevant background facts, certain phenomena come to the researcher's attention and are ordered by detecting patterns in the phenomena. Once ordered, these phenomena are explained by abductively inferring the existence of an underlying mechanism. Here, abductive inference involves reasoning from a presumed effect (the phenomenon) to its explanation in terms of an underlying cause. From an initial judgement of the plausibility of such a hypothesis attempts are made to elaborate on the nature of that mechanism, frequently by way of constructing plausible models. The developing theory is evaluated on a number of dimensions including empirical adequacy, explanatory depth and simplicity, and is modified as necessary. Research problems function to guide the clear description of puzzling phenomena and theory formation (Ward et al., 1999).

THEORY APPRAISAL

Typically, more than one theory is able to account for the evidence (i.e. under-determination) and therefore empirical adequacy alone does not provide a sufficient basis for deciding between competing theories or even deciding whether or not it is worth persevering with one model. Because of this, proper theory appraisal has to be undertaken on evaluative dimensions in addition to that of empirical adequacy. It must be noted that the kind of under-determination we are referring to is transient in nature and is usually resolvable over time (Kitcher, 2001). That is, as two theories are compared critically, a clear winner typically emerges from the testing and evaluation process. A further point is that it sometimes makes sense to develop theories that initially lack empirical adequacy because they are particularly promising in some other respect, for example, because they refer to deep underlying mechanisms (*explanatory depth*) or open up new avenues of enquiry (*fertility*).

Because of the issue of under-determination, philosophers have suggested that epistemic values (i.e. theory appraisal criteria) such as explanatory depth and fertility are equally important for making judgements about which theories are best and for helping researchers choose among competing theoretical explanations (Hooker, 1987; Newton-Smith, 2002). Epistemic values arguably track truth in some respect. In other words, the set of epistemic values in question point to a theory's likely truth. The key idea is that theories exhibiting such epistemic values have proved over time to be deeper and more satisfactory explanations: that is, they seem to be giving us a more accurate picture of the world and its workings. Because of this fact, scientists are prepared to argue that the theory in question is more likely to be true. It is important to note that the majority of the specific values proposed are conceptual. The following list captures the epistemic values commonly accepted to be good indicators of a theory's truth (Hooker, 1987; Newton-Smith, 2002). We will now outline the major theory appraisal criteria:

- *Predictive accuracy, empirical adequacy* and *scope* concern whether the theory can account for existing findings and the range of phenomena requiring explanation. An example of an empirically adequate psychological theory, with predictive accuracy and scope, is Bowlby's attachment theory (Ainsworth, 1989). It has been the focus of a considerable amount of empirical research and many of its predictions concerning the relationship between insecure attachment, self-esteem, coping style and socio-emotional intelligence have been supported.
- *Internal coherence* refers to whether a theory contain contradictions or logical gaps. An example of a psychological theory with severe problems of coherence is Freud's theory of infantile sexuality (Davison, Neale & Kring, 2003). A major issue here is the degree to which the theory is testable and whether it covers all possible empirical consequences. That is, critics have argued that it cannot be supported or falsified.
- *External consistency* is concerned with whether the theory in question is consistent with other background theories that are currently accepted. An example of a psychological theory with good external consistency is Pennington's cognitive neuroscience theory of psychopathology (Pennington, 2002). A notable feature of this theory is its consistency with findings and theories from neuroscience, neuropsychology, behavioural genetics and descriptive psychopathology.
- *Unifying power* relates to whether existing theory is drawn together in an innovative way and whether the theory can account for phenomena from related domains; does it unify aspects of a domain of research that were previously viewed as separate? A good example of a theory exhibiting this value is again Pennington's. In his naturalistic theory of psychopathology, he argues that a good explanation will need to explicitly build in genetic, developmental, neuroscience, neuropsychological, phenomenological and environmental factors.
- *Fertility or heuristic* value refers to a theory's ability to lead to new predictions and open up new avenues of inquiry. In a clinical setting this may also include a theory's capacity to lead to new and effective interventions (for a good example, see Marshall and Barbaree, Chapter 3).
- *Simplicity*, as the name suggests, refers to a theory that makes the fewest special assumptions. An example of a relatively elegant psychological theory is Skinner's radical behaviourism (Skinner, 1976). This theory sets out to explain virtually all aspects of human functioning from language development to instances of psychopathology using very basic behavioural processes.
- *Explanatory* depth refers to the theory's ability to describe deep underlying mechanisms and processes. An example of a theory exhibiting explanatory depth in cognitive science is connectionism (Marcus, 2003). Connectionism

provides a computational account of human psychological capacities in terms of simple, interacting units. It also allows for a reduction of complex mental processes to neural networks.

The use of multiple values in evaluating theories, however, does create some problems for researchers and clinicians. First, it means that theory appraisal is a complex process involving tradeoffs between the different values outlined above. Such tradeoffs between epistemic values occur because there is no algorithm for infallibly choosing the strongest theory; human judgement is inevitably required in making such determinations. In addition, different criteria may be preferred depending on the context of a research project, and the presence or absence of strong competitors. In the early stages of a theory's life it may make sense to favour its heuristic value and downplay its relatively poor showing on the more empirical criteria such as empirical scope and predictive accuracy. Of course, this partly depends on what the competing theories are like, or even if there are competitors. Sometimes, there may be only one promising theory in a given domain. Second, thinking through the different strengths and weaknesses of a theory takes quite a bit of cognitive labour and is a demanding process. This is probably why in most mature sciences there is a cognitive division of labour between theoreticians and experimental scientists. Theoreticians formulate, develop and evaluate theories while experimentalists test them, a time consuming task requiring high levels of technical and practical skill.

An important point when evaluating any theory is to keep in mind that theory appraisal is always a comparative process. Theories are usefully construed as cognitive tools that provide clinicians and researchers with maps to navigate their way through the complexities of clinical practice. Considering theories from a pragmatic perspective means that it may be the case that two different theories have quite different strengths and offer something unique in both research and clinical arenas. In this situation, it would be prudent to use both in their respective domains of application while remaining on the lookout for a more comprehensive theory that combines the virtues of each of these less satisfactory alternatives. For example, Finkelhor's precondition theory is marred by a lack of internal coherence and scope but is clinically very useful in helping offenders to grasp the dynamic nature of the offence process (fertility or heuristic value; see Chapter 2). The important thing to keep in mind is that because theories are tools, each may have a narrow domain of application and perform quite a restricted job. It is necessary to be aware of the function and scope of different theories in order to capitalise fully on their strengths and avoid falling victim to any weaknesses.

In summary, the evaluation of a theory or model involves the explicit consideration of a number of different epistemic values (Hooker, 1987; Newton-Smith, 2002). The ability of a theory to account for research findings and to survive hypothesis testing is certainly a necessary requirement for scientific acceptance. Of equal or even greater importance is its ability to extend the scope of existing perspectives and to integrate competing or diverse approaches to the study of the relevant phenomena. In addition, logical consistency, simplicity and heuristic worth represent important epistemic values against which a theory can be evaluated. Ambiguity, inconsistency, vagueness and undue complexity may restrict the overall value of a theory and should be noted whenever they are evident. Theory evaluation is a comparative process and the fact that a theory contains gaps or logical inconsistencies does not mean that it should necessarily be abandoned or rejected. Its value depends on how it compares with its competitors, and its overall explanatory capacity (Hooker, 1987). Overall, the basis for a belief in the success of science in accounting for the world and the truth of the above realist approach to theory construction and evaluation resides in realism's track record. This record provides the best explanation for the explanatory and predictive power of science and, relatedly, the utility of technologies based on these realist theories. When talking about the clinical domain, technologies are the assessment and therapeutic strategies derived from aetiological theories.

THEORY CONSTRUCTION AND DEVELOPMENT IN SEX OFFENDING

We will now illustrate briefly how the process of theory construction, development and appraisal functions in the sexual offending domain by using the example of intimacy deficits. This will help to highlight the role of theories in the sexual offending area and to clarify what constitutes good theoretical work.

In the 1980s researchers noted (see Chapter 12) that sexual offenders appeared to have difficulties relating effectively to adults, often resulting in loneliness and unhappiness (Marshall, 1989, 1999). A first suggestion was that the cause of these social and emotional problems resided in a lack of social skills. Therefore the solution was to give sexual offenders social skills training (Overholser & Beck, 1986). However, subsequent research failed to find convincing evidence of social skills deficits (failure of prediction), casting doubt on the adequacy of the social skills deficit hypothesis. Marshall (1989) proposed that one way of accounting for the relationship problems noted in sexual offenders was to adopt an attachment perspective. He argued that sexual offenders' childhood rejection and abuse resulted in the acquisition of an insecure attachment style and feelings of emotional loneliness, hostile attitudes, and a lack of intimacy and some social skills. This innovative theory encouraged clinicians to focus on self-esteem and intimacy problems and to develop a suite of new interventions to address these problems.

The attachment theory was an advance on the social skill deficit hypothesis and offered considerable heuristic value, greater explanatory depth, external consistency (with theory from developmental psychology), and greater unifying power (integrated evolutionary, cognitive and behavioural views of interpersonal problems). However there did seem to be some predictive failures and problems accounting for the range of intimacy issues noted in sexual offenders. A critical clinical observation was that some offenders did not appear to be particularly lonely or to report feeling insecure. This issue was not easily dealt with by Marshall's initial attachment theory. In response to this and other problems, Ward and his colleagues (Ward, Hudson, Marshall & Siegert, 1995b) reformulated the theory and proposed that different types of insecure attachment were associated with quite distinct clinical problems and offence styles. Subsequent empirical work has supported aspects of this theory and thrown doubt on others (e.g. Smallbone & Dadds, 1998). Further refinements in theory and research design by Smallbone and others have led to a rich body of research findings, and more tailored treatment strategies (Smallbone, 2005).

The point of this example is that a critical conceptual analysis of Marshall's original theory helped to identify its strengths and weakness and led to the construction of better theory, research, and arguably more precisely targeted treatment. By focusing explicitly on the strengths and weaknesses of this attachment perspective it was possible to draw upon the deeper resources of attachment theory and reformulate it in a way that improved its scope and explanatory depth.

We have argued above that theoretical discussion and critique are necessary steps in the development of effective treatment of sexual offenders. A significant question is what kind of theory are we referring to?

LEVELS OF THEORY

Typically, in the few book chapters actually devoted to discussion of sexual offending theories, theories tend to be classified according to the types of source theories utilised in their construction, for example, cognitive, learning, systems, psychodynamic or biological theories (see Lanyon, 1991; Schwartz, 1995). In our view this is not the most promising way of categorising theories and results in the conflation of level of generality (or focus) with type of psychological systems (e.g. behavioural, cognitive, biological) and theoretical tradition (e.g. psychodynamic versus behavioural). Additionally, theories of the same type (e.g. learning theories) may vary greatly in terms of their breadth and degree of detail. For example, a learning theory framework could be used to explain one type of problem (e.g. deviant sexual arousal) or to provide a comprehensive explanation of all aspects of sexual offending (e.g. Marshall & Barbaree, 1990).

A meta-theoretical framework for classifying theories based on their level of generality of focus, and also upon the extent to which the relevant factors are anchored in both developmental, or contemporary, experiences and processes has been provided by Ward and Hudson (1998a). In this framework, they distinguished between level I (multifactorial), level II (single factor) and level III (micro-level or offence process) theories. Level I theories represent comprehensive or multifactorial accounts of sexual offending (e.g. Marshall & Barbaree, 1990). The aim is to take into account the core features of sexual offenders and to provide a complete account of what causes these phenomena and how they manifest in sexually abusive actions. Level II, or middle level theories, have been proposed to explain single factors thought to be particularly important in the generation of sexual crimes: for example, the presence of empathy deficits (Marshall, Hudson, Jones & Fernandez, 1995). In this approach the various structures and processes constituting the variable of interest are clearly described, and their relationship with each other specified. In a sense, level II theories expand on the factors identified in level I theories. Level III theories are descriptive models of the offence chain or relapse process (e.g. Pithers, 1990; Ward, Louden, Hudson & Marshall, 1995d). These micro-models typically specify the cognitive, behavioural, motivational and social factors associated with the commission of a sexual offence over time; they constitute temporal or dynamic theories. The levels of theory model is meant to help researchers distinguish between different types of theory and ultimately to facilitate their integration through a process of theory knitting (see below). It should be noted that the levels of theory framework is only intended to function as a heuristic for locating theories according to their primary explanatory focus. Therefore, the distinctions between the different levels of theory is not intended to be overly rigid and some theories may in fact fall somewhere in between the three levels (see Chapters 14 and 15 on relapse prevention and offence chain models). Furthermore, the ultimate aim for theorists is to construct a global theory that integrates theories from the different levels into a unified explanation of sexual offending (Ward & Hudson, 1998a).

In addition to the distinction between levels of theory, Ward and Hudson also emphasised the importance of taking into account the distal–proximal distinction. Distal factors constitute vulnerability factors that emerge from both developmental experiences (e.g. sexual abuse) and genetic inheritance (e.g. anxious temperament). These *trait* factors make a person vulnerable to offending sexually once precipitating factors are present: for example, relationship conflict. Although vulnerability factors have their origins in a person's developmental history, they are always causally implicated in the onset of sexually abusive behaviour. For example, deficits in emotional regulation skills may have been acquired during a man's childhood but actively contribute to the onset of sexual offending several years later.

Proximal factors are triggering processes or events, and interact with the vulnerability factors to cause sexual offending. These factors fall naturally into two distinct groups: psychological *state* factors and situational events. The state variables are the manifestation of individuals' underlying vulnerabilities and are activated by situational events such as interpersonal conflict. For example, emotional coping deficits are likely to produce powerful negative affective states following an argument with a partner or a stressful social event such as losing a job. Both the negative emotional state and the loss of employment are proximal causes that, in conjunction with a person's longstanding difficulties in coping with emotions, directly result in a sexual offence. In this situation, sexual activity is used as a means to reduce or modulate powerful emotions and as such, represents an inappropriate coping response.

In our view, the levels of theory model provides a useful way of arranging theories by their domain of application and focus. This is likely to be of help in promoting a greater degree of collaborative research and theory development in the area. Essentially, our view is that by carefully specifying the level of a theory and its explanatory focus it will be possible to engage in more fruitful critical analysis and comparisons between competing theories. There is not much point in deciding which of two (or more) theories is better if they belong to different levels; it is a bit like comparing apples and oranges. Additionally, mapping theories across the three levels of the model enables researchers to notice possible areas of convergence and ultimately results in more unified and deeper explanatory theories. For example, it may become apparent that theories of empathy deficits and cognitive distortions can be unified by a single theory of mind approach (see Chapters 8 and 9). This process of theoretical integration is called theory knitting (Kalmar & Sternberg, 1988).

THEORY KNITTING

A theory knitting strategy stipulates that researchers should seek to integrate the best existing ideas in a given domain within a new framework (Ward & Hudson, 1998a). This strategy involves identifying the common and unique features of the relevant theories, so that it is clear what constitutes a novel contribution and what does not. The major virtue of this approach is that good ideas do not get lost in a continual procession of 'novel' theories that appear briefly in the literature and then disappear forever, often for no good reason.

Kalmar and Sternberg (1988) contrast this perspective with the traditional segregative approach to the process of theory development in psychology. According to the segregative perspective, different theories are set up in competition and compared for their ability to predict data satisfactorily. Rather than attempting to combine and develop the best elements of each theory, this approach tends to compare individual theories and view them as mutually exclusive and self-sufficient. A major disadvantage of this perspective is that it can trap theorists into seeing things only from the point of view of their preferred theory. It can also lead to researchers focusing unknowingly on different aspects of the same phenomenon. The failure to ask 'What can I usefully take from this theory or model?' frequently leads to the premature dismissal of other points of view and a kind of insular arrogance among researchers, each convinced their theory is superior to all others.

An example of the theory knitting process being applied to the sexual offending domain is the way in which the Pithers and Marques model of the offence chain (Pithers, 1990) has been integrated into the self-regulation model developed by Ward and Hudson (Ward & Hudson, 1998a). According to the original Pithers and Marques (Pithers, 1990) model, offenders lacking effective coping skills fail to manage a variety of internal and external risk factors. This failure results in a lapse, catastrophic thinking (an abstinence violation effect) and subsequent reoffending (a relapse). Ward and Hudson recognised that the relapse pathway identified in this model was applicable to some offenders and provided a useful treatment framework for these individuals (see Chapters 14 and 15 for more detail on this theory). However, their own empirical research and conceptual analysis of the traditional model led to the conclusion that there were in fact at least four quite distinct relapse pathways, each associated with different treatment needs and issues. They also used self-regulation theory to reformulate traditional relapse prevention concepts such as the abstinence violation effect and seemingly irrelevant decisions. Using two major types of treatment-related goals (approach and avoidant), in conjunction with three distinct types of self-regulatory style (under-regulation, mis-regulation and intact regulation), they developed a four-pathway model that was able to cover the majority of offence and relapse patterns evident in sexual offenders. The content validity of the Ward and Hudson theory has been established subsequently by several groups of researchers (e.g. Bickley and Beech, 2002). The availability of a more complex model meant that treatment was able to be tailored to offenders' specific needs as opposed to adopting a 'one size fits all' approach (see Chapters 14 and 15). Ward and Hudson knitted together the best aspects of the Pithers and Marques approach with some new ideas from self-regulation theory and their own research findings to construct a more comprehensive relapse prevention treatment model.

STRUCTURE OF THE BOOK

Theories are indispensable resources for clinical work with sexual offenders. They provide a framework for assessment by noting the difficulties offenders are likely to experience, outlining how such problems are interrelated, and specifying their psychological, social, biological and cultural causes. In other words, case formulation (the end product of assessment) is crucially dependent on the existence of sound aetiological theories. A good case formulation for a sexual offender should outline the developmental factors that made him vulnerable to committing a sexual offence. The relevant developmental variables may include inconsistent parenting, being a victim of sexual abuse, experimenting sexually at an early age, or compulsively masturbating as an adolescent. These learning events could lead to the formation of dysfunctional psychological mechanisms that later play a role in sexual offending. For example, inconsistent caring might lead to insecure attachment and resulting loneliness or difficulties in adult relationships. For another individual, a lack of capacity to modulate negative emotions or an inability to utilise social supports in times of emotional distress could be a partial cause of subsequent sexual abuse. Strong negative mood states might result in a loss of control, which, in conjunction with sexual desire, lead an individual opportunistically to use a child to meet his sexual needs. From a clinical perspective, the presence of different deficits or vulnerability factors requires the application of distinct therapeutic strategies, or at least, the placement of different priorities on existing treatment approaches. For example, some individuals may need to acquire relatively greater levels of relationship skills to address attachment difficulties while others would benefit from learning how to manage their moods more effectively.

   In this book we use the levels of theory framework developed by Ward and Hudson to structure the discussion of sexual offending theories. Our aim is to present the key ideas underpinning each theory as clearly as possible, and to examine their merits from both a research and a clinical point of view. We are particularly concerned with focusing on the clinical utility of the theories, believing that most have a positive contribution to make to assessment and treatment.

   In Part II we critically evaluate the major multifactorial theories of child molestation and rape. These theories have been selected because of their current popularity or potential to illuminate important aspects of sexually abusive behaviour. The emphasis in Part III is on single-factor theories employed to explain the characteristics most associated with sexual offending: empathy deficits, cognitive distortions, deviant sexual arousal, impaired social functioning, cultural factors supporting abuse and risk factors. For each topic, the two or three most influential theories will be described, evaluated and their clinical implications drawn out. In Part IV, descriptive models of the offence and relapse process are discussed and in Part V, a number of treatment theories are critically scrutinised. The last section is an interesting innovation in a theory book, included becase we wanted to examine explicitly a number of recent treatment frameworks that are currently the focus of intense discussion.

The epistemic values or theory appraisal criteria outlined above will be used to guide each theory evaluation. In order to make our discussion as user friendly as possible we will not systematically consider every value for every theory. That would prove to be rather cumbersome and time consuming. Rather we will focus on the most salient strengths and weaknesses of each approach. At the end of each chapter an overall summary of the merits and utility of the theories examined will be presented, helping the reader to appreciate the overall picture for each topic and perspective. Our focus will be on male perpetrators and primarily on the sexual crimes of rape and child sexual abuse.

It should be apparent by now that we view theory as an indispensable tool for clinicians as well as researchers. In our opinion, theory formation and appraisal has been somewhat neglected by workers in the field, with most current interest centring on risk assessment, classification and treatment efficacy. These are worthy and important topics but all are dependent on underlying aetiological and treatment theories. It is time to expose the aetiological assumptions residing deep within current practices and to shed some critical light on the way we think about sexual offending, and by implication, provide more compelling justifications for intervention.

PART II

LEVEL I THEORIES
(MULTIFACTORIAL THEORIES)

Chapter 2
FINKELHOR'S PRECONDITION MODEL

Finkelhor's precondition model (Finkelhor, 1984) is one of the most popular and widely cited theories of child sexual abuse (Morrison, Erooga & Beckett, 1994). At the time of its proposal, it represented a landmark achievement because it was the first multifactorial explanation developed to account for child sexual abuse. Its influence is felt in a wide variety of professional groups, including probation officers, social workers, psychologists, sexual offender therapists and correctional officers (Fisher, 1994). A particularly attractive feature of this theory is its simplicity and systematic way of linking aetiological factors to aspects of the offence process. Because of its simplicity, offenders can easily grasp its basic ideas and so it is often used in treatment programmes to explain the rationale and nature of treatment.

In this chapter, we examine this popular multifactorial level I theory and evaluate its strengths and weaknesses. It is important to point out that the criteria and material we are drawing on to appraise the theory are contemporary and were not available to Finkelhor at the time he formulated it. This may seem a little unfair in that we are judging the adequacy of a relatively old theory according to contemporary standards and evidence. However, it must be kept in mind that Finkelhor's theory is currently thriving and is used by countless practitioners in the course of their day to day practice. Therefore the assumption of those using it must be that it provides a good explanation of child sexual abuse by today's standards. On a related note, because the theory is still used by clinicians to formulate cases and to guide treatment, we speak of it in the present tense. To refer to it in the past tense may mislead readers into thinking it is purely of historical interest: nothing could be further from the truth.

In our view, Finkelhor has constructed a theory, not a model (see Chapter 1), although he does seem to use the terms interchangeably. To avoid confusion, we will use the term 'precondition model' when referring to this theory by name and the term 'theory' when speaking in a more general sense about it.

FINKELHOR'S FOUR PRECONDITIONS MODEL

Finkelhor (1984) was probably the first to make the observation that child molestation is a complex phenomenon and is caused by a number of different factors. These include the psychological needs and motives of the offender, situational and contextual variables, parenting practices, and social attitudes toward children and sex. This list of possible causes is certainly comprehensive and reminds clinicians and researchers that an adequate theory should be wide ranging. According to Finkelhor a good theory needs to be able to accommodate the heterogeneity of child molesters and to provide therapists with the theoretical resources to develop treatment plans based on an individual's particular problems. A feature of Finkelhor's approach to the topic is his insistence that any theory worth its salt should be able to explain why the offence is a *sexual* one. The danger is that simply providing a catalogue of the underlying psychological needs and problems offenders exhibit fails to explain why they committed sexual offences as opposed to another kind of criminal activity. Furthermore, in the absence of such an account, it is puzzling why motives such as desires for intimacy or power are not expressed in socially more acceptable ways, such as pursuing an occupation that involves caring for children. A major task for researchers according to Finkelhor is to elucidate the link between psychological needs and sexual offending in a convincing way.

Finkelhor proposes that different types of child molesters may be motivated by different needs and therefore display distinct patterns of offending and psychological characteristics. His point is that a good theory has clear implications for the classification of child molesters and should provide a justification for any such system. He also assumes that individual psychopathology is only likely to take us so far in explaining sexually abusive behaviour. Most child molesters do not have a major mental illness or demonstrate a severe degree of psychological maladjustment. In many respects, they resemble normally functioning men. An account of why certain individuals do have sex with children should spread the aetiological net a little more widely and include socialisation patterns and cultural norms and values. This will incorporate such phenomena as the sexualisation of children in advertisements and films, and the way young males are socialised to view sex on demand as their natural right (Marshall & Barbaree, 1990).

The upshot is that for Finkelhor, a satisfactory theory of child sexual abuse should be able to explain why some individuals are sexually aroused by children, why children are chosen as preferred sexual partners, and why despite the fact that sexual relationships with children are socially reviled and severely punished, certain individuals still go ahead and act on their impulses. The answers to these questions are likely to explain why individuals who experience disappointment in their intimate relationships with adults choose to establish sexual relationships with children rather than nonsexual ones.

One of the unique things about Finkelhor's model is the way he explicitly sets out to build previous aetiological work into his own theory. Closely examining the existing sexual abuse literature, he concludes that four underlying factors have consistently been involved to account for sexually abusive behaviour. These factors have typically been used as solo explanations (i.e. single factor or level II theories) and as such have proved to be quite limited in their ability to describe the generation of child molestation. These factors are: (i) sex with children is emotionally satisfying to the offender (emotional congruence); (ii) men who offend are sexually aroused by a child (sexual arousal); (iii) men have sex with children because they are unable (blockage) to meet their sexual needs in more socially appropriate ways; and, finally, (iv) men become disinhibited and carry out acts outside of their usual behavioural repertoire (disinhibition). He proposes that the function of the first three factors is to explain why certain individuals acquire deviant sexual interests in children and the fourth attempts to account for the translation of such interests into sexually abusive actions. According to Finkelhor, the four factors may interact in a number of distinct ways. They may: (i) function together to cause child molestation; (ii) work antagonistically by frustrating or blocking each other; or (iii) synergistically interact to increase the potency of specific factors. The factors are viewed as groups as each may contain slightly different mechanisms or clusters of causes.

The essential thrust of Finkelhor's argument is that the factors can be grouped into four preconditions that must be satisfied before the sexual abuse of a child occurs. What this means is that each factor occurs in a temporal (i.e. unfolds over time) sequence with the first creating the necessary conditions for the second, the second for the third and so on. All are necessary and rely on the preceding ones to create the conditions required for their appearance. The preconditions are as follows: motivation to abuse a child sexually, overcoming of internal inhibitions, overcoming of external inhibitions, and dealing with a child's possible resistance to the abuse. Three of the four factors mentioned earlier belong in the first precondition, that is, they constitute different motives for committing a sexual offence against children. They are emotional congruence, sexual arousal to children, and blockage. According to Finkelhor, the final factor, disinhibition, belongs in precondition 2, and as such functions to overcome internal inhibitions. The remaining two preconditions, overcoming external inhibitions and the victim's resistance, spell out how the abuse occurs over time and therefore are usefully viewed as phases in the offence process. They represent the situational and external conditions supporting the abuse and give the theory an important contextual and social dimension. As stated above, these preconditions are hypothesised to occur in a temporal sequence and each is necessary for the next to occur. A interesting feature of the theory is that it can also function as a typology. In other words, Finkelhor proposes that offenders can be allocated into discrete groups depending on their primary motive (i.e. emotional congruence, blockage, or sexual arousal), each group having distinct treatment related needs. We will now describe each precondition in turn.

Precondition 1: Motivation to Sexually Abuse

Finkelhor proposes that the sexual abuse of children is associated with three distinct motives, each with its own unique psychological features and history: emotional congruence, sexual arousal and blockage. *Emotional congruence* is concerned with the way the emotional needs of the offender are met by a child. The notion of congruence suggests that there is a reasonable fit or match between what certain individuals need and what children can provide. Clearly, *congruence* implies some degree of psychological vulnerability that contributes to the man's expectation that children are more likely to respond optimally to his needs for closeness, safety or some other such need. For example, a need to feel powerful and in control of a close relationship could cause difficulties with adult partners, who are likely to require respect for their autonomy and rights as individuals. Children are conditioned to expect adults to be in charge of interpersonal encounters and are frequently eager to gain their approval. Finkelhor also hypothesises that some individuals may psychologically identify with young children due to their distorted emotional development. The critical dynamic in this situation would be a desire to feel safe and on an emotionally equal footing with children. Adults are seen as dangerous and likely to harm the individual concerned through rejection or possibly physically abusive actions.

As stated above, Finkelhor incorporates social and cultural factors as well as psychological motives into his theory. He suggests that males are socialized to behave in a dominant and powerful manner in sexual relationships and can come to regard children as legitimate sexual partners. The relevant characteristics of children are the fact they are smaller, younger and physically weaker. This may attract males who rely on these features as cues indicating the availability of a suitable sexual partner. The emotional congruence in this situation lies in the match between such men's strong preferences for younger and vulnerable individuals and the fact that children tend to exhibit these qualities more often that adult men or women. A critical issue concerns why some offenders possess these strong preferences; presumably the answer lies in some combination of genetic factors and learning histories (see Chapter 10).

The second motive is that of deviant *sexual arousal* to children. Finkelhor speculates that such distorted sexual responses may have been caused by a variety of maladaptive early learning experiences. These include being exposed at a young age to sexual activities involving children, perhaps in the form of pornography, or the sexual abuse of other children by an older person. Another possibility concerns the occurrence of particularly intense and rewarding sexual encounters with another child. Such situations can condition or forge connections between sex and children, experiences so powerful that for some individuals they become a primary source of excitement and pleasure from then on. A final example of adverse early learning is that of the offender's own sexual abuse as a child. Finkelhor is not explicit about the impact this may have on the developing child, but obvious consequences include the acquisition of conditioned sexual responses to stimuli associated with children. The difference between the above two types of experiences resides in the *type* of learning event: a sexual encounter with another child versus being sexually abused by an adult. A further possibility, not really explored by Finkelhor, is the reliance on sexual activities to control or modulate negative emotional states, which Marshall calls *sexual coping* (Marshall, Anderson & Fernandez, 1999a). In this situation, adolescents use sexual activities such as masturbation to reduce feelings of anxiety, depression or anger. Reliance on sex as a means of coping can, in conjunction with the availability of victim and other circumstances, result in a sexual offence.

Whatever the developmental cause, the suggestion is that some individuals acquire entrenched sexual interests. What this means is that as a consequence of powerful learning experiences, sexual contact with a child becomes an established way of meeting sexual and emotional needs. Finkelhor points out that early sexual experiences of abuse on their own are unlikely to result in the formation of sexual preferences for children. Instead, he speculates that such experiences must have been especially meaningful or strong for them to have long-term effects. He also considers the possibility that biological factors such as abnormal hormonal levels may increase sexual desire in certain individuals, lowering their threshold for engaging in sexually illicit activities such as child molestation. Consistent with his attention to social and cultural variables, Finkelhor hypothesises that the availability of child pornography in many western countries, associated with the tendency for males to sexualise emotional needs, may also result in deviant sexual arousal to children.

We now turn to Finkelhor's final motivating factor, *blockage*. The key idea here seems to be that normally functioning men who experience stressful or unusual situations are unable to met their sexual and emotional needs in adaptive ways. A major consequence of this disruption in functioning is that children can become surrogate partners or sexual outlets. An important question concerns the nature of this disruption: whether it is temporary or persistent. In order to accommodate both possibilities, a distinction is drawn between developmental blockages (e.g. fear of intimacy) and situational blockages (e.g. marital problems). These factors may work in combination or independently. This classification seems to cross the distinction between internal and external conditions and it is possible that some internal forms of blockage are quite transitory and that some situations are enduring.

According to Finkelhor, blockage may result from a number of causes. In detailing these possible causes, he draws upon rather diverse psychological paradigms such as learning theory (e.g. inadequate social skills), psychodynamic approaches (e.g. fear of adult females, castration anxiety) and family systems perspectives (e.g. marital problems). Finkelhor sets out to be as inclusive as possible in his search for plausible causal mechanisms and even includes some socio-cultural variables thought to contribute to the phenomenon of blockage. An example is restrictive sexual norms concerning the nature of sexuality and its legitimate expression. It is hypothesised that restrictive sexual norms may leave some men feeling guilty about having sex with adults, and as a consequence of this guilt, avoid adult sexual relationships. The subsequent lack of intimacy and sexual experience might result in individuals failing to acquire the skills necessary to establish and maintain intimate sexual relationships, and if they do seek them, make it more likely that they will experience rejection. Avoidance of this type is unlikely to extinguish sexual need and might simply lead the individual concerned to seek sex with children: by comparison, a relatively guilt free and less socially demanding activity.

Finkelhor proposes that the three types of motives or causes described above can interact to produce the genesis of a sexual offence or can operate quite independently.

Precondition 2: Overcoming Internal Inhibitors

The simple fact of being motivated to have sex with a child is unlikely on its own to cause an individual to abuse a child sexually. The translation of this desire into a sexually abusive act requires a further step: the overcoming of a person's internal inhibitions against engaging in sexual acts with children. Clearly, the critical questions to be answered by any satisfactory theory are why do some men overcome their internal inhibitions, what are the processes involved, and how do they operate? Finkelhor lists a number of possible factors that may diminish a man's capacity to control the desire to have sex with a child. The internal, psychological factors include alcohol intoxication, impulse disorder, senility, psychosis, failure of the incest inhibition mechanism (e.g. with a stepdaughter the father may have not lived with the child since birth and therefore the normal inhibitions against sex with children might not be in place), and the presence of severe stress (e.g. loss of a job, death of a relative). According to Finkelhor, this set of proximal causes effectively disengages a person's self-regulatory mechanisms and makes it hard for him to resist the desire and subsequent urge to behave in a sexually abusive manner. In addition to these internal causes, he states that there are a number of relevant external factors such as socially entrenched attitudes supporting patriarchal rights for fathers and a social tolerance of sexual interest in children. These may also function to undermine individuals' attempts to control their inclination to offend sexually. In a sense, these attitudes and beliefs function as cognitive distortions and cause men to interpret potential sexual situations with children in self-serving ways. Furthermore, the availability of child pornography on the Internet and the inability of males to identify the needs of children are additional social mechanisms contributing to this failure of control. Some of these disinhibiting factors are temporary in nature (e.g. alcohol ingestion) and some are more enduring (e.g. distorted beliefs).

Precondition 3: Overcoming External Inhibitors

So far, according to the precondition model, individuals have acquired a motive (or motives) to have sex with a child and overcome their internal inhibitions against doing so. The next step in the offence process is the surmounting of external constraints or obstacles in order to create the opportunity to abuse a child sexually. This process may or may not involve systematic planning and the careful grooming of a victim and his or her family. Some sexual offenders may insinuate themselves into a family and cultivate a relationship with the parents. The goal is to encourage the parents to trust them and therefore facilitate easier access to the child for sexual abuse opportunities. Additionally, the possibility for an offence may occur quite unexpectedly, for example, encountering a child who is on his or her own. In these situations, there is no need to intervene intentionally to groom a child or ingratiate himself into a family. According to the precondition model, there are a number of conditions that make it easier for an offender to circumvent the supervision of parents and generally to overcome the external barriers that protect a child from sexual abuse. These include: an absent or ill mother, or a mother who is emotionally distant, poor supervision of a child, a socially isolated family and atypical sleeping arrangements (e.g. children sleeping with a father). Relevant social factors include a lack of social supports for mothers, erosion of family networks, a belief in family sanctity and reluctance to intervene to protect children, and finally sexual inequality and discrimination.

Precondition 4: Overcoming the Resistance of the Child

Once an individual is motivated to commit an offence, and has successfully overcome both internal and external constraints (inhibitors), the next step needed is to overcome any resistance from the child. An offender may employ a number of strategies at this point in order to gain and maintain sexual access to a child. These range from giving gifts, desensitising children to sex by introducing them to sexual stimuli and ideas (e.g. pornography) in a gradual way, encouraging emotional dependence, and using threats or violence to force a child to have sex. Emotionally insecure children, or those who do not understand the nature of sexual abuse, are particularly vulnerable to sexual exploitation. In addition, social situations where a child is taught to obey or trust particular individuals (e.g. a priest) may facilitate abusive situations (see Sullivan & Beech, in press). Other social facilitators of sexual abuse include lack of good sex education programmes for children and society's view of children as powerless.

Finkelhor is clear that child molesters are a mixed group who commit offences for different reasons. He traces their sexual preferences for male or female victims back to the nature of early conditioning experiences, which entrench a proclivity for particular types of victims. Furthermore, he draws upon the dimensions of strength and exclusivity of sexual interest in children to account for individual differences in motivation and degree of preoccupation. These additional constructs enable him to refine his theory considerably. For example, according to the precondition theory, some men may have strong sexual interests in adults as well as children (i.e. such interests are not exclusive), while others may be exclusively interested in sexual relationships with children but possess a weak sex drive.

EVALUATION OF THE PRECONDITION MODEL

The precondition model is an interesting mixture of a level I and level III theory. On the one hand, the explicit recognition that sexual abuse involves multiple aetiological factors (in various combinations) does point to it being a comprehensive or level I aetiological theory. On the other hand, the explicit emphasis on the temporal process of offending, and the critical role of preconditions 3 and 4, are indicators of an offence process model. It also attempts to account for the variety of child molesters, and the fact that different individuals exhibit diverse offending goals and styles.

We will now make a few comments about the precondition model. Our aim is to highlight only the most striking strengths and weaknesses rather than present a systematic and detailed evaluation (for this see Ward & Hudson, 2001). We will start with some general points and then move onto some specific issues.

The precondition model displays a number of theoretical virtues. First, it provides a useful framework for the comprehensive assessment of child molesters and clearly describes problems evident in these individuals (*empirical scope*). Second, it outlines simply how offenders' thoughts, feelings and behaviour interact to create a desire to commit an offence (*simplicity*). Third, it provides a justification for tailored treatment and is persuasive in its recommendation that individuals may require different types of treatment strategies (*heuristic value*).

General Problems

However, alongside these undoubted strengths it does contain some serious problems relating to its lack of internal coherence, explanatory depth and unifying power. We will now discuss these issues.

Finkelhor developed his theory at a time when theoretical work on sexual offending tended to be fairly partisan and reflect distinct theoretical allegiances (e.g. behavioural and psychodynamic theory). What is impressive about the precondition model is that it sets out to be more wide ranging in terms of its theoretical constituents and explicitly incorporates a range of psychological theories from markedly different traditions (e.g. psychoanalytic, attributional and learning theories; Howells, 1994). While this theory building strategy ideally results in a flexible and comprehensive explanation, there is a real danger of being left with a set of conflicting and mutually exclusive ideas. Unfortunately, the precondition model does display this problem; in other words, it lacks *internal coherence*. To speak of castration anxiety alongside skill deficits and classical conditioning engages very different theories and competing causal mechanisms that threaten both the internal coherence and meaningfulness of the theory.

Another general problem is that Finkelhor makes the very mistake he is so (justifiably) critical of in other theories of sexual offending. He agrees that an adequate theory should explain why a person with certain psychological and social characteristics commits a sexual offence rather than engaging in other types of behaviour. However, according to the precondition model each of the three motivational factors (i.e. blockage, emotional congruence and sexual arousal) can operate independently or in tandem to produce sexually abusive behaviour. On the one hand this seems quite sensible; after all, some men appear to have a variety of problems and motives for having sex with a child while others may only have one clear goal (e.g. sexual satisfaction). But on the other hand, if these motives can function independently to cause sexual crimes, then it is far from clear why emotional congruence and blockage result in a *sexual* offence. Why doesn't the individual involved simply seek to spend time with children as a coach, teacher or in some other such child-centred activity? Clearly, the precondition model fails to provide an account of why, in certain circumstances, nonsexual needs are expressed in a sexual rather than a nonsexual manner. This problem suggests that the theory lacks sufficient *empirical scope* and *unifying power*; it is incomplete as an explanation and does not convincingly integrate these ideas.

A final general criticism concerns the model's lack of detail on the developmental origins of the causes of sexual offending. It is unclear how the primary motives emerge and develop over time, and most importantly, why they converge at a particular point in time to cause a sexual offence. The precondition model is very good at linking motives to the different phases of offending, but is relatively silent on the trajectory leading from early developmental experiences to the onset of sexually abusive actions. This points to a lack of *explanatory depth*.

Specific Problems

When constructing a theory, it is important to ensure that terms used to refer to the core phenomena and their underlying mechanisms are clearly defined and do not overlap to any significant degree. Failure to keep terms distinct in meaning can threaten the *internal coherence* of the theory and run the risk of undermining its overall *explanatory depth*. Unfortunately, there appears to be some overlap in meaning in the Finkelhor model between the constructs of developmental blockage and emotional congruence. Both of these ideas play a key role in precondition 1 and refer to factors that motivate men to sexually abuse children. They both refer to developmental conflicts and vulnerabilities that leave some adults ill equipped to deal with the demands of adult relationships. These difficulties are hypothesised to lead such men to seek emotional comfort and sexual gratification with children. In a nutshell, they lack the necessary skills to achieve high levels of intimacy with adults. For example, poor attachment experiences as a child may cause an individual to avoid taking risks in relationships with his peers for fear of rejection, and result in a long-term pattern of unsatisfactory relationships. Children are perceived as trustworthy and less likely to hurt or punish the person concerned. In other words, there is a significant degree of emotional congruence between the characteristics of children and the psychological needs of an offender (Ward, Hudson & Marshall, 1996). In a similar vein, developmental blockage (hence the use of the term 'developmental') is thought to have its origin in early experiences with attachment figures such as the mother and leave an individual experiencing anxiety with potential female partners. For example, according to Finkelhor, castration anxiety may mean that an adult male feels extremely uncomfortable with women and views children as more accepting and less threatening. This is surely a wonderful depiction of emotional congruence! Finkelhor also proposes that social skill deficits in sexual offenders might occur as a result of developmental blockage and make it hard to have a satisfactory relationship with another adult.

Hopefully, the brief description of these two ideas makes it clear that it is difficult to understand exactly how they make separate contributions in the Finkelhor theory. If developmental blockage and emotional congruence both have their origins in early experiences, and both can result in a lack of intimacy skills and failed relationships, then why are both needed? They just do not seem to be different ideas. Perhaps it would be best to restrict the notion of blockage for situations where stressors cause an offender to revert to maladaptive coping strategies and make sex with children more probable. The difficulty with this perfectly sensible possibility is that it would make it unclear why situational stresses constitute motives to offend sexually rather than simply triggers. That is, situational blockage simply collapses into one type of disinhibiting factor, and the difference between situational blockage and factors that contribute to disinhibition disappears. In our view, the best solution is to absorb the developmental strand of the blockage motive into emotional congruence and to delete the construct of blockage completely. The situational form of the construct could then be placed into precondition 2 and facilitate the overcoming of internal inhibitions, when they exist.

A second point is that the whole idea of overcoming internal inhibitions is only applicable to a small subset of child molesters. In our work on the relapse and offence process in sexual offenders we have presented data that suggests that once a desire to have sex with a child is present many offenders do not experience any conflict or attempt to inhibit this desire (Hudson, Ward & McCormack, 1999; Ward & Hudson, 2000a). An important mediator between desires and a successful outcome is the degree to which an offender can control his feelings and desires, and formulate plans designed to satisfy them. The ability to set goals, construct a plan, put a plan into action and, finally, evaluate its effectiveness, are all components of self-regulation (Carver & Scheier, 1981). Three types of dysfunctional self-regulation have been identified in the literature (Baumeister & Heatherton, 1996; Carver & Scheier, 1990). First, individuals can fail to control their behaviour or emotions, and subsequently behave in a *disinhibited* manner. Second, despite possessing generally effective self-regulation skills individuals may use ineffective strategies to achieve their goals, resulting in a loss of control in a specific situation: a *mis-regulation* pattern. In the third type of self-regulatory failure, the major problem resides in the *choice of goals* rather than a breakdown in the components of self-regulation.

For the individual with intact self-regulation skills and the desire to establish a sexual relationship with a child, there is no need to overcome internal resistance; the individual desires to have sex with a child and formulates a plan of action to make this possible. Thus, there is intact self-regulation but inappropriate, harmful goals. The notion of disinhibition does not apply to such individuals; they do not lose control and do not use sex to escape from or reduce powerful negative mood states. The inability of Finkelhor's precondition model to accommodate different self-regulatory styles reflects a lack of *empirical adequacy* and *scope*, *unifying power*, *explanatory depth* and *fertility*: particularly relating to a lack of guidance for assessment and treatment practice.

A third, related point is that the precondition model does not have sufficient conceptual resources to deal with the fact that child molesters frequently exhibit different clusters of offence-related problems, each associated with a distinct set of causes (Bickley & Beech, 2002; Marshall, 1999; see also Chapter 5). Each of these trajectories is characterised by the use of distinct strategies to create sexual access to a child and to overcome his or her resistance (Hudson et al., 1999). For example, offenders motivated by emotional congruence should be more likely to attempt to establish 'loving' relationships with children because of their need to feel at ease and safe in intimate relationships. These abuse situations are unlikely to involve high levels of physical violence. Alternatively, offenders whose motivation is purely sexual in nature might view children simply as sexual objects to be exploited whenever the opportunity arises. The offender's tendency to focus exclusively on meeting his own needs and to view the child as a means to this end could result in physical violence. The precondition model seeks to explain these different profiles of problems and issues simply in terms of contrasting motives. However, what is really needed is an account of how motives, beliefs, strategies and goals interact with contextual cues such as the presence of a child and with broader cultural factors, in order to cause a sexual offence. What we are saying is that the theory fails to do justice to the heterogeneity of offenders' psychological and behavioural features, and therefore, does not provide a sufficient basis for assessment and treatment planning.

The failings of the theory noted above indicate it lacks *heuristic value* or *fertility*, *explanatory depth*, *unifying power*, *internal coherence*, and some degree of *empirical adequacy* and *scope*.

CLINICAL UTILITY OF THE PRECONDITION MODEL

We have discussed the precondition model in some detail and made some positive and critical remarks about its status as a theory of child sexual abuse. Now we turn to examine how this theory could be used in clinical settings.

The Finkelhor theory has many failings as an aetiological theory of child sexual abuse, some of which have been highlighted in this chapter. It does not provide a comprehensive explanation of child molestation and so cannot be used reliably on its own to guide assessment and treatment. A danger of using it as an explanatory theory is that important aspects of individuals' offending will be missed, resulting in poor clinical decisions. Assessment and treatment is always underpinned by aetiological assumptions, and if the theories we rely on when undertaking these tasks are flawed, then the quality of our practice will suffer accordingly. For example, the fact that some offenders do not need to overcome their internal inhibitions indicates that they are likely to have pre-existing offence-supportive beliefs, and be proficient at both securing victims and overcoming any resistance on the part of the child or family. That is, they exhibit high degrees of offence-related *expertise*. Such expertise may well be reflected in their ability to set goals, plan, execute plans, control their emotions and to learn from experience. There is not much point in attempting to give sexual offenders like this self-control skills; what is required are alternative core values, beliefs and goals. Furthermore, an adequate risk assessment of a sexual offender should take into account his specific array of risk factors; clearly these risk elements are directly related to the particular causes associated with his offending. What is needed to provide clinicians with the resources to achieve the tasks outlined above is a comprehensive and rich theory. In our opinion, the use of Finkelhor's precondition model in this role is likely to result in unacceptably high costs. Because of its lack of scope, its exclusive use would result in ineffective treatment because some offender criminogenic needs would go unrecognised.

The precondition model is, however, useful in helping individuals understand that their offending involves a number of distinct phases that collectively lead them to abuse a child sexually. Because of this, we suggest it should only be used as a level III practice model to educate offenders rather than providing a basis for therapy planning. The utilisation of the theory in this way enables offenders to reflect on their specific offence pattern and to comprehend the role of cognitions, emotions, sexual desire, personal circumstances and developmental histories in creating offence-related vulnerabilities. By becoming aware of each stage in the offence process, the individual can identify his specific risk factors or warning signs, and therefore learn how to manage them effectively in the future, giving him a simple and useful rationale for treatment.

In our experience, most offenders are defensive about what they have done and reluctant to talk about it in any detail. A consequence of this refusal to reflect on the circumstances and issues preceding and maintaining their sexually abusive actions is that they often fail to appreciate that their offending emerges from a unique combination of social and psychological factors. That is, it occurs in a patterned way and does not simply arise 'out of the blue'. It can be clinically useful to provide individuals with a framework that helps them to think about their behaviour in a systematic and dynamic way. The Finkelhor model fulfils that role admirably.

Furthermore, clearly identifying the fact that sexual offending has a number of distinct causes conveys the idea that not all offenders are the same and that treatment will vary from person to person depending on the specific set of problems. The explicit message that there are different causes for child sexual abuse also helps individuals to be more tolerant when they encounter group members who differ from them in some way. Another advantage is that by allowing individuals to understand why they did what they did, it takes the mystery (and anxiety to some extent) out of the treatment process. It also encourages offenders to regard themselves as individuals who have committed a sexual offence and not as 'sex offenders', who are unchangeable. In this respect, it strikes an optimistic note and offers some hope of change for the individuals concerned.

CONCLUSIONS

Finkelhor's preconditions model was one of the first comprehensive theories of child sexual abuse and in our view is an impressive accomplishment. Not only did it provide the first systematic framework for understanding why men sexually abuse children, but it also led to the formation of clear treatment goals and a number of clinical innovations. For example, from the perspective of the precondition model, it made sense for researchers to target deviant sexual arousal in some men and not others, and to construct individually tailored intervention plans. Finkelhor was an early pioneer of the 'one size does not fit all' approach to offender treatment, a lesson, alas, lost until relatively recently (see Chapters 14, 18 and 19). He also helped to legitimise research into emotional regulation skills (sexual coping), intimacy issues, socio-cultural factors and the offence process (Marshall et al., 1999a). All of these areas are now the foci of intensive research activities, new treatment techniques and assessment methods (Bickley & Beech, 2002; Cortoni & Marshall, 2001; Marshall et al., 1999a; Smallbone, 2005). The problems noted in this chapter highlight the need for reformulation in the light of current theory and empirical research. In a sense, its primary value resides in helping sensitise offenders to certain aspects of therapy (Fisher, 1994). Problems such as its lack of scope, conceptual vagueness and incoherence, and lack of unifying power mean that it no longer stands as an adequate explanatory theory.

Chapter 3

MARSHALL AND BARBAREE'S INTEGRATED THEORY

In this chapter we critically examine an extremely influential and conceptually rich, multifactorial theory of sexual offending: Marshall and Barbaree's integrated theory (1990). The integrated theory was developed as a *general* theory of sexual offending and has been used to explain the development, onset and maintenance of child sexual abuse, rape and other types of sexual deviance (Marshall & Barbaree, 1990; Marshall & Marshall, 2000). In view of the focus of the integrated theory on sexual offending in general, we will refer to examples of both rape and child sexual abuse when outlining and evaluating it. To our knowledge, the adequacy of its basic ideas has never been independently evaluated, although it has been primarily responsible for generating research on such topics as attachment, self-esteem, sexual coping and situational determinants of offending. In addition, the development of therapeutic strategies for enhancing intimacy is due partially to the fact that the integrated theory provided important insights into the development of these offence-related vulnerabilities (Marshall, Anderson and Fernandez, 1999a).

THE INTEGRATED THEORY

The integrated theory is somewhat of an exception among the theories examined in this book. It is a dynamic evolving entity and has been subject to several evaluations and subsequent developments by Marshall and his colleagues. Alongside this conceptual work, Marshall has overseen research into specific strands of the theory, which has yielded data that have subsequently been used in the elaboration of its core concepts. In the preparation of this chapter, we concentrated on three primary sources: the chapter in which the theory was first outlined (Marshall & Barbaree, 1990), an authored book, which updated the attachment aspect of the original theory (Marshall et al., 1999a) and a recent journal article in which the origins of offenders' vulnerability factors was clarified

(Marshall & Marshall, 2000). In our view, the earlier version is the most comprehensive statement of the theory, although we will use the later formulations to supplement this version when we deem it necessary. For simplicity throughout this book, when referring to this theory, we will simply refer to it as the Marshall and Barbaree integrated theory.

According to the integrated theory, a critical developmental task for adolescent males is to learn to discriminate between aggressive and sexual impulses, and to acquire the ability to control aggressive tendencies during sexual experiences. This task is made much more difficult if individuals are insecurely attached, and as a consequence of this fact, have low self-esteem, a poor coping style and inadequate interpersonal skills. The basic idea is that the presence of such vulnerability factors, in conjunction with an influx of male hormones in puberty, increases the chances of a young man behaving in a sexually aggressive manner. From the perspective of the integrated theory, early development is of critical importance in creating offence-related vulnerabilities, although transient situational variables play an important role in triggering sexual crimes. Men are hypothesised to vary in terms of their vulnerability to commit a sexual offence, with some displaying a marked predisposition to engage in sexual crimes and others a significant degree of resilience against offending. Resilience is thought to consist of characteristics (abilities, skills, attitudes, preferences, values and beliefs) that enable individuals to resist the impulse to offend sexually. Marshall and Barbaree propose that sexual crimes such as rape and child molestation are the result of multiple, interacting factors that converge at a particular point in time, in a given context, to result in offending. In the integrated theory, the salient causal factors are developmental experiences, biological processes (e.g. influx of male hormones at puberty), cultural norms and attitudes about sex and gender roles, and the psychological vulnerabilities resulting from these causes.

The Development of Vulnerability

Marshall and Barbaree suggest that early developmental experiences are especially significant in the formation of psychological predispositions to behave in sexually deviant ways. They argue that it is during early childhood that males acquire the basic interpersonal skills necessary to facilitate the transition from childhood to adult relationships. If a child is neglected or abused then he is unlikely to develop trust in others and will typically view himself as an individual who is unworthy of love and respect from others. In short, he will become insecurely attached to his caregivers and experience real difficulties relating to other people. In addition, insecure attachment is often associated with poor emotional coping and a sense of personal ineffectiveness and lack of autonomy. The consequences of insecure attachment are enduring problems with emotional regulation, low self-esteem, impaired problem solving, poor judgement, impulsivity and low self-efficacy.

Thus, Marshall and Barbaree propose that adverse early experiences result in children believing that their parents and other significant people in their lives are emotionally unavailable and do not value them highly. As a consequence of this mistrust and perception of rejection, the world may seem a threatening and dangerous place. A direct consequence of a child's belief that danger lurks in every situation is a tendency to avoid disclosing his thoughts and feelings to other people. This means that when he feels lonely and distressed the child will not know how to elicit support from others or be able to soothe himself effectively. He will simply lack these crucial intimacy and self-regulation skills and may turn to less adaptive forms of mood management, for example, masturbation. This is especially likely to occur if a child has been sexually abused. In fact, according to Marshall and Barbaree, insecure attachment is often associated with being the victim of sexual abuse.

Another aetiological factor contributing to the formation of antisocial attitudes and offence-related vulnerabilities is exposure to antisocial and misogynist behaviour in the home itself. The culprit could be a parent or relative, but the result of seeing a mother physically abused and denigrated may have devastating effects on a young male. For one thing, he might start to consider females as inferior to males and as merely objects to satisfy his own needs. Alternatively, intimate relationships may become associated with fear and anger, encouraging the developing male to avoid seeking intimate relationships in the future. The experience of being sexually abused as a child, particularly if it is seen as rewarding in some respects, might result in a child believing that sex between children and adults is normal and beneficial to all concerned. It could, in fact, lay the foundation for the individual's later sexually abusive behaviour. As Marshall and Barbaree (1990) state, 'the acquisition of attitudes and behaviors during childhood sets the stage for the developing male to respond to the sudden onset of strong desires characteristic of pubescence with a prosocial or antisocial mental set' (p. 260).

In this part of their theory, Marshall and Barbaree aim to demonstrate that negative developmental experiences (e.g. neglect, physical or sexual abuse) make it difficult for children to form positive attitudes toward intimate relationships, and also to cope with their emotional and life problems in an adaptive manner. They conclude that such inappropriate early experiences cause the person concerned to enter puberty with a number of crucial skill deficits, deficits that make it harder for him to successfully master the developmental tasks of adolescence. In brief, individuals have a greater chance of being rejected socially, feeling inadequate, and harbouring resentment and anger toward those they consider responsible for their troubles. A further complication is that an individual might also find it difficult to discriminate between sexual and aggressive impulses and inclinations (see below).

Vulnerability and the Challenge of Adolescence

The above discussion makes it clear that according to the integrated theory, adolescence is likely to be a stressful period for vulnerable individuals. This is because adverse early experiences have left these individuals unable to form and maintain same-sex and opposite-sex relationships. While problems dealing with negative mood states and relationships create all sorts of difficulties at any age, the occurrence of these factors during early adolescence is hypothesised to be a particularly ominous sign, for two major reasons. First, it can mean social ostracism at a point in life when individuals are forming social identities. Second, chronic problems in controlling emotions and negotiating relationships may make it harder to learn to deal with sexual feelings and desires, perhaps leading to episodes of acting out behaviour. According to Marshall and Barbaree, puberty is the developmental stage during which the sexual preferences of individuals are shaped and they begin to understand the subtleties and norms governing sexual encounters. The onset of puberty is a *critical period* for the acquisition of sexual scripts, interests and attitudes. The marked increase of sex hormones in males during this period increases the salience of sexual cues. The young adult suddenly becomes aware of powerful sexual urges and feelings but at the same time is unsure of what to do about them and how to behave in the presence of possible sexual partners. From the perspective of the integrated theory, individuals who lack effective self-regulation and interpersonal skills are more likely to be confused and defeated by these hormonal and biological challenges. Therefore, the chances are greater that they will learn to meet their sexual and emotional needs in a socially unacceptable manner. Marshall and Barbaree propose that deviant inclinations manifest themselves in a number of ways, ranging from the direct occurrence of sexually abusive behaviour to the reliance on deviant sexual fantasies to regulate sexual desire and problematic mood states.

The fact that vulnerable individuals have entered puberty without a satisfactory repertoire of social and intimacy skills makes it more probable that their relationship overtures to women will be met with rejection, resulting in lowered self-esteem, anger and negative attitudes toward females. According to Marshall and Barbaree, the negative emotions caused by experiencing social and romantic rejection can trigger the onset of deviant sexual fantasies. These fantasies could be characterised by sadistic and aggressive themes or contain relatively benign content. The really significant issue is that the young offender masturbates to these fantasies to alleviate unhappiness or to express rage and disappointment. The fact that he does this means that they will increase in strength and frequency, by virtue of their positive and negatively reinforcing properties of arousal and masturbation. An additional possibility is that masturbatory episodes can function as mental rehearsals in which future sexual offences are planned.

A key idea in the integrated theory is that individuals frequently meet a number of psychological needs through sexual activity. In addition to providing pleasure and tension release, sex can function as a means of increasing a person's sense of personal effectiveness and control, alleviate low mood, promote interpersonal closeness, enhance self-esteem, and consolidate a sense of masculinity. The same idea holds for deviant sexual behaviour: if someone becomes dependent on using masturbation to deviant fantasies as a form of sexual expression, the meeting of the above needs can be potently reinforced. Consequently young men are likely to seek goals such as solace, elevated esteem and confirmation of their attractiveness to females through deviant sexual activities. In addition, Marshall and Barbaree propose that if adolescent males feel inadequate they are more vulnerable to accepting cultural messages that confirm their perceived superior status as males, even if these are essentially misogynistic in nature. Cultural messages that elevate males to positions of dominance and power are likely to be particularly attractive to those individuals who have had few rewarding encounters with females. From the perspective of the integrated theory, pornography, with its adversarial and reductionist portrayals of sexual relationships, is a good example of a cultural medium that promotes dysfunctional attitudes toward gender roles. In support of their argument that cultural factors are part causes of sexual aggression, Marshall and Barbaree provide evidence that societies characterised by high levels of interpersonal violence, male domination, and disparaging attitudes toward females have higher rates of sexual crimes.

Marshall and Barbaree argue that the task of distinguishing between sexual and aggressive impulses is a difficult one for adolescent males because both types of impulse are generated by the same brain structures and are hypothesised to cause qualitatively similar experiences. According to Marshall and Barbaree the brain structures responsible for sexual and aggressive behaviours are in the midbrain and include the hypothalamus, amygdala and septum. They propose that sex steroids also have a key role to play in contributing to offenders' tendency to fuse sex and aggression. This is thought to occur because sex steroids are involved in the activation of both types of behaviour. Essentially, these biological factors present adolescent males with the developmental task of discriminating between sexual and aggressive impulses, and furthermore, learning how to inhibit aggression in sexual situations. In order to function in a sexually appropriate manner it is necessary for individuals to be able to control the way sexual arousal is expressed and to ensure that subsequent sexual behaviour adheres to the norms of their culture. From the perspective of western cultures, this involves understanding that a potential sexual partner should be competent to consent to sex and that there are limits to what count as sexually permissible activities. In an ideal world, adolescents learn that legitimate sexual activity should occur between persons of roughly the same age and stage of development, and that coercive or abusive practices are absolutely forbidden. The integrated theory proposes that for individuals already predisposed to behave in an antisocial manner, the biological changes occurring in puberty (e.g. the massive release of male hormones) may fuse sex and aggression and result in sexually aggressive actions in certain contexts. This means that vulnerable adolescents will find it difficult to know whether they are feeling angry, sexually aroused, or even experiencing both states at the same time.

Marshall and Barbaree draw similarities between the psychological characteristics of psychopaths and sexual offenders. They suggest that because both groups are likely to have experienced physical and sexual abuse as children, they may share certain features such as deficits in intimacy skills, lack of empathy, social ineptness, a tendency to egocentricity and negative attitudes toward women.

Situational Factors

Marshall and Barbaree hypothesise that vulnerability factors derived from a dysfunctional childhood, in conjunction with the social and biological processes of puberty, interact with situational disinhibitors (e.g. substance abuse, emotional states), availability of a victim and opportunity, to cause a sexual offence. Thus the integrated theory is centrally concerned with vulnerable adolescents' inability to control their sexual and aggressive inclinations in face of specific stressors; it is a disinhibition approach.

According to the integrated theory, no man is really immune from committing sexual offences; it all depends on individuals' degree of vulnerability and their personal circumstances. The basic idea is that offence-related vulnerabilities interact dynamically with situational factors such as loss of a relationship, social rejection and extreme loneliness. The more vulnerable a person is to committing sexual offences the less intense stressors need to be for an offence to occur. An interesting addition to the integrated theory by Marshall and his colleagues is the proposal that states initially associated with sexual arousal may later acquire the capacity to elicit sexually deviant urges on their own, through conditioning processes. For example, the repeated pairing of sexual arousal with feelings of loneliness could explain why rejection experiences may lead to deviant sexual urges on future occasions. If an individual frequently uses masturbation to cope with loneliness, the two states (i.e. loneliness and sexual arousal) become associated and cues indicating loneliness then directly elicit sexual arousal. Of course, this assumes a classical conditioning process, where cues indicating psychological states such as loneliness coexist to some extent with sexual arousal and masturbation. In addition, if the person finds that masturbation reduces his unhappiness and produces feelings of pleasure, the combination of negative and positive reinforcement will ensure that masturbation is used in the future as a coping strategy; an operant conditioning process. The themes of the sexual fantasies might also be paired with sexual arousal and acquire the power to elicit directly sexual desire when cues associated with them are encountered in the world (e.g. cues indicating dependence and vulnerability in a victim).

The above factors account for the onset of sexual offending, but why does it continue? Marshall and Barbaree suggest that the positive and negative reinforcing effects of sexual abuse effectively maintain it, and in addition, consolidate the individual's array of psychological and behavioural problems (i.e. his vulnerability factors). A good example is a person who lacks the capacity to manage effectively his feelings of unhappiness and anxiety. He discovers as an adolescent that masturbation to deviant fantasies reduces the intensity of these negative emotions, making him feel better, more powerful and important. The tendency to utilise sex as a coping strategy not only contributes to his initial offending, it also helps to maintain it. The difference now is that the person regulates his mood by offending rather than through masturbatory practices. The sexual offending is maintained through a combination of negative and positive reinforcement. The final piece of the puzzle as far as the maintenance of sexual offending is concerned is the acquisition of rationalisations to legitimate and excuse the offender's sexually abusive actions. The cognitions used in the service of this goal are called cognitive distortions.

EVALUATION OF THE INTEGRATED THEORY

The integrated theory proposes that sexual offending is caused by a number of interacting distal and proximal developmental, social, biological and situational factors. Marshall and Barbaree suggest that abusive or neglectful environments leave individuals with a number of psychological deficits, including antisocial attitudes, impulsivity, low self-esteem and poor interpersonal skills. These deficits constitute offence-related vulnerabilities that interact with the biological and social factors evident in puberty to result in sexual offending. The failure of adolescents to discriminate between sexual and aggressive urges (partly due to the vulnerabilities listed above) may result in their fusion and a subsequent tendency to act aggressively in sexual contexts. Furthermore, the discovery of sex in puberty may encourage a vulnerable young male to use sexual activity as a means of coping with unhappiness and inadequacy. The combination of insecure attachment, poor coping and relationship skills means that the social and biological challenges of puberty are unlikely to be resolved effectively. In the face of these deficits, situational factors such as stress, intoxication or sexual stimuli will overwhelm a person's inadequate coping skills and result in a sexual offence. Offending is maintained by the reinforcing effects of deviant sexual activity and the development of cognitive distortions that legitimise offensive sex. This reinforcement may be positive (e.g. sexual arousal, sense of importance) or negative (e.g. reduction of unhappiness) in nature.

In our view, Marshall and Barbaree's integrated theory of sexual offending is an outstanding achievement. It is both dynamic and complex, portraying sexual abuse as the outcome of biological, psychological, social, cultural and situational factors. Its focus on early developmental processes and attachment theory to explain why offenders have difficulties coping with emotions and intimate relationships is innovative and compelling. In addition, the explicit focus on resilience and psychological vulnerability constitutes a real advance and clarifies how developmental adversity contributes to sexual offending. The detailed explication of these vulnerability factors in terms of psychological mechanisms such as insecure attachment and sexual coping is a model of good theory-building practice. The causes are deep structural ones, stated clearly enough to deduce testable predictions. These strengths of the theory point to its *explanatory depth, external consistency* and *unifying power*.

The integrated theory has also resulted in multiple avenues of research and subsequent treatment innovations, illustrating its *fertility*. For example, the claim that interpersonal deficits are important causes of sexual offending has resulted in the development of therapeutic strategies to enhance intimacy skills in offenders (Marshall, 1999). In addition, many of Marshall and Barbaree's hypotheses have been supported and are the focus of continued research activities (Marshall, 1999; Smallbone & Dadds, 1998). All these facts underline its *empirical adequacy* and *predictive accuracy*.

However, despite these strengths, there are a number of puzzling features of the theory that merit closer examination. We highlight the most significant weaknesses, and refer the reader to Ward (2002) for a more detailed critique.

Before outlining more significant difficulties with this theory, we will briefly mention some *minor* difficulties. First, its attempt to explain all types of sexual offending is a problem because there are significant differences between different types of offenders, and also between those who have committed the same type of offence (Cohen, Seghorn & Calmas, 1969; Knight & Prentky, 1990). Relatedly, while the integrated theory is able to explain early onset offenders, it is unclear how it would account for those individuals who start offending as adults (Abel, Mittleman & Becker, 1985). Second, in the integrated theory, *low* self-esteem is viewed as a core component of offenders' predisposition to abuse others sexually. However, Baumeister, Smart and Boden (1996) have convincingly argued that aggression is more typically associated with unstable high self-esteem. For violent offenders low self-esteem may not be a risk factor for engaging in violent actions. Therefore, it would be expected that violent sex offenders such as rapists are more likely to have unstable high self-esteem rather than low self-esteem. These minor difficulties in the theory indicate its lack of *empirical scope*.

In terms of major weaknesses, the integrated theory places great emphasis on loss of control in the genesis of sexual offending. The theory states that individuals commit sexual offences because of their failure to inhibit deviant desires and impulses. Of course, some sex offenders do have real difficulty effectively dealing with sexual desires and strong emotional states, but this is not the case for all offenders. Recent research shows that only a relatively small number of sex offenders have enduring problems with self-regulation (Hudson, Ward & McCormack, 1999; Proulx, Perreault & Ouimet, 1999). For example, in their research on the offence process of 44 extrafamilial child molesters, Proulx et al. found that 33% planned their offences and did not appear to be particularly impulsive. In another study Yates, Kingston and Hall (2003) found that 36% of rapists and 58% of child molesters displayed an approach-explicit self-regulation pathway to their offending. Offenders allocated to this pathway tended to be characterised by sound planning skills, and the ability to postpone immediate gratification in the service of longer-term goals (see Chapter 14 for more details). In summary, then, many offenders seem quite capable of setting goals, formulating plans, and setting in place strategies designed to achieve these goals. So, the integrated theory seems to place too much emphasis on impulsivity and ignores the fact that sometimes the real problem lies with the content of the beliefs underlying offenders' goals and values. This weakness indicates a *lack of scope*, *external consistency* and *explanatory depth*.

A further major problem concerns the issue of embedded offence pathways and the implication these raise for the theory's *coherence*. Close scrutiny of the integrated theory reveals that there are distinct and possibly competing offence pathways contained within it. These pathways are essentially trajectories leading from different types of vulnerability factors to the commission of a sexual offence. The presence of multiple offence pathways is a problem because they are *implicit* and not clearly articulated, thus running the risk that the theory as a whole is somewhat incoherent. In our view each pathway represents a distinct offence trajectory and should be considered separately rather than simply examined under the general rubric of developmental and biological factors. Failure to do this means that the deficits uniquely displayed by offenders will not be readily identified during assessment and subsequently directly targeted in treatment. As we stated in Chapter 1, poorly specified theories result in inadequate formulations and interventions.

What are the different offence pathways embedded in the integrated theory? First, Marshall and Barbaree state that some individuals develop hostile attitudes toward females through early exposure to problematic relationships between their parents or other family members. In these social situations, females are portrayed as untrustworthy and inferior to males in some important respects. The theory then proposes that a lack of respect for the rights of others can result in offenders elevating the value of meeting their own needs over those of women and children. The tendency to dismiss the value of other people's needs can lead to sexual offending in certain circumstances.

A second offence pathway occurs when adolescent males become distrustful of females following unsuccessful attempts to establish intimate relationships during adolescence. This type of social rejection is thought to occur because the offender lacks satisfactory interpersonal skills. The resulting feelings of resentment can manifest in a desire to punish women for their perceived harsh treatment of the offender, possibly culminating in episodes of sexual aggression or child sexual abuse. The individual's lack of trust toward females may generalise to all adults and he could see children as the only persons capable of providing him with affection and sexual intimacy.

The third offence trajectory revolves around the use of masturbation as a mood regulator and the maladaptive consequences for offenders who rely on this kind of self-regulation strategy. What this means is that in stressful circumstances, such individuals turn to their favourite sexual fantasies to alleviate their feelings of unhappiness and tension. Eventually, reliance on sexual activities in this way can result in offenders seeking out sexual encounters whenever they feel bad: in some circumstance this may lead to sex with children or rape. Alternatively, an inability to control intense emotional states can result in a loss of control and some form of aggression.

It is possible to detect a fourth trajectory in the integrated theory, where offenders utilise deviant sexual fantasies to enhance their self-esteem and express their dissatisfaction with the world. This is different from the third trajectory (above) because the pathway is connected to social identity and is more cognitive in nature. The fantasies and associated thoughts can assume either a violent (e.g. 'Someone will pay for this!') or a non-violent (e.g., 'I want to love someone') form, although both may culminate in sexual offences of one kind or another. Finally, a fifth group fails to learn to discriminate between aggressive and sexual motives and are therefore inclined to behave in an antisocial manner in sexual contexts.

Once the multiple aetiological pathways are identified and separated, a problem emerges concerning exactly why some of these offence routes result in a *sexual* offence. For example, why do individuals who acquire hostile or misogynistic attitudes toward women (pathway one) sexually molest children or adults as opposed to engaging simply in verbal or physical aggression? Additional theoretical elaboration is needed to explain how psychological characteristics such as hostility and distrust are expressed sexually. These problems point to the *internal incoherence* of the theory in its current form.

A third major weakness stems from the integrated theory's claim that offenders are likely to confuse sexual and aggressive drives and that this confusion is causally related to their subsequent offending. There are a number of problems with the line of argument that because psychological functions arise from the same brain structures they are identical in some respects, can give rise to similar types of experience and therefore become fused in a person's mind. The first point is that midbrain structures are extremely complex and subserve a wide range of psychological functions and drives (Kolb & Whishaw, 1995). Therefore, claims about the neural underpinnings of human behaviour need to be specific about the functions concerned and the particular brain structures thought to be causing them. Failure to be clear about the exact nature of the claims being made is likely to lead to confusion and vague speculation. This degree of clarity is missing from the integrated theory and therefore it is difficult to be sure what is actually being claimed to be the case.

A concrete example will make our point clearer. The hypothalamus is the neural source of a variety of physical drives and the amygdala is associated with a number of distinct emotional states (Kolb & Whishaw, 1995; Strongman, 1996). The claim by Marshall and Barbaree that sexual urges and aggression are generated by the same general neurological structures is not precise enough. What we need to know is the specific location of the microstructures under-pinning aggression and sex. It is not sufficient to state simply that sex and aggression are mediated by the same neural substrates, structures that subsume a wide range of quite distinct drives and responses. Moreover, physical proximity in the brain does not necessarily entail functional similarity. In fact, depending on the level at which one categorises the part of the brain in question, it is possible for the same neural structures to underlie different psychological functions. A good example of this fact is the frontal cortex. The executive brain, as it is often called, is the site for a plethora of capacities and functions (e.g. self-regulation, planning and verbal fluency; Kolb & Whishaw, 1995).

A second point is that the assumption that basic human drives and capacities may share neurological structures has been thrown into doubt by recent work in evolutionary psychology. Symons (1979) has argued that males are predisposed to commit rape by virtue of their greater sexual drive and strong inclination to engage in impersonal sex whenever an opportunity emerges. By contrast, aggressive behaviour is hypothesised to be related to males' tendency to protect their kin and personal status under perceived conditions of threat. According to evolutionary psychology, the modules (i.e. psychological mechanisms) that interact with environmental conditions to produce these behaviours have evolved quite independently and therefore are unlikely to overlap to any significant degree neurologically or phenomenologically (Tooby & Cosmides, 1992). Evolutionary psychologists argue that these modules evolved to solve unique and distinct evolutionary problems. Therefore, the claim that sexual aggression can occur when these two types of drive are experientially 'fused' is a dubious one. The difficulties in the theory outlined above indicate that it lacks *external consistency*, *explanatory depth* and *empirical adequacy*.

A fourth major weakness in the integrated theory revolves around the claim that sex and aggression can be 'fused'. The notion of fusion is vague and may be interpreted in several ways in the context of the integrated theory. First, the term 'fused' could refer to the derivation of sexual and aggressive urges from a common factor such as physiological arousal. In this sense of the term, the underlying neural substrates are hypothesised to generate a generic state of arousal that in certain contexts is transformed into distinct affective states: for example sexual desire. Exactly what states physiological arousal becomes differentiated into depends on situational and learning factors. From the perspective of the integrated theory, this interpretation of the term 'fused' suggests that this process has not occurred and the offender may only be aware of feeling physiologically aroused and unsure of the meaning of such a state. Faced with uncertainty, it is likely the individual would rely on external cues to provide guidance on how to make sense of his aroused state. In this situation the offender would be unable to discriminate clearly between the two concepts and their referents, simply regarding them as manifestations of arousal. According to Marshall and Barbaree, this confusion could lead to sexually abusive behaviour in certain circumstances.

In a second interpretation of the term 'fused', the two *distinct* states of sexual arousal and aggression are causally linked and therefore if one state is activated the other is as well. They remain distinct states whereby the individual concerned is able to identify each clearly, and understand what actions need to be mobilised in the service of the drive in question. The fact that each state is likely to activate the other is probably due to powerful conditioning experiences.

According to a third interpretation of the term 'fused', offenders are unable to reliably differentiate between sexual and aggressive *mental* states. The inability to make such a discrimination indicates that they are aware of the differences between sexual and aggressive actions and their meanings, but are simply unable to distinguish them in their own minds. They may mistakenly infer that they are sexually motivated when in fact they are angry, and then seek sexual satisfaction in the wrong context.

Finally, a fourth interpretation stipulates that an offender might interpret all sexual cues as aggressive ones and be unable reliably to identify sexual states at all. In this example, one type of mental state is mistaken for another, for example, all sexual cues might be construed as revealing other people's aggressive intentions. Thus, the concept of aggression is the predominant one and sexual stimuli are in a sense reduced to, or interpreted in terms of, this particular construct. The presence of fusion in this sense would make it highly probable that sexual needs would be experienced by an individual as aggression, and also ultimately manifested in violent actions.

Our major point is that the idea of fusion as used by Marshall and Barbaree is inherently ambiguous and may well result in conflicting interpretations. This is important from both theoretical and clinical viewpoints because contrasting treatment strategies follow from the varying interpretations. For example, the first interpretation would result in treatment focusing on teaching the offender how to *identify* both aggressive and sexual urges, while treatment based on interpretation two would focus on *weakening* the link between the two distinct states. Therefore, it is important for the relationship between sex and aggression to be more precisely outlined in the integrated theory. This issue suggests that the theory lacks *internal coherence* in some respects.

CLINICAL UTILITY OF THE INTEGRATED THEORY

We have already discussed the undoubted virtues of the integrated theory; it is one of the strongest, if not the best, aetiological theories of sexual offending currently available. The characteristics that make it a very good theory also translate into clinical virtues. First, its focus on developmental factors is useful during assessment as it reminds therapists to look for adverse early experiences and their associated vulnerabilities when developing case formulations. Attachment style, sources of self-esteem, attitude toward females, masculine identity, emotional competence and sexual attitudes arguably are all strongly influenced by early learning. Second, the stress in the integrated theory on socio-cultural influences and how they interact with offence-related vulnerabilities is a timely reminder to clinicians to incorporate explicitly situational and social factors into a case formulation and also into any intervention plan. Third, related to this issue, it seems that the integrated theory is really a generic theory of criminal behaviour rather than simply an explanation of the origins of sexually abusive behaviour. Intentionally or not, Marshall and Barbaree have shifted the theoretical ground somewhat and have made it clear that many sex offenders commit a wide variety of antisocial acts, that is, they are generalists not specialists. What this means for therapy is that in a comprehensive assessment all offending behaviours should be accounted for, not just sexual offending. A fourth clinical contribution is to remind clinicians to consider the role of biological variables in the aetiology and maintenance of sexual abuse. It may be appropriate for individuals who are sexually preoccupied to be prescribed anti-androgen medications alongside a comprehensive cognitive-behavioural programme for sexual offending. Finally, the multifactorial nature of the integrated theory means that an adequate assessment will need to address a wide range of distal and proximal biological, social, psychological, developmental and situational causal factors. The causal impact of these variables upon specific offenders' offence processes should be noted and taken into account during treatment. In short, assessment of sexual offenders is a multifaceted task.

CONCLUSIONS

In this chapter we have critically examined Marshall and Barbaree's integrated theory. Our evaluation has revealed it to be a subtle and rich theory that explicitly incorporates a broad range of developmental and social factors in the explanation of sexual offending. Its explicit focus on resilience and psychological vulnerability is also a valuable innovation and constitutes a real advance over other theories. In our view it is an outstanding achievement, and the fact that Marshall and his colleagues are continuing to refine and develop its core ideas augers well for the future of this significant theory.

However, alongside its strengths the integrated theory displays a number of conceptual weaknesses. The primary focus on disinhibition, the failure to explicitly address the possibility of different offence pathways, confusion surrounding the notion of fusing aggressive and sexual drives, and the vagueness over the biological 0substrates of sex and aggression are problems.

Just how the theory fares in the long run remains to be seen. But what is clear is that clinicians should find it an extremely useful tool when assessing and treating offenders.

Chapter 4

HALL AND HIRSCHMAN'S QUADRIPARTITE MODEL

Hall and Hirschman's (1992) quadripartite model of sexual abuse has not fared as well as Finkelhor's and appears to have slipped from the research and clinical radar over the last few years. There has been little recent discussion of its key ideas in the literature and the only contemporary reference to it we could find was in a book on the assessment and treatment of sexual offenders by Hall (one of the authors of the theory) in 1996. In our view, this is rather puzzling as the quadripartite model exhibits a number of virtues and merits continued attention. The theory was originally formulated as an explanation of rape and later reworked to give an account of child sexual abuse (Hall & Hirschman, 1992). In this chapter for reasons of clarity (i.e. it may be confusing to focus on two types of problems) we will focus primarily on its application to child sexual offending, although our critical comments also apply to the rape version of the theory (Hall & Hirschman, 1991).

In this chapter, we first describe the quadripartite model, then we critically evaluate its adequacy as a theory, and finally, we consider its clinical utility in the light of our critical comments. Like Finkelhor, Hall and Hirschman have constructed a theory—not a model—and therefore we will use the term 'quadripartite model' when referring to this theory by name and the term 'theory' when speaking more generally.

HALL AND HIRSCHMAN'S (1992) QUADRIPARTITE MODEL

In Hall and Hirschman's (1992) reformulation, the quadripartite model was modified to account for the sexual abuse of children as well as rape. In particular, they were keen to capture the heterogeneity of child molesters. In their view, the majority of contemporary theories of child sexual abuse tended to single out one or two factors as the sole causes of child molestation and therefore utterly failed to capture the complexity of this phenomenon. They saw this as a problem for two main reasons. First, the various theories were incapable of explaining all aspects of child sexual abuse, often highlighting some problems and neglecting others. Second, because of this failing, existing theories were unable to provide adequate guidance to therapists for assessment and treatment, promoting a 'one size fits all' approach to both of these tasks. In their view, the empirical evidence pointed clearly to offenders demonstrating a wide range of difficulties that were causally related to their abusive behaviour. Therefore, they argued, it made good clinical sense to develop individual treatment plans. Hall and Hirschman felt that the way to remedy the lack of tailored interventions was to build a theory based on the four factors that had been the focus of research in the arena of sexual abuse. In essence, they hypothesised that inappropriate physiological sexual arousal, distorted cognition, affective dyscontrol and problematic personality factors could lead to sexually abusive behaviour against children. The first three were viewed as state factors and personality problems as a trait factor. Hall and Hirschman proposed that these factors could function either independently or in combination to generate sexual abuse. Furthermore, they argued that it was possible to construct a classification system for child molesters by using the four factors, with one type of cause tending to be predominant for any given individual.

Based on existing research and clinical work, Hall and Hirschman hypothesised that *physiological sexual arousal* was a major contributor to sexual abuse against children. Although the results were inconsistent, some studies at least concluded that it was possible to discriminate between child molesters and other offenders on the basis of their sexual arousal to child visual and auditory stimuli (for a more recent discussion of this issue see Marshall, 1999; Marshall, Anderson & Fernandez, 1999a). Hall and Hirschman also noted that clinical experience indicated that the presence of persistent and intrusive deviant sexual urges and fantasies involving sex with children was often observed in individuals subsequently diagnosed with paedophilia. In other words, it was intuitively appealing to view deviant sexual preferences for, and subsequent arousal to, children as a core feature of child molestation.

The core clinical features of individuals characterised by the physiological arousal subtype are, according to Hall (1996), their tendency to have multiple victims, low levels of physical violence against the victim, and the fact that such individuals are unlikely to exhibit nonsexual aggression.

The second factor, *cognitive distortions*, was viewed by Hall and Hirschman as a central feature of child molesters that helped to explain both the initial and continued abuse of children. By thinking of children as competent sexual agents who are able to make informed decisions about when to have sex, and with whom, it is possible for individuals to justify their offending behaviour (for a recent review of this literature see Gannon, Polaschek & Ward, 2005; Marshall, 1999; Marshall et al., 1999a; Ward, Hudson, Johnston & Marshall, 1997). Hall and Hirschman noted the clinical and research evidence showing that children are often described by offenders as sexually provocative and seductive, and as experiencing significant psychological benefits from sexual encounters with adults. For example, offenders may blame children for the fact that abuse occurred, make excuses for their offending by appealing to external causes such as stress or the effects of drugs, and typically justify their sexually abusive behaviour by, for example, referring to the sexual practices of the ancient Greeks. These cognitions have been labelled by Hall and Hirschman and others (e.g. Abel et al., 1989) as 'cognitive distortions' because they constitute inaccurate and self-serving interpretations of offence-related situations (see Chapter 8).

Hall and Hirschman suggested that offenders are more likely to act on the basis of these beliefs if the perceived benefits of sexual aggression (e.g. sexual pleasure) are thought to outweigh the estimated threats (e.g. risk of punishment). Therefore, the picture that emerges from this theoretical analysis is that child molesters are rational agents who systematically weigh the benefits and costs of sexual offending and then choose the course of action that is thought to have the greatest utility.

The core clinical features of individuals characterised by the cognitive subtype are a high degree of planning, little impulsivity in offending behaviours, and higher rates of incestuous offending compared to the *physiological sexual arousal* type (Hall, 1996).

The third factor incorporated into Hall and Hirschman's theory is that of *affective dyscontrol* (i.e. problems with the identification and management of emotions). Affective dyscontrol is essentially what other researchers have termed emotional regulation (Ward, Hudson & Keenan, 1998) and refers to the capacity of individuals to detect, control, modulate and manage their emotional states. The multicomponent nature of the emotional regulation system means that problems may crop up in a number of places. In terms of emotional recognition, an individual may not be able to identify accurately certain affective states or may confuse them in some way: for example, loneliness and sexual desire. Another type of problem involves the use of ineffective strategies to modulate or reduce the intensity of emotions such as anxiety. Examples of this type of difficulty are the reliance on masturbation to control deviant sexual fantasies or the use of alcohol to reduce feelings of sadness. While in the short term a person might experience momentary relief, in the longer term these strategies often backfire and result in greater unhappiness. Hall and Hirschman acknowledged that negative affective states such as depression and anxiety in child molesters can trigger an offence process and ultimately result in sexually abusive behaviour (see Knight & Prentky, 1990; Pithers, 1990). An extreme example of inappropriate ways of dealing with emotions such as fear and loneliness outlined in the theory is the sexual abuse of children. In this situation, the link is directly between emotional coping and sexual abuse rather than sexual abuse occurring as a consequence of using ineffective strategies such as masturbation or alcohol and drug use. A further way in which intense emotional states can result in child molestation is where they erode an individual's ability to adhere to a relapse prevention plan so that he subsequently ends up in a high-risk situation. Hall and Hirschman also proposed that negative affective states may disrupt the normal inhibitors of sexually aggressive behaviour such as victim empathy, guilt, moral conviction and anxiety regarding prosecution. Powerful negative emotions create this situation by focusing offenders' attention on the objects evoking the emotion in question (e.g. a threatening or desirable person) and diverting mental resources needed to respond empathically to others or to act in accordance with personal ideals.

The core clinical features of individuals characterised by the *affective dyscontrol* subtype are opportunistic offences, high levels of violence, a tendency to engage in both nonsexual and sexual violence, and depression (Hall, 1996).

The fourth and final factor of the Hall and Hirschman theory is *personality problems*. This component is comprised of more enduring trait-like features and as such, is usefully seen as a cluster of offence-related vulnerabilities. According to Hall and Hirschman, personality problems emerge from adverse developmental experiences such as physical or sexual abuse, or parental divorce. Events like these function to shape offenders' antisocial attitudes and problematic interpersonal strategies, for example, learning to use threats to force other people to give them what they want. Unfortunately, these attitudes and the resultant skills deficits tend to restrict individuals' opportunities for social and personal success and increase the likelihood they will embrace an antisocial lifestyle (see Bard et al., 1987; Hall & Proctor, 1987; Lipton, McDonel & McFall, 1987).

In the quadripartite model, this last factor is intended to incorporate the developmental variables and therefore constitutes a *distal* vulnerability factor. What this means is that the experience of events such as neglect and abuse leave an individual with problematic ways of thinking about the world and an inability to manage developmental tasks in an adaptive manner. The personality traits and attitudes directly caused by a hostile and neglectful upbringing (i.e. developmental vulnerabilities) are hypothesised to be activated in certain contexts (e.g. for affective dyscontrol following an episode of social rejection) and result in the three classes of state variables described above: that is, deviant arousal, affective disturbance or distorted thinking. Hall and Hirschman suggested that the presence of vulnerability factors, in conjunction with an opportunity to offend, will lead a person to commit child sexual abuse.

The core clinical features of individuals characterised by the *personality problem* subtype are chronic personality problems, a disregard for social norms and rules, a tendency to behave aggressively, and a poor treatment outcome (Hall, 1996).

Hall and Hirschman stressed that while each of the four factors may contribute in some way to the occurrence of a sexual offence, typically one factor tends to be prominent in individual cases. That is, different individuals will offend for different reasons. The fact that one of the four factors may be dominant over the others in a given situation means that it effectively 'drives' the offence. In a sense, by exerting a powerful influence on the other factors, it pushes individuals over the offence threshold, the boundary between non-abusive and abusive behaviour. The vulnerability factor can do this because it constitutes the underlying basis of an offender's sexual abuse; it is this factor that is hypothesised to predispose him to abuse children sexually in the first place. Hall and Hirschman viewed the interaction between the primary causal factor and the other three as mainly synergistic in nature; they propose that the activation of the primary factor functions to increase the intensity of the others. They labelled the primary factor in this situation the *primary motivational precursor*. Thus, the activation of the primary factor and its subsequent impact on the other three factors is thought to propel an individual above the critical threshold for performing a sexually deviant act. Offenders have different threshold gradients for committing a sexual offence and this threshold is exceeded when the benefits of such an act are perceived to exceed the estimated threats. According to the quadripartite model, the threats may either be self (e.g. chances of getting caught) or victim (e.g. harming the victim) generated. If an offender believes that the victim will enjoy or benefit from sex with an adult he is more likely to view this threat as low and go on to molest the child in question. This idea accounts for the fact that individuals vary in their predisposition to commit a sexual offence, and also suggests that there are individuals who desire to have sex with children but who do not do so because their threshold is so high. Some men are fairly easily persuaded and others will only abuse a child in extreme circumstances. Situational factors such as watching pornography or encountering a child alone function as activators and cause individuals with one of the four primary motivational precursors (i.e. one of the four factors) to commit abusive acts. The situational variables do this by raising a primary factor above its threshold gradient, overcoming the individual's inhibitions against abuse.

A concrete example will make it easier to understand Hall and Hirschman's conceptualisations. An individual may have narcissistic personality traits and hence may have problems understanding other people's perspectives in an argument or when faced with a difference of opinion. In addition, such an individual may have some minor difficulties handling negative emotions in a healthy and adaptive way. Following an argument with someone at work (situational determinant) he becomes increasingly angry (affective dyscontrol) and falls back upon his usual way of dealing with such emotions: fantasising about having sex with a child (sexual arousal). The masturbatory fantasies in turn cause this individual to justify the idea of sex with children (cognitive distortions) and to be primed to respond to an opportunity should it present itself. In this case, the primary motivational precursor is the personality defect, which in conjunction with the presence of a child, causes the individual to commit a sexual offence.

For another child molester, the primary motivational precursor might be the presence of maladaptive beliefs such as the view that children are sexual beings or that the offender is entitled to have sex with whom, and when, he pleases. The major point is that it is the primary motivational precursor that triggers the subsequent chain of events and pushes the individual concerned over his particular offence threshold. The fact that the other elements are present will not in itself result in a sexual offence; the critical ingredient is the activation of a primary factor. An important thing to note about this theory is that offenders vary in terms of their primary causes and therefore will require quite different treatment approaches.

In Hall and Hirschman's theory of child sexual abuse, the focus is squarely on the psychological structures and processes that predispose men to commit sexual crimes against children. Cultural and environmental variables only really figure in a secondary sense: as facilitators of sexual offending (e.g. arguments, presence of a child) and adverse early learning events (e.g. sexual and physical abuse). While external factors such as having access to children or the availability of pornography may trigger offences, they will not do so in the absence of a psychological predisposition. That is, external factors are viewed as situational determinants that raise the thresholds of vulnerable individuals above that required to commit a sexual offence.

According to the quadripartite model, each of the four primary factors can be used to identify a particular type of child molester. This is an example of theory-directed assessment and treatment because membership in one of the four groups directly informs the type of treatment to be implemented. This is because each group has a unique set of problems and issues that requires a distinct type of intervention:

- The physiological sexual arousal subtype is hypothesised to exhibit strong sexual preferences for children and typically has a long history of sexual offending; the classic preferential offender would belong to this group. Critical treatment strategies would include the reduction of deviant sexual arousal using a range of conditioning strategies: for example, covert desensitisation and directed masturbation.
- The cognitive subtype is hypothesised to possess good self-regulatory skills and entitlement beliefs, but tends to misinterpret the innocent behaviour of children in a sexual manner. This group frequently contains a high number of incest offenders. From the perspective of the quadripartite model, therapy should involve challenging this individual's sense of entitlement and expectation that sex with children is likely to benefit rather than harm them.
- Individuals belonging to the third subtype are thought to experience problems in managing emotions effectively, and their offences are typically impulsive and unplanned. According to Hall and Hirschman, learning how to control and regulate negative emotions should be the focus of treatment for these individuals.
- The final subtype has developmentally based personality problems and it is proposed that they will display a wide range of interpersonal and personal deficits, for example, attachment difficulties. Treatment should be intensive and pervasive in scope, seeking to modify maladaptive beliefs about themselves and other people.

Each subtype has a distinct risk profile. What this means is that the primary factor associated with each subtype will be activated (i.e. pushed above the threshold gradient) by a unique set of situational determinants. For example, experiencing rejection may overcome the inhibitions against committing a sexual offence in an individual belonging to the affective dyscontrol subtype, whereas for someone in the physiological arousal group, watching child pornography may be the crucial determinant.

EVALUATION OF THE QUADRIPARTITE MODEL

The quadripartite model of sexual aggression against children is based on four primary factors: physiological sexual arousal, cognitive distortions, affective dyscontrol and personality problems. Hall and Hirschman suggest that physiological, affective and cognitive factors are all primarily state and situation dependent (i.e. state factors) while the category of personality problems represents enduring vulnerability factors (a trait factor). These four factors are viewed as motivational precursors that increase the probability of child sexual abuse occurring by lowering the offence threshold for a given individual in a specific set of circumstances. In addition, the factors are also used to classify child molesters into four distinct subtypes, each with its own set of treatment needs.

The quadripartite model has a number of strengths, and has been unjustly neglected. First, the focus on multiple causal factors is sensible and reflects the heterogeneity of child molesters and the fact that child sexual abuse is a final common pathway for a number of distinct aetiologies. In other words, there are a number of distinct pathways that will lead men to sexually abuse a child. This aspect of the theory shows its *fertility*, *empirical scope* and *unifying power*. Second, the introduction of the idea of a critical offence threshold is valuable and helps to explain why offenders only sexually abuse children under some circumstances, and also why non-offenders may display some characteristics of sexual offenders (e.g. an interest in child pornography). It also helps to explain how enduring vulnerability factors interact with situational variables to produce sexual offending. These features of the quadripartite model also indicate its *unifying power* and *empirical scope* and *adequacy*. Third, the fact that it proposes there are subtypes of offenders and that assessment and treatment should track these differences is of immense clinical value. The basic idea here is that individual offenders frequently display contrasting problems and therefore require different types of intervention. The attention to individual differences indicates that the quadripartite model has significant clinical and research heuristic value or *fertility*.

However, alongside these strengths the quadripartite model has a number of weaknesses that limit its overall clinical utility. We intend only to outline the most important weaknesses and will not attempt a systematic and detailed critique (for this see Ward, 2001).

First, it suffers from the problem of construct vagueness, which threatens its conceptual *coherence* and *explanatory value*. Each of the four factors constituting the theory are only really defined in a general way and actually contain within them a number of diverse and distinct forms. In other words, the theory is not really fleshed out in much detail. For example, *cognition* can be further broken down from a functional perspective into positive distortions that explicitly permit sexually abusive actions and negative distortions characterised by denial and minimisation (Marshall et al., 1999a). Furthermore, it is possible to analyse cognition into its structural components, ranging from cognitive products, operations and underlying schemata (Ward et al., 1997). Or to cite another example, affective dyscontrol is a multifaceted construct and encompasses a number of distinct processes and associated competencies (Thompson, 1994). These include the ability to detect and label one's own emotional states, being able to utilise the information conveyed by emotions and to integrate this into an overall response to life situations, having the skills to discern other people's emotions based on contextual and nonverbal cues (e.g. tone of voice, facial expressions), and the degree to which individuals are able to control or modulate the intensity of emotions (Saarni, 1999). This problem indicates a need for explication and theoretical refinement. Otherwise it is difficult to understand just what the factors refer to and how they impact on each other. The issue of construct vagueness threatens the *internal coherence* of the theory. The trouble with vague ideas is that it is possible to interpret them in any number of ways and therefore be unable to decide whether research data supports or falsifies the theory in question.

A second difficulty with the quadripartite model is that it lacks *explanatory depth*. It is not clear from Hall and Hirschman's description of the four factors whether they are mechanisms or phenomena (i.e. clusters of symptoms and effects or underlying causes). The distinction between cause and effects is not explicitly made and while it is plausible that sex offenders as a group display deviant sexual arousal, affective dyscontrol, cognitive distortions and relationship problems, it is not obvious from the theory what causes these phenomena. We have argued in Chapter 1 that a theory should clearly specify the nature of the causal mechanisms generating sexual abuse. It should explain how biological, psychological, social/cultural and contextual factors interact with each other to result in sexual aggression. Unfortunately, this does not occur in the quadripartite model and all we are really left with is a list of possible factors. For example, it is unclear exactly how cognitive distortions or affective dyscontrol actually generate sexual offending.

A third, related problem, is that Hall and Hirschman did not describe in any detail how the four factors interact with each other in order to cause sexual abuse. According to the theory each factor can directly cause sexual offending or may do so in combination with the others. However, aside from the proposal that once a threshold is reached a primary factor may activate the others, the relationship between the various factors and the actions constituting sexual offending is not explicitly commented on. It is all a little vague and metaphorical. Exactly how does the primary motivational precursor of affective dyscontrol result in a sexual offence? What are the links between feeling sad, becoming sexually aroused and having sex with a child? The trouble is that the failure to provide answers to these questions about causal links leaves one with the suspicion that each factor can independently lead to child sexual abuse. If this is the case, then it is hard to understand how personality problems or affective dyscontrol on their own result in *sexual* activity, let alone child molestation. The theory lacks specificity here and runs the risk of lacking *internal coherence* and having sufficient *empirical scope*.

A fourth weakness is the way Hall and Hirschman distinguish between state and trait factors in the explication of their theory. In the quadripartite model, physiological arousal, affective dyscontrol and cognitive distortions are construed as state factors and personality problems is a trait factor. The problem is that state factors do not function as causes in any scientifically significant sense and are most usefully regarded as products of more fundamental causes, such as skill deficits or dysfunctional schemas. That is, state factors are generated by underlying causal processes, which may reside in the environment or inside an individual. An example of a psychological state factor is a panic attack experienced as a result of encountering a large unknown male when walking alone in an unlit city street at night. The underlying cause of the individual's state of intense anxiety could be the implicit theories that the world is a dangerous place and that he is particularly vulnerable to a physical attack and incapable of defending himself. In other words, a deeper explanation of human behaviour is more likely to be found in psychological traits, predispositions or learned behaviours than in moment to moment experience (i.e. states).

In the light of these comments we argue that it is reasonable to infer that the key mechanisms associated with sexual abuse are not transient and typically reside within the offender in the form of vulnerability factors. If this inference is accepted it follows that state factors such as affective dyscontrol, sexual arousal and cognitive distortions are unlikely on their own to provide satisfactory accounts of sexual abuse. It would appear that the explanatory value of the quadripartite model resides entirely within the factor of personality problems, which must directly create the problematic states described by the other three. Therefore the theory is really a one-factor, three-state model and not a four-factor theory at all.

This state of affairs is quite unsatisfactory. For one thing, it is not clear how personality problems can result in deviant sexual arousal or either of the other two types of psychological states. What is required is for the theory to be fleshed out to demonstrate the required connections or else to be reworked in another way.

In our view, the best way to salvage the theory is to propose that each factor has both a trait and state form. For example, the tendency to become sexually aroused by children often reflects enduring sexual preferences, which in combination with other variables such as sexual deprivation or the presence of children, can result in deviant sexual arousal. This line of reasoning applies to cognitive distortions and affective dyscontrol as well. With respect to cognitive distortions, researchers have made a useful distinction between cognitive products, cognitive processes and underlying schemas (Fiske & Taylor, 1991). Schemas (trait factors) are thought to be activated in specific circumstances, and in conjunction with certain cognitive processes create conscious thoughts and images (state factors). The origins of offence-supportive schemas are hypothesised to emerge from an offender's early developmental experiences and to represent attempts to explain salient interpersonal and social events in his world. It is the underlying cognitive structures that are the major cause of offenders' distorted thoughts concerning children; it is the trait rather than the state factor that is of most importance.

A similar case can be made for affective dyscontrol, which can be seen as a form of self-regulation failure. There is a number of components constituting self-regulation: identification of current states and outcomes, recognition of a discrepancy between a goal and these states, formulation of a plan to reduce the discrepancies and to move toward a valued goal, implementation of a plan, and evaluation of its effectiveness (Baumeister & Heatherton, 1996; Carver & Scheier, 1990). The ability to achieve these tasks, and the manner in which they are achieved, collectively define a particular person's self-regulation style: a trait factor. The psychological states and behavioural outcomes are the result of the application of this style in the world, and are state factors. For example, a man may habitually respond to interpersonal problems by trying to make himself feel better (emotion focused coping) rather than attempting to solve them—a trait factor. This strategy could worsen things in the long run, and result in high levels of emotional distress—a state factor.

In the light of the above comments, we argue that it is a mistake to conceptualise affective dyscontrol, cognitive distortions and physiological arousal purely as state factors. They all have state and trait forms, both of which play critical roles in causing sexual offending in some individuals. These weaknesses in the quadripartite model highlight its *internal incoherence* and lack of *empirical scope* and *adequacy*.

A fifth problem in the theory is the fact that the four factors are not conceptually distinct and seem to overlap to some degree. Deviant sexual arousal is frequently underpinned by enduring sexual preferences pertaining to sexual objects (e.g. children) or activities (e.g. sadistic acts). These preferences must involve some form of representation of the desired sexual partners and sexual acts, and judgements relating to their particular characteristics (e.g. degree of attractiveness, age, gender), interest in sex, likelihood of participation, and so on. Clearly such preferences are at least partly cognitive in nature and, in this sense, contain, or are associated with, cognitive distortions. The obvious conclusion following from this line of argument is that physiological arousal necessarily contains cognitive elements. There appears to be a close and systematic relationship between cognition and deviant sexual arousal that is not easily accounted for by the quadripartite model.

Furthermore, a similar argument can be constructed for the affective dyscontrol factor. Human emotion is a multifaceted phenomenon, consisting of behavioural, physiological and cognitive elements (Strongman, 1996). Primary cognitive appraisals are thought to alert an individual that important goals are either being pursued successfully or are in danger of being thwarted. The resulting secondary appraisals concerning the source and nature of the threat or facilitators directly lead to a cascade of physiological responses and the mobilisation of action sequences designed to deal with the situation in an appropriate manner (Saarni, 1999). If these appraisals are distorted in some manner, individuals may experience problematic emotions and engage in antisocial behaviour. For example, viewing a child as a possible romantic partner is likely to create tender and 'loving' feelings in a vulnerable man and encourage him to seek subsequent sexual encounters with the victim.

The key point is that the four factors overlap to a considerable degree and an adequate theory of child molestation should seek to explain how and why this interaction occurs. Unfortunately Hall and Hirschman do not account for the issue of overlapping factors and therefore the quadripartite model suffers from a lack of *explanatory depth* and *internal incoherence*.

A final problem with this theory concerns the relationship between primary motivational precursors and the threshold for sexual offending. As stated above, the concept of an offence threshold set at different levels for different offenders is an attractive and innovative idea. What is not clear, however, is why and how each causal factor exerts a powerful effect on the others. It is even less obvious why a primary motivational precursor should 'intensify' each of the other factors.

The difficulty here is that the nature of this interaction is not outlined clearly in the quadripartite model, making it unclear how to interpret the metaphor of a threshold. Furthermore, there are a number of ways the threshold and primary motivational precursor metaphors could be interpreted. Did Hall and Hirschman mean that the energy or pressure attached to a primary factor increases dramatically in the presence of certain internal (thoughts of children) or external (presence of children) cues? If so, how does this occur? Furthermore, once the primary motivational factor possesses more energy and therefore exceeds the threshold for an offence to occur, how does it become attached to the other three factors in order to cause a sexual offence? If it proceeds independently, how does this translate into sexually abusive actions rather than some other type of behaviour? More importantly, how can such a model apply to cognitive states or personality problems? They seem to be relatively 'cold' and do not appear to be energy conduits in any straightforward sense of the term. In our view, there could be something of value in these ideas but there are simply too many unanswered questions.

One way of resolving some of the difficulties described above is to conceptualise a threshold as representing the transition point between a vulnerability factor and its subsequent mental state. What this means is that an individual's predisposition to behave in a sexually abusive manner is activated in certain circumstances, resulting in the experience of sexual arousal, thoughts about having sex with children or negative emotional states. The kind of mental state that occurs depends on which factor is activated. For example, the possession of deviant sexual preferences by an offender (a trait factor) will cause sexual arousal (a state factor) in certain circumstances. The point at which the state of sexual arousal emerges constitutes the critical threshold. What remains to be clarified are how these vulnerabilities emerge, how threshold values are set and whether they can be modified, and how the four types of factors interact to produce a sexual offence.

A related point concerns the issue of whether cognitive distortions are able to function as primary motivational precursors. The difficulty is that cognitive distortions are *typically* defined as knowledge structures that convey information about people, the world and the offender himself. In a nutshell, they are 'cold' and relatively insulated from motivational processes and factors such as emotions, desires and drives. Cognitive distortions are essentially propositions or statements that refer to (presumed) facts about victims or the offender. They can be true or false and are not in any straightforward sense capable of motivating actions on their own; a desire or some other type of motive is also required for an action to occur. On the other hand, affective dyscontrol, sexual arousal and personality disturbance do not have this problem by virtue of their association with desires and emotions. Sexual arousal reflects desires, affective dyscontrol elicits motor tendencies (because of the composition of emotions), and personality factors embody attitudes all capable of motivating action. These three primary factors all involve goals (desired states) and therefore can help to push an individual to pursue certain outcomes. Therefore Hall and Hirschman's theory is vulnerable to the criticism that cognitive distortions cannot function as motivational precursors. Of course, if cognitive distortions are conceptualised as attitudes this is not a problem. But then the problem is to explain how distorted thoughts such as 'women desire sex all the time' which appear to be truth claims are really evaluative in nature: that is, attitudes. Attitudes convey evaluative responses to aspects of the world and are not capable of truth or falsity. The critical remarks outlined immediately above indicate that the quadripartite theory suffers from *internal incoherence*, a lack of *unifying power*, lack of *simplicity* and lack of *explanatory depth*.

CLINICAL UTILITY OF THE QUADRIPARTITE MODEL

We have critically evaluated the quadripartite model and ascertained that it contains a number of strengths and weaknesses. It is now time to turn to its clinical utility, and in the light of the above remarks, discuss how the theory can be applied in clinical settings.

The quadripartite model should not be used on its own to explain child sexual abuse or rape. It suffers from problems of incoherence, a lack of explanatory depth, lack of empirical adequacy and scope, unnecessary complexity and lack of unifying power. From a practical perspective, these failings mean that it will lead to inadequate case formulations and poorly specified intervention plans. Clinicians will need to fill in the explanatory gaps themselves by drawing upon additional theoretical resources: for example, theories of cognitive distortions and intimacy deficits, models of the offence process and other multifactorial theories of sexual abuse.

However, in our view, the quadripartite model does an excellent job of describing the types of phenomena evident in groups of child molesters (see Chapter 1). It is interesting that the four factors bear a remarkable resemblance to the dynamic risk domains detected by researchers such as Thornton (2002). These risk domains are (i) sexual interests/sexual self-regulation; (ii) attitudes supportive of sexual assault; (iii) interpersonal functioning and (iv) emotional lability. Hall and Hirschman's category of personality problems does not neatly map onto these domains but could be interpreted to refer to interpersonal functioning. It must be stressed that the risk domains are in fact clusters of phenomena, not underlying causal mechanisms, and therefore should not be used in the construction of case formulations. What we are suggesting is that the quadripartite model provides a helpful way of classifying or categorising the types of problems offenders exhibit. Therapists are recommended to keep the four problem domains in mind when assessing individuals and to ensure that they have asked questions that tap the various content domains clearly and comprehensively. Once a clear description of an offender's difficulties has been obtained, the next step is to infer the psychological dispositions hypothesised to cause these problems, and also to link them directly to the onset, development and maintenance of his sexually abusive behaviour.

In a sense, we agree with Hall and Hirschman that their theory can also function as a classification system for sexual offenders. But in our opinion, its real value lies in the categorisation of clinical phenomena rather than the allocation of offenders into four distinct aetiological groups.

CONCLUSIONS

Our overall impression of Hall and Hirschman's theory is that it has much potential, but is essentially incomplete. It is vague about the mechanisms thought to generate deviant sexual arousal, distorted cognitions, affective dyscontrol and personality problems, and does not convincingly outline how such factors interact. In addition, the current distinction between state and trait factors drawn in the quadripartite model is deeply problematic and reveals a lack of explanatory depth. Some of the four factors also seem to overlap, and the construct of primary motivational precursor is incomplete and requires fleshing out to clarify how the different factors intensify each other and combine to result in a sexual offence.

On the positive side, the quadripartite model does a marvellous job of identifying the significant clinical phenomena evident in sexual offenders. The division of the myriad difficulties exhibited by offenders into four major groups is a important conceptual innovation and we are sure will be of assistance to subsequent generations of researchers and therapists. A particularly valuable aspect of the outlining of the four factors or clusters of problems is that they constitute a focus for future aetiological theories. Furthermore, the quadripartite model's depiction of sexual abuse as being the outcome of distinct aetiological trajectories, each with its own unique cluster of problems, is particularly useful. In addition, the introduction of the construct of an *offence threshold* is innovative and helps to explain why psychological vulnerabilities only result in a sexual offence under certain circumstances. In our view, the theory still has much to offer and we encourage researchers to test directly its adequacy and reformulate it to avoid the problems noted in this chapter.

Chapter 5

WARD AND SIEGERT'S PATHWAYS MODEL

Ward and Siegert's pathways model was constructed initially as a theory knitting exercise (Ward & Siegert, 2002b) to further the scope and explanatory power of aetiological theories of child sexual abuse. Following systematic critiques of Finkelhor's precondition model (Ward & Hudson, 2001), Marshall and Barbaree's integrated theory (Ward, 2002) and Hall and Hirschman's quadripartite model (Ward, 2001), Ward and Siegert 'knitted' together the best elements of each of these theories into a comprehensive aetiological theory. The primary aim was to integrate the common and unique features of each of the above three theories into a theory that addressed explicitly a wide range of aetiological variables and was therefore able to provide a deep explanatory account of child molestation (Ward & Hudson, 1998a). Ward and Siegert were particularly keen to ensure the theory could account for the wealth of cognitive, emotional, interpersonal and sexual factors evident in child sexual offenders. Because Tony Ward was one of the theorists behind the pathways model, we sometimes use the first person perspective when referring to it throughout this chapter.

THE PATHWAYS MODEL OF CHILD SEXUAL ABUSE

In brief, the pathways model proposes that there are a number of distinct aetiological pathways that culminate in the sexual assault of a child. Each of these independent pathways is hypothesised to have at its centre a unique array of mechanisms that cause the problems typically seen in subgroups of child sexual offenders. In other words, different causal pathways will each have their own core set of dysfunctional mechanisms derived from varying developmental experiences which, in conjunction with circumstantial factors, result in an offence. The causal mechanisms include those associated with emotional regulation, interpersonal competence, cognition and sexual preferences. In the earlier version of the theory, we argued that there were five fixed aetiological pathways but we have recently adopted a more flexible approach that simply regards the five pathways as illustrative and allows for other possible trajectories. While the theory is named the *pathways model*, it is in fact a multifactorial theory (see Chapter 1) and therefore we will use the term 'pathways model' when referring to this theory by name and the term "theory" when speaking more generally.

Clinical Phenomena

A novel feature of the Ward and Siegert theory is that all of the problems evident in child sexual offenders can be organised into four sets of clinical phenomena. The four clusters of problems frequently found among adults who sexually abuse children are: (i) difficulties in identifying and controlling emotional states, (ii) social isolation, loneliness and dissatisfaction, (iii) offence-supportive cognitions (cognitive distortions) and (iv) deviant sexual fantasies and arousal. Sexual offenders' lack of empathy for their victims is subsumed under the cognitive distortions and emotional dysregulation categories. In the pathways model, each of the four clusters of clinical phenomena may be broken down into more fine-grained subcategories: for example, the category of intimacy deficits can be further subdivided into components such as interpersonal detachment or dependence. Furthermore, the overarching construct of emotional competence can be broken down into at least eight specific skills, including empathic responsiveness and the ability to cope adaptively with aversive emotional states (Saarni, 1999).

The pathways model recognises that sexual offenders are likely to vary in terms of the particular profile of clinical phenomena they display. Some individuals may struggle to establish and maintain close personal relationships while others report no problems in this aspect of their lives and instead experience difficulties monitoring their emotional states. In other words, child sexual offenders constitute a diverse group who reveal considerable variation in the type, severity and range of problems they present. According to the pathways model, the causes of these differences reside in distinct psychological dispositions or traits, essentially vulnerability factors.

Outline of the Pathways Model

A key assumption of the pathways model is that all human sexual actions are the outcome of a number of interacting psychological and physiological systems. From a social cognitive perspective, these will include motivational/emotional, interpersonal and cognitive, as well as physiological, systems (Pennington, 2002). Every human action involves emotions or motives (e.g. setting of goals), an interpersonal context (e.g. broader social setting in which actions take place), cognitive interpretation and planning (e.g. implementation of goals) and physiological arousal and activation (e.g. physical basis of actions). The different systems are comprised of subsets of causal mechanisms that interact with each other to cause human actions. From the perspective of the pathways model, there can be problems in any one of these general systems or their component structures and processes. What this means is that a satisfactory explanation of a complex phenomenon such as child sexual abuse will need to incorporate multiple levels of analysis and specifically address its biological, social, cultural, emotional, cognitive, physiological and interpersonal dimensions. Each set of mechanisms (i.e. each system) is thought to cause one of the specific clusters of clinical phenomena evident in child molesters. The inclusion of social and cultural contextual factors means that human beings are viewed as complex systems embedded within an array of social environments that facilitate their acquisition of skills and competencies, and also provide opportunities for goal satisfaction and further growth.

Thus, according to the pathways model the clinical phenomena evident among child molesters are generated by four distinct, and interacting, types of psychological mechanisms: emotional dysregulation, intimacy and social skill deficits, cognitive distortions, and distorted sexual scripts. Learning events, biological and cultural factors exert an influence through their effects on the structure and functioning of these sets of mechanisms. Psychological mechanisms generating child sexual abuse constitute *vulnerability* factors.

Psychological Mechanisms in Child Sexual Abusers

We will now describe examples of the four sets of mechanisms hypothesised to cause the clinical phenomena typically noted in child molesters. The mechanisms proposed in the pathways model are only meant to be examples and do not exhaust all of the possible causes of child sexual abuse. However, they are considered to be plausible mechanisms in light of contemporary research in both the general psychological domain and in the sexual offending area more specifically (Ward & Siegert, 2002b). In the future, however, theories of sexual offending are likely to have a more pronounced biological and developmental orientation (see Chapter 20).

It must be stressed that the pathways model was constructed with the strengths and weaknesses of Finkelhor's precondition model, Marshall and Barbaree's integrated theory, and Hall and Hirschman's quadripartite model firmly in mind. In a sense, it is a theory knitted together from the three most influential theories of child sexual abuse existing at the time of its development. However, were another aetiological theory to be developed today, we are sure it would now take quite a different form (see Chapter 20).

Intimacy and social skill deficits

For some time, clinicians and researchers have observed that sexual offenders frequently exhibit deficits in intimacy and social competence skills. In the past 15 years theorists have gone beyond simple social skill deficit models to postulate that many of these difficulties are the outcome of insecure attachment styles (Marshall, 1989; Smallbone & Dadds, 1998).

From an attachment perspective, early abusive experiences can result in distorted internal working models of attachment relationships and lead individuals to expect other people to be emotionally unavailable when they need them (see Chapter 12). An internal working model is simply a cognitive representation (i.e. schema) of individuals' potential interactions with others and contains judgements about the trustworthiness and value of other people, and the worth of the person concerned. There are different types of insecure attachment, each associated with different beliefs, interpersonal strategies and intimacy issues (Ainsworth, 1989; Ward, Hudson, Marshall & Siegert, 1995). But generally speaking, insecurely attached offenders may construe the world as a dangerous place and come to believe that disclosing their personal feelings and views to other people is unwise and likely to result in rejection or even punishment. One of the pitfalls of being insecurely attached is that infants are too anxious to explore their environments and therefore may become unduly concerned about personal safety issues at the expense of developing a rich understanding of their interpersonal and natural world (Ainsworth, 1989). In other words, they become socially handicapped and unable to function in a truly independent and mature way. One of the worrying things about insecure infant attachment is that it provides a template for individuals' adult intimate relationships and as such may result in a person who is unable to experience real intimacy with other adults.

Research indicates that insecure attachment might also result in problems with controlling mood states, overly critical self-evaluations (e.g. low self-esteem), poor problem solving, interpersonal dependence, impulsivity and low self-efficacy (Sperling & Berman, 1994). For example, individuals with a dismissive attachment style fear other people will reject them or behave in an aggressive and punishing manner toward them. The way individuals with this style resolve expected rejection is to distance themselves emotionally from close relationships and to be somewhat contemptuous of what they perceive as vulnerability in others. Therefore, they often impress as uncomfortable in intimate social situations and adopt a somewhat aloof and cold demeanour.

Sexual scripts

A primary way of explaining deviant sexual arousal in the past has been in terms of deviant sexual preferences. Typically, this idea has been introduced within a conditioning paradigm, with the acquisition of deviant preferences thought to be the outcome of learning experiences. In their presentation of the pathways model, Ward and Siegert argue that a valuable alternative approach is that of social cognition, or more specifically, the application of script theory to the sexual offending domain. Sexual scripts are the cognitive representations individuals acquire during the course of their development that specify how to behave in sexual encounters. They also help individuals interpret the meaning of other people's behaviour in sexual episodes and to identify the internal and external cues that signal the possibility of sex (Gagon, 1990; Money, 1986). Gagon (1990) states that 'Sexual scripts are involved in learning the meaning of internal states, organising the sequences of specifically sexual acts, decoding novel situations, setting the limits on sexual responses and linking meanings from nonsexual aspects of life to specifically sexual experience' (p. 6). In Gagon's theory of sexual scripts, there are three levels: the internal, interpersonal and cultural. The *internal* level involves a person understanding the physical, emotional and cognitive cues associated with sex and how they interact with specific contexts to create sexual opportunities. The *interpersonal* level focuses on the cues learned by an individual during his development that indicate when another person is interested in sex and how to respond appropriately. The *cultural* level involves the incorporation of norms, values, rules and beliefs into a sexual script. This type of information helps the individual to comprehend what is culturally permissible, and also provides an understanding of the broad cultural norms and practices associated with gender roles. In summary, a sexual script spells out when sex is to take place (i.e. context), with whom, what to do, and how to interpret the internal, interpersonal or cultural cues associated with different phases in a sexual encounter.

According to Gagon, all sexual scripts have the same components, although their form (i.e. the order of the different components) and content (i.e. the type of preferred partner, the kinds of sexual activities and the context for such activities) may vary from person to person. According to Gagon, the variability of sexual scripts is a function of individuals' particular learning histories. For example, sexual abuse may result in distortions in children's sexual scripts due to their cognitive and emotional immaturity. Because they do not really understand what sex involves and its place within human relationships, they are likely to develop dysfunctional attitudes and potentially harmful sexual practices (e.g. behave in sexualised ways with adults). The kind of distortions that occur in a sexual script include inappropriate partners (e.g. a significant age discrepancy or sex with an animal), maladaptive behaviours, (e.g. sadistic practices or indecent exposure) or inappropriate contexts (e.g. impersonal sex, sex when angry).

Emotional dysregulation

Self-regulation consists of the internal and external processes that allow an individual to engage in goal-directed actions over time, and in different contexts (Baumeister & Heatherton, 1996). They include the monitoring, evaluation, selection and modification of behaviour to accomplish one's goals in an optimal or satisfactory manner (Thompson, 1994). Emotional competence is basically the application of self-regulation processes to the emotional domain and consists of at least eight sets of skills (Saarni, 1999). These are: (i) awareness of one's emotional state, (ii) the capacity to identify other people's emotions, (iii) the ability to use the emotional vocabulary of one's culture, (iv) possessing the capacity to respond empathically to other people, (v) the ability to adjust one's emotional presentation depending on circumstances, (vi) the capacity to manage aversive emotions through a range of adaptive strategies, (vii) understanding that emotions play a critical role in establishing and maintaining intimate relationships and being able to act on this knowledge appropriately, and (viii) the capacity for emotional self-efficacy, that is, being able to experience the kind of emotions considered appropriate in specific situations: emotional authenticity. Saarni argues that emotionally competent people possess enhanced self-esteem and a considerable degree of resilience when confronted with particularly difficult problems and situations (Saarni, 1999).

A child develops emotional competence through the successful navigation of social encounters, thereby acquiring the skills necessary to control emotional states and to modulate effectively interpersonal experiences. Lack of appropriate experiences and of the modelling of emotional skills by others will probably result in deficits in one or more of the eight sets of skills and lead to numerous personal and interpersonal difficulties. For example, having problems in identifying other people's emotions will increase the chances that an offender will misinterpret a child's responses to sexual abuse, and come to believe that the child is not harmed, and may even benefit from the experience. Alternatively, maladaptive coping strategies such as a reliance on masturbation or sexual activity to modulate distressing feelings also constitutes a risk factor for sexual offending.

In summary, emotional regulation, therefore, involves the control of affective states in the service of individuals' goals. For example, reducing interpersonal anxiety by withdrawing socially may help a young man to feel less vulnerable. Problems with emotional regulation might be a function of dysfunctional goals (e.g. to avoid feelings), inadequate coping strategies (e.g. use of alcohol), inability or a disinclination to utilise coping skills, or poorly modulated affective states (Ward & Hudson, 1998a).

Cognitive distortions

In the pathways model, Ward and Siegert observe that in the sexual offending area the term 'cognitive distortions' is typically used to refer to maladaptive beliefs and attitudes, and problematic thinking styles (Ward, Hudson, Johnston & Marshall, 1997). One recent suggestion has been that underlying schemata (Ward et al., 1997) generate the cognitive distortions evident in offenders' descriptions of their sexually deviant behavior. Ward and Keenan (1999) have argued that sexual offenders' cognitive distortions emerge from underlying causal theories about the nature of their victims rather than stemming from unrelated, independent beliefs. These implicit theories function like scientific theories and are used to explain empirical regularities (e.g. other people's actions) and to make predictions about the world. They are relatively coherent and constituted by a number of interlocking beliefs and their component concepts. The relationship of these beliefs and categories to one another gives each theory its unique explanatory power and form. Thus categories are theory-impregnated and can only really be understood via their relationships to other concepts within a theory's network of constructs. This means that the core ideas constituting an implicit theory partially gain their meaning from their relationship to the other ideas; an implicit theory is basically a network of concepts and their interrelationships. Evidence that does not 'fit' the theory's basic assumptions and predictions is rejected or interpreted in light of these core assumptions. The offender draws upon his implicit theories about victims and infers their mental states, interprets their behaviour and makes predictions about their future actions and mental states.

Ward and Keenan (1999) have identified five implicit theories held by child molesters, and recent experimental research has provided evidence that they have good content validity (Marziano, Ward, Beech & Pattison, in press; Mihailides, Devilly & Ward, 2004). These five implicit theories are:

1. *Children as sexual beings*: where children are thought to possess the capacity to identify sexual practices and behaviours that satisfy them and to make decisions about when, with whom and how their sexual needs will be fulfilled.
2. *Nature of harm*: this implicit theory is concerned with the nature of harm and is based on two general beliefs: (i) there are degrees of harm and (ii) sexual activity in itself is beneficial and unlikely to harm a person.
3. *Entitlement*: here the core idea is that some people are superior to and more important than others. Because of their superior status such individuals have the right to assert their needs above others, and to expect that this right will be acknowledged and agreed to by those who are judged to be less important.
4. *Dangerous world*: this implicit theory is based on the core belief that the world is a dangerous place and that other people are likely to behave in an abusive and rejecting manner toward the offender in order to promote their own interests.
5. *Uncontrollable*: the key assumption here is that the world is essentially uncontrollable and people can therefore do little to combat its influence. Human beings are thought to be comprised of structures and processes that cannot be substantially altered or managed; emotions, sexual feelings, events all just happen to people; they are unable to exert any major personal influence on the world.

The 'implicit theory' theory is based on the idea that some individuals have ways of thinking about others, themselves and the world that make them vulnerable to behave in a sexually abusive manner. In this approach, the focus is on the content of offenders' beliefs rather than the processes generating those beliefs. Another way of understanding sexual offenders' cognitive distortions is that they are simply rationalisations constructed after an offence has occurred that function to excuse individuals' morally reprehensible actions (Gannon, 2002; Ward et al., 1997). The mechanisms underlying this type of distortion are those associated with excuse giving and self-esteem maintenance. They do not originate from maladaptive schema (implicit theories), and in fact from the viewpoint of the functional perspective, it makes little sense to speak of cognitive distortions such as excuse giving as constituting cognitive vulnerability factors as all. They occur after an offence has occurred to deflect social and personal criticisms (see Chapter 8 for a fuller examination of this distinction).

Aetiological Pathways

We will now describe a number of aetiological pathways derived from the pathways model. It is important to keep in mind the earlier caution that the five pathways to be discussed are not meant to exhaust all possible combinations of mechanisms. They are simply included for illustrative purposes and in a sense represent relatively 'pure' types. According to the pathways model, the offence pathways described are associated with different psychological and behavioural profiles, each reflecting separate aetiologies (Figure 5.1). Each pathway has a distinctive profile in that the relevant primary causal mechanism will result in a unique set of symptoms. The term 'primary' is used to mean that the causal mechanism in question impacts more on other mechanisms than they impact on it: that is, it has more causal influence. In the model, each aetiological pathway has its own unique array of causes. The number and types of causes will vary depending on a pathway's particular developmental trajectory.

In the pathways model, although each pathway has a primary mechanism at its core, *every* sexual offence involves the presence of all the symptom clusters and the activation of their underlying mechanisms. Thus all sexual crimes against children are hypothesised to involve emotional, intimacy, cognitive and arousal components. What is claimed to vary from pathway to pathway is the strength and range of the problem clusters and the particular set of causes that generate them. In the pathways model, the primary causal mechanism is hypothesised to *recruit* other types of mechanism in order to generate the range of symptoms typically seen in child molesters, and ultimately to cause a sexual offence. Yet only the primary mechanism is thought to be necessarily dysfunctional and the others may typically function quite normally and only exert a harmful effect because of the driving force of the primary mechanism.

For example, an offender may lack several emotional regulation skills and therefore on certain occasions turn to sex as a way of ameliorating his feelings of inadequacy. Following a particularly stressful period of his life, the need to enhance his mood through sexual activity is particularly intense and his usual masturbatory fantasies do not work. Lacking a sexual partner, he exploits a child to gratify himself sexually, resulting in a temporary lift in his mood. During sex with the child he fantasises about a woman he knows in order to get an erection.

This individual's primary dysfunctional mechanism is his lack of emotional competency and it is this deficit that effectively drives his offending behaviour. Sexual arousal is recruited as a means to improve his mood. The offender's social competency mechanisms are also utilised to obtain access to a child but do not in themselves display any marked dysfunction or problems. He is a reasonably socially skilled individual who sexually exploits a child to reduce his unhappiness. Finally, there are no enduring offence-supportive implicit theories and he normally regards sex with children as morally wrong and has no previous history of sexual offending. During the offence process he disengages his normal self-evaluation mechanisms by focusing on the anticipated pleasure and relief and it is only afterwards that he is overcome with guilt and remorse. All four sets of causal mechanism are involved in the offence, but the offender's social competencies, sexual scripts and cognitive system are all reasonably intact and are simply co-opted in the service of mood regulation on this particular occasion.

Pathway 1: multiple dysfunctional mechanisms

The first aetiological pathway derived from the Ward and Siegert theory contains individuals who have pronounced flaws in all the primary psychological mechanisms. However, at the heart of this pattern of multiple deficits will be

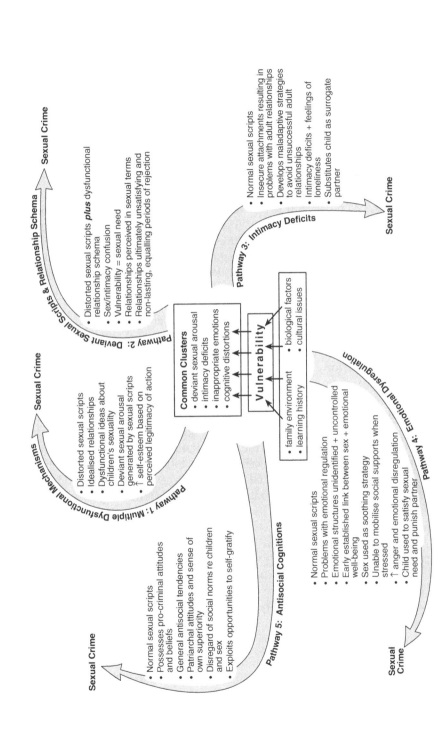

Figure 5.1 Aetiological pathways emerging from a base of vulnerability. Reprinted by permission of Sage Publications Ltd from Connolly, M. (2004). Developmental trajectories and sexual offending. *Qualitative Social Work*, 3, 39–59 (© Sage Publications, 2004)

distorted sexual scripts, usually reflecting a history of sexual abuse or exposure to sexual material or activity at a young age. The difficulty for this group is that early sexualisation and the acquisition of deviant sexual scripts are likely to have a cascading effect on the other domains of human life and therefore result in the creation of 'pure' paedophiles. In the case of uncomplicated paedophilia, the sexual scripts of offenders will contain distortions in the specification of preferred or ideal sexual partners. The 'ideal relationship' will be depicted as one between an older person and a child. However, the other elements comprising sexual scripts may also contain distortions and it is expected that such additional flaws will be correlated with additional sexually deviant behaviour. For example, a specified action or sequence of sexual behaviours might contain sadistic and aggressive elements or unusual practices.

As stated above, offenders following this pathway will also have marked dysfunctions in all the other mechanisms. They will have dysfunctional implicit theories about children's sexuality and their ability to make informed decisions about sex, inappropriate emotional regulation, and impaired relationships and attachment mechanisms (Ward et al., 1997). The existence of distorted sexual scripts, in conjunction with the other distorted mechanisms, will create all four clusters of problems evident in child sexual abusers: namely, inappropriate emotions (an emotional regulation problem), intimacy deficits, cognitive distortions and deviant sexual arousal. Sexual scripts contain cognitive components referring to the features of a preferred partner, and therefore incorporate distorted beliefs concerning children's needs and inclinations. Additional dysfunctional beliefs concerning children's needs in general, the threat posed by others, and the offender's ability to effect change in himself and others will also be involved in the production of sexually abusive behaviour. Deviant sexual arousal is generated in certain contexts (when confronted with sexual, affective or situational cues) by the activation of the sexual script. Just as the activation of a restaurant script will lead to the desire for, and actions designed to consume, food, so a sexual script contains goals concerned with the achievement of sexual satisfaction. Intimacy problems may occur as a function of the fact that an individual's preferred sexual partners are children and therefore it is probable that he would be unable to relate to adults in a way likely to lead to an open and mature relationship. The mechanisms generating intimacy deficits are suggested to be independent of—although causally interactive with—sexual scripts. Finally, emotional problems may be evident in the experiencing of positive emotions when sexually abusing a child and negative emotions such as anxiety when in potentially intimate situations with adults.

Pathway 2: deviant sexual scripts

In a second aetiological pathway, individuals are hypothesised to have subtle distortions in their sexual scripts and dysfunctional relationship schemas (Sperling & Berman, 1994). These individuals may have experienced sexual abuse as children and as a consequence become prematurely sexualised. However, the sexual script distortion is thought to reside in the *context* in which sex is sought rather than in terms of an inappropriate preferred sexual partner. In other words, this type of child molester will tend to seek impersonal sex when feeling aroused. Sex is seen as a purely physical means of release and is totally divorced from intimacy and emotional depth. As adults, individual following this pathway are likely to seek reassurances through sex and equate sex with intimacy (Marshall, 1999). This occurs through the confusion of sexual cues with those signalling affection and closeness, and a fear of rejection by others if they were to attempt to establish intimate relationships. Interpersonal closeness is, therefore, only achieved via sexual contact and feelings of vulnerability are misinterpreted as indicating sexual need. The avoidance of intimacy, coupled with a drive for impersonal sex, is expected to lead to ultimately unsatisfying encounters and relationships that do not last. Sexual offences against children may occur following periods of rejection by adults, if children are perceived as more trustworthy and accepting. The fact that children are chosen as sexual partners is largely a question of opportunity and sexual or emotional need. Cognitive distortions exhibited by offenders following this pathway will reflect the drive for impersonal sex, and the legitimacy of treating others as mere conduits for sexual gratification.

Pathway 3: intimacy deficits

The third aetiological pathway contains individuals hypothesised to possess an insecure attachment style and to have subsequent problems with intimacy establishment. These individuals will have normal sexual scripts and generally prefer to have sex with adult women or men. However, in certain situations individuals following this pathway might be prepared to substitute a child in the place of an adult, essentially regarding the child as a 'pseudo-adult'. There is no conflation of sex and intimacy (as in pathway 2), but rather an inappropriate choice of a sexual partner. The primary cause of the sexual abuse of a child in this situation resides in intimacy deficits and the subsequent experience of intense loneliness. For such individuals, their needs for sex and closeness will be transferred to children, because of their perceived acceptance of the offender.

The type of intimacy deficit experienced by this group of child molesters is related to their romantic attachment style. For example, child molesters with a preoccupied attachment style are characterised by a craving for acceptance and seek reassurance constantly from potential partners concerning their worth and acceptability. In contrast, fearful-dismissively attached offenders seek emotional independence from others because of a fear of rejection from potential or actual partners. In other words, it is better to be emotionally safe than run the risk of disappointment and social rejection. Both these individuals would be expected to have problems communicating in an open and adaptive manner with other people and in certain circumstances exploit children to meet their intimacy needs (Bumby, 2000).

The substitution of children for adult sexual partners is likely to be accompanied by cognitive distortions revolving around issues of intimacy (e.g. 'she understands me') and possibly a dangerous world implicit theory (e.g. 'he will not hurt me'). Intimacy needs will probably be expressed in a sexual way under certain circumstances, for example, when feeling sexually aroused. Sexual desire is a cyclic phenomenon in most people and sexual offenders are no different. What this means is that because an individual following this pathway turns to children to meet his intimacy needs, when he periodically experiences sexual desire, it is likely to be focused on children, rather than adults. After all, children are viewed as potential intimate partners and sexual needs are typically met within the context of an intimate relationship.

If adults are regarded with suspicion, children could be perceived as suitable sexual partners; sex however is always in the service of intimacy needs and not the other way around. This will result in sexual arousal in the context of a sexual encounter with a child, possibly intimate and 'loving' emotions, and often in an attempt to create an adult-like relationship with the child.

Pathway 4: emotional dysregulation

A fourth aetiological pathway derived from the pathways model contains individuals who lack some or many of the core sets of skills constituting emotional competence (Saarni, 1999; Thompson, 1994). The resulting deficits may involve any of eight types of emotional incompetence, and range from problems identifying emotions in themselves, a lack of empathy or poor emotional integrity, to difficulties managing strong negative emotional states. According to Ward and Siegert, two kinds of emotional dysfunction are especially probable and are directly associated with sexual offending. First, individuals might primarily have problems controlling their emotions (e.g. anger) and sexually abuse children either as a way of punishing partners or simply because they have lost control of their actions, and therefore behave in a self-destructive and antisocial manner. This is an under-regulation issue and involves a loss of emotional control. Second, individuals who have difficulty calming or soothing themselves may use sex as an emotional modulation strategy. It is not clear in this situation why sex would be utilised as an emotional coping strategy but one possible scenario is that compulsive masturbation during early adolescence, and the absence of alternative means of increasing self-esteem or mood, could create a strong link between sex and emotional well-being (Cortoni & Marshall, 2001). If such individuals are stressed it is probable they will look to sex as a means of ameliorating their mood. On some occasions, this might involve sex with children or coercive sex.

Individuals with enduring emotion regulation problems are likely to rationalise the offence once it has occurred (e.g. 'I lost control') and make little attempt to create an intimate relationship with a child. The presence of sexual arousal in the context of powerful emotional states should increase an offender's risk of committing a sexual offence, either through a loss of control or because sex is a preferred coping strategy. Thus, an association between negative emotions and sex, or simply the presence of sexual desire in conjunction with poor impulse control, increase the chance that individuals following this pathway will molest a child sexually.

Pathway 5: antisocial cognitions

A fifth aetiological pathway derived from the Ward and Siegert theory contains individuals who hold beliefs and attitudes supporting criminal behaviour in general. They are hypothesised to have no sexual script distortions but are characterised by a history of criminal offending across multiple domains. Sexual offenders following this pathway are *generalists* rather than specialists, and are likely to have committed a wide variety of criminal acts, including property crimes, violent assaults and driving offences (Smallbone & Wortley, 2000). In support of these observations, research reveals the existence of child molesters who have extensive criminal histories in addition to their sexual offences (Smallbone & Wortley, 2000; Soothhill, Francis, Sanderson & Ackerley, 2000). The offending of these individuals may be facilitated by endorsement of the dangerous world and entitlement implicit theories. If other people are regarded with suspicion in some situations, offenders are expected to behave aggressively in order to forestall any punitive actions toward themselves, in a sense, to undertake a 'pre-emptive strike' (Polaschek & Ward, 2002). Furthermore, those offenders endorsing the entitlement implicit theory frequently have patriarchal attitudes towards children and possess a strong sense of their own superiority. If they have an opportunity to indulge their sexual urges at little perceived cost, it is highly probable they will do so. This group of child molesters is hypothesised to have engaged frequently in criminal actions as children and adolescents, and may receive a diagnosis of conduct disorder (Andrews & Bonta, 1998). Their sexual offences against children will be part of this general picture of antisocial behaviour and may not reflect any enduring deviant sexual preferences.

The major type of mechanism underlying this group's sexual offending resides in their antisocial attitudes and beliefs. These cognitive distortions in conjunction with sexual desire and opportunity will result in the sexual abuse of a child. Such individuals disregard social norms forbidding sex with children and are expected to exploit any opportunity for self-gratification if it presents itself. They are likely to experience positive emotional states when abusing a child because of the pleasure experienced, and the fact that they are meeting their needs in a personally acceptable manner.

Conclusions

In the pathways model, situational triggers are hypothesised to interact with the various predispositions of individuals to sexually abuse children. The nature of the situational triggers will vary according to the particular profile of causes underlying each individual's offence trajectory or pathway. For example, it is suggested that for offenders who have distorted sexual scripts, sexual need in conjunction with the judgement that it is safe to abuse a child will result in sexual abuse. However, for an offender with deficits in emotional competence, intensely stressful situations can precipitate an offence.

EVALUATION OF THE PATHWAYS MODEL

The pathways model was constructed as a provisional framework and needs further refining. However, it does meet the required features of a comprehensive theory of child sexual abuse outlined in Chapter 1. This has been achieved by knitting together the strengths of Finkelhor's precondition model, Marshall and Barbaree's integrated theory, and Hall and Hirschman's quadripartite model. The pathways model highlights the view evident in these theories that child molestation is caused by multiple factors and that offenders sexually abuse children for very different reasons. In addition, the claim that vulnerability to commit an offence is fashioned from learning, cultural and psychological mechanisms is a core assumption in the pathways model. The concepts of diverse aetiological pathways and interacting mechanisms have been utilised to provide an overarching framework with which to integrate the best elements of the above three theories. We see this theory as having a number of distinct strengths, which we outline next.

A first strength is that the pathways model stipulates that child sexual abuse can occur via a number of distinct, and interacting, pathways. Each of these pathways involves a range of psychological factors and social and cultural variables. In this respect, it builds on the work by Finkelhor, Marshall and Barbaree, and to a lesser extent, Hall and Hirschman, by suggesting that cultural, social, psychological and situational factors converge to cause sexually abusive behaviour. The range of variables integrated into the pathways model points to its *unifying power* and *explanatory depth*.

Second, the pathways model explicitly identifies the four problem clusters (social problems, mood difficulties, deviant arousal and cognitive distortions) typically discerned in child molesters, thus providing a clear focus for its application in clinical interventions: empathy training, social skills interventions, reconditioning interventions, cognitive restructuring, stress management, and anxiety, depression and anger management. This is clearly an element derived from Hall and Hirschman's theory, although the specification of mechanisms which cause these problems has been advanced in the pathways model.

However, while the pathways model does explicitly refer to developmental constructs, its scope is clearly limited to adults: it does not constitute an explanation of child or adolescent sexual offenders. Arguably these require theories of their own although it should be noted that many of the ideas developed in the pathways theory are likely to be applicable directly to these populations. For example, the importance of distinct developmental trajectories and the insight that the sexual abuse of children might be related to distinct, and interacting, causal mechanisms (Araji, 1997). These aspects of the theory indicates its *empirical scope* and potential *fertility* with respect to treatment.

Third, a good theory should postulate mechanisms capable of generating the core clinical phenomena associated with sexual offenders and detail their inter-relationships with each other; that is, it should be dynamic in nature. The pathways model states that different offender groups and offence pathways are characterised by different core pathologies, that collectively map onto the four clusters of clinical problems evident in child molesters. Moreover, it is able to explain why offenders who exhibit entrenched sexual deviance may differ in their clinical presentation. Pathological sexual scripts may vary in terms of the desired partner or focus of sexual attention, the contexts in which this occurs (internal and external) and their preferred sexual strategies. Child molesters may resemble each other in respect of having distorted sexual scripts, but have different kinds of problems, or even possess multiple scripts. These diverse representations of sexual goals, partners and practices will result in different symptom profiles. Perhaps this feature of the pathways model reflects its greatest asset, the ability to unify promising aspects of other theories and also its description of the mechanisms thought to generate sexually abusive behaviour. It speaks to the theory's *explanatory depth, unifying power* and *fertility*.

Finally, the pathways model has gone beyond the other three major explanations of child sexual abuse when describing in detail some of the mechanisms thought to result in this phenomenon. In doing this, existing theories and research have been used that, while not universally accepted, constitute important and powerful perspectives in contemporary psychological science. These include the use of script theory, attachment research, work on implicit theories, self-regulation theory and emotional competence. This aspect of the theory indicates its *unifying power*.

Despite the strengths of the pathways model, it has a number of weaknesses. First, there are still areas of vagueness and the theory is lacking a substantive evidential base. The data that support its major ideas tend to come from other areas in psychology and there is little direct support from the sexual offending domain. That is, as yet it has not been subject to explicit testing and evaluation. This points to the relatively weak *predictive accuracy* of the theory and its limited *empirical support*.

Second, the postulation of four sets of mechanisms underlying the four clusters of problems evident in child molesters is perhaps a little too neat and does not really work. What we need to know is exactly how the four sets of causal factors interact with each other. There is evidence from neurocognitive researchers such as Pennington (2002) that a more parsimonious and theoretically fruitful way to parse psychological functions is to divide them into three major neuropsychological systems: a *motivational system* characterised by emotional and psychological needs, the source of goals; an *action selection* system responsible for the selection and control of behaviours designed to realise intrapersonal and interpersonal goals; and a *perception and memory* system responsible for processing and retaining perceptual information and declarative and procedural knowledge. Each system is associated with different brain systems and, in certain circumstances, specific types of psychopathology. This weakness in the theory indicates it could lack *simplicity*.

Third, while the idea of dysfunctional mechanisms recruiting normally functioning ones to generate sexually abusive actions is interesting, it is essentially metaphorical and needs to be fleshed out in more detail. This problem suggests a lack of clarity in the theory and possibly some degree of *incoherence*.

CLINICAL UTILITY OF THE PATHWAYS MODEL

In our view, the pathways model is a rich and useful aetiological theory. The fact that it was intentionally knitted together from the strengths of Finkelhor's precondition model, Marshall and Barbaree's integrated theory, and Hall and Hirschman's quadripartite model means that it exhibits a number of the clinical virtues of these important theories.

First, the theory is able to provide clear treatment targets, and if used to structure assessment, will ensure that clinicians do not miss critical problems. In addition, the recognition that a major problem such as empathy could be due to one of several related psychological components is extremely helpful. One offender's failure to respond empathically to his victim could be related to an inability to infer accurately mental states in others, possibly due to the distorting effects of implicit theories or poor emotional identification skills. Another's problems could be the result of a lack of skill in managing effectively strong emotional states. This might cause the offender in question to avoid intense negative emotions for fear of being overwhelmed by feelings such as despair. Each of these problems with empathy would be expected to be associated with distinct clinical presentations and to be relatively easy to distinguish provided therapists have the theory in mind during the assessment process.

Second, the fact that the four risk domains identified by Thornton (2002) correspond to the four sets of mechanisms identified in the pathways model supports its value as an explanation of why certain offenders are at risk of further offending. Thornton's domains are deviant sexual interests, distorted attitudes, socio-affective functioning and poor self-management (Thornton, 2002). The mapping of risk domains onto underlying mechanisms suggests that the type of risk factors likely to trigger reoffending will vary according to offenders' causal pathways. This should focus therapists when undertaking risk assessments on the subset of dynamic risk elements suggested by each person's case formulation.

Third, in the pathways model individuals are expected to have distinct underlying causes for their clinical problems and to require different types of interventions to ameliorate the impact of these causal mechanisms. It would seem, therefore, a good idea to base individual treatment plans on case formulations that reveal the unique causes of a person's sexually abusive behaviour. The upshot of this approach is that because people commit sexual offences for different reasons they will only benefit from some of the treatment strategies currently utilised in the area. It does not really make clinical sense to agree that an offender's sexual offending is primarily a function of his problems with mood regulation and then to insist he receive therapy for deviant sexual preferences. Furthermore, offenders with attachment-related deficits might need to reduce their level of distrust and to be prepared to disclose their feelings and thoughts to potential partners. Finally, those persons with distorted sexual scripts should respond to intensive reconditioning interventions to remove their entrenched deviant sexual preferences and beliefs. The idea underlying this point is actually very simple: only give sexual offenders the treatment they require in order to stop offending.

Finally, the pathways model proposes that all of the causal mechanisms associated with human beings' sexual actions will be involved in every sexual offence. Although only one of the underlying mechanisms may be dysfunctional, it is hypothesised to recruit or enlist the others in the process of generating child sexual abuse. For example, an individual with attachment-related deficits may see children as potential intimate partners without necessarily preferring them sexually. The sexual aspect only enters the picture within the context of intimacy seeking and is not the driving factor in this particular man's offending. The important thing to take away from this aspect of the theory is that just because a person sexually abuses a child (and is aroused etc.) it does not necessarily follow that he prefers children sexually or has any deviant sexual preferences. The sexual aspect of the offence could simply be a downstream effect of the primary causal mechanism such as intimacy seeking or emotional regulation. The value of keeping this possibility in mind is that therapists will not then erroneously infer that dysfunctional causal mechanisms underlie relatively peripheral clinical phenomena. Instead, the aim will be to isolate the factors that are effectively driving the offence and to focus therapeutic attention squarely on them when designing a treatment programme.

CONCLUSIONS

The pathways model is a useful addition to the sexual offending literature and represents an attempt to *build* on existing theoretical work rather than run the risk of continually reinventing the wheel. A major feature of the theory is the notion of multiple offence trajectories and the subsequent implication that a 'one size fits all' approach to treatment is unlikely to be successful. The evidence supporting this claim is tentative at this point in time, although the idea of multiple offence pathways is commonly accepted in the wider area of clinical psychology (Pennington, 2002). Perhaps the most enduring aspect of the theory will be its theory knitting approach to research and the assumption that it is better to absorb the lessons of history (prior theory construction) than to ignore them and repeat our mistakes. We owe our colleagues and our clients more than that.

Chapter 6

MALAMUTH'S CONFLUENCE MODEL
OF SEXUAL AGGRESSION

Over 15 years—from about 1980 to the mid-1990s—Neil Malamuth and his colleagues built up an impressive corpus of empirical investigations into sexual aggression and its correlates. Constructed mainly with college students, this body of work facilitated the development of a theory of sexual assault on several different levels. Malamuth began this research and theorising using feminist and social learning frameworks (e.g. Malamuth, 1981, 1986) but later became interested in evolutionary analyses of rape, because he saw these approaches as better able to explain *why* patriarchal dominance developed and widespread dominance of men by women did not (Malamuth, 1996). The evolutionary psychology approach is covered in more detail in the next chapter. Here, we will touch only on those aspects relevant to Malamuth's model.

From evolutionary psychology, Malamuth adopted the important distinction of *ultimate* and *proximate* causes, and the confluence model encompasses both. Ultimate causes are concerned with whether a particular characteristic or pattern of behaviour arises from natural selection. In the context of rape, evolutionary psychology asks whether the ancestral environment caused selection directly to favour men who raped women over those who did not (the 'rape as an evolved adaptation' position), or whether instead, selection promoted related behaviours (e.g. the ability to function sexually in the absence of a responsive partner). This is the 'rape as a by-product of selection' argument (Thornhill & Thornhill, 1992). Whereas ultimate causes can explain *why* humans may have developed particular behavioural tendencies, proximate causes explain *how* these patterns develop (Symons, 1979). Proximate causes focus on how a particular genetic inheritance comes to be expressed in a specific individual's life course. What developmental processes are necessary? What types of environment? Because evolutionary psychology includes both types or sources of causes, its proponents argue that it provides the most complete explanations of human behaviour (Ward & Siegert, 2002a).

MALAMUTH'S CONFLUENCE MODEL

Ultimate Causes of Sexual Aggression Against Women

Malamuth (1996) provided the most detailed account of this facet of his model. Evolutionary theorists of rape observe that ancestral environments favoured different mating strategies for women and men, based on the markedly disparate levels of parental investment necessary to produce offspring. For women, total number of possible offspring will be small, and the minimum investment is nine months of gestation. Therefore choosing partners on the basis of genetic quality and commitment to parenting is the optimal strategy. For men, the issues are different. With viable offspring produced from just a few minutes of effort, men can potentially contribute their genes to an almost infinite number of offspring, but they can never be sure offspring they are raising are actually theirs.

A key tenet of Malamuth's model is that two pathways converge to produce sexually aggressive behaviour: *sexual promiscuity* (i.e. a preference for impersonal sex with many partners) and *hostile masculinity* (i.e. hostile, dominating and controlling characteristics). The above observations about sexually dimorphic strategies (i.e. different optimal strategies for men versus women) were important to Malamuth (1996) because of the prominence in his model of the concept of impersonal sexual preference. Profound differences in optimal strategies suggest to an evolutionist that natural selection will have created fundamentally different psychological mechanisms in the brains or minds of men and women. Men— although *capable* of sex in the context of long-term affectionate pair-bonding— will be more capable than women of performing sexually in the presence of a fertile stranger (Symons, 1979). Conversely, women will prefer sexuality with men who are invested in them.

It follows that if men are adapted for sexual performance in impersonal contexts, a disinterested, or even unwilling, woman partner will not inhibit sexual performance. In summary, although men are likely to vary in the degree to which they prefer impersonal sex, and although environmental factors and life experiences influence the development of a preference for sexually coercive behaviour, essentially sexually differentiated evolutionary pressures make men far better equipped for such coercion than women.

Turning now to the *hostile masculinity* pathway, Malamuth (1996) drew first on the work of others who theorised that differing reproductive interests commonly underlie human conflict (e.g. Alexander, 1979). Of course, force and coercion are tried-and-true measures for asserting one's interests when they directly conflict with those of another. Furthermore, it is in women's reproductive interest to selectively withhold sex from insufficiently invested male partners. Malamuth noted that Buss (1989) found that withholding sex produces anger in men, and argued that if women thwart a particular man's sexual access often enough or at a developmentally formative time, he may develop a chronically hostile interpersonal style. Thus he will be easily angered and capable of using coercion and force to assert his dominance whenever he perceives that a woman may be threatening his reproductive success (Malamuth, 1996).

Second, men cannot be sure of the paternity of their offspring. So selection pressures may have favoured the development of proprietary sensibilities in male minds, leading to a desire to dominate and control women (Malamuth, 1996). This dominance motive is hypothesised to operate for men across all of the domains of a partner's life, not just in a sexual context, because a broad approach gives better control of sexual access. To summarise, chronic anger at being denied optimal sexual access by women, and anxiety about paternity in the face of possible rivals, foster hostile, controlling behaviour towards women.

Like other evolutionary theorists, Malamuth (1996) took the view that it is primarily sexual/reproductive mental mechanisms that determine rape from a male perspective. Further, these same mechanisms also generate motivation to dominate and control women more generally, and thus may be important in nonsexual violence and other antisocial behaviour towards partners.

A Model of Proximate Causes

Malamuth, Heavey and Linz (1993) first proposed this model—which is referred to as the *interactive* or *interaction* model—and its four central elements: (i) that sexual offending results from a convergence of risk factors, (ii) that the causes of aggression against women are somewhat specialised and do not predict as effectively men's behaviour toward other men, (iii) yet the causes of sexual aggression also predict other controlling and coercive behaviour toward women, and (iv) non-evolutionary factors—referred to here as *environmental* factors—are important in explaining variations in actual behaviour. We now describe each of these in turn, drawing mainly on Malamuth (1996) and Malamuth, Heavey and Linz (1993, 1996).

Convergence of risk factors

Malamuth and colleagues' approach is explicitly multivariate: three types of risk variables—motivating, disinhibiting and opportunity—need to converge for an individual to be at high risk of sexual aggression. In that sense, it is a prototypical rather than a typological approach, emphasising the melding together of crucial risk variables rather than the salience of individual variables (Malamuth et al., 1993). Indeed, their empirical research suggests that these variables may have a synergistic rather than an additive action in generating risk (Malamuth, Sockloskie, Koss & Tanaka, 1991). The impressive empirical research programme that has served to underpin and develop this model is based primarily on the use of six predictor variables, which we discuss below. These variables operationalise the two hypothesised pathways to sexual aggression: hostile masculinity (HM) and sexual promiscuity (SP; Malamuth et al., 1993). So the important point here is that rather than seeing these pathways as alternatives, Malamuth et al. postulated that they merge to provide the most complete theoretical and empirical account of sexual violence.

Domain-specific causes

Second, although there is likely to be overlap in the factors that predict men's aggression against women *and* men, Malamuth et al. (1993) expected that there are *specific* causal factors for aggression towards women, as a consequence of the evolved sexual dimorphism we discussed in the previous section. So, they speculated that some of the causes of the sexual assault of women will not be predictive of aggression towards other males.

Within-domain generalisation

Third, Malamuth and colleagues (1993) theorised that the same proximate factors that predict sexual aggression will also predict other forms of aggression, coercion, control and domination of women, since these are all manifestations of a motive to enhance paternity confidence, and express dissatisfaction with conflict over sexual access.

Environmental influences

Fourth, rather than taking a deterministic view of evolution, Malamuth et al. (1993) accounted for individual differences in the risk of sexually coercive behaviour through variation in the environmental activation of inherited psychological mechanisms. So, all men are postulated to inherit mechanisms that give them a degree of readiness to coerce women sexually, in order to achieve optimal reproductive success. However, differences in childhood developmental experiences, peer influences, cultural contexts and immediate stimuli all contribute to whether or not those mechanisms are activated.

In the confluence model, the ontogeny of coerciveness (Malamuth, 1996) is based in early childhood experiences. Parental violence, and sexual and physical abuse of male children lay the bases for developments that later put women at risk. Abused boys may develop cynical, adversarial schemata regarding relationships and women, and a disinterest in affection-based bonds with women. They may also fail to develop important life skills such as frustration tolerance and conflict mediation. Such children are at enhanced risk of association with delinquent peers and engagement in delinquent activities. If they also engage in premature independence from their families they may adopt adult sexual behaviours without having developed the interpersonal skills they need for mature socio-sexual relationships. Consequently they use domination and coercive tactics to gain what they want, rather than negotiating outcomes, because they do not value preserving the mutuality of the relationship (Malamuth et al., 1991). Both of the hypothesised trajectories (HM and SP) evolve from this background.

Impersonal sex/sexual promiscuity (SP) path

Involvement in a delinquent peer subculture may foster the development of 'a noncommittal, game-playing orientation in sexual relations' (Malamuth, 1996, p. 281), where peer status and self-esteem are mainly determined by sexual conquest, and so strategies to get women to engage in sex become highly developed. However, Malamuth (1996) stated that not all males who are promiscuous use sexual coercion, so the contribution of promiscuity to rape may well be moderated by hostile, controlling characteristics (Malamuth et al., 1991).

Hostile masculinity (HM) path

The second path refers to a constellation of personality traits made up of two overlapping elements: (i) an orientation—especially to women—that is defensive, adversarial, mistrusting and insecure, and (ii) satisfaction from dominating, humiliating and controlling women. High HM men use sex to put women 'in their place', and express hostility toward them. So this pathway both motivates and disinhibits sexual aggression. Disinhibition occurs because hostility disables otherwise empathic responses that would usually disrupt or prevent coercive behaviour. HM and its associated anger towards women correlate in adulthood with feelings of having been rejected, harmed and picked on by many women. A high HM man may experience women as threatening, and may deprecate and degrade them to reduce their potential to control (i.e. hurt) him. He is likely to feel that he is failing in the competition to attract and retain a desirable mate, and deals with his anxiety about imminent rejection by trying to prevent it through control of his partner's life (Malamuth, 1996).

A summary of the proximate model, as proposed and tested by Malamuth et al. (1991), is depicted in Figure 6.1. Longitudinal research discussed below led them to suggest that sexually aggressive behaviour in young adulthood may

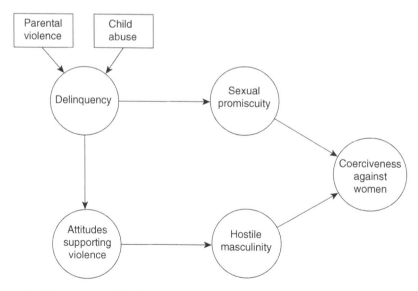

Figure 6.1 Malamuth's (1991) model of the characteristics of coercive men
Source: From Malamuth, N. M. (1996). The confluence model of sexual aggression: feminist and evolutionary perspectives. In D. M. Buss & N. M. Malamuth (Eds), *Sex, power, conflict: Evolutionary and feminist perspectives* (p. 284). New York: Oxford University Press.

signal poor relationship health later in life, including relationship conflict and distress, social isolation from women, repeated infidelity, and verbal, physical and sexual aggression.

EVALUATION OF THE CONFLUENCE MODEL

Strengths

Malamuth's confluence model (CM) is important for several reasons. First, it rests on an impressive programme of research, giving it the most solid and direct empirical basis of any theoretical framework for adult sexual assault. Second, the database was generated entirely with sexual assaulters outside the criminal justice system: in this case, male college students. To the degree that it converges with research and theorising on adjudicated offenders, it goes some way to allaying the gnawing uncertainty many writers express about the generalisability to all sexual assaulters of research and theorising based heavily on convicted offenders. Third, multivariate theories generally are based on the premise that single risk factors are of little relevance on their own and must come together somehow to create an offence. However, the synergistic confluence aspect of the model addresses the interaction of risk factors more fully than other level I theories.

The CM is *externally consistent* with several other theories and models. Although Malamuth did not mention an important contemporary—Marshall and Barbaree's (1990) integrated theory of sexual offending (see Chapter 3)—the two bear a strong resemblance, especially in the childhood and adolescent developmental aspects. However, although it falls short of providing a fully filled-out evolutionary psychology account, the CM contains a more complete outline of the ultimate causes of sexual aggression than Marshall and Barbaree's theory. The CM also acquits itself better in the area of explaining why the same childhood and adolescent factors that have been established to precede chronic and diverse adult criminality (e.g. Loeber, 1990) come to be specific to *sexual* offending.

The CM also is broadly consistent with Hall and Hirschman's (1991) quadripartite model, but Malamuth's criticism of that model—that different forms of sexual aggression are said to be dominated by one of four individual risk factors—is borne out by his data showing no great increase in risk until perhaps four or more of these risk factors come together. The other fundamental difference in the two models is that Hall and Hirschman describe three of their four factors (physiological sexual arousal, cognitive distortions, affective dyscontrol) as state factors, whereas Malamuth's risk factors are all viewed as relatively enduring (i.e. traits).

Without question, because of the strategy leading to its development, the greatest strength of the CM is in the area of *predictive* or *empirical* accuracy. Other sex offender theorists' work is obviously informed by data and clinical practice (e.g. Marshall and Barbaree, Chapter 3; Ward and Siegert, Chapter 5). However, in the sexual offending domain, the CM is the clearest and most coherent longitudinal example of the 'theory-informs-data-informs-theory' model of scientific development in the sex offender area, exemplifying as it does, 15 or 20 years of theory development and refinement informed by gradually more elaborate empirical studies. A number of early studies hold important places in this progression (e.g. Malamuth, 1983, 1988), but because of space limitations and our primary focus on conceptual rather than solely empirically based theory evaluation, these will not be reviewed here. Instead, we examine briefly empirical investigation of the main assumptions of the CM, and then concentrate on two important later studies that are the most sophisticated tests of the proximate model itself: Malamuth et al. (1991) and Malamuth, Linz, Heavey, Barnes and Acker (1995). Before doing this, we describe the core constructs in this programme. These constructs feature in a number of studies, though they have been operationalised in a variety of ways. As described by Malamuth et al. (1993), they are:

- *Sexual responsiveness to rape*: Malamuth and colleagues have recorded relative arousal to rape depictions compared to consenting sex stimuli, using plethysmography. This is the only one of these core independent variables that has been measured by using a method other than self-report questionnaire.
- *Dominance as a motive for sex*: assessed using questionnaire items, this variable is concerned with the extent to which men's desire to have sex is motivated by a desire to control and dominate women (i.e. sexual conquest).
- *Hostility toward women*: both a motivational and disinhibiting variable, hostility toward women refers to a pervasive attitude of irritability, suspiciousness, resentment and bitterness exclusively directed to women. It is usually measured here using the Hostility Toward Women (HTW) scale (Check, Malamuth, Elias & Barton, 1985).
- *Attitudes facilitating aggression against women*: the key attitudinal variable, this term actually refers to a bundle of highly related attitudes that include acceptance of the use of force in sexual interactions with women, rape myths and adversarial beliefs about heterosexual relations. Burt's 1980 scales—especially the Acceptance of Interpersonal Violence (AIV) against women scale—have usually been used to measure this variable.
- *Antisocial personality characteristics*: current research demonstrates that in incarcerated serious offenders, psychopathy—at least as it is measured using the Psychopathy Checklist—Revised (Hare, 1991)—is quite a good predictor of sexual offending risk (e.g. Serin, Mailloux & Malcolm, 2001). Malamuth et al. (1993) included this construct despite believing at that time that there was little relationship between measures of antisocial personality characteristics and sexual offending. They used Eysenck's (1978) Psychoticism scale.
- *Sexual experience*: sexual experience has been viewed as both an indicator of the degree of opportunity to use sexual aggression, and as an individual difference variable in its own right. Malamuth et al. (1993) have used several inventories to measure research participants' exposure to a variety of heterosexual sexual experiences, and also to record number of sexual partners and age of first sexual experience.
- *Use of sexual aggression*: Koss and Oros's (1982) Sexual Experiences Survey (SES) is a self-report measure that assesses levels of sexual aggression on

a continuum from psychological pressure through to acts that meet legal criteria for rape. The *dependent measure* in these studies has usually been SES scores.

Malamuth (1986) used the first six variables above to predict self-reported sexual aggression. Using data from 95 men, he found that deviant plethysmography scores produced the biggest correlation with SES scores. All variables except antisocial personality were significantly related, and four (deviant sexual arousal, hostility to women, attitudes supporting violence towards women and sexual experience) made unique contributions in multiple regression analyses. Furthermore, regression equations with interactive terms accounted for more variance than equations with additive effects only, indicating statistically the confluence (or synergistic) aspect of the variable combinations. Figure 6.2 illustrates support for the central assumption that risk factors must converge for sexual aggression to occur. Here, the amount of self-reported sexual aggression is depicted as a function of the number of predictor variables on which each participant scored in the top half of the distribution. It demonstrates clearly that the risk of sexual aggression rises markedly above near-zero levels only when individuals are high on four or more risk factors.

In addition to this confluence aspect, other main assumptions have generally been supported by empirical investigation, for example, *domain specificity*. In an experimental paradigm in which subjects delivered noise blasts to confederates as punishment for errors, Malamuth (1988) found no relationship between

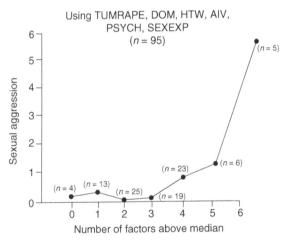

Figure 6.2 Mean level of sexual aggression by number of high-risk factors. TUMRAPE, tumescence arousal to rape index; DOM, dominance motive; HTW, Hostility Toward Women scale; AIV, Acceptance of Interpersonal Violence (against women) scale; PSYCH, psychoticism scale; SEXEXP, sexual experience measure
Source: From Malamuth, N. M., Heavey, C. L. & Linz, D. (1993). Predicting men's antisocial behavior against women: the interaction model of sexual aggression. In G. C. N. Hall, R. Hirschman, J. R. Graham & M. S. Zaragoza (Eds), *Sexual aggression: Issues in etiology, assessment, and treatment* (p. 79). Washington, DC: Taylor & Francis.

dominance, AIV scores or rape arousal, and aggression towards male confederates. However, correlations between 0.25 and 0.41 were found between these variables and aggression towards a woman confederate. SES sexual aggression scores correlated 0.34 with aggression toward men, showing—as would be predicted—that men who are aggressive towards women are also sometimes general aggressors. Importantly, this study demonstrates that the power of these variables is not limited to prediction of sexual aggression. They also can be used to demonstrate *domain generalisation* (i.e. other forms of antisocial and coercive behaviour towards women).

Another series of studies has examined a completely different variable from this same domain: sexually aggressive men's conversational behaviour with women. Malamuth et al. (1993) reported several unpublished studies showing that observer ratings of domineering conversational behaviour towards women were significantly correlated with predictors of sexual aggression such as the dominance motive and attitudes to violence towards women. Domineering behaviour has been defined to include such things as boasting, criticising, interrupting, disagreeing, overriding the wishes of and obstructing the replies of a female conversational partner (Malamuth et al., 1993).

Now to the two studies that form the most elaborate tests of the CM. The first, (Malamuth et al., 1991) tested data obtained from a large nationally representative multisite US college sample of between 1713 and 2652 predominantly European American men with a mean age of 21 years.

Using structural equation modelling, Malamuth et al. (1991) constructed a model with half of the sample and then largely confirmed it by replication using the data from the remaining half. The tested model is identical to Figure 6.1 in every respect but one. Social isolation—defined here as the tendency to avoid friendships and closeness with women—was added to the model, and was strongly predicted by HM. In this study, HM was measured using three scales: the HTW scale, Burt's (1980) Adversarial Sexual Beliefs scale, and a measure of destructive masculinity, characterised as an exaggeratedly self-autonomous version of male identity, in which self-protective and self-assertive actions dominate all other interpersonal behaviour (Malamuth et al., 1991).

All relationships in the model were strong and significant except for two. The relationship between Parental Violence and Delinquency and the relationship between Delinquency and Attitudes Supporting Violence were both weak. In conclusion, the design of this study was impressive, particularly because the sample size permitted testing model fit with unused data. However, two important weaknesses are (i) the absence of independent data because all data were obtained from self-report questionnaires, and (ii) the cross-sectional nature of the study. Both are addressed in the next study.

Malamuth et al. (1995) used an unrelated sample of college students to test the cross-sectional model, elaborate it with new variables, and then extend it to prediction of behaviour 10 years later. Time 1 data were collected between 1979 and 1981 from approximately 350 mainly European Canadian men. Time 2 data were collected 10 years later on the 176 men and 91 of their women partners who could be found using official records, and who responded to the initial invitation to participate.

The original model (see Figure 6.1) was again replicated. Better operationalisation of variables may have contributed to the strong relationship found this time between the early risk factors and adolescent delinquency (previously measured using just two items). New variables included sex drive, coercive sexual fantasies, general hostility-proneness, and masculine gender role stress (i.e. the extent to which men experience stress in non-traditional sex role situations such as having a woman manager, a taller partner or being unemployed). Outcome variables included sexual aggression, nonsexual physical aggression, verbal aggression and relationship distress. Women partners also provided data on outcome variables. Finally, couples at Time 2 were invited to participate in videotaped problem-solving discussions in which observers rated the extent to which the man dominated his partner and expressed hostility toward her.

This study produced extensive results and just a few are reported here. Using Time 2 data cross-sectionally, General Hostility predicted HM scores, and also made a direct contribution to both Relationship Distress and Verbal Aggression. Masculine gender role stress made only weak contributions to the model. The longitudinal model is depicted in Figure 6.3.

There are several important theoretical implications of the models tested with this sample. First, sexually aggressive behaviour by men in their early 20s was a significant predictor of problematic relationship behaviour 10 years later. This

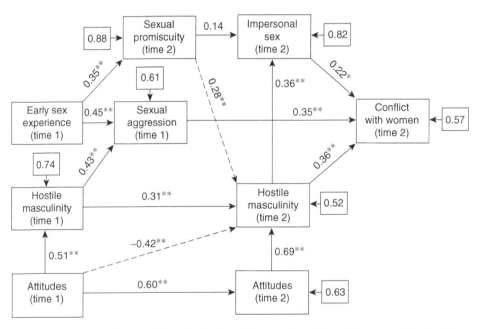

Figure 6.3 Longitudinal path analysis of predictors of conflict with women. Broken lines indicate path added on the basis of modification indices. $^*p < 0.05$; $^{**}p < 0.01$
Source: From Malamuth, N. M., Linz, D., Heavey, C. L., Barnes, G. & Acker, M. (1995). Using the confluence model of sexual aggression to predict men's conflict with women: a 10-year follow-up study. *Journal of Personality and Social Psychology*, 69, 363.

finding suggests common mechanisms, supporting the contention among domestic violence researchers that marital rape is often part of men's relationship violence, even though neither partner may disclose it (Yllö & Finkelhor, 1985). Malamuth et al. also point out that early sexual aggression—which in their study was probably not against long-term partners or even meaningful partners at all—may be an early warning sign for long-term relationship antisociality.

Second, Malamuth and colleagues suggested that they had found no clear evidence that sex drive per se predicted sexual aggression risk, in contrast to Ellis (1991) and others who have predicted that it does. Rather, they interpreted their findings as supporting the multifactorial nature of sex drive, partly because preference for impersonal sex was more clearly related to sexual aggression than preference for more personal, intimate sex (Malamuth et al., 1996).

Another theoretically interesting finding relates to the specificity of predictor variables. Malamuth and colleagues' results suggest that some variables predict both sexual and nonsexual aggression while others performed poorly except with sexual aggression. Thus Malamuth et al. proposed that future investigation be shaped by a hierarchical model of risk factors, from general to specific. Drawing on the work of Malamuth (1988), they suggested that the most general level comprises factors that contribute to general criminal behaviour (e.g. impulsivity, criminal attitudes). At the second level are variables relevant especially to types of intergroup conflict, such as those that predict harassment of weaker outgroups. Third are variables that predict antisocial interactions with women, and finally, at the bottom, are the factors that specifically predict sexual coercion.

There has been little independent research as yet on the CM. Murnen, Wright and Kaluzny (2002) independently confirmed the predictive accuracy of the HM construct. In a meta-analysis of hyper-masculine ideology as a predictor of sexual aggression, they found Malamuth's HM construct produced one of the two largest effect sizes in this literature. Wheeler, George and Dahl (2002) replicated the cross-sectional prediction of sexual aggression as conducted by Malamuth et al. (1995). They found again that HM and SP interact to predict sexual aggression, using the same types of measures.

In addition to the strength of its *empirical* and *predictive accuracy*, the CM has other virtues. One obvious one is *scope* in that the model insofar as it is explanatory at all (see below) predicts both temporally contiguous and temporally distant nonsexual violence and other obnoxious behaviour towards women. Its *unifying power* lies in the way the CM draws together feminist theories that specify that rape is about power and domination of women with evolutionary (and other) theories that say that not only rape, but relationship conflict, partner assault and even conversational domineeringness are sexually motivated. The longstanding and quite fruitless debate about whether rape is 'about sex or about power' (e.g. Brownmiller, 1975; Burt, 1980; Groth, Burgess & Holmstrom, 1977) is quite elegantly dealt with in the CM (Malamuth, 1996).

There are other strengths too. It is a *simple* model, yet it has high *fertility*, which Malamuth and colleagues have demonstrated with their own empirical research and suggestions for future development. Regrettably—as is too often the case in psychology—few others have seen this model as a stimulus for future research.

One important exception is Wheeler et al. (2002). Malamuth et al. (1993) suggested that generalised empathy deficits may form a unique, and as yet uninvestigated, aspect of HM. Wheeler et al. set about investigating this suggestion and it proved accurate, with scores on a general empathy measure (the Interpersonal Reactivity Index; Davis, 1980) predicting which high-risk men (high on both SP and HM, low on empathy) were most likely to report sexual aggression. Numerous other testable predictions can be derived from this research. To give one other example, the suggested mechanism behind the HM pathway is the perception of having been hurt and rejected by many women. This is a suggestion that would fit neatly with existing implicit theory research on rapists (Polaschek & Ward, 2002).

There may also be *treatment fertility* in the CM, particularly when intervening with this unadjudicated college population. We discuss this aspect in a later section.

Problems

The confluence model does not purport to be a mature scientific theory. Nor is it a metaphor- or analogy-based model in the sense we described in Chapter 1. In fact, one of the most frustrating aspects of the model is that much of its strength is unrealised, although it contains a number of potentially worthwhile and elegant features (e.g. specific recognition of motivating, disinhibiting and opportunity factors; two interacting pathways and so on). The sketchiness of both the evolutionary psychology-based ultimate-causes aspect of the model and the proximate statistical modelling-based model is evident, but we concentrate here on evaluating the latter. A more detailed examination of the ultimate-causes evolutionary theories of sexual offending follows in Chapter 7.

It is not entirely clear how the latent constructs (e.g., HM, parental violence, delinquency) in the structural equation models were obtained in the first place, and why these particular constructs were chosen and others were not. For example, generalised hostility was originally omitted, as were alcohol and drug use, empathy deficits, impulsivity, sexual fantasy, intimacy deficits, attachment difficulties and other variables commonly implicated in sexual aggression by other theorists.

However—and more importantly—because of the heavy emphasis on statistical modelling, there is only cursory detail about what drives the relationships between variables. In other words, for the CM to become a fully-fledged theory, the actual mechanisms that link related variables together need to be described in much more depth. This observation has two key aspects. First, developmental mechanisms are missing. To take an example, just two variables—parental violence and childhood sexual and physical abuse—adequately predicted adolescent delinquency. However, they do not constitute a full theoretical picture of the relevant childhood factors leading to the development of juvenile conduct problems. And even if they did, what are the effects of these experiences? What is it that an abused child carries into adolescence and expresses in delinquent behaviour?

Second, the cross-sectional aspect of the model—the interaction of HM and SP—is also vaguely specified. Although, at least in student samples, three or four or more of their risk factors need to co-occur for there to be a high risk of sexual aggression, does it matter which variables? And if they do co-occur, again, how does that interaction actually work? An example here is that Malamuth et al. (1991) speculated that HM characteristics moderated the expression of SP characteristics. They tested this hypothesis using moderated multiple regression and found that the interaction was significant for sexual aggression but not for nonsexual aggression. Thus they found statistical support for their hypothesis, but there is no real explanation of the theoretical mechanisms.

In other words, we have referred to the predictors as 'risk factors' and they are statistical markers of risk. However, it is not clear if these markers are actually causal factors that *explain* behaviour, or simply predict it by reliable association with the behaviour.

As with Hall and Hirschman's (1992) model (see Chapter 4), each of these important predictive factors is likely to contain distinct subforms within it. Concordant then with the colloquial observation that 'the devil is in the detail', much of the *explanatory depth* of this model is yet to become visible, and awaits future work.

Relatedly, the age of the CM has compromised its *explanatory potential*. Much of the foundational research to which Malamuth and colleagues refer is from the 1980s or earlier. Important theoretical work on victim empathy, attachment style, intimacy deficits and self-regulation styles that could help provide plausible mechanisms for the CM has been conducted since that time. For example, the childhood experiences described by Malamuth and colleagues may generate dismissive attachment style, which may explain how delinquency comes to be acted out sexually (Malamuth et al., 1991).

Malamuth et al. (1995) offered Berkowitz's (1993) construct of 'associative networks' as having the potential to account for risk factor convergence, but without explaining how. And the confluence aspect implies that there is some notional 'critical threshold' at which risk level gets expressed, as with Hall and Hirschman (1991, 1992). This issue is also not addressed.

The model gives a heavy emphasis to trait variables in the aetiology of sexual aggression. There is no room currently for situational influences, despite the significant theoretical and practical limitations now recognised in models that do not take a person–situation interactional view of human behaviour (Wortley & Smallbone, in press).

Finally, the model appears to ignore the issue of offender and offence heterogeneity (Knight & Prentky, 1990; Polaschek & King, 2002). Indeed the emphasis on a common pathway to sexual offending, in which factors converge, suggests some degree of uniformity.

There are at least two possible explanations for this impression. It may be that offenders who are high-functioning enough to attend university and are still available in the community 10 years later *are* less heterogeneous than convicted populations, perhaps. Although we think it unlikely, if this suggestion is true then the model has a *scope* limitation. Alternatively, the design hides possible heterogeneity because the aim was predictive accuracy. Malamuth et al. used median splits in the risk convergence analysis to define high scores in a population in which most scores were probably heavily skewed towards the lower end. Thus the range of scores that fall into the high category, and the variable combinations of higher and lower high scores across variables may involve a diversity of mechanisms that regulate heterogeneity. The model also does not report on variations in sexually aggressive acts. We assume such variation exists, and the SES covers quite a wide range of behaviour, and so would have the capacity to detect some variation. Examining offence characteristics data may also provide more evidence of heterogeneity.

CLINICAL UTILITY OF THE CONFLUENCE MODEL

The confluence model of sexual aggression is not adequate as a comprehensive aetiological theory of sexual aggression against women, as we have explained above. Nor does it profess to be. It is a model, rather than a theory, with seriously compromised explanatory depth, but a strong empirical infrastructure. Thus it could be argued to offer useful suggestions about assessment areas worthy of attention, but cannot inform formulation because it lacks a 'story' that would integrate those assessment findings together in a way that can be used to plan intervention.

We can speculate that the CM applies best to relatively intellectually competent, superficially socially skilled offenders who can maintain a heterosexual relationship to some degree, and avoid prosecution for interpersonal aggression. The offences they commit may well be at the low-violence end of the spectrum. Perhaps the most useful application of the model to intervention then is in the design of prevention programmes for college populations (e.g. Schewe & O'Donohue, 1996), especially for men at high risk of, or reporting minor acts of, sexual coercion. Furthermore, the scales used in testing the CM could be useful instruments in identifying which men should be targeted for such programmes, and in monitoring risk after intervention.

In the context of programming for rapists on criminal sentences, the model is less helpful in a wholesale sense. However, it broadly affirms the importance of hostility, hostility towards women, violence-supportive attitudes and so on in underpinning rape risk. And we think the sexual promiscuity/impersonal sexual preference pathway is a relatively novel contribution to considerations about the criminogenic needs of rapists. Rather than a high level of sexual interest per se being the problem, it suggests that a construct like dismissive attachment—found to be quite prevalent in rapists (Ward, Hudson, & Marshall, 1996)—fosters not only disinterest in closeness, but interest in high levels of uninvolved sex. Do current interventions for rapists adequately recognise that even continuing to maintain a preference for consenting impersonal sex would seem to be a risk for rapists, and may help maintain a dismissive interpersonal style? What are our current interventions for sexual promiscuity (i.e. the formation of many short-term sexual liaisons in which consenting sex may be the aim, at least some of the time)?

CONCLUSIONS

Malamuth and his colleagues developed an elegant statistical model of the proximate causes of sexual aggression, and embedded it in a combination of evolutionary, feminist and social learning precepts. The resulting CM has an impressive empirical entourage but fails to recognise its full theoretical potential, at least in part because its development appears to have stalled about a decade ago. The CM exhibits a poverty of explanatory depth resulting from generally vague or unspecified mechanisms. Although Malamuth takes care to distinguish the CM from Hall and Hirschman's theory (Chapter 4), it is similar in some ways. Its division of risk factors into two paths—or trajectories—is interesting, and the sexual promiscuity pathway is quite novel. Its convergent risk feature suggests, as Hall and Hirschman do, that there is a critical threshold to offence risk, but this aspect is not developed. And it considers only trait factors. On the appealing side, it covers the important area of unadjudicated offenders, and it easily accommodates domain generality in harmful behaviour directed against women, a common clinical finding. It offers some useful aspects for intervention though it is not complete enough to stand alone. However, we believe it is an unjustly neglected theoretical approach that would benefit from considered integration with more recent work on level II mechanisms (e.g. attachment, intimacy deficits, fragile high self-esteem).

Chapter 7
EVOLUTIONARY THEORY
AND SEXUAL OFFENDING

Human beings are hybrid creatures, and in this respect, something of an enigma. On the one hand, we are beings of flesh and blood, subject to biological laws and processes like any other animal. On the other hand, we are artefacts, products of a culture, animals who use technology as a means to achieve valued goals but who in turn are shaped substantially by this technology. The puzzle is that it is possible to portray humans in two fundamentally different and arguably mutually exclusive ways, a finished product versus a self-constructing entity. How can they be both? Surely there is an element of truth in both descriptions and therefore it would be unwise to embrace one image of human nature at the expense of the other. We propose that this dichotomy is not just a reflection of the gap between social science and biological explanations, but is also evident *within* the camp of evolutionary perspectives on human behaviour. These two perspectives are *evolutionary psychology* and *gene–culture co-evolution theory*.

Evolutionary theorists (the evolutionary psychology perspective) emphasising the biological aspects of human nature argue that over thousands of years, natural selection sculpted the brain into a complex, multipurpose instrument capable of helping organisms survive and reproduce in a hostile world (Tooby & Cosmides, 1992). Theorists espousing this perspective propose that human beings have a 'thick' nature: that is, they arrive into the world with a dense structure and complex array of psychological competencies. These structures or modules collectively constitute the human mind, which is hardwired with solutions to ancient problems such as finding a mate, identifying and escaping from predators, detecting nutritious foods, and ascertaining whether or not a fellow tribe member is honest or deceptive (Buss, 1999). Tooby and Cosmides claim that the architecture of the human mind can only be properly understood in terms of our evolutionary past and that 'Our modern skulls house a stone age mind' (Cosmides & Tooby, 2000, p. 13). The role of the environment is hypothesised merely to activate and calibrate latent capacities, while culture constitutes a wrap of ideas and values around a hard core of genetically determined traits. In other words, culture does not really create people's traits much at all; at best, it exerts no more than a moderating effect on preset causal processes. Our natures are thought to unfold effortlessly in certain environments; they are in a real sense *preformed* by eons of evolutionary processes (Buller & Hardcastle, 2000).

In contrast, gene–culture co-evolution theorists, who advocate that human beings are characterised by psychological plasticity and a capacity to be significantly shaped by their environment, tend to be more interested in the relationship between biology and technology. According to Andy Clark (2003, p. 3), humans are 'natural-born cyborgs': part animal, part machine. What he means by this is that humans construct and utilise technology to change themselves and their world in accordance with specific intentions and plans. In a real sense, people are (increasingly) biological artefacts. Technology extends the reach of human agency into regions formerly though impossible and does not diminish or reduce individuals to the status of mere machines. According to Clark, brains are scaffolded from the moment of birth by an impressive suite of learning opportunities, deliberately engineered environments, that allow each person to construct a self and the skills and competencies to pursue his or her vision of a good life. Individuals are born into a world replete with a number of different developmental resources, including genetically encoded predispositions, a culture, parents, and the presence of teachers and learning institutions. These resources equally influence the development of children and are all important in the process of facilitating their growth from birth to maturity. In a nutshell, humans are co-constructed through the delicate interplay between biological, psychological, social and environmental variables.

The theoretical positions sketched above represent only two of the possible ways of applying evolutionary ideas to the domain of human behaviour (Laland & Brown, 2002). Human beings can be studied through a variety of different biological lenses, each focusing on a subset of causal factors and possible mechanisms. An additional layer of complexity is added once the terms 'nature' and 'natural' are analysed (Lee, 1999; Sterelny, 2003). The concept of nature is a slippery one and has many different meanings. In view of this indeterminacy of meaning, theories claiming to explain human behaviour naturalistically are systematically ambiguous. It is important for any such theory to provide an account of how the term 'nature' is being used and what it refers to. We suggest that some of the problems evident in the dispute between evolutionary psychologists and gene–culture evolutionary theorists noted above are in part due to the fact that they use the term 'nature' in different ways.

In a penetrating examination of the relationship between the natural and the artefactual, Lee (1999) distinguishes seven different ways of defining 'nature'. These are: (i) nature as contrasted with 'culture': unintended as opposed to intended products; (ii) nature contrasted with the supernatural: the latter term referring to objects and events that exist outside time and space as we currently understand it; (iii) nature as evident in parts of the world that are unaffected by human actions: intentional or unintentional; (iv) nature as adversely affected by human actions through, for example, pollution or forest clearing; (v) nature as contrasted with the artefactual: that which is not the product of human intentions in any sense; (vi) nature as natural kinds: fundamental essences of things; and (vii) nature as naturally occurring physical elements, for example, biological or chemical (Lee, 1999). In the latter definition, 'nature' refers to a type of matter; the contrast here is between artificial human-made elements (e.g. plastic) and the raw biological material of the earth and its various life forms.

We contend that evolutionarily inclined theorists who claim our minds are preformed and genetically determined are presupposing the meanings of 'nature' evident in (iii), (v) and possibly (vi); essentially, nature is that which we cannot really dramatically modify or alter. Human beings are thought to have a hardwired internal structure that causes them to interpret the world and the actions of others in clearly demarcated ways and also generates human behaviour within specified parameters. In other words, there are very few degrees of freedom available to human beings when contemplating what to do or how to interpret a chain of events.

In contrast, evolutionary theorists who state that behaviour is the product of biological and cultural/technological structures allow for the possibility of human beings altering their internal nature in some manner. People's psychological plasticity enables researchers and practitioners of various stripes (e.g. medical scientists, doctors, psychologists, teachers, parents) to treat them as biological artefacts: beings that can be redesigned through the use of technology embodying human intentions. An emphasis on the possibility of shaping biological beings in ways that embody human intentions reflects the meaning inherent in Lee's seventh definition. This perspective allows theorists to view human beings as part of the natural world and to admit also the possibility that their basic nature is capable of being altered intentionally by human intervention and planning (e.g. genetic engineering, drugs, use of certain parenting practices and so on).

In our view, the application of evolutionary theories to the sexual offending field has been heavily influenced by evolutionary psychology's assumptions concerning the meanings of 'nature'. We consider this a mistake and believe that a more promising way of explaining human behaviour naturalistically resides in the utilisation of some form of gene–culture co-evolutionary perspective (Odling-Smee, Laland & Feldman, 2003).

In this chapter, we first briefly outline the basic ideas comprising Darwinian approaches to *Homo sapiens*, in order to provide an appropriate context for understanding the significance of evolutionary theory for human behaviour. We will then discuss five different evolutionary theories of human behaviour, three of which are also briefly described. Next we critically examine evolutionary psychology and niche construction theory, evaluating the ability of each perspective to account for sexual aggression. In the final section we discuss the clinical utility of evolutionary theories of sexual offending.

THEORY OF EVOLUTION

The fundamental idea in evolutionary theory is that organisms slowly evolve over time, and through a process of natural selection either adapt to environmental challenges or become extinct. The process of change is gradual, comprised of small, incremental modifications in existing organs or characteristics, which can lead to the emergence of new characteristics or even new species. The gradual sculpting process typically results in life forms that appear to be intentionally designed, and frequently are exquisitely equipped to live in certain environments. The effect of millions of years of evolution is to present developing organisms with stern challenges, problems which, if they remain unsolved, are likely to result in their extinction. Through the processes of natural selection and sexual selection animals that are the winners in the evolutionary struggle develop specific physical and psychological adaptations that enable them to meet these challenges.

As we noted in the previous chapter, there are two major forms of evolutionary explanations of human traits, *ultimate* and *proximate*. Ultimate explanations attempt to identify the function of a given trait or mechanism by determining its role in solving a particular adaptive problem within the ancestral environment. A proximate explanation focuses on the nature of the causal mechanisms that underpin its current functional role (Buss, 1999). Ultimate causes include such things as the ancestral environment, sexual selection and natural selection. Proximate causes include such variables as the person's genes, their developmental history, learning and environmental stimuli. An important strength of evolutionary psychology is that it explains behaviour in terms of both *ultimate* and *proximate* causes.

There are three essential elements in Darwin's ideas about natural selection (Darwin, 1859). First, individual members of a species all *vary* with respect to their physical and psychological traits. Second, some individual members of a species will demonstrate variations that make them better able to survive or adapt to changing environmental conditions. For example, the faster deer is more likely to escape predatory animals. Third, those individuals that are better equipped to survive will be more likely to breed and in doing so will pass on these characteristics to their progeny. Consequently, these inherited characteristics will become more common within that species.

In addition to natural selection, Darwin also discerned one other important process in evolution: *sexual selection*. This is the idea that male and female members of a particular species will demonstrate distinct preferences in their choice of mates based upon the physical or behavioural characteristics of such organisms. Consequently, individuals with characteristics or traits that are highly preferred in mates will leave behind more offspring and these characteristics will become more frequent in the population. For example, in certain species of birds (e.g. peacocks), the females demonstrate a preference for males with extravagant, brightly coloured plumage. An interesting point is that on some occasions natural and sexual selection might work against each other, for example, while the gaudily coloured male peacock tail is likely to lead to increased mating opportunities it could also make it easier for predators to detect and catch them. In this example, the very feature that increases the peacock's inclusive fitness also diminishes it on some occasions!

Evolutionary Perspectives on Human Behaviour

There are at least five different ways of applying evolutionary theory to human behaviour (see Laland & Brown, 2002, for an excellent discussion of the five theories: sociobiology, human behavioural ecology, memetics, evolutionary psychology and gene–culture co-evolution theory). The alternative evolutionary perspectives adopt distinct views on a number of related issues, including the relationship between genes and human development, the role of learning in explaining human behaviour, and the degree to which human nature is hard-wired or subject to modification through intentional (cultural) interventions (Laland & Brown, 2002). Each of the five evolutionary theories has its strengths and weaknesses and is the focus of continued research and theoretical development (Laland & Brown, 2002). For reasons that are not entirely clear, evolutionary psychology has had the most influence in psychology and is the approach underpinning the majority of the current evolutionary work in the sexual offending area (e.g., Quinsey, 2002; Quinsey & Lalumiere, 1995). Since we will be examining evolutionary psychology and gene–culture co-evolution theory in considerable depth later in the chapter, in this section, a brief description of the other three perspectives will be given.

First, the *sociobiological approach* to explaining human behaviour was introduced to the general public by Edward Wilson in his landmark book *Sociobiology: The new synthesis* (1975). Wilson and his colleagues adapted methods and ideas from ethology to the study of human beings and systematically investigated the functional significance of human social behaviour. The essence of the sociobiological perspective is nicely captured in a quote by Wilson where he states that it is 'the systematic study of the biological basis of all social behavior' (1975, p. 4). The basic assumptions underlying this theory are actually quite straightforward. First, human beings are animals and therefore should be studied using methods derived from researchers studying other animals because all are part of the natural world. Second, humans inherit the capacity for culture and social behaviour. It is only the fact that genes code for language and higher cognitive capacities that makes it possible for people to construct artworks, philosophy, and engage in cultural activities. Third, the ways in which human development proceeds is deeply influenced by genetic constraints. Fourth, these inherited traits constitute human nature and are evident in all cultures; they are universal. Fifth, genes are the basic units of selection, not organisms or groups, and are selected upon the basis of increasing organisms (essentially vehicles for genes), reproductive success and survival. Therefore, a successful gene is more likely to be represented in greater numbers in a future population than its less successful competitors. Finally, genetic processes influence human *behaviour* directly, as is evident in such phenomena as incest avoidance, sexual division of labour and male dominance.

The second approach, *human behavioural ecology*, is concerned directly with investigating the degree to which human behaviour is *currently adaptive* in the environments in which it is expressed (Laland & Brown, 2002). It is important to note the distinction drawn by evolutionary theorists between two quite different, although related, questions: (i) is a behaviour an adaptation?, and (ii) is a behaviour adaptive? The former refers to a trait selected for in the past because it increased reproductive success; it may currently be adaptive or maladaptive. By contrast, an adaptive behaviour is defined as one that *currently* results in increased reproductive success. It may not have been selected for directly in the past and could be the by-product of another trait that was subject to natural selection. Human behavioural ecologists focus on the second question: is the behaviour in question currently adaptive? Typically, researchers construct mathematical models depicting the most adaptive or optimal behaviour (based on efficiency considerations) in a specific context and then evaluate its accuracy in predicting behavioural outcomes. Examples of problem domains are the relationship between food choice and caloric value or the best size for a hunting party. If the model is supported it is assumed that the behaviour in question could have evolved via natural selection. The populations used to test the models are chosen because of their presumed similarity to prehistoric humans and are typically engaged in hunting and gathering practices in order to survive (Laland & Brown, 2002).

The third approach is the *memetic perspective*, which adapts a gene-focused evolutionary approach to the issue of cultural evolution and was first articulated by Richard Dawkins in his book *The selfish gene* (Dawkins, 1976). In this theory, memes are viewed as units of cultural knowledge and function to instruct behaviour in some respects: that is, they inform individuals about how to behave and what to do in certain situations. Examples of memes are songs, ideas, rituals and skills. In formulating the theory of memes, Dawkins used the gene–organism relationship as a model for the meme–human mind relationship. Memes are viewed as cultural replicators; the vehicles or carriers of memes are human brains. According to Dawkins, memes spread throughout the population through social learning processes such as imitation, and are transmitted across the generations as well as throughout a society (and the world potentially) at a given period of time. Their primary purpose, to use anthropomorphic language, is to replicate. In a real sense then, human beings are exploited by memes in order to propagate themselves. Memes may confer little or no functional advantages on hosts and in some situation may in fact prove quite deadly (e.g. memes associated with terrorism or suicide). A powerful—although disturbing—way to think of memes is that they infest or infect the minds of persons and, in this sense, are cultural viruses. Some memes are grouped together in larger complexes to form clusters of ideas such as religions or political ideologies. A disturbing feature of some memes is that they 'defend' themselves against rejection. For example, some types of religious or ideological doctrines may contain component ideas that make it practically impossible to falsify them.

EVOLUTIONARY PSYCHOLOGY

Evolutionary psychologists argue that evolution has resulted in human beings acquiring a range of specific cognitive mechanisms designed to solve certain adaptive problems. As a consequence, the mind is believed to be a set of hundreds or thousands of domain-specific mental modules which operate independently but in a coordinated fashion (Tooby & Cosmides, 1992). Such modules are considered to be independent, self-contained information processors that function quickly and automatically, mostly outside of conscious awareness. The fact that they are self-contained or informationally encapsulated means that they are unable to be altered by external factors such as learning or cultural processes. Rather, external influences simply function to trigger or calibrate the mechanisms to one of several predetermined settings. For example, sexual competition for access to females might result in one of three mating strategies being adopted by a particular male: honest courtship, deception or rape (Ward & Siegert, 2002a).

Each of these modules represents an adaptation that has evolved to solve a specific problem facing our ancestors, such as avoiding predators, forming friendships and alliances, selecting mates and communicating with others. Failure to solve these problems satisfactorily would have lessened an individual's chances of surviving and passing on his or her genes to future generations. Modules are psychological structures or information processing mechanisms that operate according to specific rules in certain domains, and only when exposed to quite specific information. For example, a predator-avoidance module would function to detect designated predators and instruct individuals to adopt certain strategies to avoid or escape from them, while a mate selection module would help males and females to maximise their chances of finding a suitable mate and producing offspring that survived.

According to evolutionary psychologists, it is these modules or information processing mechanisms that are selected for, rather than specific behaviours (as argued by behavioural ecologists). It is important to note that these inherited mechanisms are not necessarily operating at birth. In fact, they may come 'online' at different developmental stages. So for example, mate selection modules only really start to exert a profound influence during adolescence. Additionally, modules are only activated once the relevant environmental conditions obtain, and specific information is available as input to the mechanism. The nature of these inputs may also channel individuals down one of several possible developmental pathways by virtue of their effects on the relevant mechanism. For example, the absence of a father during childhood may result in a male adopting short-term mating strategies and not investing in a permanent relationship (Malamuth & Heilman, 1998). In a sense, environmental events serve to activate a mechanism and to calibrate it, thereby setting its threshold of activation and the particular form it takes.

From the perspective of evolutionary psychology, the psychology of human mating is best understood in terms of the different strategies that evolved for males and females over millions of years in the ancestral environment. Moreover, while cultural evolution has occurred very rapidly in the past few centuries, biological evolution by comparison is very slow and incremental. This means that, in terms of sex and relationships, our modern minds function in much the same way as our ancestors' did a million years ago. Sexual offending is assumed to reflect the workings of the mental modules or adaptations associated with human mating behaviour, and as such, is not easily influenced by social learning, including treatment (Thornhill & Palmer, 2000).

Thornhill and Palmer's Evolutionary Theory of Rape

A number of theorists have applied evolutionary theory to sexual offending (e.g. Ellis, 1989; Malamuth & Heilman, 1998; Quinsey & Lalumiere, 1995). In this chapter we have chosen to present Thornhill and Palmer's theory because it relies extensively on evolutionary psychology and has also been the focus of sustained critical attention. In a way it is representative of the some of the worst and best aspects of biologically informed theories of sexual offending.

Thornhill and Palmer appear to accept the basic assumptions of evolutionary psychology outlined earlier: for example, a view of the mind as radically modular. They emphasise the biological nature of the mind and are extremely critical of social science explanations of rape because they believe that they are based on erroneous assumptions about the mind's architecture and functioning. Thornhill and Palmer argue for an evolutionary theory of rape on the grounds that human beings are essentially animals and part of the natural world. They are therefore dismissive of rape theories that emphasise the role of culture and learning in the acquisition of rape-prone traits, arguing that culture is only possible because individuals have evolved capacities that enable them to learn.

Thornhill and Palmer view rape as a consequence of the mating strategies that evolution must have favoured among men and women. Finding a mate was an intensely competitive process with high-quality males likely to dominate the sexual arena and secure exclusive sexual access to females. Therefore, males with the highest status and the most resources were more likely to obtain sexual access to females, thereby increasing the chances that their genes would be passed on and their offspring would survive. Males evolved to prefer females who were fertile and therefore more likely to conceive. Because fertility is not directly observable, they developed preferences for females with features associated with reproductive success, for example, a youthful appearance. In addition, Thornhill and Palmer argue that males would have most likely evolved to possess intense sexual desires that increased their motivation for sexual experiences and activities. The tendency to seek multiple sexual partners was also facilitated by the fact that because fertilisation in females occurs internally, males could never be certain of their paternity. By attempting to have sex with as many women as possible, males thereby increased their chances of reproductive success.

Thornhill and Palmer assert that rape is either an adaptation *directly* selected for because it resulted in a reproductive advantage for males or it is the *by-product* of other psychological adaptations that were selected for because of their ability to solve adaptive problems. An example of the latter possibility is males' relatively strong interest in low-commitment sex (Symons, 1979). Thus rape is viewed always as a sexually motivated action rather than occurring as a consequence of nonsexual motives such as needs for power and control.

Thornhill and Palmer assert that rape is likely to be a conditional strategy only employed when circumstances are judged to be favourable. They suggest that from this perspective rape represents one of three condition-dependent strategies, along with honest courtship and deceptive courtship. An individual is hypothesised to use rape to secure sexual access to a female only if he believes that the advantages outweigh any disadvantages relative to the other possible strategies. Therefore, rape as an adaptation will not occur under every possible circumstance: rather only when the circumstances are considered to favour it as a sexual strategy. Several factors are hypothesised to increase the chances of males utilising rape under conducive conditions, including a lack of physical and psychological resources, social alienation, limited sexual access to females, and unsatisfying romantic relationships. Thornhill and Palmer argue that such circumstances may function as developmental switches that shift males into relying primarily on a rape strategy. Therefore, the combination of inheriting a propensity to engage in sexual aggression, in conjunction with specific environmental conditions, may result in the development (proximate mechanisms) of rape-supportive attitudes and strategies.

If this argument is to be supported it is necessary to establish that any suggested mechanisms are designed for rape and therefore solve an adaptation problem, and develop reliably, efficiently and economically (Tooby & Cosmides, 1992). Thornhill and Palmer review a number of possible proximate mechanisms that could conceivably represent adaptations to rape in human males. These include psychological mechanisms that help males detect potential rape victims, motivate men who lack resources or sexual access to rape females, cause males to sexually prefer victims who exhibit certain characteristics such as a younger age, and patterns of sexual arousal that facilitate rape such as sexual arousal to violence. They conclude after examining the relevant evidence that none of these candidates is supported unequivocally, and that the research data could either be equally well explained by other mechanisms (by-products) or are of insufficient quality to warrant any substantive conclusions. For example, the fact that high-status men sometimes rape females suggests that vulnerability evaluations may be due to a cost–benefit evaluation mechanism that is not specific to rape. Therefore, they concede that at this point there is little evidence to support the strongest form of the evolutionary theory of rape. However, they still view it as a promising theoretical possibility.

Thornhill and Palmer next consider the hypothesis that rape may occur as a by-product of adaptations that evolved to establish sexual access to a consenting partner. They consider just one possibility: Symons' (1979) suggestion that the primary adaptations causing rape are males' greater sexual drive and their predilection to engage in impersonal sex (i.e. be less sexually discriminating). This is nicely captured by the following quote: 'the typical male is at least slightly sexually attracted to most females, whereas the typical female is not sexually attracted to most males' (Symons, 1979, p. 267). According to Symons, rape is a side effect of the adaptations producing this situation, but is not an adaptation itself because none of the evolved mechanisms involved were specifically selected for rape. Thornhill and Palmer assert that while rape may be a by-product of other adaptations, only adaptations associated with sexual behaviour are likely to be involved. In other words, because rape is a sexually motivated transgression, the mechanisms associated with it will always reflect aspects of human sexual functioning. Factors such as power and control are considered by Thornhill and Palmer to have no important causal relationship to rape.

EVALUATION OF EVOLUTIONARY PSYCHOLOGY

In our view, the development of biologically informed explanations of sexual abuse is timely and very exciting. We are animals, and the tendency of psychological research on sexual crimes to ignore this fact over a number of decades is disappointing, and possibly misguided and wrong. The assumptions of evolutionary psychology—that the mind is modular in nature and that it was fashioned by natural selection over the last million years or so—may help to unify psychological and biological theories and data. It may also enable researchers to explain sexual offending in much greater depth, by referring to deep psychological mechanisms and processes. Because Thornhill and Palmer explicitly argue, using animal data, that human rape is a natural phenomenon, it seems that the theory holds both external consistency and empirical scope. In summary, these features of evolutionary psychology and Thornhill and Palmer's theory indicate that it has, at least at first glance, some degree of *unifying power, explanatory depth* and *external consistency*.

We do not have the space systematically to critique evolutionary psychology and Thornhill and Palmer's evolutionary theory of sexual offending, and will simply summarise our concerns (for a detailed critical examination see Ward & Siegert, 2002a). We will make some general criticisms about evolutionary psychology first and then add a couple of specific remarks about Thornhill and Palmer's theory of rape.

First, there is evidence from cognitive neuropsychology and developmental psychology that our minds are not massively modular in the way depicted by evolutionary psychology and by Thornhill and Palmer (Buller & Hardcastle, 2000). Rather, a critical human adaptation appears to be our cognitive plasticity and ability to learn from experience and each other (Clark, 2003), and this capacity is likely to involve domain general learning mechanisms (Griffiths & Stotz, 2000). Second, we actively construct our environment by using technology and social learning, and so any explanation of robust human characteristics will always involve cultural factors (Odling-Smee et al., 2003). Third, our minds are constructed throughout the process of development and are not preformed in any meaningful sense; rather they emerge out of a matrix of developmental resources. This means that social scaffolding by parents, peers and other social actors plays a critical role in the development of the mind (Tomasello, 1999). We do not house ancient minds within modern skulls but rather inherit the capacity to acquire a mind (Clark, 2003). Thus, we argue that individuals' ability to construct and, in turn, be shaped by their environments, in conjunction with their cognitive and behavioural plasticity and the role of culture and social learning in creating minds, means that it is a mistake to view human nature as biologically fixed in the way evolutionary psychology does. Clark (2003) noted that human beings do not have a set nature with a 'simple wrap-around of tools and culture; the tools and culture are as much determiners of our natures as products of it' (p. 86).

These criticisms indicate that despite initial impressions, evolutionary psychology suffers from a lack of *empirical adequacy* and *scope, unifying power* and *explanatory depth*.

The first critical point regarding Thornhill and Palmer's theory relates to the lack of *explanatory depth* and limited *scope* of the theory. In our view, Thornhill and Palmer do not develop a systematic theory of rape. There is no attempt to specify systematically a set of mechanisms that reliably generate rape and its associated phenomena. Although they considered the idea that rape is an adaptation, they either rejected all the possible candidates, or deferred judgement about their possible validity. The second possibility, that rape is a by-product of adaptations relating to male sexuality, is also not systematically explored, nor is a theory explicitly constructed. Thornhill and Palmer simply present a case for the plausibility of an evolutionary explanation of rape. Their style of argument is tentative and general. A theory of rape needs to specify the nature of the causal mechanisms in more detail and demonstrate how biological, psychological, social/cultural and contextual factors interact to result in sexual aggression.

Our second point concerns the extensive sections of their book that Thornhill and Palmer devote to attacking the 'standard social science model' (SSSM) of rape. This is a theme throughout their book and forms the subject of an entire chapter. The assumption here seems to be that if this model is proven inadequate then somehow this substantiates their own theory. This is a 'straw man' argument at best. In fact, the version of an SSSM they critique so fiercely borders upon a caricature, and reflects just one influential dimension of modern theories of rape (i.e. the feminist/political approach which argues that rape is about power, not sex). They largely ignore any other 'social science' accounts of rape, particularly those models that include a broad range of causal variables or allow for biological influences (e.g. Marshall & Barbaree, 1990). These weaknesses in the Thornhill and Palmer theory point to its lack of *explanatory depth*, *coherence* (the theory does not actually explain rape despite the stated aim) and *unifying power*.

GENE–CULTURE CO-EVOLUTIONARY THEORY AND NICHE CONSTRUCTION

Gene–culture theory is a flexible evolutionary model claiming that the evolution of human beings is propelled by genetic, individual learning and cultural processes. Because of this, the explanation of human traits is likely to involve these three sets of processes (Odling-Smee et al., 2003). Genetic factors may result in a predisposition to seek certain types of goods, while learning events, within a particular cultural context, provide socially constructed ways of achieving these valued experiences, activities and outcomes. From a correctional perspective, this means that the causes of sexually aggressive behaviour are likely to have a naturalistic basis, and that motivational and cognitive biases lead individuals to seek basic human goods in socially unacceptable ways. An intriguing aspect of this naturalistic picture is the powerful influence of genetic and cultural processes; neither dominates the other, giving both biological and social learning oriented researchers an important role in accounting for sexually abusive behaviour.

The version of gene–culture co-evolutionary theory we prefer is that developed by Odling-Smee et al. (2003), and is best defined by its focus on the construct of 'niche construction'. According to Odling-Smee et al., niche construction is environment modification driven by an organism, that changes the relationship between themselves and the environment. A good example is that of the leaf-cutter ant, where the ants store plant material in their nests in order to cultivate a specific type of fungus (i.e. they construct fungal gardens), which they use as a food source. The process of constructing this niche results in systematic changes to the soil and ecosystem within and around the nest and also alters the selective environment for their offspring. This may effectively reduce selection pressures in ways that benefit or harm the long-term survival chances of the leaf-cutter ant and its offspring. An example of niche construction in human beings is the building of houses, implementation of farming practices (e.g. dairy farming) and the development of technology. All these changes modify the niche in which human beings live their lives and thereby change the relationship or match between themselves and features of the environment.

According to Odling-Smee et al., there are three types of processes involved in niche construction in a population of living organisms: *genetic processes, onto genetic processes* (individual learning within a lifetime) and *cultural processes*. Each of these processes is associated with unique ways of acquiring, storing and transmitting information, and also with distinct means of interacting with the environment. An example of genetic processes is that of the orb-web spider, where the spinning of webs on a nightly basis is thought to be rigidly determined by genes (Avital & Jablonka, 2000). An example of ontogenetic or learning processes is the use of pine needles by woodpecker finches in the Galapagos Islands to dislodge insects from the bark of trees; this is thought to be relearned by each generation of finches on a trial and error basis (Avital & Jablonka, 2000). This behaviour enables the finches to exploit resources (i.e. create a new niche) that were not previously available to them, and in doing so, has 'created a stable selection favouring a bill able to manipulate tools rather than the sharp, pointed bill and long tongue characteristic of woodpeckers' (Odling-Smee et al., 2003, p. 22). The advantage of an ontogenetic process such as learning is that organisms are able to adapt rapidly to changing circumstances and not rely on inbuilt genetic solutions. Odling-Smee et al. state that this type of learning may well be regulated by a general principle such as the law of effect, and therefore actions that are followed by a positive outcome are more likely to be repeated in the future. An example of cultural processes in animals is the discovery by macaque monkeys that washing potatoes nested in the sand improves their edibility (Avital & Jablonka, 2000). A human example is the cultural discovery of dairy farming practices, resulting in the widespread development of lactose tolerance (Durham, 1991). The existence of culturally stored knowledge means that organisms do not have to learn themselves all the information critical for survival, and therefore do not have to repeat the mistakes made by those who have gone before them. This confers greater flexibility on a species and the opportunity to gradually develop increased technological expertise and environmental control.

These three types of behavioural strategies are hypothesised by Odling-Smee et al. to affect causally and interact with each other and, in some instances, they may reduce or exacerbate selection pressures. For example, the development of medications in human beings to cure hereditary diseases means that individuals with these diseases are able to survive and reproduce, reducing the evolutionary pressure to select for genes that protect individuals from developing the disease in the first place. In other words, a cultural response is able to solve the problems and reduce the need for a genetic solution. However, in some situations cultural responses may in effect exacerbate problematic situations and prevent the chances of genetic solutions even appearing. A good example is the pollution of waterways, the air and the earth.

The three types of processes outlined above are thought to result in the modification of the environment, and are also implicated in the creation of three quite different types of inheritance: genetic inheritance, cultural inheritance and ecological inheritance (the altered ecological niche). *Genetic inheritance* consists of the genetic resources (i.e. the genome) available to the next generation, and is responsible for some of the cognitive, motivational and behavioural characteristics comprising the nature of the species in question. *Cultural inheritance* consists of the knowledge, values, practices and technology passed on to offspring by way of social learning (i.e. imitation and modelling). *Ecological inheritance* refers to the changed environment and ecology passed on to the new generation and, as such, constitutes a new selection environment; this is the constructed niche and it is built by genetic, cultural and ecological inheritance. An interesting observation is that the availability of an externally structured learning environment makes the reliance of young organisms on innate genetic programmes such as mental modules less essential, and in a sense, can be seen as an external nervous system or knowledge resource (Sterelny, 2003). Each of these inheritance systems makes a potentially valuable contribution to the offspring of the organisms in question and may equip them to exist successfully within their niche, or in some situations, result in additional problems. The crucial point is that the selection environment is fundamentally altered in some way, thereby modifying the relationship between the traits of the organism and the features of the environment. There are two basic types of niche construction: (i) inceptive niche construction, the original modification of the environment; and (ii) counteractive niche construction, modification in an attempt to counteract a previous change or problem. In addition, organisms may choose to alter an existing niche or to move and create a new one.

Applying Gene–Culture Co-Evolutionary Theory to Sexual Offending

We will now apply these ideas to the example of rape in order to grasp their significance for the field of sexual offending. From the perspective of the niche construction model, we assume that there are three sources of cognitive and behavioural strategies involved in human mating behaviour: *genetic constraints or predispositions, individual learning processes* and *cultural resources and processes*. In addition, we assume that the population of human beings is characterised by cognitive flexibility and behavioural plasticity. In other words, while there may be modifiable genetic predispositions that initiate human development and the construction of different capacities, the final architecture of our minds and capacities is strongly affected by social learning and scaffolding. Our minds are constructed during development rather than simply unfolding when triggered by environmental cues.

An example of a genetic predisposition might be males' hypothesised tendency to seek impersonal sex and also to attempt to exert power and control over females (Ellis, 1989; Symons, 1979). An example of an ontogenetic process leading to impersonal sex is learning to use sex as a way of coping with negative mood states and feelings of inadequacy (Marshall & Barbaree, 1990). An example of a relevant cultural process might be the portrayal of females as sexual objects and males as entitled to have sex when and where they want (Polaschek & Ward, 2002). These three sets of processes will individually, and in interaction, result in the construction of the mating domain: that is, the individual, social, physical (e.g. nightclubs, bars etc.) and cultural environment or arena where sexual interests, meaning and opportunities converge. Individuals will enter this arena with heterogeneous combinations of these sets of factors, resulting in varying degrees of rape-proneness (Sanday, 2003). For some males, the weak genetic predisposition toward sexual promiscuity may interact with a learning environment where females are routinely ridiculed and presented as inferior, and a culture where females are not valued and are underrepresented in positions of power and influence. In other cases, this weak predisposition may be modified by socialisation in a household where sex is viewed as an essential component of intimacy and females are viewed as equal to males.

We suggest that counteractive niche construction in a rape-prone society is possible at each of the three levels outlined earlier. First, it may be possible for genes that code for sexual cooperation to be selected if females consistently reject aggressive and sexually promiscuous males. In this scenario, the mating domain (i.e. constructed niche) has been modified to make it less likely that aggressive sexual behaviour will result in reproductive success, and this change is hypothesised to select out males with rape-supportive dispositions. Second, individual men might decide to cease their sexually aggressive behaviour following powerful learning experiences: for example, consistent rejection by females or becoming aware of the suffering they have inflicted on others. In this situation, the salient causal factor is offenders' specific learning experiences rather than genetic or cultural factors. Third, at a cultural level there may be a commitment to rehabilitation and also changes to the way sexuality is represented, and the way males and females are socialised. The impact of such a cultural change is likely to be pervasive and alter the context in which males are socialised, thereby lessening the likelihood of developing rape-supportive attitudes and beliefs.

EVALUATION OF GENE–CULTURE THEORY
OF SEXUAL OFFENDING

The niche construction variant of gene–culture co-evolution theory is a flexible and powerful framework for explaining sexually abusive behaviour. In view of the fact that it has not been applied systematically to the domain of sexual offending it is difficult to make more than preliminary evaluative comments.

In terms of its strengths, niche construction theory is able to bridge the gap between the biological and cultural aspects of human behaviour. The postulation of three types of inheritance: ecological, cultural and genetic, in conjunction with the recognition that human beings can intentionally alter and shape themselves and their environment, is a marked advance on simple evolutionary psychology models. The theory allows for genetic predispositions and human flexibility. There is room for different levels of explanation and an explicit acknowledgement that cultural and individual learning can contribute partly to the onset of sexually abusive behaviour. Thus the niche construction perspective on sexual offending has good *unifying power* and *external consistency*.

A second strength of niche construction theory is its *explanatory depth*. The theory posits the existence of genetic, cultural and psychological structures and processes capable of generating a wide range of human phenomena. The cognitive plasticity of human beings in conjunction with their cultural inventiveness means that they can sometimes act in ways that violate fitness requirements: for example causing wide-scale environmental damage that may in the end destroy life itself. On the positive side, it also means that humans are able to counteract problematic genetic predispositions and through the construction of interventions (e.g. development of drugs to ameliorate the symptoms of inherited diseases) ultimately improve human welfare.

A third strength is that it avoids the preformist implications and genetic reductionism problems evident in simple versions of evolutionary psychology. Genes are not viewed as crude blueprints that simply come 'online' at specific points in time and instruct the body how to build a person. Rather, human beings are hypothesised to be constructed through the dynamic interplay of biological and cultural processes. This feature of the theory speaks to its *explanatory depth*.

From a critical perspective, a first problem is that it has not been evaluated systematically and therefore there is a lack of empirical evidence to support its contentions. Data that do exist tend to come from animal models and a few human case studies. This problem reveals a lack of *empirical adequacy*.

Second, a lack of detail concerning the interaction between the three forms of inheritance raises the suspicion that the theory, when suitably fleshed out, may suffer from *internal incoherence*. A key question is 'how do cultural and individual learning processes overcome, or wash out, genetic effects?' In our view the theory does have room to move here and it is notable that a form of niche construction theory has been implemented in developmental psychology under the auspices of developmental systems theory (Griffiths & Stotz, 2000). This type of research is progressing well and indicates that the broader model may eventually evolve into a powerful theory with a strong evidential base.

CLINICAL UTILITY OF EVOLUTIONARY THEORIES OF RAPE

In our discussion of the clinical utility of evolutionary theories of rape we will focus more on the possible contribution of evolutionary psychology and will only comment on the potential of niche construction theory where appropriate. This is mainly due to the fact that there has been little attention paid to this very promising application of evolutionary theory to human behaviour at this point.

A major contribution of evolutionary perspectives in the sexual offending domain is the way they could inform the construction of aetiological theories. The inclusion in theories of sexual offending of distal and proximate elements might help therapists to trace the origins of certain human traits and to detect proximate mechanisms currently generating sexually abusive behaviour. An evolutionary perspective can provide a broad and unifying theory that integrates the study of psychopathology and connects it with other biological and social sciences. It allows for the integration of data from a variety of aetiological models (genetic, biochemical, developmental, cognitive, etc.) through its emphasis on the role of ultimate causes and their interaction with proximate causes.

Another important insight from evolutionary psychology concerns the possibility that mental disorders may be the product of mechanisms functioning normally, but in currently nonadaptive circumstances (Gilbert, 1998a). There may be a discrepancy between modern and early ancestral environments that make evolved mechanisms currently maladaptive. For example, because of access to lethal weapons, male jealousy may result in more serious crimes than in the past, despite jealousy having the evolved function of mate guarding. Furthermore, problems may emerge because normally functioning mechanisms may occasionally result in mistakes. For example, males' tendency to infer sexual interest in females when there is none may result in sexual aggression in certain contexts.

Perhaps the most fundamental influence upon treatment will spring from adopting a radically different concept of mind from that advanced under the 'standard social science model'. Instead of a general computing device moulded largely by culture, from an evolutionary psychology perspective the mind is a highly specialised biological computer that has evolved to perform a number of specific functions. Thus, in designing therapeutic interventions we may need to be more specific about which cognitive modules they are intended to influence or interact with. In terms of sexual offending, it is necessary to keep in mind whether the issue is one of sexual jealousy, problems of status maintenance (e.g. grievance-related rapes—getting back at women) or group solidarity (e.g. gang rapes). While the gene–culture co-evolutionary model is not so strongly committed to a modular view of the human mind, it still accepts that there are genetic constraints on the development of the brain and natural inclinations to interpret the world in certain ways that should be factored into any explanation of, and attempt to modify, human behaviour.

Another implication for treatment is that we may also have to adopt a different, and more complex, model of mental disorder. Current models of pathology in clinical psychology frequently conceptualise mental disorders as either illness or as learned behaviours. An evolutionary perspective implies a radical shift in our thinking concerning the nature of mental disorder. Many of what clinical psychologists call 'maladaptive behaviours' may actually be behavioural systems that had survival value and have been selected by evolution over millions of years.

There are also some broad ethical implications for practitioners as well. Therapy goals are based on judgements concerning the best possible outcomes for clients, ones that are likely to increase their welfare. Accepting a naturalistic model of human nature means that clinicians need to evaluate carefully their clinical theories to ensure they are not seeking outcomes that frustrate natural goods. For example, attempting to foster non-violent conflict resolution skills in males while ignoring their proclivity to engage in competitive behaviour may prove fruitless. Finally, striving to help couples develop a better understanding of each other should arguably take into account evolved gender differences. This process involves ethical judgements because of the relationship between natural goods and ideal therapy outcomes.

The niche construction theory also focuses our attention on modifying cultural institutions and the importance of public policy initiatives to reduce the chances of environments directly reinforcing biologically based inclinations. For example, careful attention to the way male and female relationships are portrayed could facilitate young men in developing less adversarial attitudes toward gender relationships.

CONCLUSIONS

In this chapter, we have critically discussed the application of two evolutionary theories to the domain of sexual offending: evolutionary psychology and niche construction theory. Our evaluation of the two perspectives revealed niche construction theory to be less problematic and to offer great promise in integrating biological and cultural/technological approaches to the explanation of human behaviour. The fact that niche construction theory is consistent with a broad, naturalistic view of human behaviour is also attractive and in our opinion it is able to accommodate the insight from developmental psychology that we actively construct our environments and, in turn, are partially shaped by them. In other words, the form of naturalism we espouse is one that accepts that human beings do not have fixed unalterable essences but with knowledge and foresight are able to deliberately redesign deep aspects of themselves in the hope of ultimately increasing human welfare and reducing crimes such as sexual abuse.

PART III
LEVEL II THEORIES
(SINGLE-FACTOR THEORIES)

Chapter 8
THEORIES OF COGNITIVE DISTORTIONS

This is the first of six chapters examining individual factors implicated in the aetiology of sexual offending. Of these factors, cognitive distortions is the most well known, widely discussed and theoretically developed. Most (or all) of the theories reviewed in Part II identify cognitive distortions as a key theoretical building block. Many practitioners feel considerable confidence about their importance as a treatment target.

We begin by reviewing briefly key assumptions and issues in the study of cognition in general. Then we examine definitions of cognitive distortions, before outlining and evaluating the major theories. Because of the high volume of empirical research in this area, we have separated the conceptual and empirical critiques of each theory. The scope of this chapter is limited to cognitive distortions; it is important to be mindful from the outset that cognitive distortions are only one aspect of any account of the role of cognition in sexual offending. Cognitive processes and products—normal or distorted—occur throughout the offending cycle.

THE ROLES OF COGNITION IN SEXUAL OFFENDING

To evaluate adequately cognitive distortion theory, and even to understand what cognitive distortions are, they need to be placed within the framework of modern cognitive and social-cognitive psychology. The term *cognition* refers to a general system with many different aspects that can be defined and labelled to enhance understanding (Kendall & Dobson, 1993). *Information processing theory* remains the dominant perspective in cognitive theorising and research on psychopathology. In information processing terms, individual differences in experience and behaviour are viewed as resulting from differences in information stored and organised in long-term memory (i.e. information *content* and *structure*), and in how this stored information biases individuals' attention, encoding and retrieval (information *processing*; Hollon & Kriss, 1984; Ingram & Kendall, 1986). Put simply, life experience leads individuals to build up a knowledge base or framework of highly associated content (i.e. a schema) that contains assumptions of what to expect from the world and people in it (Ward, Hudson, Johnston & Marshall, 1997). Schemata provide a view of the world based on what is *expected* rather than what is objectively true. Of course, interpreting the world as one expects to find it is efficient; time and energy are not wasted entertaining possibilities that rarely occur. However, it also means that schemata become self-fulfilling knowledge bases. Schema-supportive information is attended to and encoded preferentially, and selective 'detection' by the schema only serves to reinforce its veracity. When information is scant, schemata dissolve ambiguity by providing a plausible context for interpreting likely causes and mechanisms.

Generally, people appear not to have direct access to the content and structure of their own cognition. More often than not, it is inferred from individuals' reports of their cognitive *products* (i.e. the end-stage cognitions resulting from the interaction between cognitive content, structures and processing; Hollon & Kriss, 1984). The most common cognitive products examined in sex offender research are self-statements (e.g. 'I was only fooling around'; Murphy, 1990) or attitudinal propositions such as those included in questionnaires (e.g. 'Having sex with a child is a good way for an adult to teach a child about sex'; Abel and Becker Cognition Scale, Abel et al., 1989). When we use terms like *cognitive distortion* or *offence-supportive cognitions* here, we are referring to both of these types of products.

Much of the work on information processing theory was developed largely in the study of non-social or impersonal cognition. In an offending context, much of the activity of interest is social in nature; both the offence process and the process of formal rehabilitation occur in a social context. The study of social cognition differs from that of impersonal cognition in that it refers to all aspects of understanding the social world, including not just cognition, but motivation and affect (Kunda, 1999). In particular, social cognition recognises that an individual's goals and emotional state at a particular point in time will influence perceptions of social situations.

One final distinction is important. Much of the business of making sense of the social and non-social world is achieved *automatically* (i.e. outside of conscious awareness), and thus is rapid, effortless and cannot be tampered with easily by the conscious mind (Toderov & Bargh, 2002). By contrast, *controlled* processes are effortful, intentional and aware. They are resource-intensive, and thus easily disrupted when affect or other demands constrain these finite cognitive resources (Kunda, 1999).

DEFINING COGNITIVE DISTORTIONS

The exact theoretical roots of the term *cognitive distortion* when applied to sex offenders are not immediately clear. The first usage in the sex offending literature was 20 years ago, when Abel, Becker and Cunningham-Rathner (1984) defined cognitive distortions as belief systems that supported having sexual contact with children, but also as 'justifications, perceptions and judgements used by the sex offender to rationalize his child molestation behavior' (Abel et al., 1989, p. 137).

Many other terms have been used since to refer to the same phenomena, including *excuses* (Pollock & Hashmall, 1991), *rationalisations* (Neidigh & Krop, 1992) and *justifications* (Murphy, 1990). Thus cognitive distortions are defined as both processes and products. To confuse things further, writers in this area use the word 'process' to mean two different things: both information processing and social processes (e.g. Murphy, 1990; Ward, 2000). We discuss this confusion again later in the chapter.

ABEL'S COGNITIVE DISTORTION THEORY

Abel et al. (1984) provided the first theory of sexual offenders' cognitive distortions. The term *cognitive distortion* was already in use to explain thinking related to disparate psychopathologies in clinical psychology. For example, Beck (1976) used the term to refer to the perceptions (or cognitive symptoms) of depressed individuals that were thought to be driven by stable, negative beliefs about themselves, the world and the future. However, rather than drawing on the clinical literature, Abel cited the influence of Bandura on his theory, and Bandura (e.g. 1986) used the term *faulty thinking* rather than cognitive distortion. So Abel appears to be responsible for taking a term that hitherto referred to thinking habits that maintained a mental disorder and applying it to a new domain of *antisocial* behaviour.

Abel and his colleagues did not articulate their theory fully in any single published source, and so we describe it here by piecing it together from several publications. As we just noted, their cognitive distortion theory is embedded in a broader aetiological theory of child sexual offending (Abel et al., 1984). In this account, most boys learn in childhood which sexual arousal patterns are considered societally inappropriate, and inhibit such interests. However sometimes they still fantasise about prohibited material, and so for these boys, a pattern of deviant arousal develops that is carried into adulthood unless there is disapproval from significant others. Abel et al. suggested that in the late teens or early 20s such a young man becomes gradually cognisant that his sexual preferences deviate from social mores. His response is to develop idiosyncratic beliefs, which Abel called *cognitive distortions*. Abel et al. (1984) suggested that cognitive distortions are externally reinforced by masturbation, so that they apparently precede the onset of offending. But later, Abel et al. (1989) gave cognitive distortions a maintenance role when they identified the source of their reinforcement as actual offending.

As we also noted above, Abel et al. (1989, p. 137) wrote that cognitive distortions were 'internal processes, including the justifications, perceptions, and judgments used by the sex offender to rationalise his child molestation behavior'. They went on to say:

> Clinically, a child molester's cognitive distortions appear to allow the offender to justify his ongoing sexual abuse of children without the anxiety, guilt and loss of self esteem that would usually result from an individual committing behaviors contrary to the norms of his society ... [they are] the products of conflict between external reinforcements and internal self-condemnation. (pp. 137–138)

What does this statement mean? Clearly, Abel et al. saw cognitive distortions as protecting the offender's self-image from condemnation, while he continued to experience the external reinforcement of ongoing offending. By inference then, Abel saw cognitive distortions as facilitating or maintaining—not causing—sexual assault propensity, since they arise from behaviours that are already being contemplated or carried out (see Abel, Rouleau & Cunningham-Rathner, 1986, for a clear statement of this view). Abel et al. (1986) also suggested that such cognitive distortions gradually become more entrenched over time.

Do they become so entrenched that offenders lose awareness or recognition of their distorted nature? Abel and colleagues (1989) made the intriguing observation that established offenders appear to avoid opportunities to evaluate their beliefs against those of other adults, in order to be able to sustain their self-justifications. So it would seem that Abel et al. viewed offenders as maintaining some minimal level of awareness of the self-serving inaccuracy of their cognitive distortions, a phenomenon that might now be referred to as motivated self-deception (Baumeister, 1996; Wright & Schneider, 1997).

Much of Abel's theorising and empirical research on sex offenders is on those who target children. However, some of his writings imply that this version of cognitive distortion theory generalises to rapists (e.g. Abel, Becker & Skinner, 1987; Abel, Mittelman & Becker, 1985).

EVALUATION OF ABEL'S THEORY

As with all of the chapters in Part III, cognitive distortion theory is an example of a level II theory, dealing with an individual factor at the heart of sex-offending aetiology. The conceptual strength of single-factor theories is based on how full an account they provide of the factor's relevant structures and processes, and how these relate to each other. It is against this standard that we evaluate Abel's cognitive distortion theory.

Conceptual Issues

Abel's contribution to the early cognitive-behavioural treatment of sexual offending was substantial (Marshall, Anderson & Fernandez, 1999a). Clinicians working with child molesters had observed offence-supportive statements for decades before the ascendancy of cognitive psychology in the 1970s and 1980s, and interventions certainly recognised their possible importance by the 1970s (Marshall et al., 1999a). However, Abel's was the first conspicuous attempt at articulating a theoretical understand of the significance of these statements for child sex offending, in what became the cognitive-behavioural era of sex offender treatment. It is a deceptively simple preliminary proposal that over 20 years has dramatically shaped both research and practice (i.e. it has had high *heuristic value*, or *fertility*). It remains the dominant theoretical viewpoint on sex offender cognition even now.

In one sense its durability is puzzling, because it represents a skeletal and confusing account that leaves important questions unanswered (*internal coherence*). This lack of clarity, examined in more detail below, has allowed for important misunderstandings of interpretation. As we noted earlier, we think that Abel and colleagues clearly viewed cognitive distortions as maintaining, not aetiological, factors. Others have also interpreted his theory that way (e.g. Mann & Beech, 2003; Murphy, 1990). However, cognitive distortions have a prominent place in many level I aetiological theories of sexual offending (e.g. Hall, 1996; Ward & Siegert, 2002a). Yet Abel, the leading theorist in the area, suggested that cognitive distortions arise when the offender is already contemplating offending, but is aware that his interest is morally reprehensible and threatens his good image of himself. Therefore the *scope* of the theory does not clearly include an aetiological role for cognitive distortions, thus making the theory *externally inconsistent* with currently accepted level I theories. Arguably this point actually does not indicate a fault on the part of Abel et al. since they may be correctly describing an important aspect of cognitive distortions in sexual offenders. However, it does point to a gap in level II theorising: if cognitive distortions can cause sexual offending as level I theorists have suggested, where is the level II theory that explains how?

Another *scope* issue is Abel and colleagues' suggestion of a single aetiological path: adolescent-onset life-course-persistent sexual offending. This path certainly does exist, but what about adult-onset offenders? Late onset of sexual offending may be common: in a sample of imprisoned adult offenders, Smallbone and Wortley (2004b) found the average self-reported age of first sexual contact with a child to be 32 years.

As we noted above, Abel and colleagues' theory also has some difficulties with *internal coherence*. Recall that the main stimulus for this theory comes from the spontaneous statements child molesters make to therapists and interviewers (Abel et al., 1984). When discussing their offending, child molesters make statements like 'but she enjoyed it', and 'it didn't do him any harm, at least not that I could see'. Did Abel think that cognitive distortions—once developed early in an offence career—became a virtually impermeable barrier against negative self-evaluation? Or did he theorise that cognitive distortions are employed more dynamically, so that they are more likely to dominate offender cognition in contexts where he is particularly likely to feel guilt and anxiety about his offending?

Abel's work seems contradictory on this point. On the one hand he observed that offenders did not seek to test their beliefs with others. Rather they cloaked them in secrecy, suggesting that the holders of such beliefs have at least tenuous conscious awareness that their distortions are a fragile shield indeed against anticipated condemnation. On the other hand, Abel set about establishing an empirical basis for his theory by developing a transparent self-report questionnaire and then asking identified offenders to fill it in (Abel et al., 1989), a design that many, many others have emulated. Such an approach suggests that Abel thought that by the time an offender has been caught for offending, his cognitive distortions were sufficiently stable and entrenched that he would admit them openly even when in conditions that were likely to make him feel threatened.

And are these beliefs conscious or unconscious (Marshall et al., 1999a)? This problem is akin to that of covert planning in the relapse prevention model (see Chapter 14). Consciousness is unlikely to be a dichotomous state, but Abel made no explicit comment about this issue. The questionnaire approach seems to presume simultaneously that offenders are consciously aware of their own beliefs, but unaware of how others see them. Other, more robustly designed studies suggest that some aspects of sex offenders' distorted cognition (e.g. rapists perceiving women as hostile)—which show up both in transparent questionnaire measures (Malamuth, Linz, Heavey, Barnes & Acker, 1995) and in how men interpret behaviour in social interactions (Malamuth & Brown, 1994)—are genuinely unconscious misperceptions (Marshall et al., 1999a). These points suggest difficulties with *explanatory depth, internal coherence* and *empirical accuracy*.

Another fundamental issue of *internal coherence* concerns the mechanism by which cognitive distortions are learned. Abel et al. suggested that Bandura's social learning theory (1977) provided the best basis for sexual offending aetiology. Yet they also noted the secrecy associated with sexual offending. Secrecy appears inconsistent with learning by observation; surely a hallmark of social learning theory. In fact, the way they described Bandura's theory makes it more closely resemble earlier, non-social learning theories. They suggested that cognitive distortions are learned by (i) classical conditioning processes, when they are repeatedly paired with (deviant) sexual arousal, and (ii) operant learning when they are negatively reinforced because they alleviate painful self-referential affect (e.g. guilt).

Abel and colleagues' use of the term 'processes' (1989, p. 137) began an area of conceptual confusion that has proliferated through 15 years of literature. The study of cognition in sex offenders has drawn repeatedly on two distinct psychological traditions. The first is personality and social psychology, which is concerned with attitudes and attitude formation. This is a very old branch of psychology. In recent years social psychology has also embraced the 'cognitive revolution' of the 1950s. Melding itself together with cognitive psychology resulted in the domain we now call *social cognition* (Kunda, 1999), which was interested not only in attitudes, beliefs and attributions, but also in affective and motivational issues. The second—and younger—tradition then is cognitive psychology, which for a long time was primarily concerned with non-social cognition, or a more static or 'cold' approach to cognition (Kunda). Non-social cognitive psychology's heartland is a raft of *processes* by which we learn, think and remember.

One specific approach to non-social cognition has dominated cognitive approaches to psychopathology. In information processing theory the brain is viewed as a computer-like system for processing, storing and retrieving information (Huesmann, 1988). So we might speak of attention and retrieval processes and this is what we mean. Social cognitive information processing theories have developed from this basis. For example, Huesmann (1988) developed just such a theory of aggression.

The processes of *justification, excuse-making* and so on that are often referred to in the cognitive distortion literature are *not* cognitive processes in this sense. They are psychological processes having to do with protection of the self image, and in some cases, the image of others (Schlenker, Pontari & Christopher, 2001). Just like the social information processes involved in sexual aggression, they can certainly be viewed as *social cognitive* processes themselves. However, in the sex offender cognitive distortion literature, they have no obvious theoretical basis at present. A theory of these processes would be centrally concerned with the development, maintenance and protection of the self, not simply with the acquisition, storage and retrieval of 'knowledge' about sexual offending.

So, when Abel et al. (1989) referred to the 'internal processes, including justifications, perceptions and judgements' (p. 137), they appeared to be referring to these self-protective processes. On the other hand, when they operationalised their theory with a standardised attitudinal questionnaire, they were drawing either on an older tradition from social psychology of surveying 'cold' attitudes to sexual offending, or on the impersonal cognitive psychology tradition of assessing knowledge about non-social phenomena in a written test. Again this contradiction implies *internal incoherence* within the theory itself.

This conceptual evaluation exposes Abel's theory as a preliminary offering with some important limitations to be resolved. In addition to these limitations, there are significant concerns about its empirical accuracy and, relatedly, how researchers have set about testing it empirically.

Empirical and Predictive Accuracy

What light can data shed on whether child molesters' offence-supportive comments and statements represent pre-existing beliefs, or post-offence (i.e. post-hoc) justifications and excuses, or both (Marshall et al., 1999a)? The vast majority of research on cognition in sex offenders uses a variant of one design: a questionnaire of relevant beliefs is administered to sex offenders and to one or more comparison groups, chosen to enable any differences in the resulting mean scores to be attributed to type of current offence. Reviews of these studies sometimes find differences between groups on mean scores and sometimes do not. At best, they find that, on average, child molesters either disagree or strongly disagree with cognitive distortion items (Gannon & Polaschek, 2005). In other words, generally sex offenders disagree a bit less than do comparison nonsexual offenders. Examination of individual responses usually reveals only occasional agreement with any cognitive distortion item, a much lower rate of responding than would be expected from Abel's theory.

Quite plausibly, researchers and practitioners have argued that the transparency of many of these tests renders them vulnerable to socially desirable response (SDR) bias (e.g. Langevin, 1991). So some researchers have included separate SDR measures and found unexpectedly equivocal results about whether SDR *is* related to questionnaire scores (Bumby, 1996; Hanson, Gizzarelli & Scott, 1994; Hogue, 1994).

The most common response from researchers to (i) very low rates of endorsement of cognitive distortion items on pencil and paper questionnaires, (ii) unclear results about whether offenders are 'faking good', and (iii) the high frequency of distorted statements articulated by offenders when talking about their own offending, is that Abel's theory is correct: offenders really *do* hold stable distorted beliefs about sex offending, but they lie on questionnaires.

But do they? More sophisticated designs that could provide better empirical investigation of Abel's theory have rarely been used. We mention two exceptions here. Gannon (in press) had child sex offenders complete a cognitive distortion questionnaire on two separate occasions. On the second occasion, half of them were attached to a fake lie detector. There were no differences in questionnaire responding either within or between offender groups, suggesting no significant role for conscious lying in explaining low distortion rates. On the other hand, Neidigh and Krop (1992) found that, on average, sex offenders reported 3.5 cognitive distortions about their own offending, but endorsed only 1.8 on average, on a paper-based cognitive distortion scale. If offenders are trying to 'look good' by pretending their cognition is not distorted, why do this less in an interview with a potentially judgmental audience than on paper? Taken together, these findings suggest several possible interpretations. At the very least, they argue that the version of Abel's theory that has been empirically tested in these questionnaire studies—the idea that established offenders hold entrenched offence-supportive beliefs that are chronically accessible, in conscious awareness and unaffected by study context—represents an incomplete account of how cognitive distortions operate for sex offenders.

Pollock and Hashmall's research suggests a different picture. They found that when offenders were in a context in which the anticipated condemnation of others seemed imminent (i.e. pre-trial assessments), a predictable, rational syntax of cognitive distortions emerged. Pollock and Hashmall's findings suggest a common vocabulary among offenders, that seems to us to be similar to what 'normal' people say in response to social transgressions, and supporting the contention that offenders are using a normative process for protecting themselves and their sense of control over the world when they talk about their offending to researchers (Snyder & Higgins, 1988). Whether this process itself becomes stable and entrenched so that it causes subsequent offending, or remains simply a dynamic correlate of talking and thinking about past offences, neither Abel's theory nor empirical research can currently tell us.

Conclusions

Although highly innovative at the time, hindsight suggests that Abel's theory was never fully developed and contains some conceptual weaknesses. Although it has not been evaluated empirically with any sophistication, some interpretations of it are not well supported by existing data. By recent standards, it is founded on a simplistic view of human cognition and so it is no longer externally consistent with social cognition theory. Its longevity is explained by the absence of any significant additional theory development in this area.

SCHEMA THEORIES

Schemata are variously defined in cognitive literatures as organised storage devices that hold knowledge acquired from experience and also act on incoming information according to both the nature and structure of that existing knowledge (Ward et al., 1997). More recently, some theorists have proposed that this dynamic processing aspect is a form of causal theorising (see Ward, 2000, for a review). Schemata are considered to represent *deep* cognition (Kwon & Oei, 1994), and can be assessed only indirectly through cognitive products. Their accessibility (i.e. the degree to which they dominate information processing at any time) can vary from occasional to chronic (Anderson, Anderson & Deuser, 1996).

The suggestion that schemata play a role in psychopathology and in antisocial behaviour is not new. Extensive literatures exist in the study of both aggression and clinical disorders such as depression and anxiety. However, whether schemata have an aetiological role in behaviour of interest to clinicians is still contentious (Williams, Watts, MacLeod & Mathews, 1997).

As we noted, Abel and colleagues' theoretical account of cognitive distortions in sex offenders has stood in lonely isolation for two decades. Surprisingly, new proposals in the form of schema theories appeared in the sex offender literature only in the late 1990s, when Ward and his colleagues articulated the first schema-based theory of sexual offender cognition. It was followed by Mann and Beech's (2003) schema-based model. Both are reviewed below.

SEX OFFENDERS' IMPLICIT THEORIES

Ward (2000) proposed that research on children's development of theory of mind, and on implicit theories in psychology, could provide a theoretical way to integrate sex offender cognitive distortions. From a cognitive psychopathology perspective such integration is certainly needed. Despite widening recognition of the idea that cognitive structures are essential to understanding day-to-day cognition—whether disordered or normal (Alford & Beck, 1997; Brewin, 1988; Kendall & Dobson, 1993)—previous research on sex offenders mainly treated the statements articulated by offenders as if each was somewhat unrelated to any other, or grouped them only on surface semantic criteria. If these statements are cognitive products, Ward (2000) argued, it follows that they are generated by schemata. The concept of schemata is used broadly and does not necessarily inform about *how* such structures operate; Ward went one step further, suggesting that these schemata be regarded as causal theories, interacting with personal and interpersonal experiences to form coherent structures that help explain and predict our own and others' behaviour (Ward, 2000). Yet these implicit theories are largely outside of conscious awareness: individuals are generally not aware that they think this way and others may not.

Specifically, Ward (2000) argued that many offenders' cognitive distortions are generated by theories about their beliefs and desires and those of the people around them. Ward suggested that sex offenders' distorted theories exist at several levels: from those about individual victims, to categories of entities (e.g. women, children) and at the most abstract, beliefs about how people operate in the world (e.g. understanding that people generally put their own needs first). However, each theory is coherent in itself, containing well-organised components that operate in concert to explain relevant phenomena.

There may be a number of distinct difficulties associated with the implicit theories of offenders. Ward (2000) suggested that first—at the broadest level—an offender may lack a fully mature theory of mind. For example, he may not understand that a joint experience he may have enjoyed was very unpleasant and unwanted by the other person. Second, he may have a flawed entity-level theory. For example, he may believe that children are as capable as adults of giving informed consent for sexual interaction, or that women appear unwilling to have sex whether they are interested or not. And third, he may develop distorted victim-specific theories. So, while accepting that in general wives have a right to refuse sexual approaches from their husbands, a rapist may believe that *his* wife does not have this right because she had sex with another man earlier in their marriage.

Ward (2000) contended that implicit theories most often develop early in childhood in response to specific experiences and are therefore adaptive at that time, as well as more general in form. As the offender begins sexual development, they come to be applied specifically to the sexual domain.

Ward and Keenan (1999) and Polaschek and Ward (2002) proposed implicit theories for child molesters and rapists, respectively, that were reconstructed mainly from existing psychometric scales of cognitive distortions, despite, as we noted earlier, there being little evidence that sex offenders actually agree with these items.

Ward and Keenan (1999) outlined five child sex offender implicit theories:

1. *Children as sexual beings*: children are inherently sexual creatures who enjoy, and even seek out, sex with adults.
2. *Nature of harm*: sexual contact between adults and children is harmless unless it involves significant physical violence. *True* harm results from physical force and injury only. If harmed, children quickly recover.
3. *Uncontrollability*: events just happen, and behaviour is directed mainly by powerful urges and emotions. Offenders do not have agency over their own actions.
4. *Entitlement*: the offender is inherently superior to others and so entitled to use inferior individuals such as children to meet his needs—including sexual needs—as he wishes.
5. *Dangerous world*: the world is a menacing environment, teeming with hostile and abusive individuals. There are two variants: child molesters either perceive all individuals, including children, as hostile and rejecting, and believe that the only effective way of dealing with them is to dominate and control them (i.e. through sexual abuse), or they perceive only adults to be dangerous. By comparison, a child represents a safe haven and so a preferred sexual partner.

Again using existing questionnaires as a starting point for their analysis, Polaschek and Ward (2002) proposed five implicit theories for rapists:

1. *Women are unknowable*: women are fundamentally different from men, with minds so inherently alien that men cannot easily grasp how they work. Therefore, heterosexual encounters are adversarial and women will seek to deceive men about what they really want.
2. *Women are sex objects*: women are constantly sexually receptive to men's needs but are not always consciously aware that they are. Women's body language is actually more relevant to ascertaining their receptiveness than is their speech. Furthermore, women cannot be injured by sexual activity unless they are physically injured.
3. *Male sex drive is uncontrollable*: men's sexual energy can build up to dangerous levels if women do not provide them with reasonable sexual access. Once men start to get sexually aroused, it is difficult for them to contain themselves if a woman then prevents them from continuing to orgasm.
4. *Entitlement*: referring again to the idea that one's needs should be met on demand, including one's sexual needs. In addition to having sex when they want to, entitled men are also justified in punishing—by rape—a woman who is not suitably subservient to their needs.
5. *Dangerous world*: as for child molesters, the world is a hostile and threatening place, where actors must be constantly on guard against exploitation by others. However, for rapists, there is no safe haven. Incidentally, this theory was not found to be represented in the rape-related attitudinal scales, probably because it has no specific focus on women or sex, but was included because the authors' clinical experience suggested its relevance. It is captured in the phrase 'it's just a dog-eat-dog world'.

EVALUATION OF THE IMPLICIT THEORY THEORY

Conceptual Evaluation

Ward's (2000) implicit theory theory has considerable potential to provide a rich and fruitful underpinning for the disparate beliefs that have been implicated as cognitive distortions in sex offenders, thus filling a much needed gap in theory. It also finally provides an explicitly aetiological role for cognitive distortions, filling a glaring gap in the links between level I and II theories (*external consistency*).

It is quite a complex theory but it has strong *unifying power*, bringing together several disparate areas (e.g. development of theory of mind, implicit or folk theory theorising and more traditional sex offender cognitive distortion theory). It has *fertility* and *heuristic value* too, suggesting new research into relationships between sex offender types and types of cognitive distortion, and new approaches to intervention.

Ward's implicit theory theory is still very new: the most detailed description of it is contained in Ward's (2000) article, which draws on a wide range of theoretical and research sources that give the implicit theory theory much of its potential *explanatory depth*. However, this first account of the theory also contains some areas of possible *internal incoherence*. For example, in the 2000 article, Ward imported a key idea from the literature on the development of theory of mind in children: that children develop implicit theories by functioning like scientists, 'forming hypotheses, testing them, and discarding those that fail to predict behavior. Therefore just as science progresses through the development of successively more adequate theories, so does children's understanding of other peoples' mental states' (2000, p. 497). Ward goes on to say that essentially the most consistently supported perspective at this time is that implicit theories transform during the lifespan through a similar process of revision to that proposed by Kuhn to occur in science (see Kuhn, 1989).

Do sex offenders use their implicit theories like scientists? Scientists need training in order to avoid the naturally occurring cognitive biases like the availability heuristic and confirmation bias. They learn to try to stand back from data and be 'objective'. However, schema theories in psychopathology propose that established schemata automatically bias interpretation at a pre-aware level, so that the information that comes in for interpretation is already skewed in a schema-consistent manner, especially in situations of ambiguity (Todorov & Bargh, 2002; Williams et al., 1997). What evidence is there that offenders attempt to overcome these processes by reflective 'objectivity'? Abel suggested that offenders may actively avoid opportunities to test their thinking. Of course scientists sometimes do this too, but that does not make their behaviour scientific!

Relatedly, Ward recognises that cognition is often influenced by goals and affect, and so is dynamic. However, this aspect is not really developed; often the theory seems to be taking a 'cold' cognition view: assuming that schemata function in a more static, impersonal way (Kunda, 1999; Williams et al., 1997).

In the aggression literature, there is substantial experimental and other evidence for the importance of priming phenomena in understanding distorted cognition in social interactions (Toderov & Bargh, 2002). The evidence for dynamic cognitive functioning in sex offending seems to be sparse. The most obvious candidate for a priming stimulus in the sex offender literature is sexual arousal. But we know of no studies that have tested whether affective or sexual arousal-based priming affects the accessibility of cognitive distortions or schemas in empirical research on sex offenders. However, qualitative analysis of offenders' and victims' accounts of offences suggests that offenders substantially distort their interpretations of victim behaviour in line with their own goals, even when such behaviour appears unambiguous to others (Polaschek, Hudson, Ward & Siegert, 2001). The degree of loss of objectivity that is necessary to explain how offenders overlook that the child was crying and asking to be allowed to leave, or that the offender broke into the victim's house and held a knife to her throat throughout the offence and then maintained that she sought him as a lover is very hard to explain without resorting to powerfully distorting states such as self-centred goal-directedness and sexual arousal. The explanatory depth of the implicit theory theory would be greatly enhanced by more explicit discussion of dynamic cognition issues.

Ward has not yet fully spelled out the mechanism for how implicit theories come to cause *sexual* offending, particularly in later onset offenders. Ward (2000) proposes that implicit theories mainly develop early in childhood and come to apply to the sexual domain as offenders become sexually active. However, several of the reconstructed theories—both for rapists and child molesters—are not sexual in nature, e.g. *entitlement*, *dangerous world* and *uncontrollability* for child molesters (Ward & Keenan, 1999); *women are unknowable*, *entitlement* and *dangerous world* for rapists (Polaschek & Ward, 2002). How exactly do they develop a sexual component in adolescence that supports the maintenance of later sexual offending, and do they support other forms of interpersonal violence or offending if they are not specific? And in adult-onset offenders, how do they develop at puberty without causing offending until much later?

Lastly, there are connections still to be made to other literatures that would increase the theory's *unifying power*. *Entitlement*, for example, may relate to narcissism, which has been implicated in facilitating general aggression (Baumeister, Bushman & Campbell, 2000), as has the hostile attributional bias (Matthews & Norris, 2002) which may overlap as a construct with the *dangerous world* implicit theory.

Empirical Adequacy

Given its youth, there is little research yet directly investigating the implicit theory theory's empirical adequacy, and the two most directly relevant studies were conducted by the original proponents (Polaschek & Ward, 2002; Ward & Keenan, 1999). They have since tested their proposed implicit theories using interview-based data (Beech & Ward, 2004; Marziano, Ward, Beech & Pattison, 2004; Polaschek & Gannon, 2004). The findings of these preliminary studies generally have been supportive. An experimental study by Mihailides, Devilly and Ward (2004) recently used the Implicit Association Test (Greenwald, McGhee & Schwartz, 1998) with child molesters, nonsexual offenders and non-offenders, and found stronger evidence for the *children as sexual beings* and *uncontrollability of sexuality* implicit theories in molesters compared to both other groups. The *sexual entitlement* implicit theory was only more evident in molesters when compared with non-offenders.

Mann and Hollin (2001) conducted independent qualitative analyses of both rapists' and child molesters' self-reports. In their first investigation, the main categories of schemata identified from self-reports of rapists were:

1. *Grievance*: a perception of being victimised by women and being justified in taking revenge against them.
2. *Self as victim*: a more passive view of being unable to respond agentically to the demands of living.
3. *Control*: believing that one needed to be in charge of others.
4. *Entitlement*: believing that one could do as one wished in the world, regardless of whether or not this conduct impinged on others.
5. *Disrespect for certain women*: the view that women with certain characteristics (e.g. prostitutes) had obviated their right to respectful treatment.

A second study with both rapists and child molesters found evidence of both the grievance and control schemata. Interestingly, Mann and Beech observed both that rapists gave 'grievance' as the most common cause of their offences, and that child molesters' reports suggested that their offending was *less* schema-driven than that of rapists.

Experimental research on sex offenders' schemata is very sparse. A single study by Malamuth and Brown (1994) found evidence in men at risk of rape for a suspiciousness-toward-women schema, perhaps consistent with Polaschek and Gannon's (2004) implicit theory *women are dangerous*.

Conclusions

Ward's implicit theory theory provides a much-needed theoretical basis for organising disparate cognitive distortions into themes arising from a common structure, the schema. A strength is the idea that these schemata function as causal theories that are tested by experience. The theory is likely to prove very fertile in an area where no significant theoretical innovation has occurred in two decades. However, its internal coherence and explanatory depth will increase when Ward has more clearly specified some aspects of the mechanisms, and the types of cognition the proposed implicit theories regulate.

MANN AND BEECH'S SCHEMA-BASED MODEL OF SEXUAL ASSAULT

Mann and Beech (2003) outlined the second schema approach to sexual assault in the form of a model of how schemata interact with environmental variables (e.g. life events) and with other risk factors to produce sexual offending. After examining both the socio-cognitive and cognitive therapy approaches to schema theories, they concluded that neither provided clear guidance about the form of a schema theory for sexual assault. However they judged the cognitive therapy tradition to hold the most promise because of (i) a research history that more closely aligned with sex offender issues, and (ii) explicit links to existing therapeutic approaches with sexual offenders.

Their model is depicted in Figure 8.1, and proposes that dysfunctional schemata operating in tandem with negative or ambiguous life events process incoming information in a schema-congruent manner. Once activation occurs, then the schemata or beliefs generate surface cognitions followed by affective and motivational states, which act to make the idea of carrying out a sexual assault seem 'appropriate, necessary, or attractive' to the offender (Mann & Beech, 2003, p. 147).

Having outlined the process above, Mann and Beech emphasise that they view schemata as taking only a minor role in offending, in interaction with other risk factors such as sexual arousal and poor emotional regulation.

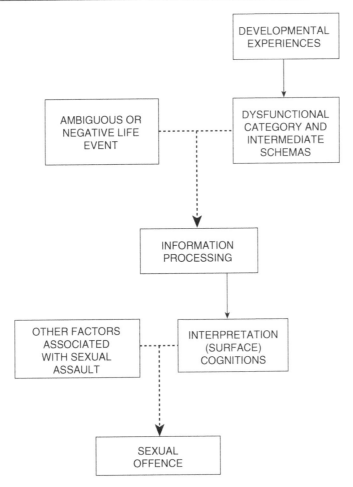

Figure 8.1 A schema-based model of cognition in sexual offending
Source: Mann, R. E. & Beech, A. R. (2003). Cognitive distortions, schemas and implicit theories. In T. Ward, D. R. Laws & S. M. Hudson (Eds), *Sexual deviance: Issues and controversies* (p. 146). Thousand Oaks, CA: Sage.

EVALUATION OF THE MANN AND BEECH SCHEMA MODEL

As we noted, the Mann and Beech (2003) schema model is clearly intended as a preliminary framework for the role of schematic cognition in sexual assaults, rather than as a fully fledged theory. Mann and Beech report later in their 2003 chapter on an intervention using Young's schema therapy (e.g. Young, Klosko & Weishaar, 2003) with sex offenders. Theoretical models of schematic functioning can provide an important rationale for such interventions, and this appears to have been one of their aims.

Its preliminary nature is reflected in some difficulties with conceptual clarity. For example, it is unclear whether Figure 8.1 depicts an episode of offending, or the onset of an offending career (i.e. is it an aetiological or event model?). Second, Figure 8.1 refers to 'ambiguous or negative' life events, described as 'threatening' in the accompanying text (Mann & Beech, 2003, p. 147). This feature may limit the *explanatory scope* to offences triggered by negative affect. If so, and if the model is event-based, this feature would be *externally inconsistent* with research on the offence process that suggests that negative life events are often not present (see Chapters 14 and 15).

A third, minor problem concerns *external consistency* and *internal coherence*. Both schema literatures from which Mann and Beech draw—and their own model—recognise that schemata can be activated by life events. In contradiction with these literatures, they have defined schemata as 'chronically accessible' (Mann & Beech, 2003, p. 145). Fourth, because this is a model, Mann and Beech have not suggested how schematic processes actually *interact* with the other sexual assault factors they mention. Most of the *explanatory power* of a model like this lies in mapping out those interactions which, if done, could make this a level I theory!

Finally, Mann and Beech report that their model is influenced by schema approaches from both social cognition and cognitive therapy. With respect to the latter, they particularly referred to the work of Kwon and Oei (1994), who drew up several different models of the role of cognitions in both the aetiology and maintenance of depression. Kwon and Oei noted a problem in schema models of depression that is equally problematic with sex offenders: there is little in the way of agreement about how negative cognitions relate to depression, nor the mechanisms for change in treatment. It may be, for example, that dysfunctional attitudes—to use Kwon and Oei's term—come into play only once a mild depression has already developed (i.e. the differential activation model of depressive cognition; Teasdale, 1983, 1988).

The choice of a depression-based model as a template for sexual offending could be arguable, particularly if sexual assault is viewed as a criminal behaviour rather than as a form of clinical psychopathology. There are at least two important differences between each of these types of problems. Depression is a (sometimes recurring) disorder of mood that persists for days, weeks and months and then often remits. It is present, more or less, when sufferers are on their own, or in the company of others. By contrast sexual offending comprises an event or series of events: an interaction over a limited time span that often ends when the perpetrator obtains sexual gratification. And it is a social event, involving at least one other person, a victim. Depression pervades every aspect of the sufferer's life whereas many sexual offenders may behave and experience life in a manner that is indistinguishable from others between offending episodes. Depressed individuals evince a variety of stable cognitions that are easily detected. Not so sex offenders. And depression is unlikely to be motivated—as sex offending often is—by appetitive drives and approach goals. Lastly, and perhaps most obviously, depression is not by definition a socially condemned behaviour resulting in potentially substantial damage to others. And no one has credibly suggested that depressive cognition develops to help protect the sufferer from getting well. Yet this is exactly what has been suggested for sexual offending. Indeed, a defining feature of sexual offending is that it involves the pursuit of one's own pleasure at the expense of someone else's well-being. This conflict creates psychological tension in all but the most psychopathic of individuals, and has no parallel in depression. To reduce the conflict and the tension that results from it, perpetrators must do some form of mental gymnastics as Abel has suggested. This feature of sexual offending is shared with criminal behaviour in general. It follows that in the next stage of development of schematic models, integration with schema theories for behaviours more closely parallel to sexual offending may be fruitful (e.g. aggression: Anderson & Bushman, 2002; Huesmann, 1998).

Conclusions

Mann and Beech have proposed a novel preliminary model of how schemata may be involved in sexual assault. Further work is needed to clarify it, and give it more consistency, fertility, scope and explanatory depth.

CLINICAL IMPLICATIONS OF COGNITIVE DISTORTION THEORIES

We currently have little evidence that any cognitive distortion interventions are effective (or ineffective) in reducing risk, despite their widespread inclusion in sex offender treatment programmes. One possible reason for this lack of evidence may be an inadequate theoretical rationale for such interventions. An adequate level II theory should seek to specify the key mechanisms and Abel's account falls short, providing a rather fuzzy theoretical basis for clinical use. Consequently, confusion about whether cognitive distortions represent errors of knowledge or fact, or examples of motivated self-deception (or both perhaps) has been proliferated throughout the sex offender treatment literature.

Marshall et al. (1999a) suggest that understanding the mechanisms that generate cognitive distortions will not ultimately affect intervention. We think this conclusion is premature. Abel and colleagues suggested that sexual offenders have developed cognitive distortions to avoid anxiety, shame and guilt. Intervention needs to be tailored to recognise that correcting such distortions will require careful management by therapists of the consequent negative impact on self- and social identity that must result from an accurate understanding of each man's offending. Yet most interventions for cognitive distortions in sex offenders appear similar to those used in cognitive therapy for clinical disorders, where self-loathing or expectations of social rejection would not be an anticipated consequence of successful treatment. Some of these traditional cognitive-behavioural approaches to recognising distorted thinking use quite aggressive, rational disputation processes (e.g. RET; see Murphy, 1990). When such methods are directed at cognitions that are protecting an offender from self-censure, these processes surely only can serve to enhance resistance to change. Cognitive approaches can be ineffective or even damaging if used without an adequate understanding of the function of the cognitions concerned (Fox, 1999).

Marshall et al. (1999a) have recently focused on the enhancement and preservation of self-esteem in both their research and intervention, as a way of increasing responsivity. This approach implicitly recognises the self-protective functions of cognitive distortions for sex offenders. Furthermore, their description of their treatment approach (Marshall et al., 1999a) suggests that they directly manage the potentially threatening self-referential consequences for offenders of stripping away these protections when they work with them on their cognitive distortions. Their work is consistent with the spirit of Abel's theory, yet confusingly they identify Ward's implicit theory theory as providing the best account of cognitive distortions as they understand them. Recall that implicit theories are thought to develop prior to puberty, rather than in response to motivation to offend. As such, they will be difficult to change, but are unlikely to be as intertwined with maintaining a tolerable sense of identity as are cognitions that function as Abel has suggested.

By contrast to Abel and colleagues' theory, both of the newer schema approaches emphasise cognitive products resulting from erroneous early learning experiences that have a specific effect on offending that can be distinguished from cognitive distortions generated by offenders to avoid self- or external condemnation. However, neither provides guidance about how to distinguish one form of cognitive distortions from the other. Each suggests a different therapeutic approach.

Ward (2000) advocates instructing sex offenders in how to be better scientists by making their own assumptions more explicit, and teaching them how to stand back from what they believe to be true so that they can gather genuine evidence. Ward and Keenan (1999) speculate that targeting these *core* theories' (p. 836) will make therapy far more efficient, since a single theory may be capable of generating dozens of individual cognitive distortions. Drake, Ward, Nathan and Lee (2001) have set about documenting a therapeutic intervention approach based on the implicit theories of child molesters (Ward & Keenan, 1999). They report that offenders understood the implicit theory approach readily, and speculate that the approach will be more effective than previous interventions.

Mann and Beech's schema-based model was designed to support a schema-based treatment programme for high-risk sex offenders piloted in the UK prison service in the mid-1990s (Mann & Beech, 2003). Aside from the weak theoretical status of cognitive distortion theory in general, there are at least two other reasons to exercise some caution in adapting Young's schema-focused therapy (Young et al., 2003) for widespread use in sex offender programmes. First, there is no compelling empirical evidence that Young's approach is more effective than other forms of cognitive therapy in the treatment of clinical disorders. Few relevant studies have been undertaken as yet, and those examining the theory have not always supported it (e.g. Halford, Bernoth-Doolan & Eadie, 2002). Second, there is no theoretical rationale for adoption. Young's early maladaptive schemata (EMSs) are not in any way specific to particular behavioural domains, such as sexual functioning, but are thought to generate diffuse psychopathology. Further, Mann and Beech's (2003) schema model of sexual offending is not based around EMSs, and their own empirical research (Mann & Hollin, 2001) produced very different types of schemata to Young's. There is a need for a better match between theory and practice if we are to achieve treatment integrity with schema approaches.

As we noted, Mann and Beech (2003) reported encouraging preliminary data from Thornton and Shingler (2001) on a UK schema-based intervention. In this evaluation, sex offenders were provided with conventional cognitive restructuring in the first phase of treatment, and with a Young-type schema-focused approach in the second phase. Using a traditional questionnaire-based data collection strategy, they found incremental decreases in distorted cognition at the end of each treatment phase. Unfortunately, the different types of intervention were not able to be counterbalanced and only higher risk offenders received the second one. Therefore this study on its own cannot establish whether one approach is more effective than the other. The results may simply be a good demonstration of the risk principle in offender rehabilitation (i.e. the principle that high-risk cases benefit more from high-intensity interventions; see Andrews, Bonta & Hoge, 1990).

CONCLUSIONS

Cognitive distortions are one of the best-known treatment targets in sexual offender intervention. The relevant theory has stood in a preliminary state of development for over two decades and there is significant confusion about its central tenets and what they mean for intervention. Recent new offerings based on schema theory are promising, but may be describing different forms of cognitive distortion to those originally identified by Abel and his colleagues. Therefore some fundamental conceptual problems with the nature and functions of cognitive distortions remain to be resolved before theory development can really advance. Of equal importance is more scientific research, including experimental investigations and investigations using less direct and less conscious measures of cognition. Indeed this point is stated in *every* review of cognitive distortions (e.g. Gannon, Polaschek & Ward, 2005; Ward et al., 1997) Despite these imprecations, the general sophistication of research in this area remains quite low, and hampers theory development.

A good cognitive distortion theory would cover how cognitive distortions develop, whether they are aetiological, whether they are stable or more transiently available, whether they represent faulty 'fact-learning' or approaches to managing negative self- and social evaluative needs, or both, whether they can differentiate between different types of offenders (e.g. different levels of risk), and whether they can themselves motivate offending. This is a tall order.

In the meantime there is no evidence of a need to make radical changes to current intervention approaches. Unfortunately nor is there evidence we should stay with them! Intervention is likely to proceed more smoothly and efficiently if therapists and offenders attempt to establish and work on altering clusters of cognitive distortions rather than individual statements. This is the most obvious implication of schema-based approaches, and Drake et al. (2001) set out some clear guidelines for getting started. Finally, recognising that Abel was saying that cognitive distortions protect those who articulate them gives explicit emphasis to the importance of restructuring them in a gentle and graduated manner, in a supportive, group environment (Marshall et al., 1999a).

Chapter 9

THEORIES OF DEFICIENT VICTIM EMPATHY

The sex offender literature is replete with interventions for empathy, but there is little in the way of level II theory that outlines adequately the mechanisms by which empathy deficits contribute to the risk of committing a sexual offence. Consequently, the widespread inclusion of victim empathy components in cognitive-behavioural treatment programmes rests more firmly on intuition than on scientific principles. As with cognitive distortions, even the *concept* of empathy is remarkably difficult to define. After considering definitions and components briefly, we examine the four-stage model of empathy and several fledgling theories about the causes of victim empathy deficits. We conclude with clinical implications.

WHAT IS EMPATHY?

The roots of the term empathy are said to originate in the German concept *einfühlung*, which translates as 'feeling into' (Oxford English Dictionary, 2002). Theodore Lipps has been credited with introducing it into psychology at the very end of the 19th century (Mahrer, Boulet & Fairweather, 1994). Examination of dictionary definitions immediately suggests confusion about what empathy is. The Merriam-Webster's Collegiate Dictionary (2002) defines it as:

> The action of understanding, being aware of, being sensitive to, and vicar-
> iously experiencing the feelings, thoughts and experience of another of either
> the past or present without having the feelings, thoughts and experience fully
> communicated in an objectively explicit manner.

This definition allows for empathic responses to a full range of human experiences, not just negative ones. In contrast, the related term *sympathy* is usually applied selectively to feelings of compassion and sorrow directed at another person's negative experiences (Oxford English Dictionary, 2002). In practice, in the sex offender domain empathy refers usually to perceiving that another person has been harmed, frightened or otherwise subjected to a negative experience, and to feelings of concern, caring and compassion towards that person. In that sense the victim empathy component of treatment programmes could more accurately be called 'sympathy training' than empathy training (Hanson, 1997b), where the aim would be for the offender to experience a parallel range of affects to the victim (e.g., fear, helplessness, despair; Marshall, Hudson, Jones & Fernandez, 1995).

COMPONENTS OF EMPATHY

Empathy can be treated as an individual difference (or trait) variable, or as a process. Either way, it can be broken down into related components. A number of authors propose two semi-distinct components: *perspective taking* (i.e. intellectually taking the viewpoint of the other, 'putting oneself in her shoes') and *vicarious emotional responding* (i.e. experiencing a range of emotions that are the same or similar to those actually experienced by the other; Kerem, Fishman & Josselson, 2001; Mahrer et al., 1994; Moore, 1990). Gladstein (1983) labelled the first component *cognitive empathy* and the second *affective empathy* to minimise confusion.

Davis (1983) developed a multiple-component view of the empathic response, which is reflected in the structure of his commonly used global empathy scale, the Interpersonal Reactivity Index (IRI). Davis's four components are (i) perspective taking, (ii) fantasy: the extent to which respondents report that they can imagine themselves in the roles of fantasy characters; (iii) empathic concern, or feelings of compassion for others, and (iv) personal distress; the extent to which respondents become upset and distressed by their experiences.

EMPATHY AND SEXUAL OFFENDING

Several level I theories note lack of empathy as a defining characteristic of sexual offenders. Marshall and Barbaree (1990) likened the empathic functioning of sex offenders to that of psychopaths: globally absent. Others (e.g. Araji & Finkelhor, 1985; Scully, 1990) also note empathy deficits, but are unclear about the extent of such deficits. Nevertheless, these theories suggest simply—and circularly—that empathy must be absent because the offence would not have occurred if the offender had adequate levels of understanding and concern for the harm he was causing. But *how* do empathy deficits contribute to sexual assault? For example, does a lack of empathy motivate sexual offending, or simply fail to stop such offences?

Global Dispositional Empathy Deficits

The simplest theoretical idea is that offenders have global, stable deficits in their ability to experience empathy for others. Marshall and Barbaree (1990), for example, proposed that a punitive, neglectful childhood led to widespread emotional indifference to others, typical of that found in psychopaths (Hart & Hare, 1997). Such a theory implies that the main mechanism is one of inhibition failure: when such an offender desires to do something that will—whether incidentally or intentionally—harm another, he will pursue that desire without any constraints. Although an empathic person might have the same desire, according to this argument, he would not pursue it because feeling for others would inhibit him.

Global deficits, if they work by the mechanism proposed above, should predict widespread and diverse offending. This is the pattern seen in psychopaths (Hart & Hare, 1997). However, many sex offenders are not psychopaths, and although offending histories are quite varied, sex offenders, particularly child sex offenders, can show evidence of offence specialisation (Smallbone & Wortley, 2004a). Furthermore, empirical examination of global empathy—admittedly using weak designs and dubious measures—has not usually found differences between sex offenders and other offender or non-offender samples (see Polaschek, 2003b). So this theory, besides having little *explanatory depth*, also appears lacking in *predictive accuracy*.

More specific theories predict stable deficits that apply only to classes or categories of people such as children (Abel et al., 1989) or women (Barbaree, Marshall & Lanthier, 1979; Polaschek & Ward, 2002). Empirical investigation is also unsupportive of this idea, at least with child molesters. Research currently suggests that deficits *are* stable (i.e. present during routine assessment, not just during the offence process), but appear strongest for the offender's own victim, and sometimes for those who have experienced similar harm (e.g. Fernandez, Marshall, Lightbody & O'Sullivan, 1999; Marshall, Hamilton & Fernandez, 2001). In Marshall and colleagues' research, child molesters' self-reported empathy for child accident victims was no different to non-offenders' empathy. The picture for rapists is less clear at this stage (Fernandez & Marshall, 2003; Marshall & Moulden, 2001).

So, when a person is able to suppress concern for others and persistently harm them through sexual assault, it may not be a result of the absence of normal empathy development per se. Some other mechanism may be in operation. Just what is it?

The Empathy Process

One approach to answering this question is to unpack the process of developing an empathic response. Earlier, we described the common two-component model of empathy: perspective taking and vicarious emotional responding (i.e. cognitive and affective components). Of course a component analysis does not imply any particular temporal relationship between the components, but it is intuitively appealing to assume that emotional responding naturally follows on from the cognitive process of perspective taking, at least in normal empathy.

This simple, two-step model developed out of psychological research on altruistic and prosocial behaviour (Gladstein, 1983; Mahrer et al., 1994). However, in an antisocial context, we are interested in empathy for its absence. This model is not adequate for the task of explaining why empathy does not always unfold as it should. Psychopaths—individuals who are by definition chronically deficient in caring feelings for others—reportedly can learn to take others' perspectives and then use such knowledge to exploit others better (Rice, Harris & Cormier, 1992). Therefore their emotional responding may be either indifferent or positive in situations where others would feel vicarious negative affect. In a more transient way, an individual with a grudge against another may inflict harm and experience cognitive empathy along with emotions like satisfaction in response to the other person's suffering. In both of these examples the first component is present but the second component does not follow, suggesting that at least one other element is needed: some form of motivation to experience vicarious emotion. In prosocial situations where empathy has mainly been studied, research participants were implicitly motivated. What motivates a person to experience empathy towards another? Hanson and Scott (1995) suggested the addition of a third element to this model, labelled *caring or compassion*, to imply a motive to respond sympathetically (i.e. in tune with) another's experience. More recently, Hanson (2003) has renamed this aspect of his empathy model a *caring relationship goal*.

THE FOUR-STAGE MODEL OF THE EMPATHY PROCESS

The utility of empathy process models in understanding deficits lies in the ability to examine at what point(s) the process goes awry. Marshall and colleagues in a seminal review paper on empathy in sex offenders (Marshall et al., 1995) proposed a four-stage general model of empathy, which they then applied to sex offenders. The four stages of the model of the empathy process are '(1) emotional recognition, (2) perspective-taking, (3) emotional replication, and (4) response decision' (Marshall et al., 1995, p. 101).

Marshall and colleagues (1995) described *emotional recognition* as the process of identifying—with some degree of accuracy—the emotional state of another. They suggested that this first phase has been overlooked by most previous investigators and so little relevant research exists. In the context of sexual offending, the information available to the perceiver is likely to include several different types of sensory input (e.g. visual information, sound). They argue that the ability to recognise accurately distress in, for example, the facial affect of a victim, is a necessary part of the empathic process that could terminate a sexual attack.

Consistent with the remainder of the empathy literature, *perspective taking*, the second stage, is defined by Marshall et al. (1995) as the ability to comprehend the world from another's frame of reference. The main issue they identified here is the degree of similarity to the victim; greater perceptions of difference have been found to reduce empathic inhibition; it is easier to harm a distinctly different other. The implication is that sexual assaulters may see victims as belonging to a group of people with unfamiliar characteristics (e.g. attitudes).

The third stage, *emotional replication*, refers to the generation of an emotional response to perspective taking that approximates the other's response. According to Marshall et al. (1995), emotional replication can only occur if (i) the potential offender has been sufficiently accurate at both stages I and II, and (ii) has the ability to experience the appropriate emotion. Here they noted that offenders often seem to have access to a truncated range of either emotional labels or emotional experiences, and suggest that such a problem leads to difficulties both at stage I and stage III.

The fourth stage, *response decision*—also called 'empathic responding' by Marshall et al.—refers to 'the observer's decision to act or not on the basis of their feelings' (p. 102). They suggested that having completed stages I to III in an empathic manner, a sexual aggressor may now decide to ignore his perceptions and feelings and aggress anyway. They noted that this suggestion is contrary to the research on the inhibiting effects of empathy on aggression, described no theoretical mechanism and provided no evidence to support this idea that stage IV can operate independently of stage III.

EVALUATION OF THE FOUR-STAGE MODEL

Marshall and colleagues' (1995) review is an important landmark in current clinical understanding of how empathy can unfold. Although treatment programmes at this time already appeared to have been taking an offending-specific approach to remediation of empathy deficits (e.g. Hildebran & Pithers, 1989), the research literature was sparse and confused, and formally articulated theory almost non-existent. Primarily Marshall and colleagues' (1995) goal was to 'offer a better way to understand and treat the empathy deficits in [sex offenders]' (p. 99). How successful was their offering as a theory?

Aside from its novelty at the time, the staged model has several important strengths. First, it has some *unifying power*. It provides a scaffold for organising a wide range of theoretical ideas and clinical observations (e.g. limited emotional recognition and labelling abilities). A second strength is its apparent *explanatory depth* and *scope*, particularly the ease with which it invokes a variety of mechanisms to account for predicted variation in types of empathy deficit. And relatedly, it has *fertility* or *heuristic value*. In particular it facilitates novel research questions about different patterns of empathy deficit, and suggests that different intervention responses will be required. It predicts that individual offenders may have unique patterns of competence and deficiency across the different stages. For example, a rapist may correctly recognise a woman's unwilling facial expression in the early stages of a sexual assault (stage I competence), but incorrectly believe that it arises from ignorance about his competence as a sexual partner (stage II deficit). Another rapist may both correctly interpret the victim's emotional display (stage I competence) and understand that he is harming her (stage II competence) but feel pleased about this state of affairs (stage III problem) because for some reason she is a 'bad' woman who deserves to be harmed.

However, there are significant deficits in Marshall's model, when it is viewed as a theory rather than just as an organising framework (Geer, Estupinan & Manguno-Mire, 2000). The most important issue is the lack of clarity about exactly *how* deficiencies in their model facilitate sexual offending (*internal coherence*).

In particular, *when* does this hypothetical process unfold in relation to an offence? Is it during an offence, or between offences? Stage I (emotional recognition) requires the presence of a victim or potential victim who is experiencing something sufficiently unpleasant to be displaying negative affect. These circumstances would seem to arise well into a typical offence process, in fact apparently after the offender commences his sexually assaultative behaviour (see Chapters 14 and 15). A within-offence-episode interpretation is also consistent with this passage: 'since it is clear that feeling empathy aborts ongoing harmful behaviour toward a distressed person, then the failure to recognize this distress would allow continuation of whatever harmful behaviour is being enacted' (Marshall et al., 1995, p. 101).

From a theoretical point of view, we think there is a problem with the plausibility of proposing that the empathic process only begins to become deficient at the point where the offender is in the presence of a distressed victim (i.e. he has begun the offence). Firstly, this view is inconsistent with level I theories (e.g. Finkelhor, see Chapter 2) that suggest internal empathy-like inhibitors are relevant long before the offender starts to approach a victim (*external consistency*). By this time, the offender has already passed a number of stages at which empathy should already have inhibited his behaviour. For example, knowing that sexual contact between adults and children is harmful to children, and caring about harm to children (competence at stages II and III, respectively) should prevent people from even approaching a child sexually in the first place. So if the approach is made at all, arguably empathy deficits have already emerged. Some research may support this view. Dean and Malamuth (1997), for example, found that men who were more sensitive to the feelings of others fantasised about sexual aggression as much as those who were low in such sensitivity, but reported less actual aggressive behaviour.

Furthermore, the proximity of a powerful reinforcer (positive or negative), perhaps a cognitively deconstructed state (Ward, Hudson & Marshall, 1995a), or the effects of rising arousal are all likely to disrupt the process of generating empathy during the offence. A central tenet of the relapse prevention model is that self-control—particularly self-control invoked by evaluating the costs of the prohibited behaviour—becomes more difficult as the proximity of an environment conducive to carrying out the behaviour draws closer. We would not expect an alcoholic sitting in front of a drink in a bar to be able to feel any concern for the harm that she may do to herself and others if she drinks again, even when she knows and cares about that harm at other times. For empathy to act within an offence process, it would need to be invoked much earlier, when self-control is still possible, but a distressed victim is not present yet.

Alternatively, did Marshall et al. envision their process unfolding post-offence or between offences, when the offender is presumably no longer aroused, but perhaps finds himself in the presence of a distressed victim? Pithers (1999) certainly assumes that the Marshall et al. model is a theory of empathy that unfolds post-offence, thus acting to inhibit the commencement of a subsequent offence process. This is an area of confusion that requires attention, to increase the model's clarity and utility.

Finally, the Marshall et al. (1995) empathy model primarily suggests that remediable skill deficits make an important contribution to empathic failure in sex offenders. A small amount of research supports this view, but much of the model remains untested empirically. However, their own subsequent research has diverted interest away from the model. Marshall, Fernandez and colleagues (e.g. Fernandez & Marshall, 2003; Marshall & Moulden, 2001) have led the development of self-report measures that aim to disentangle victim-specific responses from responses to sexual assault victims, and responses to accident victims. If offenders are deficient in empathy skills pertinent to their own sexual offending, why do they not show the same reduced empathy for other sexual assault victims? The epistemic value of *simplicity* is threatened if one has to postulate, for example, that offenders' emotional recognition *skills* are deficient only at reading the facial expressions of a subgroup of women or children: his victims.

In the decade since 1995, interesting theoretical innovations suggest ways to develop this model, and Marshall is one of several people who have made important advances in the proposed mechanisms underlying empathy deficits. We think the next theory offers a much more parsimonious way of dealing with this puzzling pattern; where 'empathy deficits' are largely specific to one's own victim, but sometimes may generalise to others in the same situations (i.e. other children who have been sexually abused).

VICTIM EMPATHY DEFICITS AND COGNITIVE DISTORTIONS

So far, we have examined empathy deficits from the perspective of a failure to exhibit normal empathic responses, and we have assumed that this failure suggests that offenders need help in developing normal empathy, even if only in the sexual abuse domain. This perspective is implicit in all of the material we have discussed to this point. An alternative is to go back to first principles and ask the question: is what we observe in offenders actually an independent, encapsulated skill deficit, akin perhaps to the deficits demonstrated by women who can't understand why their husbands love watching motor racing on television but can't bear to go shopping for clothes? Are the presentations we call victim empathy deficits instead just a predictable consequence of cognitive distortions, or even a subset of distortions themselves? Are cognitive distortions and victim empathy deficits produced by the same underlying mechanisms? These ideas have been promoted and discussed in recent years by several researchers (Bumby, 2000; Marshall, Anderson & Fernandez, 1999a; Ward & Keenan, 1999). Marshall et al. (1999a) propose that victim empathy deficits are *not* the result of empathy problems at all, but in fact reflect a normal empathy process unfolding from the premise that the victim has not been harmed. They review evidence that supports their 'hypothesis that apparent empathy deficits in [sex offenders] are no more than distortion about the harmful consequences of their abuse' (p. 85), and others agree (Hanson, 2003; Hilton, 1993).

Several other sources of information also seem to support Marshall and colleagues' view. Some recent victim-specific empathy measures seem essentially cognitive in nature, in line with the perspective-taking component (Polaschek, 2003b). Marshall, Hamilton and Fernandez (2001) demonstrated a very large correlation between perspective taking and cognitive distortions in child molesters. And Marshall et al. (1999a) noted that a number of researchers have found that interventions to increase victim empathy decrease cognitive distortions (e.g. Pithers, 1994). All of these findings support construct overlap, or at least very strong links between what we have called 'victim empathy' and cognitive distortions. It then follows that theory development should encompass an understanding of the mechanisms that regulate the denial of harm by the offenders who inflict it. Delineation of these mechanisms will help to establish whether displays of indifference or callousness towards victims are primarily a cognitive issue, and whether perspective taking deficits are the main source of such displays. We discuss two proposals for mechanisms next.

A THEORY OF MIND PERSPECTIVE

In the previous chapter we reviewed Ward and colleagues' 'theory of mind' theory of cognitive distortions (e.g. Polaschek & Ward, 2002; Ward & Keenan, 1999). Briefly, Ward, Keenan and Hudson (2000) and Keenan and Ward (2000) propose that not just cognitive distortions, but victim empathy deficits and intimacy deficits may all be generated by a common difficulty in understanding and making accurate inferences about the psychological states of other people. In the previous chapter our emphasis was on the development of specific erroneous implicit theories, schematic structures that have the capacity to link together disparate cognitive products. Here, we will give more attention to the process of theorising about others' mental states, and Ward and colleagues' speculations about how systematic errors in this process create inappropriate perceptions and emotional responses to victim experiences.

A theory of mind perspective asserts that from childhood we develop increasingly more sophisticated models of the workings of our own minds, and those of others. A key aspect of these models is the point at which they become representational. In normal development by about the age of 4 years a child begins to realise that people act on the basis of what they believe (i.e. subjectively) rather than what really is. Such beliefs can be false, and can differ in different people, but it is beliefs that predict behaviour, not an objective truth. Children come to understand then that needs, desires, beliefs and feelings may all differ across people, because rather than having direct access to reality, instead we each view the world using unique mental models. Although this field is still quite new, Ward and colleagues note research that suggests that the sophistication of children's theories of mind is related to the occurrence of mental state talk in the family (i.e. conversations with parents and older siblings that process experiences in terms of inner states and the like). In severely neglectful and abusive home environments, children may be delayed in developing an adequate theory of mind because of an absence of such processing, or possibly because the main method of transmission—a secure attachment relationship—is absent. Alternatively, in such a home a child may develop a theory that contains assumptions that, while true in that context, are problematic and often erroneous in the wider adult world. For example, a child in an abusive home environment may develop a 'theory of nasty minds' (Happé & Frith, 1996). As an adult, he may treat acquaintances and work colleagues as if he expects them to be 'nasty'. Although most of them are not, they respond to his communicated expectations in ways that are somewhat consistent with his theory. Consequently he suffers social and occupational disadvantage.

According to Keenan and Ward (2000), two hypothetical forms of abnormal theory of mind development may be of specific relevance to sexual offending. Theory of mind development may be delayed or completely absent. Delay or developmental failure may be global or circumscribed. Ward et al. (2000) call global deficits *framework theory deficits* and give as an example the inability of a rapist to appreciate that his victim may not want to have sex with him, although he desires to have sex with her. Such a view, according to this proposal, may be caused by the failure to recognise that people act on their own subjective realities, not on some objective, universal reality that he is privy to.

Also important are possible *specific theory deficits* (Ward et al., 2000), in which there may be a delay or failure to develop a theory about mental states only in particular contexts. So a man who believes that children's sexuality and the ways it is expressed are similar to that of adults may interpret a child showing her underwear to that adult, or climbing on his lap, as inviting a sexual approach from him. In other respects, he may understand children's mental states quite accurately.

Third, Keenan and Ward (2000) suggest that extreme stress, anger or alcohol and drug abuse can cause self-regulatory failure and loss of control over behaviour. In this instance, through disinhibition an offender may develop a temporary specific theory of mind deficit where he fails to apply his usual abilities to attend to victim cues and construct a model of the other's mental state. A state empathy failure results as he erroneously projects his own beliefs and desires onto the victim.

EVALUATION OF THE 'THEORY OF MIND' THEORY

Keenan and Ward (2000; Ward et al., 2000) gave only peripheral attention to how a theory of mind perspective links to victim empathy deficits. However, because it was primarily designed to accommodate cognitive distortions, the theory is quite easily aligned to the task, if we adopt Marshall's view that lack of victim empathy results from the denial of victim harm. Through early learning in aversive environments, offenders could develop a number of different ways of denying harm from sexual abuse. Particular experiences, both with sexual abuse victimisation, and even with having their own basic needs neglected by incapable or egocentric adults, could create fertile environments for erroneous theory development. Ward and colleagues' specific implicit theories may also predict the patterns of cognition and affect characteristic of victim-specific empathy deficits. For example, one implicit theory—*children as sexual objects*—denies harm through asserting that sex between adults and children meets 'essential' needs of the child (Ward & Keenan, 1999). With adult women, the same implicit theory views adult women as constantly receptive to men's sexual approaches. Consequently they can only be harmed by sex if they are severely physically assaulted (Polaschek & Ward, 2002).

There is considerable room to develop this approach to provide a more direct, richer and clearer account of how theories of mind produce the kinds of distortions that Marshall et al. (1999a) have suggested. As we proposed above, implicit theories can readily account for errors in the perspective taking step that Marshall identified as key to problematic empathic processing. However, the implicit theory/theory of mind approach could be extended readily to explain another type of empathy deficit: why men who know that sexual abuse is harmful may still feel no compassion for victims. For example, *entitlement* and *dangerous world* implicit theories would both predict that a man may be aware that his behaviour is harmful but be emotionally unaffected or even pleased or satisfied by this perception that he is creating harm. This scenario would suggest a stage 3 deficit in the Marshall et al. (1995) model.

Last, Ward et al. (2000) suggest that the theory of mind perspective can be used to predict differences in the extensiveness (e.g. all women, all people or just this victim) and temporal stability of empathy deficits. This is another aspect that would be valuable to unpack further.

In summary, Ward et al. have not developed their theory of mind/implicit theory theory to account explicitly for empathy deficits in sexual offenders. Indeed they mention the issue more in passing than anything. There is increasing recognition that some, perhaps a majority, of the observed empathy deficits in sex offenders are a by-product of processes that distort cognition, and mainly occur quite early in the process of empathic responding. By implication, then, Ward's work has theoretical potential in this domain, but needs significant specific development to meet epistemic criteria.

SHAME, SELF-ESTEEM AND DEFICIENT EMPATHY

A number of authors have pointed to shame as an important construct with respect to empathic functioning (e.g. Hanson, 1997b; Roys, 1997; Ward, Hudson & Marshall, 1994); however, Bumby (2000; Bumby, Marshall & Langton, 1999) provides one of the more elaborate accounts. Like Marshall and colleagues (Fernandez et al., 1999; Marshall et al., 1999a), Bumby (2000) proposes that it is not meaningful to attempt to separate what we currently refer to as cognitive distortions and victim empathy deficits from each other. He considers offenders' unempathic behaviour to be a display of 'selective inhibition' in the service of avoiding the experience of shame and guilt rather than 'a true empathic *deficit*' (p. 151, italics in original). He sees cognitive distortions as evidence that offenders are quite consciously—even intensely—aware of the harm they cause.

Ward and colleagues' theoretical and empirical analyses of the abstinence violation effect in the relapse prevention model (Hudson, Ward & Marshall, 1992; Ward et al., 1994) support the view that making different attributions for relapses leads to distinct affective responses (i.e. shame versus guilt). Of particular relevance here is the idea that if offenders attribute their failure to avoid offending to internal, uncontrollable factors (e.g. personal defectiveness), they experience shame and have low self-efficacy about preventing future offending.

Bumby et al. (1999; Bumby, 2000) built this finding into a theory of how shame and guilt responses predict both likelihood of relapse and the specific nature of cognitive distortions and empathy responses. We will concentrate here on the empathy aspects, which also drew on Tangney's writing on shame. Bumby (2000) notes that Tangney (1995, 1996; Tangney, Burggraf & Wagner, 1995) described shame as including 'painful and global self-scrutiny, self-consciousness, and perceptions of negative evaluation, all of which create self-oriented distress' (Bumby, 2000, p. 152). Offenders who feel shame in response to transgressions tend to develop high levels of self-focused distress, which is managed through a process that Tangney (1995, 1996) termed *defensive externalisation*, which includes disabling levels of self-consciousness and blaming others for transgressive behaviour. Hanson (2003) describes this phenomenon quite clearly when he notes that 'some sexual offending may be based on misunderstandings but it is unlikely that such serious misunderstanding would persist if the offender had benign intentions ... the fixed, irrational quality of [offenders'] defensive justifications [distinguishes] them from honest errors in perspective-taking' (p. 17).

So, this process of defensive externalisation creates the appearance of victim-specific empathy deficits. Thus Bumby and colleagues are proposing that a tendency to respond with shame to 'wrongdoing' is the mechanism that accounts for unempathic behaviour toward victims, and should be the target of treatment rather than empathy itself.

Proeve and Howells (2002) suggest that the Bumby et al. (1999) theory is limited by an emphasis on only the negative self-evaluative aspects of shame (*internal shame*; Gilbert, 1998b) at the expense of another important aspect, conscious awareness of others' scrutiny (*external shame*; Gilbert, 1998b). Proeve and Howell cite research that has found shame-proneness to be negatively related to empathy (Tangney, 1991), and suggest that shame restricts empathy both because (i) the person is unduly absorbed with negatively evaluating himself, but also (ii) feeling judged by others can generate hostility towards and blaming of others.

Marshall and colleagues have suggested low self-esteem to be an empathy inhibitor, and have demonstrated large correlations between social self-esteem and victim-specific empathy (Marshall et al., 1999a; Marshall, Champagne, Brown & Miller, 1997). Marshall et al. propose that offenders use cognitive distortions—including denial of victim harm—to protect an already fragile (and low) sense of self-esteem from further negative appraisal; this mechanism is consistent with wider research on self-esteem. They emphasise the problems that low self-esteem creates for maintaining offence risk and impeding treatment progress. They also suggest that low self-esteem may *cause* sexual aggression through a variety of routes, including over-reliance on sex for coping with associated low mood, loneliness resulting from intimacy avoidance, and so on.

EVALUATION OF SHAME AND SELF-ESTEEM PROPOSALS

These proposals all suggest that core aspects of self-appraisal generate the pattern of characteristics we call victim-specific empathy deficits, along with other important offender features, such as cognitive distortions, intimacy avoidance and loneliness.

Considering shame first, Bumby's (2000) chapter offers quite a rich and fertile formulation of the mechanisms by which empathic functioning, intimacy deficits and attachment difficulties are linked, and facilitate sexual offending. With respect to empathy, the use of Tangney's work in particular, gives the proposal *explanatory depth*. Although difficulties with measuring shame accurately may make establishing its *empirical adequacy* a challenge, there is tentative support. Bumby (2000) reports a study (Bumby, Levine & Cunningham, 1996) that found a positive relationship between personal distress, externalisation and shame-proneness in outpatient sex offenders. They noted that, as shame increased, so did blaming others and self-focus. In contrast, guilt-proneness was positively associated with both cognitive and affective aspects of empathic ability. Also consistent is Thornton, Todd and Thornton's (1996) study reporting that scores on the Personal Distress scale of the Interpersonal Reactivity Index (a pen-and-paper measure of general empathy; Davis, 1983) were inversely correlated with empathy and related to resistance to experiencing empathy in interventions. Others have recognised that offenders' general ability to tolerate negative affect or personal distress is a barrier to the effectiveness of empathy treatment (Eldridge & Wyre, 1998; Schwartz & Canfield, 1998). Offenders who respond with intense shame to recognition of culpability may continue to blame victims and resist victim empathy training despite adequate general empathy (Hanson & Scott, 1995).

Proeve and Howells (2002), along with Bumby (2000), demonstrate the *heuristic value* of the theory for treatment. However, the theory is not yet well enough developed to enable evaluation of some epistemic values, such as *scope* and *internal coherence*.

Moving on now to the self-esteem argument, Marshall et al. (1999a) focus on the importance of self-esteem in the context of therapeutic processes. They see self-esteem restoration as crucial in getting offenders motivated to take responsibility for their behaviour, and develop some confidence that they can learn to avoid reoffending. In that sense, the effects of self-esteem on empathy are a more peripheral aspect of their argument. Nevertheless Marshall and colleagues seem to be suggesting a broadly similar mechanism to Bumby: avoidance of negative self-appraisal or, at least, efforts to titrate negative self-appraisal to tolerable levels, lead offenders with low self-esteem to blame others, deny empathy for others and develop cognitive distortions.

Future development of this theoretical idea could usefully focus on several immediate issues. Self-esteem is multidimensional (Bandura, 1997), so one obvious issue is how Marshall and colleagues' version of self-esteem—which is operationalised as appraisal of social worth—is related to shame, particularly how each generates deficient expressions of victim-specific empathy.

Marshall et al. (1999a) suggested that 'individuals with low self esteem feel more threatened by negative feedback than do individuals with high self esteem' (p. 55). This view appears *externally inconsistent* with a growing body of theory on self-esteem and narcissism (e.g. Baumeister, Smart & Boden, 1996; Morf & Rhodewalt, 2001). Experimental evidence on responses to negative external evaluation have not shown self-esteem to be a predictor of defensively unempathic responses (Bushman & Baumeister, 1998). However, *narcissism* was a good predictor with experimental analogues of both sexual and nonsexual aggression (Bushman & Baumeister, 1998; Bushman, Bonacci, van Dijk & Baumeister, 2003). Narcissism—defined by Baumeister et al. (1996) as *unstable high* self-esteem—and shame have quite a long shared theoretical history (Tangney & Dearing, 2002), suggesting that theorising about the role of narcissism in sexual aggression may also be relevant to understanding how shame and self-esteem contribute to empathic behaviour.

This problem with *external consistency* is related to a difficulty with *internal coherence* as well. Marshall (1993a) suggested that the apparent high self-esteem of some rapists was actually a defensive response to low self-esteem. This argument is central to psychodynamic views of narcissism, and is consequently difficult to falsify because it assumes that the *low* self-esteem is unconsciously held. Putatively defensive but overtly high self-esteem is a very different clinical presentation to overtly low self-esteem, and poses different therapeutic challenges, the first of which is getting such men into treatment at all (Marshall, 1993a).

What is the relevance of these points? It appears that many sex offenders' empathy deficits are victim-specific. However, are they specific to victims of *sexual abuse*? Marshall has suggested that deficient articulations of own-victim harm are to be understood as protecting sex offenders from further insults to already low self-image. For victim empathy deficits to be specific to these offenders' sexual abuse victims and not generalise to all forms of transgressive behaviours perpetrated by the offender, this fragile self-image must be specific to their identity as a *sexual offender*. If the fragile social self-image is more general, we would expect callous responses to the experiences of any individual that an offender harms socially (e.g. by malicious gossip). Further research would be worthwhile to clarify the specificity of the mechanism.

Furthermore, some offenders have highly narcissistic personal characteristics (Kosson, Kelly & White, 1998). Narcissism would be predicted theoretically to produce *general* deficiencies in empathy, not victim-specific ones, and has recently been reconceptualised as *fragile high self-esteem* (Baumeister et al., 1996). So for a self-esteem theory to explain the full range of empathy deficits, narcissism needs to be considered.

The association between intimacy, loneliness, low self-esteem and emotion-focused coping proposed by Marshall and colleagues appears to be a feature of only one pathway to sexual offending (see Chapter 5, pathway 1). To conclude, to date Marshall's theory of low self-esteem has limited *scope* when used as a mechanism to explain victim-specific empathy deficits, but further development may make it more widely useful.

CLINICAL UTILITY OF EMPATHY DEFICIT THEORIES

Although Marshall and colleagues' (1995) four-stage empathy model can be used readily to develop sophisticated skills-based interventions for empathy, subsequent research—although still sparse—suggests that such intensive remediation is not appropriate if many sex offenders can demonstrate normal empathy, sometimes even for sexual assault victims other than their own (e.g. Fernandez & Marshall, 2003). However, among theories of sexual offending, victim empathy deficit theory is still poorly developed, and this under-development stands in striking contrast to the apparent confidence clinicians have in the relevance of victim empathy modules for reducing risk of reoffending (Knopp, Freeman-Longo & Stevenson, 1992).

For several reasons, we question whether some programmes actually are teaching offenders the skill of *empathic responding*. First, offenders often appear quite capable of normal empathy when their own victim is not the focus. Second, many empathy interventions in sex offender programmes seem to aim to educate about victim harm, and then have offenders make compassionate, not empathic, responses to that harm, regardless of who perpetrated it. As Hanson (2003) has noted, compassion and concern seem a much more appropriate aim than, say, having the offender feel frightened and distressed, truly empathic responses to many victims' assaultative experiences. So most programmes offering extensive intervention in this area are actually intending to do 'sympathy training' (Hanson, 1997b).

Victim empathy training has most commonly been understood to reduce recidivism by inhibiting—through distress responses—subsequent urges to offend (e.g. Hildebran & Pithers, 1989). However, Marshall et al. (1999a) suggest that most programmes are confused about what they are doing. There is little wonder given how confused the theory in this area is. In reality, what we have just renamed 'sympathy training' above may actually be a form of cognitive distortion retraining, to help offenders make the kind of socio-emotional development that allows them to squarely take responsibility for what they have done and feel genuine remorse about it without being crippled emotionally.

Defensiveness and fragile self-esteem are unlikely to be direct causes of sexual offending through inadequate victim empathy. Indeed, to date denial/minimisation and empathy deficits have not been found reliably to predict recidivism in sex offenders (Hanson & Bussière, 1998; Hood, Shute, Feilzer & Wilcox, 2002; but see Lund, 2000). Theorists are suggesting that defensive externalisation, shame reactions, fragile self-esteem and a restricted ability to cope with the negative affect of others work to *maintain* both cognitive distortions and victim empathy deficits (Bumby, 2000; Marshall et al., 1999a). The implication of this view is that to fully treat both cognitive distortions and especially victim harm-related defensiveness, therapists need to help offenders also develop the inner psychological resources that enable acceptance of the emotional consequences of their behaviour (i.e. guilt). If not, data suggest that victim empathy interventions can actually decrease victim empathy (Beckett, Beech, Fisher & Fordham, 1994), probably by invoking strong shame reactions that can increase anger and hostility towards the perceived source (Bumby, 2000; Hanson, 2003).

Therefore the theories focusing on self-esteem and shame as core mechanisms in producing denial of victim harm have clear treatment implications. Bumby et al. (1999) outline treatment strategies for shifting offenders' responses from shame to guilt. Following from their self-esteem theory, Marshall et al. (1999a) outline an elaborate treatment approach that includes therapist characteristics, process issues and techniques for developing a more robust sense of self-worth, motivation and personal responsibility, but limits direct focus on victim empathy to just two components: (i) discussion of a group-generated list of negative sexual abuse consequences, which are then related to each offender's victim, and (ii) hypothetical letter construction: each offender writes a letter from his victim's perspective and then a second in which he responds to the first letter (Marshall et al., 1999a).

However, empirical studies show that there is heterogeneity in victim empathy functioning among offenders (see Polaschek, 2003b), so ongoing individual assessment of the nature of deficits remains important. As discussed above, one pattern is the defensive denial of harm specific to individuals who have been injured—whether psychologically, physically or in other ways—by the offender himself. But there will be a number of other patterns of empathic deficiency with distinct underlying causes that will affect the optimum treatment approach chosen.

Turning now to the clinical implications of the 'theory of mind' perspective some offenders may have quite encapsulated faulty theories of mind about how sexual abuse is experienced by others. Survivors who experienced their own abuse as somewhat positive, or whose distress was discounted or minimised by others to such an extent that they learned to discount it themselves, are candidates for such erroneous early learning. So direct experience of sexual abuse victimisation may be a hindrance to empathy for some offenders (Simons, Wurtele & Heil, 2002), particularly if they view their childhood sexual experiences as consensual. Some abuse survivors may hold enduring views that represent exemplars of *children as sexual objects, entitlement* and *dangerous world* implicit theories. These views are not necessarily generated primarily by the need to be self-defensive about immoral motivations (i.e. a desire to abuse others sexually), but instead represent elaborate but inaccurate knowledge structures learned at the time they were abused. Education directed at altering the implicit theories may be the first approach with these men, although successfully re-educating survivors can also create the need for therapists to respond to the men's distress, as they recognise belatedly the full consequences of their own childhood experiences.

Ward et al. (2000) suggest that a crucial implication of the developmental theory of mind perspective is that occasionally, men may have a more extensive form of 'mindblindness', where an offender fundamentally is incapable of accurate inference about another's beliefs, intent, feelings and so on. Where this kind of deficit exists, widespread empathy deficits are likely to be observed, and extensive education about how people's minds work will be needed, before going on to other intervention components (Ward et al., 2000).

Also important to understanding heterogeneity is understanding why victim harm is not only acknowledged by some offenders, but is seen in positive terms. For these offenders, perspective taking during the offence may not be the problem. Rather, the deficit is created by a lack of compassion for the victim, which may be state-dependent or enduring. For example, a rapist may gain satisfaction from harming his estranged partner because he perceives that she has deliberately harmed him. Lack of compassion may also be fuelled by specific implicit theories (e.g. *women are unknowable, male sex drive is uncontrollable, entitlement*). The intervention implications of an implicit theory view are outlined in the previous chapter.

Researchers often note that sadism is another important example of a type of empathy deficit. Sadists are assumed to take perspective accurately and then derive pleasure instead of compassion from their perceptions of victim suffering (e.g. Marshall et al., 1999a). This sounds plausible, but sexual sadists who target non-consenting victims are rare, and sadism has proved very difficult to operationalise (Polaschek, Ward & Gannon, 2006).

Finally, some offenders certainly do have trait empathy deficits. Experimental research on narcissism suggests that narcissists are one type of offender with global deficits. If so they will be exceptionally resistant to entering treatment, and when they do, are unlikely to respond to the supportive strategies proposed by Marshall to enhance self-esteem. Furthermore, esteem enhancement may be harmful (Baumeister et al., 1996) and decrease empathy rather than increasing it.

Psychopathy scores should also identify men with global deficits. The extent of involvement in nonsexual offending (i.e. criminal versatility; Smallbone, Wheaton & Hourigan, 2003) may also be predictive of widespread empathy deficits. The evidence that general empathy deficits are related to offending is generally stronger for nonsexual than sexual offending (Jolliffe & Farrington, 2004). Although the theories above offer good ideas for treatment of victim-specific deficits, intervention with global deficits in sex offenders requires more theoretical attention.

CONCLUSIONS

This is a young and challenging area within the field of sexual assault theory and research. One of the frustrating elements of this domain is the degree of confusion. As Marshall et al. (1999a) note, the models of what we are doing are in serious need of clarification. Many important questions remain. For example, are we actually measuring victim empathy with current measures? Do offenders need victim empathy to avoid offending, or would the knowledge of the damage that sexual abuse does, coupled with sympathy, be sufficient? Are we teaching victim empathy, or merely making participants more comfortable with articulating the harm they have done?

Theory development needs to keep pace with the research, and most especially, practice, which is currently running well ahead of it. One fruitful avenue for such development lies in the application of 'theory of mind' to empathy. Ward and colleagues have already demonstrated how this body of thinking can accommodate different kinds of deficits, including dynamic suppression of empathy (Ward et al., 2000). Theorising and investigation of self-protective processes as aetiological agents in sexual offending is also still quite a new domain for cognitive-behavioural theorists and therapists too. The 'big picture' inferences from the theories reviewed here are that a number of aetiological features of sexual offending not only appear to be generated by common mechanisms, but these mechanisms may facilitate sexual offending and adversely affect treatment responsivity. Perhaps a few years from now, as this view develops in sophistication, we will cease to talk about victim empathy deficits as a stand-alone criminogenic need at all.

Chapter 10
THEORIES OF DEVIANT SEXUAL PREFERENCES

It is commonly thought that child molesters abuse children sexually because they have a deviant sexual interest in children, and that rapists prefer forced sexual contact with women to consensual sex. In other words, the acquisition of deviant sexual behaviour is thought to be the direct product of a deviant sexual preference. This proposal has evolved to become the *sexual preference hypothesis* (Lalumiere & Quinsey, 1994). That is, men who engage in sexually deviant behaviours do so because they prefer them to socially acceptable sexual behaviours. These deviant sexual preferences (or paraphilias) are thought by many to have become entrenched prior to the initial deviant act (Abel et al., 1987a; Marshall, Barbaree & Eccles, 1991).

Paraphilias have been defined in DSM-IV-TR as 'recurrent intense sexually arousing fantasies, sexual urges or behaviours, generally around children or non-consenting persons, the suffering or humiliation of oneself or others, or non-human objects' (American Psychiatric Association, 2000, p. 522). Kafka (1997) noted that despite there being a number of paraphilias identified in DSM-IV-TR (2000)[1] there is substantial overlap between these categories. For example, a number of large-scale studies (e.g. Abel et al., 1987a; Bradford, Boulet & Pawlak, 1992) report that individuals hold a number of paraphilias (either simultaneously or serially). Kafka also noted that paedophiles commonly acknowledge voyeuristic, exhibitionistic or rape paraphilias, and that only a low percentage actually report that children are their primary source of sexual arousal.

---

[1] The following are the paraphilias described in DSM-IV: exhibitionism, fetishism, frotteurism, sexual sadism, sexual masochism, tranvestic fetishism, voyeurism, paedophilia and paraphilia (not otherwise specified), which includes: obscene phone calling, necrophilia (corpses), zoophilia (animals), partialism (exclusive focus on specific body parts), coprophilia (faeces), klismaphilia (enemas) and urophila (urine). Polaschek (2003a) notes that rape is omitted from this scheme unless it fits the diagnostic criteria for sexual sadism.

Typically, sexual arousal to paraphilias has been measured using the penile plethysmograph (PPG). This is an instrument that measures penile tumescence to stimuli: such as slides of unclothed individuals at a variety of ages. The underlying assumption here is that penile tumescence to deviant material is indicative of paraphilic sexual arousal (Rempel & Serafini, 1995). Thus, consistent genital response to specific types of stimuli would appear to indicate sexual preference, deviant or non-deviant. To date, a number of detailed reviews concerning the measurement of deviant sexual preference have been published (e.g. Kalmus & Beech, 2005; Marshall & Fernandez, 2000; Murphy & Barbaree, 1994). Thus research offers weak support for the utility of the plethysmograph but it is still unclear exactly what is being measured: sexual arousal, sexual preferences or sexual interest. As for the relationship between (paraphilic) deviant arousal and sexual offending, Hanson and Bussière (1998) found that deviant sexual interest in children, as measured by the PPG, was the biggest single predictor of sexual offence recidivism in a sample of nearly 5000 sexual offenders.

Approaches to the treatment of deviant sexual preferences in sexual offenders from the 1960s and 1970s involved little more than behavioural procedures aimed at changing sexual preferences from paraphilic to non-paraphilic. These procedures would usually involve aversive conditioning using electric shock or aversive odours (Beech & Mann, 2002). It is fair to say that treatment has evolved considerably since the original use of such behavioural modification techniques, and now typically includes addressing cognitive distortions, victim empathy deficits, intimacy deficits and the inculcation of relapse prevention skills (Beech & Fisher, 2002). However, the treatment of paraphilic deviant sexual preferences still remains a central feature of many treatment programmes.

Early descriptions of the aetiology of paraphilic sexual preferences suggest that a symptom, or behaviour, is learned at some time in the past (e.g. Binet, 1888). More specifically, the root cause of paraphilic sexual preference results from a concurrent experience of deviant stimuli and a sexually aroused physiological state. In other words, any stimulus that regularly precedes sexual climax by the correct time interval will become more and more sexually exciting. Such a stimulus may be circumstantial (e.g. the particular time or place where masturbation or intercourse takes place), or it may be deliberate (e.g. a sexual fantasy). Therefore paraphilias can arise as a case of one-trial accidental learning from a deviant sexual experience.

This idea does not seem unreasonable until we note that the majority of those exposed to such unwanted sexual experiences in childhood do not go on to develop the particular paraphilia to which they have been exposed (McGuire, Carlisle & Young, 1965). McGuire et al. noted that early theorists were forced to add an unknown *constitutional factor* to explain individual differences in the ease of acquisition of such paraphilias.

More recently, those who have described the acquisition of deviant sexual preference have suggested a more sophisticated description of how such paraphilias are acquired. Here, fantasy is seen as being important in the maintenance of deviant interests. Leitenberg and Henning (1995) defined sexual fantasy as almost any mental imagery that is sexually arousing or erotic to the individual.

Sexual fantasies do not have to be accompanied by masturbation, although they often are. The role of sexual fantasy in the aetiology of sexual offending has been described by Abel et al. (1987a), who reported that in a sample of 400 outpatient sexual offenders, 58% stated that they had experienced, prior to the age of 18, sexual arousal to deviant ideas that were later translated into deviant acts. More recently, Marshall and Eccles (1991) reported that 41% of men who had molested boys outside of the family had experienced deviant fantasy prior to the age of 20. Hence it is hypothesised that deviant fantasies precede deviant arousal, which, in turn, leads to sexual offending.

More recently, an alternative neurobiological explanation has been used to describe the pathophysiology of paraphilic disorder. Although this approach is less well known than learning theory explanations of deviant sexual preference, it can be seen as having an impact upon the treatment of deviant sexual preference.

Therefore, the aim of this chapter is to describe some of the theories proposed to explain the acquisition of deviant sexual preferences, to evaluate critically these theories, and to assess their clinical utility. More specifically, we will outline McGuire et al.'s (1965) 'sexual deviation as a conditioned behaviour' hypothesis, Laws and Marshall's (1990) conditioning theory of deviant sexual preference and behaviour, and Kafka's (1997, 2003) monoamine hypothesis for the paraphysiology of paraphilic disorders. We do not aim to provide an exhaustive account of theories of sexual preference but merely use the most influential single-factor theories as illustrations.

Because the theoretical explanations of the acquisition of deviant sexual preference rely on basic learning principles, we will now outline these briefly. For those who are conversant with these principles we suggest that such readers should skip to the next section of the chapter.

BASIC LEARNING PRINCIPLES

The Oxford Dictionary of Psychology (Colman, 2001) describes the two major forms of behavioural learning (i.e. any lasting change in behaviour from experience) as the following:

- *Classical conditioning*, this process of learning describes what happens when an initial neutral stimulus in the environment comes to elicit a response that does not normally occur. An example being the repeated pairing of a bell with food (which normally elicits salivation in animals), such that an animal learns to salivate just to the ringing of a bell.
- *Operant conditioning*, where the relative frequency of a response increases as a result of reinforcement (i.e. reward) or decreases by the administration of an aversive stimulus (punishment). *Negative reinforcement* is said to occur when an individual escapes punishment.

However, the relationship between stimulus and reward will not last forever, and will gradually weaken and disappear by a process of *extinction*. Therefore, it is necessary to occasionally re-pair the conditioned stimulus with the conditioned response, or occasionally follow an operant response by a reinforcing stimulus for these types of learning to be maintained. This type of reward is known as *partial* or *intermittent reinforcement*. Conditioning is found to be more resistant to extinction in this kind of learning situation than when training has been established by *continuous reinforcement*.

We would also note here the concept of *locus of control*, described by Colman (2001) as a cognitive style or personality trait characterised by a generalised expectancy about the relationship between behaviour and the subsequent occurrence of reinforcement (punishment or reward). Those with an internal locus of control tend to expect reinforcements as a consequence of their own efforts, while people with an external locus of control view reinforcements as being due to chance, luck, fate or the actions of powerful others. A number of studies have demonstrated that untreated sexual offenders tend to have an external locus of control (e.g. Fisher, Beech & Browne, 2000). Laws and Marshall (1990) also noted that other principles of learning are important to consider when attempting to understand the acquisition of deviant sexual interest, including Seligman's (1970) *continuum of preparedness*, which suggests that individuals come prepared to more easily associate some stimuli and events than others. So, individuals are highly prepared to learn the association of sexual arousal to opposite sex individuals, while at the same time they are extremely resistant to learning an association between arousal and inanimate objects. They also note that there are several principles associated with the acquisition of *prepared* associations (Seligman, 1970). These include that stimuli that are high in preparedness can be acquired in one or two trials, are highly resistant to extinction and are non-cognitive. Hence they are not readily modifiable using cognitive strategies.

The final learning principles that we briefly describe in this section are associated with social learning theory. This is an approach to understanding learning described by Bandura (1973, 1977) and others, that has investigated how social influences can alter people's thoughts, feelings and behaviours. Bandura suggested that imitation and modelling of behaviour can sometimes occur without reinforcement, through three forms of observational learning: (i) *participant modelling*, where individuals observe and then copy the behaviour that they have seen; (ii) *vicarious learning*, with non-participant observation (i.e. in written form or visual media); and (iii) *symbolic modelling*, in which behaviour and its consequences are developed and elaborated in thought or mental images.

We will now examine two accounts of how learning principles have been used to explain theoretically the acquisition and maintenance of deviant sexual interest.

McGUIRE ET AL.'S (1965) SEXUAL DEVIATION THEORY

McGuire et al. (1965), in an in-depth study of 45 men described as sexual deviants, suggested that the learning is postulated to take place after their first seduction or sexual experience, which in effect only plays a part in supplying the initial aetiological fantasy for later masturbation. McGuire et al. note that this is the mechanism by which most sexual deviations develop; the precipitating incident is typically an individual's first real sexual experience rather than masturbating to something less real, such as stories or pictures. Because it is real, the sexual experience has more salience; in McGuire et al.'s terms it has a *strong initial stimulus value*. Therefore the acquisition of a deviant preference is primarily motivated by masturbation to deviant fantasy (derived from a sexual experience), because of the fact that the more attention given to this type of fantasy, the more stimulating it becomes. At the same time, arousal to non-deviant stimuli (e.g. the fantasy of having consensual sex with an appropriate other) will gradually be extinguished due to a lack of masturbatory reinforcement. Hence, as a form of operant conditioning, McGuire et al. place masturbation centre stage in the formation and shaping of sexual preference.

McGuire et al.'s model also incorporated the idea that sexual offenders may have problems in a number of areas of function, and it is these problems that actually drive their sexual deviation. For example, the majority of subjects in their study were found to hold the types of cognitions that made it difficult for them to have conventional sexual relationships. They argued that these cognitions strengthen deviant arousal by weakening an individual's idea that a conventional sexual outlet is possible.

The sexual deviation theory of McGuire et al. makes a number of specific predictions:

1. Any deviation can be acquired. Acquisition is not dependent upon previous sexual interest.
2. Any deviation can be extinguished by 'reconditioning' (see below).
3. Deviant interest is not extinguished by guilt, as proximal sexual pleasure occurs at a more effective moment for learning than distal feelings of guilt and shame.
4. A person who has acquired a sexual deviation or sexual preference is likely to acquire other deviant sexual interests.

EVALUATION OF THE SEXUAL DEVIATION THEORY

McGuire et al.'s model is very sophisticated—given that it was developed 40 years ago—because it incorporates the idea that sexual offenders may have problems in a number of areas of function and that these drive sexual deviation. For example, believing that a normal sexual outlet is not possible, or feeling socially or sexually inadequate, may strengthen a deviant sexual preference that has already formed through operant conditioning. Bringing together these concepts to explain the paraphilias shows that McGuire's theory holds a degree of *unifying power*. Its implicit treatment and evaluative component, centred on the assessment and reduction of a deviant preference, gives prominence to conditioning theory, which still remains a highly influential approach today in explaining the development of deviant sexual preference (Laws & Marshall,

1990). In other words, the theory shows good *heuristic value* (i.e. it has led to new innovations regarding treatment). However, it suffers from a number of problems in the way that it was derived.

By today's standards, only a minority of the sample of men on which the theory was based would be regarded as having committed illegal paraphilias (seven paedophiles, seven exhibitionists and three voyeurs). Therefore, most of the sample would no longer be regarded as sexually deviant (i.e. 21 homosexuals and 5 transvestites). Given the times, it is unsurprising that those with a homosexual orientation felt that a 'normal' sexual outlet was not available for them. Also, feelings of social and sexual inadequacy may well have been experienced by these individuals during adolescence due to the social mores at that time. It seems, then, that this theory lacks *empirical scope,* because it cannot account for the range of paraphilias requiring explanation today.

On closer examination—and again, by today's standards—the authors also appear to have been too ready to accept at face value the veracity of offenders' accounts of their own thoughts, feelings and behaviour. For example, the first case example consists of a man who had abused boys, including his own son. McGuire et al. described this man as having normal sexual interests with impotency due to a strict religious upbringing. They also reported that while he was in the army 'due to scruples about having relations with native married women ... [he] finally resorted to the native children of either sex ... and this remained his only sexual outlet till he was discharged ...' (1965, p. 188). In Cases 2 and 3, they took at face value that two exhibitionists 'just happened' to be urinating in a public place, when they were surprised by a passing woman. In other words, McGuire et al. appeared to believe exactly what the offenders said. Of Case 1 they stated that 'the above case shows how force of circumstances and self masturbation to a sexual memory can shape, by simple conditioning, an individual's sexual behaviour, so that behaviour which was initially substitutive can gain dominance by frequent positive sexual reinforcement' (1965, p. 188). We would argue that Case 1 is more likely to be a fixated paedophile who is trying to present himself in the best possible light than an individual who, through force of circumstance, has fallen back on children due to the preceding thoughts and feelings. With regard to Cases 2 and 3, clinical experience suggests that it is much more likely that these offenders' fantasies involved being surprised by a woman while they were exposing themselves. This problem suggests that the theory lacks *external consistency* (i.e. it is not consistent with currently accepted knowledge) and *explanatory depth* (i.e. it appears to make erroneous assumptions regarding the mechanisms underlying deviant sexual behaviour).

McGuire et al. also noted that not all of their patients fitted the conditioning theory of the acquisition of deviant sexual preferences. This admission indicates the theory lacks *scope* and therefore *empirical adequacy.*

McGuire et al.'s theory also shows itself to be very much a product of its time with respect to its ignorance of female sexuality. They took at face value Kinsey's (1935) finding that females masturbate less often than males. From this they made the assumption that females are less likely to develop sexual deviation than men. The limited understanding of sexuality points to the theory lacking *external consistency* and *explanatory depth.*

In summary, then, the theory is based on a small sample, most of whom are now not considered sexual offenders at all. Also, interestingly, the main plank of the theory appears to be that cognitive factors and problems in socio-sexual/ socio-emotional functioning precede and effectively drive sexual deviance. The evidence for this assumption is very thin indeed. Hence we would suggest that extreme caution should be exercised in taking this theory seriously even though it has been extremely influential in its clinical application. We will now describe a more recent learning theory explanation of the acquisition of deviant sexual preference before going on to address the clinical utility of such approaches.

LAWS AND MARSHALL'S CONDITIONING THEORY

Laws and Marshall (1990) have presented an influential take on the deviant sexual preference hypothesis by extending McGuire's basic ideas so that they have a firmer theoretical footing. Laws and Marshall took a lot more account of the finer detail of learning theory (both classical and operant conditioning), noting that deviant sexual preferences and cognitions are acquired by the same mechanisms by which conventional modes of sexual expression are acquired. They also took account of social learning theory (SLT), noting that human sexual behaviour is social behaviour and so the SLT concepts of participant modelling, vicarious learning and symbolic learning are useful in the understanding of the aetiology of sexually abusive behaviours. Specifically, they noted that offenders who have been abused in childhood may subsequently replicate their own victimisation experiences (participant modelling), or may use ideas that they have seen in films, or written material, or on the Internet describing abuse, to abuse others (vicarious learning) or to imagine abusing others (symbolic modelling). Symbolic modelling, Laws and Marshall noted, can be highly important in the development of deviant fantasy. We will now examine these ideas in more detail.

Laws and Marshall noted that sexual arousal is an unconditioned response which can be classically conditioned. When this occurs, it becomes a *conditioned response*. In other words, a stimulus in the environment is paired with sexual arousal, so that any subsequent stimulus relating to the original one will produce arousal. Therefore, a previously conditioned sexual fantasy, plus masturbation, can produce high sexual arousal. Laws and Marshall described how deviant fantasy can emerge in this way. Here they noted how variations on fantasies need to take place for them to continue to be arousing. One such element that might be varied in those with paedophilic tendencies would be age. Therefore an individual may start masturbating, say, to fantasies of having sex with younger and younger individuals, resulting in deviant sexual attraction. Such sexual fantasies will increase, that is to say will be operantly conditioned, if rewarded by genital stimulation and ejaculation. Therefore these types of fantasies will be operantly maintained.

Laws and Marshall also noted in their theory that many human behaviours are learned in an ordered sequence. If any of these are followed by punishment, the chain of behaviours will decrease and eventually be extinguished. They suggested that the normal acquisition of sexual preference could be disrupted if the child is punished for exhibiting unwanted sexual behaviours such as displaying their genitals or sexual talk. Therefore, according to Laws and Marshall, it is possible that an individual will learn to secure sexual reinforcement through other, undetected illegal behaviours, if the routes to 'normal' sexual behaviours have been disrupted.

The maintenance of sexual deviation is also outlined in this theory. Here, symbolic modelling is seen as becoming more important through the use and elaboration of deviant fantasy. An individual may elaborate on real-life experiences to the point where, given the right opportunity, an offender may choose to play out these fantasies in real life. As we noted in our general description of learning theory, responses established by partial, intermittent reinforcement are more resistant to extinction than responses established by continuous reinforcement. Sexually deviant behaviours have typically been set up under a partial reinforcement schedule; such behaviours will persist over a long period of time, despite setbacks and infrequent rewards.

EVALUATION OF THE LAWS AND MARSHALL THEORY

As Laws and Marshall noted, the strength of their theory, which combines elements of conditioning theory and SLT, is in its rigorous description of how deviant sexual interests are acquired (i.e. it displays *explanatory depth*). They noted that by drawing theoretical ideas from both learning theory and SLT, the development of deviant fantasy can be explained (i.e. it displays some degree of *unifying power*). Hence, by understanding the acquisition of fantasies and behaviours, ways of modifying deviant fantasy and behaviour can be addressed in treatment (heuristic value).

However, not all offenders have primary arousal to deviant fantasies (see Chapter 4 for a description of differing aetiological pathways to offending). Therefore a number of sexual offenders will have appropriate fantasies, with their offending arising primarily from emotional deregulation, intimacy deficits or cognitive distortions. Therefore a conditioning theory explanation that focuses on sexual preference as the main cause will not provide an adequate account of the aetiology of sexual offending. In other words, this theory lacks *empirical scope*. This weakness reveals that the Laws and Marshall theory is essentially a level II rather than a level I theory.

Despite the shortcomings of a behavioural explanation of how deviant sexual interests are acquired, the behavioural approach has had a major influence upon therapeutic interventions over the years. The next section of this chapter will outline some of the better-known behavioural techniques that have been used in the behavioural treatment of deviant sexual arousal and fantasy.

CLINICAL UTILITY OF LEARNING THEORY

Clinicians and researchers have commonly used a number of techniques based on learning and SLT principles in order to change existing deviant sexual interests and create new, more appropriate ones. A variety of reconditioning techniques has been used. The following is not an inclusive list but give an idea of the techniques that have been developed. These include electric aversion therapy, olfactory aversion therapy, ammonia aversion therapy, covert sensitisation, masturbatory reconditioning, directed masturbation and verbal satiation. Laws and Marshall also note that typically these procedures have not been used on their own in behavioural approaches to treatment, but have been supplemented by social skills training, assertiveness training or sex education. We now turn to examine some of the approaches taken to modify deviant sexual interest.

Electric Aversion Therapy

McGuire et al. suggested that aversion therapy could be used to re-orient those with deviant sexual interest. For this technique, an uncomfortable shock to the leg or arm of the offender is paired with thinking about deviant fantasies. McGuire et al. noted that in therapy, patients should be warned of the conditioning effect of orgasms. In other words, they should avoid thinking about deviant fantasy immediately prior to climax, as doing this will undo aversion therapy. Aversion therapy is currently no longer used due to ethical concerns and because less problematic conditioning techniques are now available (Marshall et al., 1999a).

Olfactory Aversion Therapy

This procedure involves the client pairing deviant sexual fantasy with an aversive olfactory experience, such as the smell of rotting meat. The aim is to associate the two events, so that deviant imagery becomes less arousing (e.g. Laws, Meyer & Holmen, 1978). There is some evidence that olfactory aversion can reduce deviant sexual arousal. Olfactory aversion has also been used with some success in conjunction with other techniques; for example, covert sensitisation.

Ammonia Aversion Therapy

This procedure is similar to olfactory conditioning, except that inhalation of ammonia salts is used, so that the conditioning response is mediated by the pain system, rather than the olfactory system. Marshall et al. (1999a) comment that although this procedure makes good sense, there is little empirical evidence to support its efficacy.

Covert Sensitisation

This technique involves the pairing of the imagined target behaviour with an imagined unpleasant outcome. For example, Marshall et al. (1999a) have described asking the offender to imagine that he has become sick after he has offended or has discovered sores on the body of a victim. They note that while the evidence for the efficacy of covert sensitisation is not strong, it is a very popular method of behavioural therapy. However, classic covert sensitisation alone is rarely used with sexual offenders. Rather, it has been used in conjunction with olfactory aversion (e.g. Maletsky, 1980) to increase the negative associations of deviant fantasy.

Masturbatory Reconditioning

The use of masturbatory reconditioning techniques to alter sexual preferences is described by Marquis (1970). The procedure typically involves the client masturbating to a deviant theme until the point at which he feels orgasm is inevitable. He is instructed to switch to a non-deviant fantasy (*thematic shift*), as suggested by McGuire et al. (1965). Therefore, orgasm is paired with the non-deviant fantasy. In Laws and Marshall's (1990) review of masturbatory reconditioning, they concluded that there was little rigorously conducted research into the usefulness of this technique, with the only systematic study using this technique failing to support its efficacy.

Directed Masturbation

This technique involves the client being instructed to masturbate solely to non-deviant themes. It was developed as an alternative to fantasy alternation by Laws and his colleagues (e.g. Kremsdorf, Holmen & Laws 1980; Laws & O'Neil, 1981). Kremsdorf et al. explained directed masturbation as a conditioning procedure, with increases in non-deviant arousal due to continual pairing of the non-deviant fantasy with masturbation and ejaculation. Laws and Marshall (1990) concluded that although there is not very much reported about this approach, the results would suggest that directed masturbation has been unjustifiably neglected. However, it is unclear, according to Quinsey (2003), whether the results of experimental studies that have attempted to condition sexual arousal to neutral or non-preferred stimuli actually reflect changes in underlying sexual preferences. In fact Quinsey thinks they probably do not.

Verbal Satiation

This technique was developed from Marshall's masturbatory satiation work by Laws and his colleagues (described in Laws, 1995b). Laws (1995b) described verbal satiation as the use of the repeated verbalisation of deviant sexual fantasies to reduce deviant sexual arousal. Laws suggested that the best explanation of why verbal satiation works is 'conditioned inhibition'. Laws and Osborn (1983) commented that one of the advantages of verbal satiation is that the individual will fairly quickly exhaust his existing repertoire of deviant fantasies;

he will then start to verbalise new fantasy material during treatment sessions that has not yet had the opportunity to incorporate into his regular fantasy life (i.e. the technique reduces the arousability of this material before it can be used and reinforced during masturbation).

KAFKA'S MONOAMINE HYPOTHESIS

We will now examine a very different approach, which suggests that the origins of paraphilias may lie in problems centred on neurobiological function, specifically problems in the levels of operation of the neurotransmitters (or *monoamines*) serotonin (5HT), noradrenalin and dopamine. Pearson (1990), Coleman (1991) and Kafka and Coleman (1991) were probably the first to suggest that problematic 5HT transmission underlies paraphilic disorder. More recently, Kafka (1997, 2003) has suggested that the neurotransmitters noradrenalin and dopamine may also play a role. In terms of the general function of these monoamines, current evidence would suggest that *noradrenalin* is crucial to the maintenance of alertness, drive and motivation (Colman, 2001), *dopamine* is strongly implicated in the experience of pleasure and reward (Colman, 2001), and *5HT* is involved in arousal, attention and mood. Taken together these monoamines act as 'neuromodulators mediating attention, learning, physiological function, affective states, goal motivated and motor behaviour, as well as appetitive states such as sleep, sex, thirst and appetite' (Kafka, 1997, p. 346). Kafka (1997, 2003) makes a number of arguments to suggest that problems in monoamine function underlie deviant sexual behaviour. These arguments come from (i) animal work, (ii) human work, (iii) observations that paraphilias often co-occur with Axis I disorders, (iv) observations that pharmacological agents employed to ameliorate psychiatric disorder also appear to reduce paraphilic symptomology, and (v) evidence showing that sexual offenders and non-offenders have different levels of monoamines.

Kafka's first argument is that, in animal work, there is evidence that decreased levels of 5HT may disinhibit or increase sexual appetitive behaviour, while increased central 5HT activity may inhibit or reduce sexual appetitive behaviour in some mammalian species (Kafka, 1997). Here, he observes that the depletion of central 5HT in rats appears to increase the level of excitement and mounting behaviour. Also, sexual behaviour in castrated rats cannot be restored using testosterone alone but can be restored when testosterone is used in conjunction with a pharmacological agent that reduces the availability of central 5HT. In rhesus monkeys, chlomipramine (a selective serotonin reuptake inhibitor: SSRI) has been found to increase female receptivity in the presence of male monkeys. He also notes evidence that pharmacological agents that enhance noradrenergic transmission increase mounting behaviours and decrease mounting latency in sexually naïve male rats, while noradrenalin receptor agonists have the opposite effect. Finally, as regards the monoamine effects in animals, he notes that neuroleptics that block D2 dopamine receptor sites have the effect of abolishing sexual behaviour in rats (e.g. sexual appetite, mounting, intromission and ejaculation), while dopamine agonists (e.g. L-DOPA) enhance sexual behaviour in both intact and castrated male rats. Hence, he makes the argument that sex hormones such as testosterone and progesterone can alter monoamine binding in the limbic system. Taken together he suggests that the evidence indicates that the sex hormones and monoamines may act dynamically in sexual behaviours. Thus, monoamines may play a significant role in paraphilic sexual disorders.

Kafka's second argument is about the level of measured monoamines in men and women and the effect on sexual function of pharmacological agents such as SSRIs and neuroleptics in non-paraphilic individuals. Even though Kafka (1997) notes that the neuromodulation of sexual desire in humans is poorly understood, the SSRIs chlomipramine and fluoxetine have been shown to produce a high level of sexually dysfunctional side effects when given as a pharmacological agent to reduce psychiatric problems. These effects include loss of sexual desire, ejaculatory delay, erectile dysfunction and anorgasmia. He also notes that the major tranquilliser neuroleptics (which block dopamine D2 receptor sites) have been found to reduce sexual appetite, while the level of self-reported sexual desire has been found to be increased in non-paraphilic Parkinson's patients who have been treated with L-DOPA or amphetamine.

Kafka's third argument is about the comorbidity of some psychiatric Axis I disorders and sexual offending. Axis I disorders are more prevalent among both adult and adolescent sexual offenders than would be expected. Here, he notes the co-occurrence of substance abuse, conduct disorder and attention deficit disorder, antisocial impulsivity, mixed anxiety-depression, and social anxiety with concomitant social skills deficits. As it is suggested that some of these Axis I disorders are related to problems in monoamine function, Kafka makes the argument that there may be a shared aetiology in terms of monoamine dysfunction.

His fourth argument is that the side effects of pharmacological treatment for Axis I disorders (i.e. psychostimulants, neuroleptics and antidepressant medication), which have an effect upon monoamine function, appear to have substantial effects upon human sexual functioning, including a reduction in paraphilic arousal. Specifically, he notes that there have been several case studies that report that tricyclic anti-depressants and lithium carbonate—used to treat bipolar disorder—appear to reduce paraphilic behaviours. Furthermore, a number of studies using SSRIs (used in the treatment of depression) bring about reductions in the following paraphilic behaviours: deviant fantasies, unconventional/abnormal sexual behaviours and obsessions/compulsions regarding aberrant sexual behaviour. He also notes that neuroleptics which block dopamine (D2) receptor sites have been found to reduce sexual arousal.

Finally, Kafka notes that there is evidence of a relationship between neurotransmitter dysregulation and the specific dimensions of psychopathology (antisocial impulsivity, anxiety, depression and hypersexuality) that may underpin specific paraphilic disorders. Here, Kafka (2003) notes that there is some evidence of a higher level of noradrenalin and dopamine in mixed groups of sexual offenders than might be expected (Kogan et al., 1995, cited by Kafka, 2003) and that paedophilia may be associated with a dysregulation of particular 5HT receptors (Maes et al., 2001).

EVALUATION OF THE MONOAMINE HYPOTHESIS

A virtue of this theory is the fact that it integrates the neurobiological literature with knowledge about deviant sexual interest. This indicates that the theory has a certain amount of *unifying power* and *external consistency*.

However, although these ideas seem useful, there are a number of short-comings to this approach. First, the theory says little about the aetiology of paraphilic disorder, indicating that it lacks *explanatory depth*. Second, at the present time there is not a great deal of firm evidence as to the relationship between monoamine dysfunction and deviant (paraphilic) sexual interest (a lack of *empirical adequacy*). Third, as Kafka notes, dysregulation of 5HT may underpin more general disinhibition rather than being specific to deviant sexual preference. In other words, it is unclear how dysregulation of 5HT is specifically related to deviant sexual preferences. This points to a lack of specificity and *empirical scope*.

Finally, the relevance of changes in neurotransmitters for the aetiology and treatment of sexual disorders is still unclear, revealing possible *internal incoherence* in the theory. In Chapter 12 we will consider this topic in more depth and examine human and animal studies that have looked at the neurobiology of intimacy deficits. This research suggests that problems in monoamine function—specifically 5HT deficits—may predispose individuals to offend sexually. More-over, this approach has led to the treatment of sexual offenders using SSRIs. In the next section we will examine this idea in more detail.

CLINICAL UTILITY OF THE MONOAMINE HYPOTHESIS

There have been a number of studies that suggest the clinical utility of SSRIs in reducing deviant arousal/fantasy. Kafka (2003), for example, notes that there are now over 200 examples of the positive use of SSRIs for the treatment of paraphilic disorders; most of those reported are single case studies. However, Adi et al. (2002) conclude in a systematic review of the area that only eight studies could be considered of reasonable methodological quality. Outcome measures reported in the studies included the rate of recidivism, level of aggressiveness, reduction in sex drive, and PPG responses to fantasies, or photograph and video stimuli. Studies that had any directly or indirectly related sexual behaviour outcomes were also considered in the review, but they excluded from their analysis individual case reports. Adi et al. report that the areas where improvements were found in these studies were decreases in deviant fantasies (Bradford, 1995; Greenberg, Bradford, Curry & O'Rourke, 1996; Perilstein, Lipper & Friedman, 1991), unconventional/abnormal sexual behaviours (Kafka, 1994; Kafka & Hennen, 2000; Kafka & Prentky, 1992), and obsessions/compulsions regarding aberrant sexual behaviour (Coleman, Gratzer, Nesvacil & Raymond, 2000; Stein et al., 1992). Therefore, the real benefits of this approach appear to be the decrease in the motivation/compulsion to engage in deviant fantasies/behaviours (Kafka, 2003) generally without any decrease in non-paraphilic behaviours. Adverse effects reported by some included delayed ejaculation, less interest in sexual intercourse with a partner, sexual dysfunction, worsening of sexual symptoms, impotence, gastrointestinal distress, fatigue, increased depression, headache, insomnia and blurred vision (Adi et al., 2002).

CONCLUSIONS

In this chapter, we have outlined two main approaches to explaining deviant sexual preferences; these are learning theory and neurobiological dysregulation. Both of these approaches suggest treatment approaches to the modification of deviant sexual preferences if an offender has these particular paraphilias. As regards the efficacy of these approaches, behavioural conditioning has been used to modify deviant arousal/fantasy for a number of years, though it would appear that changes brought about by such intervention may at best be regarded as modest for those whose primary sexual interest is deviant. They may work better with those who have both deviant and non-deviant sexual preferences.

Although it is probably too early to comment upon the efficacy of pharmacological interventions because of the lack of reasonable quality studies, it would appear that there is some evidence that these may be of use in reducing deviant fantasy and paraphilic sexual behaviours. However, the way forward may be to combine both of these approaches in order to work appropriately with deviant sexual fantasy and arousal. In other words, the use of SSRI medication may be a useful adjunct to the behavioural modification techniques outlined above.

Chapter 11

FEMINIST THEORIES OF CHILD SEXUAL ABUSE

In recent years, psychological theories on child sexual abuse have dominated the aetiological landscape and the development of treatment for sexual offenders. Traditionally, such approaches have focused exclusively on the psychological features of individual offenders, while simultaneously neglecting the cultural dimensions of child sexual abuse. This neglect is unfortunate, and we argue that it is timely to consider the usefulness of cultural explanations of the abuse of children. We have chosen to focus on cultural explanations of child molestation rather than rape or some other form of sexual deviancy because feminist approaches to this serious social problem are often overlooked. The key variable to consider when discussing the social facets of sexual offending is that of culture.

Culture has been usefully defined as 'a socially transmitted or socially constructed constellation consisting of such things as practices, competencies, ideas, schemas, symbols, values, norms, institutions, goals, constitutive rules, artifacts, and modifications of the physical environment' (Fiske, 2002, p. 85). Fiske argues that these components are causally related to each other, and in some cases, mutually constitutive in that the presence of one factor is entirely due to the existence of another (Fiske, 2002). Additionally, Kitayama (2002) states that culture is a dynamic system that exists 'not just in the head', but also 'out there in the form of external realities and collective patterns of behaviour' (p. 92). Kitayama and Markus (1999) offer the following thoughtful description of culture:

> Everyone is born into a culture consisting of a set of practices and meanings, which have been laid out by generations of people who have created, carried, maintained, and altered them. To engage in culturally patterned relationships and practices and to become mature, well-functioning adults in the society, new members of the culture must come to coordinate their responses to their particular social milieu. That is, people must come to think, feel, and act with reference to local practices, relationships, institutions, and artifacts; to do so they must use the local cultural models, which consequently become an

> integral part of their psychological systems. Each person actively seeks to behave adaptively in the attendant cultural context, and in the process different persons develop their own unique set of response tendencies, cognitive orientations, emotional preparedness, and structures of goals and values. (pp. 250–251)

The central message communicated in these definitions is that culture is a dynamic system consisting of interrelated components that develop to work coherently together. In sum, culture is something that greatly influences what we do, and how we do it.

Not surprisingly, the role of culture in generating human behaviour has been widely researched and discussed in different domains and contexts, including the role of culture in child sexual abuse. Gil (1995) proposed that:

> Cultural issues are relevant to child sexual abuse in three major ways: how cultural beliefs or attitudes contribute to family climates in which children can be abused; how cultural organisation prohibits or hinders disclosure; and how culture plays a role in seeking or accepting social service or mental health assistance. (p. xiii)

We suggest that feminist, sociological, cross-cultural and, to a slightly lesser extent, anthropological authors have contributed most to the study of the cultural dimensions of sexual offending. While the work of cross-cultural and anthropological writers has been more useful in understanding rape, we have found feminist theories particularly valuable in partially explaining some aspects of child sexual abuse. Feminist researchers have greatly extended our cultural understandings and practices of gender, and have theorised extensively as to how such understandings create contextualised norms and generate sexual behaviours. Furthermore, feminist literature has made a significant contribution to understanding the structural and dynamic factors that socially advantage or disadvantage women and children.

Feminist analyses of sexual offending are more varied than is generally appreciated, and differences between such analyses are frequently overlooked (see for example, Driver & Droisen, 1989; Herman, 1981; Herman & Hirschmann, 1977; Kelly, 1988; McLeod & Saraga, 1988; Rush, 1980; Russell, 1986, 1999). It is not possible simply to go to any given feminist source on child sexual abuse, and come away with an understanding of *the* feminist perspective on this crime. While it is true that a consistent feature of feminist discourse on child sexual abuse is the emphasis on gender and power and how both are influenced by culture, there appears to be disagreement within the broad range of feminist literature regarding how these processes work in relation to child sexual abuse, and consequently, a singular feminist perspective on child sexual abuse cannot be presented here. Because feminist writers form a diverse group, this chapter is not intended to be an exhaustive review of feminist literature on child sexual abuse; rather we have chosen to illustrate differing feminist perspectives by detailing and critiquing the work of selected writers.

We have chosen three types of feminist theory to examine critically: radical feminism, postmodernist feminist theories and sociological feminist theory (for an extensive discussion of feminist theories of child sexual abuse see

Purvis & Ward, in press). Although there is a large range of feminist explanations of child sexual abuse we believe that the three perspectives focused on in this chapter most usefully emphasise the cultural aspects of gender socialisation, and the influence of culture on the aetiology and maintenance of sexual crimes.

RADICAL FEMINISM

In the 1980s, when the problem of child sexual abuse became a focus of greater public awareness and concern, feminist writers sought to focus progressively more on issues of sexual violence related to children (e.g. McLeod & Saraga, 1988). For the purposes of illustrating the arguments of the radical feminist approach to understanding child sexual abuse, we have chosen to detail and critique Breckenridge's (1992) views, as her account of child sexual abuse is highly representative of a radical feminist perspective.

In general, a radical feminist perspective on child sexual abuse centres on the patriarchal nature of (western) society and the commitment of the State to maintaining patriarchal family relations. Patriarchy has been defined by radical feminist writers as 'the world view that seeks to create and maintain male control over females—it is a system of male supremacy' (Waldby, Clancy, Emetchi & Summerfield, 1989, p. 97). This perspective emphasises males' *possession* of power: 'the power that all men have and exercise over all women, explicitly or implicitly' (Lancaster & Lumb, 1999, p. 126). Consequently, sexual abuse is viewed as a concrete expression of the power men have over women. Furthermore, according to a radical feminist perspective, all men are hypothesised to acquire attitudes and behaviours through gender socialisation that directly facilitate sexual offending. It is argued that features commonly noted in sexual offenders (e.g. cognitive distortions) are derived from being socialised as males and not from any unique characteristics associated with being sexual offenders.

Thus, according to a radical feminist analysis, gender is the primary factor in child sexual abuse. Implicit within this assertion, Breckenridge (1992) argued, is the necessary 'exploration of the patriarchal power relationships that shape the social relations between men and women, adults and children' (p. 19). Essentially, the State is considered to play an integral role in the construction of the patriarchal gender order, and therefore the establishment of social inequalities based on gender. Subsequently, women tend to be distrustful of formal organisations and the kind of hierarchy they create through social stratification (Wood, 1994). Breckenridge argued that the State effectively controls sexual violence among its citizens, and because it embodies the interests of men, legislative and policy responses to child sexual abuse entrench patriarchal familial relations: relations, radical feminists argue, that are the cause of child sexual abuse.

To explain why the State situates itself in a way that favours the interests of men, Breckenridge provided an historical account of the types of theoretical developments that have influenced that State's position. She detailed the views of the psychoanalytic (Freudian) perspective, the family dysfunction theory and psychological explanations of child sexual abuse. In her account of the psychoanalytic tradition, Breckenridge cited Freud's work on child sexual abuse. In this work, Freud claimed that incest was a rare occurrence, but when it did occur it was either because the child had acted out her desire for the father, or because the mother had abandoned her wifely role. Later, Breckenridge argued, the original denial of the existence of child sexual abuse changed to that of minimising its significance; this occurred through the emergence of *family dysfunction theory*. The family dysfunction theory advocated that abnormal behaviour, such as incest, was a symptom of overall family dysfunction. The source of the blame was pinpointed as the mother, which conveniently drew attention away from the responsibility and gender of the perpetrator. Finally, development of psychological explanations of child sexual abuse shifted the focus from gender to a focus on the pathology of a defined group; a development that was fully accepted by the State. Breckenridge argued that the apparent failure of these perspectives to analyse sexual offending in its social context means they are unable to explain the gendered nature of the offence. She argued that 'the legacy of this covert misogyny and victim blaming' (p. 23) is still evident in the State's response to child sexual abuse. For example, Breckenridge made reference to a 21-year-old Wisconsin court judgment which found a 5-year old girl responsible for familial incest. In conclusion, Breckenridge asserted that the responsibility of feminists is to break down the mythology about child sexual abuse that informs the State.

Evaluation of Radical Feminist Theories

Radical feminist perspectives represent an encouraging and powerful movement toward incorporating issues of gender, power and patriarchy into an understanding of child sexual offending. Certainly, radical feminists have made a significant contribution in terms of addressing the gendered nature of law and the gendered political responses of the State to sexual (and also domestic) violence. There is no question that the radical feminist movement has achieved important goals for women, such as consciousness-raising, support for women's issues and the enhancement of women's self-esteem (Wood, 1994). Furthermore, radical feminists place a much-needed demand on researchers to analyse sexual offending within its social context. These features point to the potential *unifying power* of radical feminist theories of child sexual abuse.

However, we have identified several common problems in radical feminist perspectives that limit their use as aetiological theory. A general critical point that applies to most feminist theories is that they are often presented as level I explanations of sexual offending when in fact they are really only level II or single-factor explanations of some aspects of the social and cultural processes underlying sexually abusive behaviour. This weakness of feminist theories points to their lack of *empirical scope*. The specific critical remarks outlined below essentially underline this general observation.

First, radical feminists emphasise men's *possession* of power and the power that *all* men have over *all* women. The argument that all persons of one group possess power entirely and completely over another group is an oversimplified explanation of the dynamics between gender and power. Power is relational, complex and shifting; it has an unstable existence. In this sense, power is something that is experienced as a result of autonomy, circumstances, opportunities, knowledge and relationships; it is not possessed or owned. Power, therefore, should be understood in terms of relationships, and analysed according to who has power over whom, why, and how this changes over circumstances and time. For instance, Lancaster and Lumb (1999) write that the therapist and offender may demonstrate power over one another at any time. The therapist may have the power to return the offender to court, yet may feel powerless in the face of the offender's denial. Similar changes in power can occur in any relationship and, in this sense, no position of power is fixed; rather, power may go back and forth between two parties several times during the course of a single meeting. Consequently, the assertion that a man will always be more powerful than a woman purely because of physical sex and gender is unsustainable. The western social world is filled with examples that refute the theory that men possess power in the way that radical feminists imply (i.e. in an all-encompassing and absolute way). For example, within the media, images of women communicate conflicting representations; specifically, women are often represented as powerful, athletic, career-oriented and autonomous, while conversely being portrayed as powerless, disadvantaged and childlike. In reality, many women occupy positions of power both in public and private arenas.

Thus, power is arguably not something that men are born with or develop and own simply because they are men. Instead, power can be said to emerge out of interactions between people and between people and their environment. This criticism indicates a lack of *internal coherence* and possibly *explanatory depth* in the radical feminist position.

Relatedly, radical feminists portray gender, that is, masculine and feminine, as distinct, oppositional, fixed and coherent. However, many feminist writers are now moving away from such deterministic and reductionist views. Featherstone and Lancaster (1997) argue that it is important to stop viewing men and women as having distinct and different essential natures. Masculinity and femininity should be viewed as mutually constitutive, instead of clear-cut, opposite and competing.

Second, radical feminist theory also argues that central to child sexual abuse is patriarchy and the role of the State in maintaining patriarchal relations that are abuse-supportive. A problem is that this aspect of the theory is conspiratorial and unsustainable due to its reductionist view of men and patriarchy. Essentially, the theory argues that all men somehow share in social and material 'benefits' which result from other men behaving in sexually abusive ways, and that the socialisation of all men into abuse-supportive attitudes is unavoidable and inevitable. However, other feminist writers warn against the tendency 'to portray perpetrators as a homogenised mass, indistinguishable from other men, rationally exercising power not only on their own behalf, but also on behalf of patriarchy' (Featherstone & Lancaster, 1997, p. 52). Needless to say, this theory fails to acknowledge male diversity and imbalance, pointing to a lack of *explanatory depth*.

A third shortcoming with a radical feminist argument that sexual offenders have abuse-supportive beliefs, not because they are sexual offenders but because they are men, concerns the question of autonomy. The argument implies that men, due to their socially acquired attitudes and beliefs, have little (if any) control over actions directly springing from these attitudes. The problem is that this argument essentially strips males of their autonomy and denies the fact that a large number of human beings (without serious mental impairment) have significant control over their actions and do not offend sexually. Furthermore, the radical feminist perspective implies that all men are potentially sexual offenders because of the attitudes and beliefs they possess about sex, and women and children. If this were true, then it would be reasonable to expect a great number of men to offend sexually, if not a majority. The fact that only a small minority of males abuse children sexually is difficult to explain from a simple social structural perspective. This problem highlights a lack of *empirical scope* in the theory.

Finally, although feminist theorists clearly are interested in how to achieve change in their domain of interest, the development of feminist practice models lags well behind feminist theoretical explanations: feminist explanations have only recently begun to form the basis of therapeutic interventions (Breckenridge, 1992). Because radical feminist theory focuses on the broader societal causal factors, which are presumed to enforce patriarchy, the theory is unhelpful in terms of therapeutic work with individual offenders. In particular, the difficulty for a radical feminist perspective of child sexual abuse is that it does not provide a clinical framework for changing the dispositions and behaviour of sexually aggressive men (Lancaster & Lumb, 1999). While many practitioners recognise the socio-cultural influences causing and maintaining sexual offending, pragmatically they are required to focus on the offending individual as the primary target of change. This means basing interventions on psychological theory and research, which specifies both an understanding of why men sexually abuse children and a clear conception of how treatment should proceed with respect to aetiology. This reveals a lack of *fertility* in radical feminist theory with respect to treatment.

POSTMODERN FEMINISM

In the following section we briefly outline the postmodernist feminist view of sexual offending. It is important to note that this perspective is largely based on criticism of radical feminism and does not really offer a substantive explanation of child sexual abuse (see below).

Like most radical feminist researchers, postmodern authors have tended to concentrate their explanatory efforts on the problem of sexual violence against women. However, some theorists have directed their attention to child sexual abuse, and for this reason we have relied on the work of a few key authors to communicate the postmodern perspective. Specifically, we have located some lucid, and distinctly postmodern, themes in the work of Featherstone and Fawcett (1994), Featherstone and Lancaster (1997) and Lancaster and Lumb (1999), who provide an excellent commentary on the broader feminist approach as well.

Postmodern feminists reject the radical feminist perspective, seeing it as a somewhat simplistic way of conceptualising male power and child molestation.

Rather, feminists who write from a postmodern perspective 'are sceptical of theories which posit universal explanations and are insufficiently self critical' (Featherstone & Fawcett, 1994, p. 64). In this sense, postmodern feminists are more concerned with identifying the effects of oppression rather than discovering universal causes, and challenge the notion of gender and power being fixed and inevitable.

Featherstone and Fawcett (1994) proposed that a postmodern analysis of child sexual abuse revolves around three specific areas of debate central to feminist writers: theory, gender and power. In terms of theory, they suggest that the search for causal explanations has led to the construction of theories that 'exclude, marginalise and control those who do not fit' (p. 62). Featherstone and Fawcett (1994) noted that Flax (1990) argued that feminist discourses have gaps and omissions due to contradictory and ambivalent feelings about the issue of child sexual abuse, and the desire for certainty at all costs. This has resulted in somewhat dogmatic and at times incoherent theories. They further stated that generalisations in theory about abusive and powerful men, passive and virtuous women and powerless children are both empirically inaccurate and unhelpful in practice. They agree that explanations can exist on a variety of levels, 'and that sexual violence cannot be explained as simply part of men's nature' (Lancaster & Lumb, 1999, p. 120).

Second, in terms of gender, postmodernists have been concerned with challenging notions that portray gender as fixed or inevitable (i.e. men as aggressive and women as passive). Instead, they view gender as relational in that masculinity and femininity constitute each other, rather than being distinct and oppositional. The radical feminist idea that all men are socialised into attitudes and behaviours connected to sexual offending is rejected by postmodernists, who assert that variability among men needs to be addressed. They write:

> Hegemonic masculinity is not an end state or finished product and there is nothing automatic about the positions individuals take up. There are . . . wide variations within categories such as men and women and such variations are not recognised by feminist accounts, which frequently attach stable and unitary meanings to them. (Featherstone & Fawcett, 1994, p. 73)

The postmodern account seeks to disclose the plurality and diversity of men, their experiences, attitudes, circumstances and beliefs. Discourses that identify men as hopelessly bad and devoid of control over their sexual feelings, and women as virtuous and invisible are considered by the postmodern perspective to be theoretically unsound and politically unhelpful (Featherstone & Fawcett, 1994). A consequence of the focus on plurality and the legitimacy of diverse perspectives is that postmodernist views frequently endorse some form of relativism. What this means is there is no objective and correct solution to a problem, but rather conflicting and equally valid points of view.

Finally, postmodern feminists dispute the assertion that sexual abuse is a representation of the power that all men have over all women and children. They also reject arguments that men abuse children because they are men and do so to demonstrate the power they have over women and children (Lancaster & Lumb,

1999). Postmodernists propose that power, like gender, is relational and they therefore question absolute notions of power that place power in the possession of men or the State, as suggested by the radical perspective.

In sum, Featherstone and Lancaster (1997) argue:

> Men who sexually abuse are not outside society but neither are they wholly reducible to it. They are neither totally powerful, nor the victims of forces beyond their control. Some may 'know' exactly what they are doing and what the consequences are but others may not. Even for those who 'know', such conscious knowing will be underpinned by layers of unconscious denial and projection. (p. 67).

Evaluation of the Postmodernist Perspective

In general, postmodern feminists reject the simplicity of radical feminists' explanations of child sexual abuse for what we agree are correct reasons. They are refreshingly critical of the broader feminist perspective from which they write, and acknowledge the complexity and incongruence of gender and power. They aptly argue that gender is mutually constitutive and define power as relational rather than as an attribute of all men. These virtues highlight the perspective's *empirical scope* and *explanatory depth*.

However, ironically the conceptual richness of the postmodernist perspective is also a weakness. The difficulty is that theorists are typically unable to account for child sexual abuse clearly and succinctly. Postmodern theorists are ultimately concerned with maintaining depth and complexity in their arguments, so much so that we find they are unable to articulate concisely what their theoretical position on child sexual offending is. There are simply multiple perspectives and potential ways of legitimately interpreting sexual abuse and related ideas such as gender and power: possibly an infinite number. This is perhaps largely due to the postmodern aim of understanding the 'experience' rather than explaining the causes. This indicates a problem of *internal incoherence* and a problem of *empirical scope* (i.e. it is not clear exactly what phenomena are being accounted for).

A second set of difficulties arise from the scepticism and truth relativism typically found in postmodernist approaches and the idea that reality is constructed through language (Denzin, 1997). Consequently, theories are considered interpretations that are not fixed but, rather, ever changing according to who is giving the phenomena meaning and for what purpose the phenomena are being investigated. Important in this process, according to postmodernism, is questioning the choice of words used to describe phenomena. Featherstone and Lancaster (1997) write 'The continuum of the violence concept...at times appears to link aggressive words and aggressive actions in an unproblematic fashion' (p. 67). They therefore argue that the phrase 'sexual violence' needs to be deconstructed 'and the continuities and discontinuities between words, behaviours, images and meanings explored and worked through' (p. 67). As critical realists we argue that postmodernist theory's espousal of the indeterminacy of meaning and rejection of the possibility of arriving at an understanding of the way the world really functions, is unsatisfactory. It points to *internal incoherence* and an inability to explain how it is that science is slowly converging on the causes of child sexual abuse and the development of treatment strategies that, through the modification of these causes, reduce the recidivism rate (Andrews & Bonta, 1998; Marshall, 1999).

SOCIOLOGICAL FEMINIST THEORY: COSSINS' POWER/POWERLESSNESS THEORY

A more recent addition to sociological feminist theory is Anne Cossins' (2000) power/powerlessness theory. Although Cossins (2000) acknowledges that radical feminism has provided an excellent intellectual context for perspectives and theories to emerge, she disconnects herself from this position, stating that she 'does not adopt the radical feminist premise that patriarchy is primary' (p. 93). She also claims that such an ideological position is unsustainable because conceptualising *patriarchy* and *masculinity* is essentially reductive and deterministic.

According to Cossins, child sexual offending is the method by which some men alleviate experiences of powerlessness and establish their masculinity and power. She argues that gender is not a static property that people acquire and keep; rather, it is constructed out of the activities they engage in. Therefore, in order to experience power, a man must repeatedly engage in certain social practices that prove his masculinity; the central features of masculinity are power and sexuality. Like gender, however, male experiences of power are changing and dynamic such that men will experience instances of both power and powerlessness through their position in a social hierarchy where they are both subordinate (e.g. economically or politically) and dominant (e.g. in comparison to racial minorities and women). Sexuality is central to the construction of masculinity because sexuality is the site at which masculinity and power are established. Certain sexual practices serve to create and maintain power relations between men, and between men and women. Although specific features of a man's life (age, class, race, and so on) can alter his experiences of power, creating diversity among men, sexuality highlights the similarities of men: 'thus, like sport, it is hypothesised that certain sexual behaviours differentiate men from women, whilst creating bonds between men' (Cossins, 2000, p. 111). Cossins refers to this commonality as 'exploitative masculine sexuality' (p. 111). At the centre of masculinity is sexuality, more specifically, the 'heterosexual ideal or hero' (p. 115) who confirms his gender through endless conquests.

> [These] masculinities...can be reproduced and affirmed through child sex offending in a cultural environment where the characteristics of less powerful objects of desire include willingness, compliance, petiteness, submissiveness—in short, the characteristics of children (p. 115).

Cossins argues that sexually exploitative behaviour constitutes an expression of normative masculine sexuality that is socially constructed and, furthermore, that child sexual offending is also connected to normative masculine sexual practices, which are structured on relations of power. She describes the elements of normative masculine sexuality as being sexually in charge, dominant, sexually successful, detached and self-focused, predatory, conquest-like, phallocentric, secretive and immoral, while minimising sexual inadequacy.

Cossins argues that because sexuality is socially constructed there is no need to consider the psychology or biology of the offender in accounting for his sexually abusive behaviour. That is, there is no entrenched individual tendency or predisposition to engage in child sexual abuse. Cossins proposes that through sexually abusing a child, a man accomplishes a sense of masculinity and overcomes the experiences of powerlessness frequently felt when competing or interacting with other men. In brief, Cossins links child sexual offending to men's feelings of powerlessness or perceived threats to power and masculinity:

> For some men, therefore, sexual practices such as sexual behaviour with a child may be a key experience through which power is derived and masculinity is accomplished. In fact, a child sex offender's chronic experiences of powerlessness may then explain chronic instances of sex offending against children. Despite any structural power that a man may be able to draw on, because of the dynamic and changing characteristics of gender practices and, hence, structures of power, arguably, most men will experience a combination of experiences of power and powerlessness. Thus, it is proposed that offenders sexually abuse children in circumstances where there are real or perceived challenges to their masculine power, such as a direct experience of lack of sexual potency or an experience which constitutes a lack of power as a man in other arenas of life. (pp. 126–127)

In this sense, the powerlessness that these men feel may occur at the social level, but is more likely to be felt on a personal level: as inadequacies and real or perceived personal failings. According to Cossins, this explains why child sexual offenders range from the socially empowered to the marginalised, working-class offender. In acknowledgement of the fact that socially powerful men also offend against children, she argues that these individuals are a part of a privileged group of men, and child sexual abuse serves to maintain their experience of being 'on top'. Finally, Cossins admits that experiences of powerlessness alone do not explain child sexual abuse; rather, she argues that it is the man's particular attachment to the link between sexual prowess and experiences of masculinity that will determine how he behaves sexually and whom he chooses as a sexual partner.

Critical Evaluation of Cossins' Sociological Theory

Through her development of the power/powerlessness theory, Cossins has made a significant contribution to the feminist literature on child sexual offending. Her willingness to move beyond the reductionist position of radical feminists means that she is able to locate sexual offending within a social context, without claiming that patriarchy or the State are the unseen forces behind sexually abusive behaviour. Instead, Cossins makes some interesting assertions regarding the causes of child sexual abuse and improves considerably upon the radical feminist conception of power. These strengths reveal that her theory has some degree of *explanatory depth* and *unifying power*. However, the power/power-lessness theory does exhibit a number of conceptual problems.

First, the claim that child sexual offending can be linked to normative masculine sexuality is perplexing. Cossins argues that at the centre of normative masculine sexuality is the masculine heterosexual ideal. However, she also writes that the masculine ideal differs substantially from most men's actual identities in real life and, furthermore, men who aspire to the masculine ideal will inevitably suffer from low self-esteem and social inadequacy because they will be unable to live up to and achieve this idealised state. If this is true (and incidentally we agree that it is), then the theory is unclear on how the masculine ideal maintains its 'hold' over men (if it does not represent men's reality) and in what form men respond to the ideal (as any attempt to strive for the ideal will either be frustrated or will lead to personal and social problems). Thus it appears that the theory suffers from some degree of *internal incoherency*.

There is a second, related problem concerning Cossins' connection between normative masculine sexuality and child sexual abuse. On the one hand, Cossins argues that child sexual abuse represents normative masculine sexuality because it allows a man to be self-focused, dominant and totally detached. On the other hand, Cossins writes, 'the choice of a child as a sexual "partner" may also be a function of a lack of congruence with, or an inability to conform to, some aspects of the masculine sexual ideal' (p. 127). In this sense, the theory appears to be somewhat contradictory. Of course, the obvious problem with the first asser-tion—that child sexual abuse conforms to normative masculine sexuality which features dominance, self-focus and detachment—is that psychological literature has confirmed that men engage sexually with children for a variety of reasons (Ward & Siegert, 2002b). For instance, Hudson, Ward and McCormack (1999) and Ward, Louden, Hudson & Marshall (1995d) found three distinct foci that offenders can have during sexual contact with children: *self-focus* (the offender is dominant and focused on his own sexual needs), *victim-focus* (the offender views the sexual contact as beneficial for the child; the victim's needs feature as paramount) and *mutual-focus* (the offender views the sexual contact as occurring within the context of a 'loving' relationship; the emphasis is on perceived reciprocity). It appears that Cossins' theory refers primarily to the self-focused offender who is more predatory in nature compared to the other offender types. The self-focused offender may well be seeking feelings of empowerment through sexually abusing a child, but this may not be all he is seeking. For the other offender types, it is unlikely that empowerment is the central goal. Rather, offenders with a victim- or mutual-focus often report that they were seeking feelings such as intimacy and affection when they offended sexually. This diffi-culty indicates the theory lacks sufficient *empirical scope* and *external consistency*.

A third reason why the connection between normative masculine sexuality and child sexual abuse is problematic is because a majority of adult males do not sexually offend against children, which might also suggest that most adult males do not have sexual thoughts about children. Certainly the suggestion that men seek out the characteristics of children (e.g. compliance, petiteness, submissive-ness, etc.) in their sexual relationships with women provides an extremely limited interpretation of the male–female intimate relationship. At least in western culture, we argue that normal male sexuality is more complex than Cossins' description: namely, the seeking of power through sexual relationships with a less powerful other. Furthermore, if Cossins believes that sexuality is socially constructed, objects of desire are unlikely to be solely characterised by those characteristics of children (willingness, compliance, petiteness, submissiveness) since the social world provides a vast array of information that is contradictory, in that it is both supportive and unsupportive of this assertion. Indeed, social images exist in western media and fashion that do encourage the sexualisation of childlike images (e.g. baby-doll clothing for women, and child-like cartoon underwear that can be found for both children and women). However, contradictory examples are also highly prevalent in the same arenas, with attractive images of desirable women also being represented as non-compliant, strong, athletic, sophisticated and assertive. A further problem with the idea of socially constructed sexuality is that Cossins claims that there is no need to concern ourselves with the study of the male psyche, as sexuality is developed through socialisation. This is a contentious aspect of Cossins' theory as she neglects to fully explore and understand the origin and role of sexual preferences. There is little research evidence to suggest that sexual preferences can be easily changed or altered (Barbaree & Seto, 1997) and therefore it appears that sexuality is more than simply a social construct. Rather, sexual preferences, interests and desires arguably reflect a combination of inherited, biological dispositions and powerful social learning experiences (Symons, 1979). This issue suggests a lack of *external consistency* and *explanatory depth* in Cossins' theory.

Then there is the problem of explaining child sexual offending almost exclusively in terms of powerlessness. Such a limited conceptualisation of the causes of sexual offending only leads to a failure to understand adequately both the full array of factors contributing to sexually abusive behaviour, and the range of needs that must be addressed for offenders in treatment. It is puzzling that so many feminist writers seemingly refuse to acknowledge the decades of aetiological research evident in psychological literature, much of which delves far beyond experiences of power/powerlessness (e.g. Finkelhor, 1984; Hall & Hirschman, 1992; Knight & Prentky, 1990; Marshall, et al. 1999a). This criticism underscores our claim that most feminist theories of child sexual abuse are level II or single-factor theories and are not able to provide a comprehensive explanation of child sexual abuse. It points to a lack of *empirical scope* and *explanatory depth*.

Finally, a problem with Cossins' theory is that it does not explain how child sexual offending overcomes the real or imagined experiences of powerlessness that the offender feels in relation to other men. One could reasonably predict that the sexual abuse of a child will not help a man to regain his social power but, rather, that disclosure of the abuse would reduce his status further. Cossins initially argues that men's experiences of sexuality serve to create bonds between men (affirming masculinity and therefore power) and differences between men and women. However, this only happens when sexuality is either communicated to other men or witnessed by other men. As child sexual offending in western cultures is considered both legally and morally wrong, it operates covertly in most instances, meaning that others (men) do not validate the offender's experiences of masculinity.

CLINICAL UTILITY OF FEMINIST THEORIES

We have suggested throughout the chapter that one major limitation of feminist theories of child molestation is that they tend to dismiss the relevance of psychological characteristics of offenders. In view of this dismissal, it is unclear what clinical utility such theoretical perspectives may have. We propose that the clinical utility of feminist and/or cultural explanations can be best appreciated through the application of the Public Health Model (PHM) to the domain of child sexual abuse (Laws, 2003; Mercy, 1999). A PHM approach requires that sexual offending be treated as a public health issue, like any other condition that results in mental and physical health problems for its victims (Mercy, 1999). Employing a PHM to combat disease has been extremely effective in reducing the incidence of smallpox, tuberculosis and polio, and has also worked well against drink driving, smoking and HIV/AIDS (Laws, 2003). The identification of three levels of prevention in the PHM (see below) means that it is able to incorporate a wide variety of distinct aetiological perspectives, ranging from psychological to social/cultural factors.

The PHM distinguishes between three levels of prevention: (i) primary, (ii) secondary and (iii) tertiary (Laws, 2003; McMahon, 2000). At the *primary* level, the goal is to prevent the condition—in this case, sexually abusive behaviour—from ever occurring. Essentially, intervention at the primary level would require attempts to inculcate preventative or resilience factors into adults, perhaps through the adoption of non-sexist child rearing and interpersonal strategies. This type of intervention should identify what the problem is, the magnitude of the problem, who is at risk of abusing and being abused, how to prevent abuse from happening, and how to intervene if abuse is suspected or known (Laws, 2003). Feminist analyses of gender construction and sex roles have the potential to help in the identification of salient targets for social/cultural change.

The *secondary* level of the PHM concerns interventions with those persons who have begun to engage in sexually abusive behaviour towards children. This level requires the community to be capable of detecting signs that indicate a sexual interest in children, or that suggest sexual activity with children is taking place. At this level, it is acknowledged that sexually abusive behaviour has occurred, but it is assumed that the behaviour is not chronic and that the perpetrator is therefore amenable to treatment (Laws, 2003). Here feminist interventions might be helpful in analysing problematic dynamics in family and social relationships and locating social factors that increase an individual's chance of behaving in a sexually abusive manner.

At the *tertiary* level, chronic offenders who have been offending for years and who have entrenched abuse-supportive beliefs and patterns of abusive behaviours are identified. These offenders are in need of intensive relapse prevention treatment and typically undergo such treatment in prisons and mental health institutions. The PHA requires that the offender be treated so as to stop the behaviour now and prevent further abuse from happening again (Laws, 2003). It is not clear what role feminist ideas could have at this level other than perhaps promoting ideals of equality in gender relationships.

CONCLUSIONS

Through our review of the three types of feminist theories of child sexual abuse, we have found that feminist theorists, though often unacknowledged within the psychological literature, have made a significant contribution toward understanding and dealing with child sexual abuse. For a long time, psychological theories have seemingly neglected the finding that most sexual offenders are male, and in this regard have failed to fully understand, analyse and explain the roles of gender and power in sexual offending. In terms of child sexual abuse, feminist writers are justified in their continued focus on the role of gender in accounting, at least partially, for this crime.

Nevertheless, our evaluation of feminist approaches to child molestation has also revealed that they suffer from some serious weaknesses. A major limitation of the theories reviewed in this chapter has been their tendency to ignore or dismiss purely psychological variables. In our view, a comprehensive explanation of sexual offending should include an understanding of cultural and social factors, an appreciation of the contribution of psychological variables such as impulsivity, deviant sexual preferences and intimacy deficits, and a grasp of the role of biological processes in priming or creating offence-related vulnerabilities. It is not enough to appeal solely to male socialisation and issues of power and control. Cultural factors only constitute one small piece of the aetiological puzzle.

Chapter 12
THEORIES OF INTIMACY DEFICITS

For many years, researchers and clinicians have noted that sexual offenders appear to have great difficulty establishing and maintaining intimate relationships with other adults. But what has been missing in much of this work is a theoretically persuasive explanation of the relationship between such interpersonal deficits and sexual offending. In recent years there has been a sustained attempt to address this issue; we believe it is now timely to examine systematically these theories of sexual offenders' intimacy deficits.

In this chapter, we will examine three major theoretical approaches regarding the role of intimacy deficits in the generation of sexual offending: (i) Marshall's theoretical work linking childhood attachment with intimacy/loneliness, and its putative relationship to sexual offending; (ii) work that has related childhood attachment behaviours with adult attachment style, and specifically focused upon linking these adult attachment styles with various sexual offending behaviours; and (iii) a biological explanation of how adverse developmental experience can lead to neurobiological deficits that may predispose individuals to offend sexually. We describe each theory in turn, critically evaluate its conceptual adequacy, and examine its clinical utility in the light of our comments.

MARSHALL'S THEORY OF INTIMACY DEFICITS
AND SEXUAL OFFENDING

Marshall (1989) appears to have been the first to make clear the link between intimacy deficits and sexual offending. He noted that while behavioural and psychodynamic approaches to treatment in the 1970s and 1980s recognised that sexual offenders had problems in social functioning, they tended to argue that such deficits arose either from problems in sexual satisfaction or the need for power and control. Marshall pioneered the shift in focus to an investigation of how intimacy deficits, which have been extensively described in the developmental and attachment literatures, can lead to sexual offending.

Marshall (1989) noted that adult intimacy is a function of the attachment bond between two people and involves three relationship states: closeness and interdependence of partners, mutual self-disclosure, and warmth and affection for one another (Perlman & Fehr, 1987). He also drew upon the work of Weiss (1974), which suggested that intimacy in adulthood is best understood as consisting of the following: companionship, reassurance, support, security, and feelings of emotional comfort that provide the opportunity to develop and maintain intimacy with another person. Marshall observed that the development of intimacy is shaped by parental influences and early attachment relationships. For example, a child who experiences sensitive and responsive caregivers (i.e. is able to form a *secure* attachment to his or her caregivers) has been found to be more cooperative, and to cry less, explore more and be more comfortable with 'less familiar' adults (Ainsworth, 1979; Sperling & Berman, 1994). In later life, such securely attached individuals were also better problem solvers and were more sociable than those who were less securely attached as children (Ainsworth, 1979; Ainsworth, Blehar, Waters & Wall, 1978). Marshall proposed that intimacy confers upon adults both a sense of well-being and life meaning. He further stated that individuals who score highly on measures of intimacy are viewed by others as warm and sincere, and less self-centred than those who score low on such measures. Marshall made the argument that adults with well-developed intimate relationships are more resilient than those who lack intimacy, because they have a greater sense of purpose in life, show a greater resistance to depression, and are in better physical and mental health.

On the other hand, those who have suffered sexual, emotional or physical abuse, rejection, lack of support, emotional coldness or disruptive experiences with their parents in childhood are much more likely to be insecurely attached. Marshall reported that individuals who have experienced such *insecure attachment* during childhood have problems relating to others in adolescence and adulthood, and hence are much more likely to suffer from emotional loneliness than those who experienced secure attachments. Here he drew upon work from the wider attachment literature. For example, Weiss (1982) hypothesised that experiencing a problematic relationship with one's parents in childhood may leave a child unclear as to how to behave intimately during adulthood, because they do not hold a clear model of intimacy. An extreme expression of this failure could lead to an aggressive disposition and a tendency to pursue sex with diverse partners in the hope of finding intimacy through sexuality, or to the seeking out of less threatening partners such as children or other vulnerable individuals.

Marshall (1989) proposed that social and cultural influences may also inhibit, or facilitate, the development of adolescent and adult intimacy. Here he argued that for those who have experienced problematic attachment formation in childhood, and therefore have not been properly prepared to form intimate relationships, social and cultural influences may encourage inappropriate intimate behaviours. The kinds of influence that Marshall was describing here relate to perceived images of intimacy in the media, such as macho attitudes, and the portrayal of purely sexual intimate relations in adult pornography. In later work, Marshall and colleagues (Marshall & Barbaree, 1990; Marshall & Marshall, 2000) have outlined more specifically the processes by which a failure to achieve intimacy can lead to sexual offending. This theory is outlined fully in Chapter 3. To recap briefly, Marshall and colleagues propose that poor quality of parent–child attachments may lead to low self-confidence, poor social skills, little understanding of relationship issues and a lack of empathy (Garlick, Marshall & Thornton, 1996). Such social competence problems mean that it is difficult, if not impossible, to initiate relationships with appropriate others, therefore individuals are effectively isolated and withdrawn. These types of social competence problems may then lead individuals to engage in sexual fantasies that incorporate elements of power and control around sex. These fantasies, Marshall and colleagues argue, may become more deviant over time. Such fantasies, paired with low levels of social competence, lead to a 'disposition to offend' which may be acted upon if the right circumstances for offending occur and are coupled with disinhibiting factors such as stress and alcohol.

Empirical support for Marshall's ideas has come from two major sources: research on offenders' early experiences, and studies that have specifically investigated their current relationships. First, poor childhood attachment has been noted widely in sexual offenders' histories (Becker, 1998; Browne & Herbert, 1997; Marshall, Serran & Cortoni, 2000), while Craissati, McClurg and Browne (2002), for example, in a review of the literature, found that family backgrounds of sexual offenders are typified by neglect, violence and disruption. Furthermore, Awad, Saunders and Levene (1984) reported that parents of adolescent sexual offenders were often rejecting, abusive or emotionally detached towards their children. This was supported by the work of Craissati et al. (2002), who concluded that an 'affectionless control' style of parenting was reported as being highly prevalent in the parents of sexual offenders. Physical and sexual abuse are also highly likely to occur when there is a home life characterised by poor parental relationships and a history of parental aggression, alcohol abuse and criminality (Dhaliwal, Gauzas, Antonowicz & Ross, 1996; Langevin, Wright & Handy, 1989; Weeks & Widom, 1998). Finally, Smallbone and McCabe (2003) discovered that sexual offenders who reported an insecure attachment style were more likely to report being sexually abused than those with a secure attachment style.

A second line of evidence for Marshall's theory has been supplied by studies examining offenders' experience of loneliness, satisfaction and frustration in relationships. For example, researchers reported that child sex abusers typically exhibit higher levels of emotional loneliness, fear of intimacy and isolation than non-offenders (Bumby & Hansen, 1997; Fisher, Beech & Browne, 1999; Garlick et al., 1996). This pattern is more pronounced in preferential, fixated child abusers who also exhibit concomitant high levels of emotional identification and fixation with children (Fisher et al., 1999). In another significant study, Proulx, McKibben and Lusignan (1996) provided evidence for a relationship between emotional loneliness and deviant fantasy in child molesters and rapists. Garlick et al. (1996) also report that rapists reported a higher level of emotional loneliness than non-offenders but this was not as high as that found in their child molester sample. Furthermore, Marshall and Hambley (1996) concluded that levels of loneliness and intimacy deficits were significantly correlated with the willingness to endorse rape myths and hostility towards women in a sample of rapists. Finally, the same type of relationship between emotional loneliness and sexually coercive behaviour has been reported in non-adjudicated offenders. Check, Perlman and Malamuth (1985) found that levels of emotional loneliness were significantly associated with self-reported acceptance of violence, hostility and anger at rejection by women. They also stated that those individuals with high levels of emotional loneliness exhibited higher levels of past sexual aggression and rape than men who had lower levels of emotional loneliness.

Evaluation of Marshall's Intimacy Deficits Theory

Marshall (1989) was one of the first to note that poor attachment bonds between child and parent characterise sexual offenders' family contexts, and may later lead to difficulties relating effectively to adults, resulting in loneliness and unhappiness. As we have seen, a number of studies have provided empirical support for these observations, illustrating that this theory has some degree of *empirical adequacy*. A second virtue of this theory is that it integrates the developmental literature on attachment deficits with knowledge about adult sexual offenders' intimacy deficits. This feature indicates that it has a consider-able degree of *unifying power* and *external consistency*. However, we have also identified some general problems with this theory that warrant discussion.

   First, Marshall does not clearly restrict the explanatory scope of his theory of intimacy deficits and it sometimes appears that it is intended as a level I theory (i.e. a comprehensive explanation of sexual offending) when it is in fact a level II (i.e. single-factor) theory. This problem points to some degree of *incoherence* in the theory. Second, we argue that the conclusion that rejection, erratic parenting and abuse lead causally to sexual offending via emotional loneliness and unhappi-ness is a bridge too far. Marshall, for example, notes that delinquent adolescents come from homes where parents are often cold and violent. In other words, the theory fails to provide an explanation of why, in certain circumstances, adverse developmental experiences lead to sexual rather than nonsexual offending. This weakness points to poor specificity and a lack of *empirical scope*. On a related point, because Marshall argues that a lack of intimacy skills is a partial cause of sexual offending, a logical suggestion, in terms of treatment, is that sexual offenders should be given social and intimacy skills training. However, as yet there is no evidence that social skills training can, on its own, reduce sexual offenders' risk. Hence intimacy problems must be viewed as playing some role in the sexual offending process, but it cannot be strongly argued that sexual offending is entirely due to intimacy deficits. This problem indicates a lack of *explanatory depth* and *empirical adequacy*.

Clinical Utility of Marshall's Ideas

Marshall's theory that intimacy deficits play a causal role in sexual offending clearly indicates that social competence problems should be a focus of treatment. It also suggests that clinicians should measure the level of socio-affective problems in any comprehensive risk or treatment needs assessment of a sexual offender (Beech, Fisher & Thornton, 2003). In relation to clinical utility, Proulx et al. (1996), for example, noted the importance of working on this area with child molesters, particularly for those offenders who report that children can meet their emotional needs better than age-appropriate adults. Marshall has argued that in sexual offenders' histories, childhood rejection and abuse result in the acquisition of an insecure attachment style and feelings of emotional loneliness, hostile attitudes and a lack of intimacy. Therefore, this innovative theory has encouraged clinicians to focus on self-esteem and intimacy problems and to develop a suite of new interventions to address these problems. In particular, the Marshall and Hambley (1996) paper, which describes a treatment programme designed to enhance intimacy in sex offenders, has been the template for many of the sessions of one of the earlier prison-based sex offender treatment programmes, the Extended Sex Offender Treatment Programme run in the English and Welsh Prison Service (Offending Behaviour Programmes Unit, June 1998).

Marshall's work can be seen as part of a growing body of evidence highlighting various deficits in child abusers, such as poor self-esteem, emotional loneliness and poor emotional regulation, which can be grouped together under the heading of socio-affective functioning problems (Thornton, 2002). Thus, addressing how sex offenders relate to others must be seen as an important treatment target. These ideas have had a profound impact on practice in recent years and have led many treatment programmes to include sections on life skills and modules specifically designed to improve socio-affective skills (Beech & Fisher, 2002).

ADULT ATTACHMENT PROBLEMS AND SEXUAL OFFENDING

Another perspective concerning the relationship between intimacy deficits and sexual offending has drawn more directly from the theories and empirical work of adult attachment researchers. This theoretical perspective has tended to concentrate on the link between sexual offenders' adult romantic attachment style and their offending behaviour. Clearly, however, theorists from this perspective still recognise the importance of childhood attachment, and its relationship to adult attachment quality and subsequent offending. We will outline briefly the main patterns of childhood attachment that have typically been observed, then we will look at adult attachment styles and examine how they relate to childhood attachment styles and, finally, we outline the relationship between adult attachment styles and sexual offending.

Drawing upon the *strange situation* task devised by Ainsworth et al. (1978), in which children's reactions to separation and reunion from their caregivers are observed in the laboratory, theorists generally agree that there are four main childhood attachment styles. These are (i) a *secure* attachment (i.e. appropriate behaviours upon separation and reunion with caregiver), (ii) an *avoidant* attachment (i.e. indifference to separation, and avoidance upon caregiver return), (iii) an *ambivalent* attachment (i.e. distress at separation, yet ambivalence at reunion) and (iv) a *disorganised/disoriented* attachment (i.e. both the ambivalent and avoidant styles combined). Attachment theorists working in the area of adult personal relationships suggest that a child's relationships with his parents, whether positive or negative, provide a model or template for *future* personal and intimate relationships with others. An individual's adult attachment style is seen as a set of enduring characteristics for making sense of one's life experiences and interactions with others (Young, Klosko & Weishaar, 2003). Four adult attachment styles have been identified using the Adult Attachment Interview (AAI; George, Kaplan & Main, 1996); *secure, dismissing, preoccupied* and *unresolved/ disorganised*. Each appears to relate to one of the four main childhood attachment styles (see Table 12.1). These adult attachment styles are also postulated to have an effect upon future romantic relationships. For example, level of adult attachment security has been found to be related to the quality of adult intimate relationships (Hazan & Shaver, 1987). The essential components of such an internal model include memories of attachment-related experiences, beliefs, expectations and attitudes about relationships, as well as plans and strategies for achieving attachment-related goals (Collins & Read, 1994).

A framework for understanding how adult attachment styles affect individuals' views of themselves and others has been suggested by Bartholomew and Horowitz (1991). This framework has two dichotomous dimensions. The first dimension is a model of self: lovable (i.e. *positive view of self*) versus unlovable (i.e. *negative view of self*). The second dimension is a model of others in relation to the individual: others seen as capable of giving love (i.e. *others viewed positively*) versus others seen as not capable of giving love (i.e. *others viewed negatively*). Through this system, four types of relationship can be generated in terms of views about self and others that map clearly onto the adult types described previously (see Table 12.1).

Adult romantic love has also been likened to an attachment process, in which romantic love is 'a biosocial process by which affectional bonds are formed between adult lovers, just as affectional bonds are formed earlier in life between human infants and their parents' (Hazan & Shaver, 1987, p. 511). Hazan and Shaver also note that relationships between appropriate others can be conceptualised using the three childhood attachment styles: secure, avoidant and ambivalent. Further, they argue that these styles map onto styles of romantic attachments reported by Lee (1973), where secure attachment relates to a combination of what Lee called 'eros' (passionate love) and 'agape' (selfless love); avoidant attachment (*dismissing* in adulthood) relates to a style of romantic attachment termed 'ludus' (game-playing love); and ambivalent attachment (*preoccupied* in adulthood) relates to 'mania' (possessive love). Levy and Davis (1988) have reported evidence for this hypothesis, finding that a secure attachment was positively related to passionate and selfless love and negatively related to game-playing love; a dismissing attachment style was positively related to ludus and negatively to eros; while an ambivalent attachment style was positively related to mania.

Table 12.1 illustrates how the adult attachment styles map onto childhood attachment styles and romantic attachment styles. From Table 12.1 it can be seen that, first, a *secure/autonomous* adult attachment style emerges from the secure attachment style in childhood. The evaluation of attachment-related experience

Table 12.1 The relationship between infant, adult and romantic attachment styles

Infant attachment style	Adult attachment style	Model of self and others	Adult evaluation of attachment-related experience	Romantic attachment style
Secure	Secure/ autonomous	View self and others in a positive way	Adults with this view of the world are comfortable with intimacy, and autonomy, in that they value others but are objective regarding events/ relationships	High levels of intimacy in close adult relationships
Avoidant	Dismissing	View self in a positive way/view others in a negative way	Adults with this view of the world emphasise achievement and self-reliance at the expense of intimacy. Hence place a great deal of value on remaining independent, as sceptical of the value of close relationships	Likely to endorse the idea that sex without love is pleasurable Likely to engage in 'one night stands'
Ambivalent	Preoccupied	View self in negative way/ others in a positive way	Adults with this view of the world are preoccupied by past attachment relationship/ experiences, therefore are seeking approval of others	Individuals sexually preoccupied/ possessive in order to meet their strong needs for security and affection This romantic style is unlikely to lead to satisfactory sexual relationships
Disorganised/ disoriented	Unresolved/ disorganised	View self in negative way/ others in a negative way	Adults with this view of the world generally have a fear of attachment and are generally avoidant towards others	Fear of rejection and avoidance of closeness will lead to the seeking of impersonal sex

reported by adults with this identified attachment style is found to be consistent, whether favourable or unfavourable as regards the experience. Ward, Hudson and Marshall (1996) noted that securely attached individuals have high self-esteem and view others as warm and accepting. Their interpersonal strategies frequently result in high levels of intimacy in close adult relationships.

Second, a *dismissing* attachment style found in adults arises from having an avoidant attachment style in childhood. Here, those with this adult attachment style are disparaging about the importance of attachment-related experiences. Such individuals are more likely to be actively hostile in their interpersonal style and are viewed by others as cold and aloof (Ward et al., 1996). Sawle and Kear-Colwell (2001) note that such individuals are self-absorbed and are unwilling to approach others for support. Feeney, Noller and Patty (1993) reported that individuals with this style of attachment have more accepting attitudes towards casual sex than other attachment groups. Brennan and Shaver (1995) found that such individuals are much more likely than securely attached individuals to endorse the idea that sex without love is pleasurable and hence are likely to engage in 'one night stands'.

Third, a *preoccupied* attachment style found in adults is the product of an ambivalent attachment style in childhood. An individual with this style of attachment typically reports being preoccupied by past attachment experiences and having an inability to report a coherent view of interactions with others. Ward et al. (1996) noted that preoccupied individuals have a sense of personal unworthiness; this, coupled with their positive views of others, leads to them seeking others' approval. Hence such individuals will be sexually preoccupied in order to meet their strong needs for security and affection. Ward et al. argued that this style is unlikely to lead to a satisfactory sexual relationship with an appropriate adult.

Finally, a *disorganised* attachment style identified in adulthood (Main, Kaplan & Cassidy, 1985) emerges from a disorganised attachment style in childhood. The adult classification is also referred to as 'unresolved'. According to Ward et al. (1996), unresolved/disorganised individuals will seek intimacy in relationships but fear of rejection means that they will keep partners 'at a distance'. Ward et al. proposed that while this group may not be actively hostile in their interactions with others, they are likely to express their aggression indirectly. The fear of rejection and avoidance of closeness will, according to Ward et al., lead them to seek impersonal sex. Here, such an attachment would lead to the following socio-affective functioning problems: intimacy deficits (i.e. lack of intimate relationships, difficulty or unwillingness to create intimate relationships) and inadequacy (i.e. low self-esteem, a passive victim stance and suspiciousness).

But how do problematic attachment styles in childhood translate into an adult style of interpersonal functioning that leads to vulnerability to offend sexually? Ward et al. (1996) argued that each of the three insecure attachment styles in the four-category model would be related to a distinct type of sexual offending. Here, they argued that *dismissive* individuals would be more likely to demonstrate hostility to others, making them likely to offend violently against adult women; *preoccupied* individuals would tend to seek approval from others and sexualise attachment relationships, leading them to engage in sexual contact with children; and finally, *unresolved/disorganised* individuals would choose to seek intimacy through impersonal sexual encounters. Further to this, Burk and Burkhart (2003) note that individuals with a disorganised style of attachment are likely to use sexual offending as one of several possible strategies of externally based control in response to the intense negative emotional states which are the sequelae of such an attachment style. Smallbone and Dadds (1998, 2000) suggest that if an intrafamilial abuser has some level of disorganised attachment, distress (which normally activates the attachment system) may instead activate the sexual system, leading the man to employ sex in the service of nonsexual needs.

Empirically there has been some support for these theoretical ideas. Ward et al. (1996) found evidence that attachment insecurity was associated with specific types of sexual offending. Specifically, child abusers were more likely to report having preoccupied attachment styles compared to rapists, violent offenders and non-violent offenders. In contrast, rapists were more likely to report a dismissing style than child abusers and non-violent offenders. However, there was no difference in the level of dismissing style of attachment between rapists and violent nonsexual offenders. Similarly, Van Ijzendoorn, Schuengel and Bakermans-Kranenberg (1999) also report high rates of disorganised attachment in a forensic psychiatric population of violent and sexual offenders in comparison to a non-clinical sample, while Baker and Beech (2004) concluded that sexual offenders show more indicators of disorganised attachment style than violent offenders and non-offenders.

Evaluation of the Adult Attachment Perspective

Ward, Hudson, Marshall and Siegert's (1995c) work was an advance on Marshall's earlier work (1989, 1993b) because it predicted that different attachment styles would be related to distinct clinical problems and offence styles. The utilisation of the construct of an internal working model and the suggestion that different attachment styles are causally related to offenders' offence-related behaviour gives the theory considerable *explanatory depth* and research *fertility*. In addition, the integration of research on adult attachment styles indicates its *external consistency* and *unifying power*.

However, empirical work has upheld only some aspects of these ideas. Smallbone and Dadds (1998), for example, although finding that sex offenders reported lower maternal attachment than nonsexual non violent offenders, found no differences between stranger rapists and other offender groups in terms of reporting an avoidant style of attachment. Furthermore, Marshall et al. (2000) found no attachment differences between child sex abusers and non-offender controls, indicating that insecure attachment may be a common risk factor for criminality rather than sexual offending. To complicate things a bit more, Jamieson and Marshall (2000) concluded that extrafamilial child sex offenders were nearly five times more likely to report disorganised attachment than a non-offending control group. No difference was found between incestuous abusers and non-offenders. This interesting finding highlights the potential explanatory value of the disorganised attachment style and reveals a weakness in the Ward et al. theory, which did not systematically deal with this type of insecure attachment.

Therefore, empirical work has lent some support to the idea that different types of attachment style lead to different types of sexual offending. However, there is also contradictory evidence, suggesting a possible lack of *empirical adequacy* and *external consistency* in the adult offender attachment perspective.

Clinical Utility of the Adult Attachment Perspective

Hudson and Ward (1997) noted that individuals with disorganised or preoccupied attachment styles report higher levels of emotional loneliness than secure or dismissing men, so for men with disorganised or preoccupied styles, it is important to work on this area of socio-affective functioning. By contrast, Hudson and Ward stated that individuals with dismissive or disorganised attachment styles report high levels of fear of intimacy, hence this would be an area that needs to be worked on in men with these types of attachment styles. Part of the English and Welsh Prison Service Extended Sex Offender Programme (Mann et al., 2001) involves getting group members to become aware of their adult attachment style and, if insecure, discussing how it has affected their own relationship experience. The programme's manual describes how therapists can get offenders to work on their identified intimacy deficits with the aim of developing a secure attachment style. Ward, Hudson and McCormack (1997) noted that sexual offenders are particularly deficient in self-disclosure, expressions of physical affection, giving support, empathy and conflict resolution. Therefore, the Extended Programme aims to address these, and the deficits underpinned by attachment problems, with the aim of tailoring this part of the programme to a particular offender's dysfunctional attachment style.

THE NEUROBIOLOGY UNDERLYING INTIMACY DEFICITS

We will now examine some recent work that suggests a different approach to the explanation (and treatment) of attachment-related problems. It has its origins in the neurobiology literature. Here an argument is made that abuse, neglect and poor attachment with parents lead to very real changes in brain chemistry and brain function. Therefore it is suggested that if a sex offender has such deficits, these need to be addressed in treatment (Beech & Mitchell, 2005).

There appears to be some evidence in the biological literature, from both animal and human studies, that there are similarities in the neurobiological processes underlying attachment in childhood and adulthood. Nelson and Panksepp (1998), for example, note that the neural mechanisms that underlie attachment are organised into a *socially directed motivational system* within the brain. This neural system emerges in infancy and continues to modulate affiliative behaviours throughout an individual's lifespan. For example, Hazan and Zeifman (2003) have observed that adult sexual partners at the beginning of a relationship will spend a great deal of time 'in mutual gazing, cuddling, nuzzling, suckling, and kissing, in the context of face-to-face, skin-to-skin, belly-to-belly contact and the touching of body parts' (p. 341), all of which can also be observed in mother–infant relationships.

The most salient neurobiological system correlates of attachment are the *oxytocin* and *vasopressin* neuropeptide systems.[1] Oxytocin release, acting on limbic structures, appears to underlie certain aspects of attachment formation and associated behaviours. Oxytocin is released during suckling and nursing interactions and is hypothesised to induce infant attachment and maternal care-giving. In humans, vaginal birth and breast-feeding—which are associated with increased oxytocin release—are correlated with behavioural changes, including good attachment formation between infant and mother (Sjogren, Widstrom, Edman & Uvnas-Moberg, 2000). Oxytocin is also released at sexual climax in humans, where both males and females show large surges in oxytocin (Blaicher et al., 1999; Caldwell, 2002). Oxytocin has also been implicated in the 'afterplay' (cuddling) that often follows sexual intercourse (Blaicher et al., 1999).

The role of vasopressin receptors in the formation of partner preferences has been demonstrated (Winslow & Insel, 1993). Although its precise role is still to be determined, it appears that vasopressin plays an important role in the consolidation of social memory, a critical component of attachment behaviour (Ferguson et al., 2000).

Corticosteroids have also been implicated in problematic attachment behaviours because parents who are frightening or fearful are a source of stress for their offspring. Prolonged and severe stress can cause some infants to develop dysfunctional control of corticosteroid release so that the steroid is no longer released in response to acute stressors. Henry and Wang (1998) note that this blunted stress response may correlate with disrupted socio-affective functioning. Kraemer (1992) suggested that disrupted social functioning causes the infant to fail to solve social problems when necessary, and such failures cause an individual to continue to be exposed to 'uncontrollable, unavoidable and inescapable stressors' (p. 510) as they get older. Prolonged chronic stress, such as that induced by abuse as a child, or by prolonged military combat, is associated with hippocampal atrophy (Bremner et al., 1995, 1997; Sapolsky, 1997). These results suggest that there is the potential for stress to exert fairly direct effects upon the mechanisms that underlie attachment. For example, neonatal stress can result in long-term changes in the sensitivity of the oxytocin system (Carter, 1998).

We have noted elsewhere (Beech & Mitchell, 2005) that adverse childhood experiences are highly significant for later life, especially such adverse events as *abuse, stress* and *insecure attachment*, which produce biochemical changes in the areas of the limbic areas of the brain that modulate attachment behaviours. Therefore Beech and Mitchell argue that poor attachment in early childhood and the consequent increased exposure to stressors results in reduced serotonin 5-hydroxytryptamine (5HT) levels, oxytocin and vasopressin function, and raised

---

[1] Oxytocin and vasopressin are best understood in terms of their actions as hormones. However, in addition to acting as hormones, oxytocin and vasopressin can act as neurotransmitters within the brain. They are accordingly referred to as neuropeptides. When acting in this manner, neurones mainly within the hypothalamus and amygdala release the neuropeptides into a variety of brain structures. These target structures lie mainly within the limbic system, parts of the olfactory system and brain areas associated with controlling the autonomic nervous system.

corticosteroid release, which can result in hippocampal and striatal damage. We will now look at these systems in more detail, and pay particular attention to theory and research that has outlined what happens to brain neurobiology if there is poor attachment between the infant and parent.

Beech and Mitchell (2005) note that a reduction in oxytocin levels in humans may lead to reduced oxytocin release in sexual climax. Hence, sex may be experienced as a mechanical, unloving experience, rather than something that is accompanied by warm affiliative feelings, perhaps explaining why individuals with a dismissive or disorganised attachment style often report that they regard sex without love as a pleasurable experience.

Acute social deprivation in animals induced by separation of offspring from the mother has been regarded as modelling some aspects of problematic attachment (Hall, 1998). Stress in rodents induced by prolonged social isolation is accompanied by reductions in 5HT (Dalley, Theobald, Pereira, Li & Robbins, 2002; Muchimapura, Mason & Marsden, 2003). This reduction in serotonergic function may contribute to raised corticosteroid release. In terms of stress in humans, Lyons-Ruth and Jacobvitz (2003) note that blunted cortisol responses to stress may be an outcome of particularly deviant early attachment experiences. The mechanisms by which childhood stressors can lead to long-term changes in behaviour may include corticosteroid-induced neuronal damage. The neuropeptide oxytocin and vasopressin systems can also interact with the corticosteroid system (Griebel et al., 2002; Legross, 2001).

Therefore, there is evidence that an abusive relationship between a child and adult carer can lead to very real changes in the neurobiology of the child, and these changes are likely to persist into adulthood unless some intervention takes place. Here we would point out that levels of oxytocin and vasopressin are clearly dependent upon the level of 5HT (Insel & Winslow 1998), while levels of corticosteroids have been found to be inversely correlated with 5HT (i.e. a high level of corticosteroids is associated with low levels of 5HT; Chaouloff, 2000; Porter, McAllister-Williams, Lunn & Young, 1998; Zhong & Ciaranello, 1995).

---

[2] 5HT is one of the major neurotransmitters substances in the central nervous system and is involved in the regulation of arousal, attention and mood. Selective serotonin reuptake inhibitors (SSRIs) are so termed to contrast them with agents which inhibit the reuptake of 5HT as part of a much more widespread effect on neurotransmitters. SSRIs are selective in terms of affecting the neuronal uptake pump for 5HT. This action affects a multitude of specific post-synaptic 5HT receptors, which in turn, affect a multitude of neural systems (Hoyer, Clark & Fozard, 1994). 5HT-active drugs have been found to be useful in the treatment of major depression, anxiety disorders, pain disorders and premature ejaculation (Adi et al., 2002.). In the human brain 5HT-containing neurones are found mainly in the dorsal raphe nucleus of the brainstem. From this nucleus, the cells send out axons that end in 5HT-containing terminals innervating the diverse areas throughout the brain (Adi et al., 2002). These regions include the brainstem, the cerebellum, the hypothalamus, basal ganglia, hippocampus and associated limbic structures and the neocortex. This probably explains why 5HT is implicated in so many brain functions (pain perception, sleep, thermal regulation, appetite, gut regulation, balance, reproductive function, motor function, higher cognitive function and sensory interpretation; Adi et al., 2002), why SSRIs can produce so many diverse clinical effects, and why dysfunction of 5HT neurones has been implicated in psychiatric problems such as depression.

It would seem therefore that 5HT is implicated in the modulation of some of the systems underlying attachment/socio-affective behaviours. Therefore it could be argued that drugs that modulate the level of 5HT may be useful in the treatment of attachment-related problems. Indeed there are such anti-depressant drugs that block the reuptake of 5HT, allowing concentrations of this neurotransmitter to increase in particular areas of the brain. This class of anti-depressant drugs is collectively known as selective serotonin reuptake inhibitors (SSRIs[2]).

There are also indications in the animal literature that behaviours stemming from problematic attachment can be modified by SSRIs, such as Prozac and Seroxat. For example it has been found that social grooming is 5HT dependent (Insel & Winslow, 1998). The administration of Seroxat and amperozide (a 5HT receptor antagonist) increases social cohesiveness in male rats (Rademacher, Anderson & Steinpreis, 2002). Furthermore, primate dominance hierarchies are based on 5HT and the administration of 5HT agonists leads to dominance in the animal given 5HT agonists in unstable hierarchies. However, this is achieved by increased affiliative interactions (i.e. grooming) rather than by aggressive behaviours (Raleigh, McGuire, Brammer, Pollack & Yuwiler, 1991). Similarly, young human adults treated with Seroxat were found to show increased social affiliation, primarily by reducing indices of hostility and negative affect (Knutson et al., 1998). Taken together these results would suggest that SSRIs have positive effects upon socio-affective functioning.

There has also been some work that has suggested similarities between obsessive-compulsive behaviours—where SSRIs are often the treatment of choice—and the behaviours of sex offenders (e.g. Bradford, 1999). This work has suggested to some that SSRIs may be useful in the treatment of sex offenders.

Evaluation of the Neurobiological Perspective

This section has attempted to bring two strands of work together—attachment theory and brain neurobiology—in order to understand the putative socio-emotional problems that a number of sexual offenders may have. We have examined the literature on the neurobiology of social attachment, where investigations have been carried out looking at the effects of brain biochemistry on levels of social attachment, often using animal analogues. Here, we have been particularly interested in the evidence of what happens to the brain if neglect and abuse have occurred. Neglect and abuse are striking features in the histories of many sexual offenders, who report poorly attached relationships with their parents. Such events can cause very real changes to the brain in terms of function and biochemistry. Next, as SSRIs have been reported to be useful in the reduction of problematic thoughts, feelings and behaviours in sexual offenders, we have examined what effects SSRIs have upon brain neurobiology, particularly functions that have been disrupted by abuse and neglect. Here 5HT mediates effects upon social behaviours by a variety of mechanisms. Raising synaptic 5HT levels by the administration of SSRIs will have a range of beneficial effects upon the brain in the sex offender. Chronic administration will raise the levels of the neurotrophic factor BDNF. This will result in increased neuronal plasticity and consequently an increased capacity for behaviour to be modified (Beech & Mitchell, 2005). Furthermore, raised 5HT levels could act to increase affiliative behaviours secondary to increasing oxytocin and vasopressin release. Here, Beech and Mitchell argue that the potential for SSRIs to induce neuronal plasticity could facilitate the brain being nudged into a more normal state of functioning in the many sexual offenders who report adverse development difficulties. Evidence also suggests that child sex offenders experience high levels of emotional loneliness, fear of intimacy and isolation compared to non-offenders. This pattern is most pronounced in preferential, fixated offenders, who report high levels of emotional isolation and low mood (Bumby & Hansen, 1997; Fisher et al., 1999; Garlick et al., 1996). SSRIs have been found successfully to target such problems (e.g. Kuzel, 1999). These aspects of the neurobiological theoretical perspective indicate its *external consistency*, *explanatory depth* and potential *unifying power*.

Alongside these strengths, there are a number of weaknesses in the neurobiological approach to explaining attachment and intimacy deficits in sexual offenders. A first problem is the lack of integration with psychological interventions such as intimacy skill retraining. It seems as if the clinical contribution of the neurobiological approach amounts to little more than simply administering drugs to elevate neurotransmitter levels. What remains to be seen is whether this will add value over and above the contribution of psychological interventions. This concern suggests a possible lack of treatment *fertility* at the present time.

A second difficulty is that while it may be the case that neurobiological factors help to explain the origins of intimacy deficits in sexual offenders, this does not mean that they have any useful implications for treatment. This is a similar point to that made above and really speaks to the issue of its treatment utility and the lack of *fertility* of this approach. Finally, the relevance of pharmacological data from animal models needs to be established with sexual offenders. In the absence of clear evidence the assumption that such data are relevant may compromise the *internal coherence* of this theoretical perspective.

Clinical Utility of Using SSRIs with Sexual Offenders

Only a small number of adequately designed studies have demonstrated reductions in sexual offending behaviour through SSRI treatment. Although Kafka (2003) notes that there are now over 200 examples of the positive uses of SSRIs for the treatment of paraphilias (deviant sexual urges) or paraphilic disorders, most of those reported are single-case studies. Adi et al. (2002) carried out a systematic review, and found only nine studies could be considered of reasonable quality. Adi et al. reported that the areas where improvements were found were decreases in deviant fantasies (Bradford, 1995; Greenberg, Bradford, Curry & O'Rourke, 1996; Perilstein, Lipper & Friedman, 1991), unconventional/abnormal sexual behaviours (Kafka, 1994; Kafka & Hennen, 2000; Kafka & Prentky, 1992) and obsessions/compulsions regarding aberrant sexual behaviour (Coleman, Gratzer, Nesvacil & Raymond, 2000; Stein et al., 1992) as discussed in Chapter 10.

Although this approach is in its infancy, findings from the use of SSRIs with sex offenders suggest the possibility of developing novel treatment strategies, especially if SSRI treatment was carried out in conjunction with the type of cognitive-behavioural therapy that has been reported to be effective in the treatment of sexual offenders (Friendship, Mann & Beech, 2003; Hanson et al., 2002). Employment of SSRIs might also be useful as an adjunct to the schema-based interventions that are beginning to be used for sexual offenders, particularly in the UK Prison Service (Mann & Beech, 2003). This approach addresses enduring personality characteristics, and deficits arising from childhood problems such as abuse, neglect and insecure attachment. Here, increasing affiliative thoughts and feelings—in effect, promoting more pro-social feelings in sexual offenders, while at the same time decreasing aggressive thoughts and feelings—may increase the impact of therapy. This is because if sexual offenders start to think and feel more pro-socially they may be less likely to be motivated to engage in, or fantasise about, paraphilic sexual behaviours.

On a final note, we caution against relying solely on neurobiological models when constructing case formulations. In our view, sexual offending is most fruitfully explained by integrating biological, social/cultural and psychological variables. Sexual offenders are usefully conceptualised as social agents who meet various social and personal goals through sexual activity with children or other forms of deviant behaviour. The assumption that they suffer from some type of neurobiological abnormality is yet to be established and, in any event, is likely only to apply to a small subset of those men who behave in a sexually abusive manner.

CONCLUSIONS

In this chapter, we have examined three theoretical ideas about how intimacy deficits play a role in sexual offending. Prior to the advent of these ideas, it had been assumed that sexual offenders' social functioning deficits were the result of sexual satisfaction problems, or the need for power and control. Marshall was the first researcher to adopt an attachment perspective, arguing that poor parenting during childhood leads to an insecure attachment style, emotional loneliness and a lack of intimacy and social skills. However, although Marshall's work advanced our understanding of intimacy deficits considerably, it could not account for the range of intimacy problems commonly observed in sexual offenders. Because of this, Marshall's basic theory was refined and improved by other theorists (e.g. Ward et al. 1995c), who made associations between specific types of adult attachment styles and types of sexual offenders. In our view, although this later reformulation has received only partial support, it has led to more focused empirical research which, in turn, empirically informs our treatment of this diverse group of men. Finally, we have outlined some recent work that builds upon attachment theory, yet adds a new strand of knowledge: work outlining the neurobiological basis of intimacy deficits. Research in this area suggests that poor socio-affective functioning resulting from problematic attachment may be significantly improved with the use of SSRIs such as Prozac and Seroxat. In other words, it may be useful, in future, for therapists to consider the benefits of incorporating neurobiological interventions into cognitive-behavioural treatment programmes for sexual offenders. But of course we recognise that more empirical work needs to be conducted before considering seriously this treatment intervention for all offenders.

Chapter 13
THEORIES OF RISK

Clinicians typically use clinical judgement, actuarial prediction or some combination of these approaches to assess the future risk level of a convicted sexual offender. Clinical judgement may, or may not, be rooted in theory depending upon the clinician's knowledge of the field; in the worst-case scenario, risk assessments may even be based on idiosyncratic judgements of which variables are the most important to consider in an assessment of risk. This practice is in marked contrast to the most commonly employed actuarial risk predictions (see Beech, Fisher & Thornton, 2003, for a review), which rely almost exclusively on historical or *static* risk factors (i.e. factors that cannot change or that change slowly), such as previous convictions for sexual offences, identified lack of long-term intimate relationships and general criminality. These and other factors have been identified in various empirical studies reported by risk assessment developers: for example, Hanson and Thornton (2000), who describe the development and validation of Static-99, and Thornton et al. (2003), who describes the development and validation of Risk-Matrix 2000.

In an attempt to overcome the limitations of purely static actuarial instruments, and to take into account the fact that risk may be reduced by treatment, some researchers have developed classification schemes that additionally incorporate *dynamic* factors (i.e. long-term clinical risk factors that are amenable to change; Beech et al., 2003). Four *stable dynamic risk* areas have been identified: deviant sexual interests, attitudes supportive of sexual assault, socio-affective problems, and self-management or general self-regulation problems (Beech, 1998; Hanson & Harris, 2000a; Thornton, 2002). These have been used to characterise criminogenic need (i.e. they are changeable factors that are related to recidivism; Andrews & Bonta, 1998), as opposed to *static* risk factors that cannot change as they remain in the history of the offender. An even more recent development by Hanson and Harris (2000a, b) is the identification of a number of what they term *acute dynamic* factors. Acute dynamic risk factors are proximal/contextual characteristics that signal the onset of offending. These variables, which can be identified clinically, include evidence of severe emotional disturbance or crisis, hostility, substance abuse and rejection of supervision.

Risk assessment has made great strides in the past ten years in identifying the various factors associated with risk. However, the lack of clear guidelines on how historical factors and stable and acute dynamic risk factors link together has meant that the commonalties between current theorising, clinical expertise and empirical knowledge have not necessarily been recognised, or put into a clear framework for clinicians to use in risk assessment and clinical formulation. We would argue that it is important to consider theory in any construction of a descriptive risk assessment model. As we have suggested elsewhere, consideration of theory leads to a better understanding of the aetiology of risk (see Beech & Ward, 2004; Ward & Beech, 2004) than more 'traditional' approaches, regardless of whether they are clinically or empirically driven.

Therefore the aim of this chapter is to compare the received wisdom around risk assessment (see Beech et al., 2003) with a more theoretically driven model of risk that incorporates many of the ideas that we have covered in previous chapters. The construction of this model means that we can abductively construct a clearer theory of risk. In summary, first we aim to describe current views of risk and risk assessment. Second, we outline how some of the theories described in previous chapters can usefully inform risk assessment by describing an aetiological model of risk that draws on both empirical and clinical ideas, and theoretical work described in previous chapters of this book. Here we will argue that this model has a great deal of relevance to the practising clinician both in terms of clinical formulation and as a more holistic approach to risk assessment.

THE CURRENT VIEW OF RISK AND RISK ASSESSMENT

Doren (2002) has argued that, broadly, there are six approaches that have been employed to assess risk in sexual offenders. The first starts at a gut-level approach with an *unstructured clinical judgement* using subjective assessments typically gained from material gathered at interview with an offender (Beech, 2001). A slightly more refined approach is *guided clinical judgement*, where clinicians start with their own ideas and theories without relating these to current theories and findings in the risk area. Although these approaches are employed by some professionals currently working in the field, we would caution against over-reliance on unguided and guided clinical approaches.

An approach to assessment that is more informed clinically is *anamnestic[1] risk assessment*, where an offender's life history is examined in terms of dispositional and contextual factors and his, or her, current circumstances examined to see whether particular identified risk factors are still present. Here, models may be employed in order to consider current and previous risk factors. The strength of this type of model is that it provides a clear decision path. However the weakness of this approach is that, by its very nature, there is over-reliance on clinicians' judgements gained from interview(s) and their own potentially idiosyncratic views concerning which are the important risk factors and which are not.

---

[1] Aiding the memory.

The *research-guided clinical judgement* approach to risk assessment can be seen as a more rigorous version of an anamnestic risk assessment approach. In this approach, a clinician employs an *a priori* set of factors informed by research and theory as a guide to carry out a risk assessment. Probably the best-known research-guided clinical tool applied to sexual offenders is the Sexual Violence Risk Assessment Instrument (SVR-20; Boer, Hart, Kropp & Webster, 1997). Developed in Canada, it is described by its developers as a 'judgement after review' instrument. The SVR-20 is intended to provide a list of items that have been shown by research to be indicative of reconviction. It contains *static* or *historical* risk items (e.g. previous sexual or violent offences, relation-ship problems), *stable dynamic or dispositional* risk items (i.e. attitudes that support or condone sexual offences, substance abuse problems) and *acute or triggering* risk items (e.g. recent loss of social support network, frequent contact with potential victims). The SVR-20 gives the clinician freedom to weight items in accordance with each individual situation; this of course means that the instrument's accuracy will vary depending on the judgement of the clinician applying it.

In recent years, there has been an increasing focus on the development of mechanically driven risk prediction instruments for sexual offenders, the *purely actuarial approach* (e.g. Rapid Risk Assessment for Sexual Recidivism, Hanson, 1997a; Static-99, Hanson & Thornton, 2000; Risk-Matrix 2000, Thornton et al. 2003; The Sex Offence Risk Appraisal Guide or SORAG, Quinsey, Harris, Rice & Cormier, 1998; The Minnesota Sex Offender Screening Tool—Revised or MnSOST-R, Epperson, Kaul & Hesselton, 1998). Typically, such instruments use historical items identified in research studies and then devise ways of coding the presence of these to arrive at a score, which gives a probability of reconviction for a sexual offence for an individual over some specified follow-up period (e.g. two-, five- and ten-year time periods), across a number of risk categories (e.g. low, low–medium, medium–high, high). Although such risk prediction instru-ments commonly outperform intuitive or clinical judgement (see Beech et al., 2003), it is important to note that this approach has its own limitations. Of the most interest here is that actuarial predictors by their very nature rely almost exclusively on static factors (those factors that cannot change), such as previous offence history, lack of long-term relationships and general criminality. Hence, they are essentially atheoretical in nature and provide no guidance on which psychological factors underlie risk and hence give no indication of how risk can be reduced or when such a reduction in risk has taken place (e.g. through successful treatment). In an attempt to overcome the limitations of purely static actuarial instruments, some researchers have developed classification schemes that additionally incorporate factors that are amenable to change in terms of indicating an altered risk level in an individual; the *clinically adjusted actuarial approach*. In this approach, *stable dynamic* risk domains, such as those we mentioned earlier, are used to adjust level of risk based on current level of psychological problems or reductions in these problems after treatment. This perspective is more theoretically driven than the purely actuarial approach in that these individual factors have been clearly researched and written about in the literature as level II theories (see Chapters 8, 10 and 12).

The three most well known systems that have been developed to look at stable dynamic, 'need' factors are the Sex Offender Treatment Evaluation Project (STEP) psychometric test battery (Beech, Fisher & Beckett, 1999) used by UK probation services to measure the level of psychological problems in child abusers, the Initial Deviance Assessment (IDA) from Thornton's (2000, 2002) Structured Risk Assessment model for use with all sexual offenders and used by the Prison Service in the UK, and the Sex Offender Need Assessment Rating (SONAR; Hanson & Harris, 2000b) employed in Canada. The latest version of SONAR contains six stable dynamic predictors and eight acute dynamic predictors. *Stable dynamic variables* are: significant social influences, intimacy deficits, attitudes supportive of sexual assault, cooperation with supervision, sexual self-regulation and general self-regulation; *acute risk factors* are: victim access, emotional collapse, collapse of social supports, hostility, substance abuse, sexual preoccupations, rejection of supervision and a 'unique factor' to the individual.

All of the above systems can be employed to adjust for level of risk based on whether individuals have high or low levels of dynamic problems, and potentially whether an individual has, or has not, responded to treatment and therefore has a reduced level of risk. The question of whether one method is more appropriate than another depends on the circumstances of the assessment and the setting. For example, for those who do not have access to psychometric measures, clinical interview and file information will provide the necessary information to apply the SONAR to an offender who is in the community. The IDA is scored from clinical interview plus file data, from information gathered in treatment or from psychometrics. By contrast, the STEP assessment battery is based on a set of psychometric instruments that are put together using a weighting system to determine levels of dynamic problems, and is applicable only to child abusers.

The clinical effectiveness of a clinically adjusted actuarial risk assessment system is clearly demonstrated in the most recent revision of this framework (Beech et al., 2003; Thornton & Beech, 2002). Here, Thornton and Beech suggest that a high level of problems is defined as an individual showing difficulties within at least three domains, while a lower level of problems is when individuals have difficulties in two or fewer domains. Thornton and Beech found that, in a sample of 174 men followed over a 4-year period, those with a high level of problems (high deviance men) were nearly nine times more likely to have been reconvicted for a sexual offence compared to those with a lower level of problems (i.e. 34% compared to 4%). They also found that combining dynamic risk with static risk was a distinct improvement upon just considering level of static risk alone, in that two-thirds of those individuals who scored as high risk actuarially and had a high level of psychological problems were reconvicted over a four-year follow-up period.

CLINICAL UTILITY OF CURRENT RISK ASSESSMENT SYSTEMS

The previous discussion clearly indicates that clinical and empirical perspectives are converging in current notions of risk; research informs clinical judgement and empirically research-driven risk systems are informed by clinical judgement. The state-of-the-art in risk assessment can be seen as consisting of the following assessment components: (i) an analysis of how an offender's problems contributed to his offending (a functional analysis approach); (ii) the application of suitable actuarial risk predictors to assess the offender's level of risk (a statistical approach); (iii) the identification of psychological problems at the stable dynamic risk level in order to identify deficits that need to be addressed in treatment (a clinical/psychometric approach); and (iv) the assessment of acute dynamic risk factors that indicate offending is imminent (a monitoring/intelligence approach). Which combination of these approaches should be used will obviously depend on the characteristics of the offender, the purposes of the assessment, and the information potentially available to the clinician or assessor.

Decisions about the intensity of supervision and monitoring, or of appropriate treatment services, can be assessed cost-effectively using the relatively simple actuarial tools for assessing static or historical risk items. Such instruments are also appropriate when the offender is unwilling to cooperate with the assessment process, or where major life implications to the offender depend on the outcome of the assessment (e.g. North American civil commitment trials). This is because the evidence base for most static actuarial scales is relatively large and the historical information required for such assessments can be obtained relatively easily from official sources. However, the clinician should be aware that actuarial instruments seek to estimate long-term risk and take no account of acute risk factors that might indicate imminent risk, or of which factors need to be addressed in treatment. Also, such instruments have been developed looking at the relationship between official recidivism events (i.e. convictions) and historical information. Therefore the probabilities associated with each risk category in an actuarial assessment will inevitably underestimate the true reoffence rate of that category of risk. Also if clinicians rely totally on actuarial instruments this may lead them to ignore unusual factors that may be relevant to the individual case.

Where tailoring treatment to the needs of the offender is paramount, then static actuarial assessments should be combined with functional analysis and assessment of stable dynamic factors. Assessment of dynamic factors is also necessary if the issue is whether risk has been modified: for example, if an incarcerated offender is being considered as suitable for release. Here the combination of these approaches potentially makes it possible to judge whether an intervention has been relevant to the offender's needs, and which areas of current behaviour are potentially significant as indicators of the continuing operation of long-term risk factors. However, dynamic risk factors are relatively less well explored at the present time than static risk factors, and the level at which reduction of dynamic risk (i.e. successful treatment) relates to lower reconviction rates has still not been firmly established.

Where intensive treatment is involved for a population that may contain individuals with multiple diagnoses (personality disorder, paraphilia) then instruments that have been constructed specifically from populations of such individuals (e.g. the SORAG and the SVR-20) will have their own distinct advantages. This is because the application of standard actuarial risk instruments may produce misleading results for individuals with these characteristics. The major problem in this situation is that the more complex offenders typically are not well represented in the samples used to construct or test the actuarial instruments in the first place.

If the offender is under supervision in the community, then routine monitoring of acute risk factors is necessary at all levels of static risk, as an individual with a low actuarial risk classification may nevertheless sometimes be highly likely to offend (e.g. an untreated incest offender with continuing access to his past victim).

In our view, the domain of risk assessment is currently lacking a comprehensive theoretical framework that specifies how the various aspects of risk fit together. The research-guided clinical judgement (i.e. SVR-20) approach to risk assessment indicates a number of areas that need to be assessed but the constructors of this instrument do not indicate to which areas should be given the most weight, while the clinically adjusted actuarial approaches currently do not spell out how static and dynamic risk factors can be integrated in a properly unified assessment. In fact, in a rather scathing review of this form of assessment, Hart, Laws and Kropp (2003) comment that 'it makes no sense to take test scores and introduce guesswork (a "fudge factor") into the equation' (p. 214). Furthermore, it is unclear in the risk literature exactly what the relationship between stable and acute dynamic risk factors is. Hence, the aim of the second half of this chapter is to outline how insights from empirical research and clinical observation can be integrated in a more coherent manner.

AN AETIOLOGICAL MODEL OF RISK

In order to put risk assessment on a firmer theoretical foundation, we have developed a new aetiological model of risk. In this section, we describe this model, and discuss how it maps onto some of the theoretical ideas outlined in previous chapters. In our aetiological model of risk we have six aims. First, we aim to integrate Marshall and Barbaree's idea that developmental adversity can result in increased vulnerability to sexually abuse a child (see Chapter 3). Then we will show that stable dynamic risk factors such as deviant sexual arousal denote *psychological vulnerabilities* while static risk factors act as *markers* for these vulnerability factors (Mrazek & Haggerty, 1994). Third, we will demonstrate how Ward and Siegert's (2002b) descriptions of different offence pathways (see Chapter 5) map onto the *stable* dynamic risk factors, outlined in the first half of this chapter. Fourth, we will illustrate how the distinction between *stable* dynamic and *acute* dynamic risk factors might be reframed better in terms of the more psychologically rigorous definitions of *trait* (i.e. dispositional) risk factors and *state* (contextual) risk factors. Fifth, we suggest that acute risk factors, such as emotional collapse, collapse of social supports, hostility and substance abuse would be better conceptualised as triggering or contextual risk factors, and finally, we argue that states of high proximal risk are due to psychological traits being pushed into states of high risk by these triggering factors.

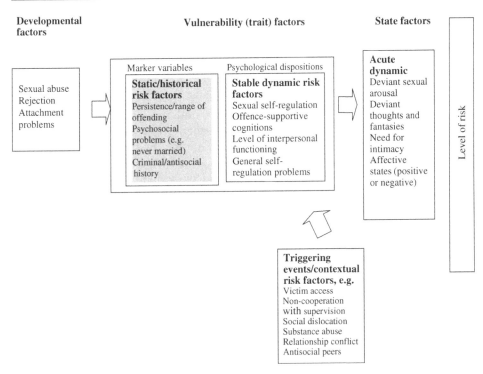

Figure 13.1 An aetiological model of risk

Source: Reprinted from Beech, A. R. & Ward, T. (2004). The integration of etiology and risk in sexual offenders: a theoretical framework. *Aggression and Violent Behavior*, 10, 31–63, with permission from Elsevier.

In Figure 13.1, the relationships between these factors are outlined. The model itself contains a developmental factors section, a vulnerability section (as measured by historical risk markers and psychological disposition risk factors), a triggering or contextual events section, and an acute risk factor section. It represents an innovative addition to the field of risk assessment, because of the way aetiological elements and risk categories are integrated within the one model.

We will now look at each of these sections in more detail, relating them to the level I and II theories described in previous chapters.

Developmental Factors

The measurement of developmental problems in current risk assessments is rather vague and underspecified, even though theoretically and empirically, a number of variables have been predicted or identified as being clear precursors to sexual abuse. This appears to be because, in the main, in the risk prediction literature there is a primary focus on the identification and measurement of offence-related variables, the presence of which are relatively easily determined from criminal justice files. This highlights the potential risks in separating risk prediction models from a wider consideration of psychological factors implicated in sexual offending. In our model, we have included three developmental variables (sexual abuse, rejection and attachment problems), as we would argue that these are important areas to consider in any future developments of risk assessment.

Craissati (2003) is one of the few researchers to have considered in detail the relationship between developmental variables and risk assessment. She notes that such variables are implicated in both treatment dropout and compliance in treatment. Specifically, Craissati found that having two or more childhood adaptive difficulties (plus never having been in a long-term relationship) correctly identified 87% of poor treatment attendees, while childhood difficulties (coupled with contact with mental health services as an adult) correctly classified 83% of non-compliers. These developmental variables are, technically, historical variables, yet the literature on static risk prediction has hardly examined these factors.

We will now consider three developmental variables—sexual abuse, rejection and attachment difficulties—which have all been written about from a theoretical perspective. This is not to say that this list is exhaustive but these three have been shown, or hypothesised, to be related to risk, and give a flavour of the areas that should be considered in any comprehensive risk assessment. Consideration of developmental variables also illustrates the aetiological course of risk in the model outlined in Figure 13.1.

Sexual abuse

A number of studies have described the relationship between being abused and subsequently becoming an abuser. For example, Briere and Smiljanich (1993) reported that sexually abused men were significantly more likely than non-abused men to report having raped a woman. Watkins and Bentovim (1992) and Beitchman et al. (1992) reported that the long-term effects of sexual abuse are psychological disorder, with marked risk for the development of alcohol and drug misuse, disturbed adult sexual functioning, poor social adjustment and confusion over sexual identity.

Rejection

Craissati (2003), among others, reports that an affectionless, over-controlled style of parenting was found to be highly prevalent among the parents of sexual offenders. The experience of childhood rejection is also likely to result in an avoidant attachment style and problems regulating affect in intimate relationships (see Chapter 12).

Poor attachment

Smallbone and Dadds (1998) found that poor paternal attachments predicted sexual coercion in adulthood and that poor relationship with mother was predictive of general antisocial behaviour. Hanson and Bussière (1998), in a meta-analysis of variables that may be related to offender recidivism, identified that 'negative relationship with mother' was related to subsequent recidivism in sexual offenders. In terms of the link with subsequent vulnerability factors, it could be argued that such attachment difficulties can lead to offenders having difficulties in forming relationships with age-appropriate adults. Marshall, Hudson and Hodkinson (1993), for example, noted that attachment difficulties lead adults to seek emotional intimacy through sex, even if they have to force a partner to participate. The causal relationships between poor attachment style and adult functioning and sexual offending are explored in more detail in Chapter 12.

Therefore, rejection, sexual abuse and attachment problems leading to substance misuse, disturbed sexual functioning, poor social adjustment, confusion over sexual identity, inappropriate attempts to reassert masculinity, and recapitulation of the abuse experience can all be seen as precursors of psychological vulnerabilities to sexually offend. The possible sequelae to childhood events are intimacy deficits (due to poor attachment), cognitive distortions, self-management problems and deviant arousal. We will now examine these vulnerability factors in more detail.

Vulnerability Factors

In the second section of the model we note the usefulness of Mrazek and Haggety's (1994) distinction between risk factors that play a *causal* role (i.e. *psychological dispositions*) and those that identify the potential risk for a disorder (i.e. *marker variables*). This idea clearly maps onto the static/dynamic risk distinction. Here we would suggest that stable dynamic variables are causal factors, (i.e. psychological dispositions), while historical risk factors are essentially 'markers' of vulnerability. We will now look at the two aspects of the vulnerability factors section of the model in more detail. By reconceptualising these concepts it is fairly easy to see how static and dynamic factors actually may be two sides of the same coin.

Psychological dispositions

As we outlined in the first half of the chapter, stable dynamic risk factors have been defined by Hanson and Harris (2000a) and Thornton (2002) as problems in sexual self-regulation, offence-supportive cognitions, problems in interpersonal functioning, and general self-regulation problems. Here, we would argue that these are in fact psychological traits. Trait theory gives a more theoretical grounding to dynamic risk assessment. Some points useful to consider here are that traits can only be inferred from behaviour or overt responses, which are indicative of deeper causal properties of a person's functioning (Cattell & Kline, 1977), and trait theory suggests that by identifying the level of a particular genetic, physiological or cognitive trait in an individual, this is likely to help predict a person's future behaviour (Matthews & Deary, 1998). We have noted elsewhere (Beech & Ward, 2004) that by conceptualising stable dynamic risk factors as traits, then the temporary state versions of these traits (deviant sexual arousal, deviant thoughts and fantasies, need for intimacy and control, and impulsive behaviour) should be considered as the real acute dynamic risk factors.[3]

We would also propose that theory has a lot to offer in explaining the aetiological underpinning of each of the four risk domains. In particular, we would note that there is a clear mapping between Ward and Siegert's pathways model of sexual abuse (see Chapter 5) and these risk domains. Table 13.1 shows these mappings and an aetiological explanation derived from Ward and Siegert's

Table 13.1 Mappings of stable dynamic risk domains and Ward and Siegert's pathways

Risk domain	Ward & Siegert's pathway	Aetiological explanation of psychological vulnerability for child abuse from theory
Offence-supportive cognitions	Antisocial cognitions	These arise out of a set of core schemas or implicit theories held by the offender, and generate the cognitive distortions that are measured at the surface level. These beliefs will centre on entitlement to sex, whenever and with whomever, they want. These beliefs, in conjunction with sexual desire and opportunity, will result in sexual offending.
Problems in interpersonal functioning	Intimacy deficits	These arise from insecure attachment and subsequent problems establishing intimacy with adults, leading to the substitution of children for adult sexual partners. This will result in sexual arousal in the context of a sexual encounter with a child, possibly intimate and 'loving' emotions, and an attempt to create an adult-like relationship with the child.
Self-management/ general self-regulation problems	Emotional dysregulation	These arise from an inability in identifying emotions, modulating negative emotions, or an inability to utilise social supports at times of emotional distress. This inability to effectively manage mood states may result in a loss of control which, in conjunction with sexual desire, might lead an individual either to become disinhibited, or else opportunistically to use sex with a child as a soothing strategy to meet his emotional and sexual needs.
Sexual self-regulation	Deviant sexual scripts	These arise from problems in the three other domains (i.e. offence-supportive cognitions, problems in interpersonal functioning, self-management problems) which, in conjunction with sexual desire (a basic physiological drive), lead an individual to abuse.

---

[3] How these states arise is described later in this chapter; see Table 13.2.

theory. In brief, each of the risk categories maps onto one of the four types of factors involved in the generation of a sexual offence: developmental factors, offence-related vulnerabilities or traits, acute or state factors, and triggering events. In this model, vulnerabilities emerge from a range of developmental adverse experiences and impaired social learning. They are activated by contextual variables to produce problematic psychological states such as negative affect or sexual arousal. We will now walk through the model in a more detailed and systematic manner.

Historical risk markers of dispositions

In the model these variables converge on psychological vulnerabilities. Thus we argue that actuarial assessments really act as marker variables or proxies for the above vulnerability factors, especially for the sexual self-regulation and self-management or general self-regulation domains, as these reasonably can be assessed in terms of previous sexual offending and general offending convictions. However, the offence-supportive attitudes and level of interpersonal functioning domains are not so well covered, with the probable exception of 'never been in a long-term relationship' as a marker variable for problems in interpersonal functioning. An advantage in thinking about risk variables in aetiological terms is that it encourages clinicians to consider a wider range of marker variables corresponding to the different types of vulnerability factors when assessing offenders. This enables them to develop case formulations more clearly linked to the different risk domains. In a sense, it improves the quality of risk assessments and also helps to tailor risk assessment procedures to the unique set of causes relevant to individual offenders. It also reminds those involved in the construction of risk assessment measures to ensure all domains are covered and to identify static factors that could function as proxies for the underlying psychological dispositions.

In the next section of the model we will outline how *state factors* become states of high risk that act as acute precursors to offending.

State factors

In our model we suggest that underlying traits can be activated to produce transient mental states (Eysenck & Eysenck, 1980) by triggering factors (which we outline in the next section of the model). Table 13.2 illustrates how, if we take each psychological disposition or stable dynamic risk factor, each trait manifests into a state that acts as a precursor to sexual offending. For example, an offender who was sexually abused as a child might have learned to cope with stressful interpersonal events through masturbating, a means of soothing himself. The reliance on sex as a means to control negative mood states constitutes a deficit in emotional and self-regulation and is hypothesised to constitute a vulnerability factor. Following an argument with someone at work the offender might resort to deviant sexual fantasies and masturbation to reduce his feelings of anger, and to induce feelings of pleasure. Unfortunately, the resultant high levels of sexual arousal in certain circumstances might increase his chances of sexual offending, particularly if his masturbatory fantasies contain aggressive themes.

Table 13.2 Mappings of vulnerability (trait) factors to contextual (state) factors via triggering factors

Trait problem area	Triggering factors operate on the particular disposition in the following way	State risk factors—acute dynamic
Sexual self-regulation	Promotes sexual arousal in the probable presence of the inability to effectively manage mood states, distorted sexual attitudes or an inability to utilise social supports in times of emotional distress	Deviant sexual arousal
Offence-supportive cognitions	Produces deviant thoughts/ fantasies from the core set of schemas held by the offender in interaction with specific triggers	Deviant thoughts and fantasies
Level of interpersonal functioning	Problematic attachment style particular to the offender (experienced as particular set of interpersonal problems) activated in times of stress	Need for intimacy/ control
Self-management/ general self-regulation problems	Triggering events produce states of tension leading to arousal of the autonomic nervous system	Experiences of negative emotional state if cognitive appraisal is negative, or positive feelings if outcome is desired

It can be seen from Table 13.2 that in the model presented here, deviant sexual arousal, deviant thoughts and fantasies, the need for intimacy/control, and negative emotional or positive emotional states can arise from the core underlying dispositions described theoretically and identified empirically (i.e. sexual self-regulation problems, offence-supportive cognitions, problems in interpersonal functioning and general self-management problems). Hence consideration of current theory allows us to get a better conceptualisation of what risk assessment is actually measuring.

Triggering/contextual events

The last section of Figure 13.1 is labelled triggering or contextual events. These may be more familiar to some as the so-called *acute dynamic risk factors* (see Hanson & Harris, 2000a, b). However, we would suggest that these items would be better conceptualised as triggering events or contextual risk factors, which interact with vulnerability (trait) factors to generate *states* likely to produce sexual offending behaviours. As we noted earlier, Hanson and Harris (2000b) identified seven types of behaviour, plus the possibility of an eighth 'unique' risk factor, that indicated increased risk in a group of sexual offenders under supervision. These clinically identified factors can be grouped as the following: cognitive, affective and behavioural triggering factors. We would suggest that victim access behaviours, rejection of supervision and substance abuse act as *behavioural* factors, hostility and emotional collapse are *affective* factors, while sexual preoccupations act as a *cognitive* triggering factor. However, a closer examination reveals that these triggering risk factors may not be that clear-cut, in that treating victim access behaviours and sexual preoccupations as acute precursors suggests that an offender is passive rather than actively engaging in these behaviours and cognitions. Therefore, by critically examining in the model some of the received wisdom in risk assessment, hopefully we have suggested a more integrated approach to this area. We will now consider the clinical implications of this model.

EVALUATION OF THE RISK AETIOLOGY MODEL

The major purpose in constructing the model shown in Figure 13.1 is to link two related clinical domains in order to further both risk assessment and theory-directed research. Here, we have attempted to incorporate static and dynamic risk factors into an aetiological framework. Our risk aetiology model represents the first explicit attempt to integrate aetiological theory with the different types of risk factors. In a sense, it provides an explanation of why certain types of factors increase an individual's risk of committing a sexual offence in the future. Furthermore, it accounts for why static factors do a reasonable job of predicting reoffending, and clearly specifies their relationship to psychological traits or dispositions: that is, offence-related vulnerabilities. These aspects of the model highlight its *unifying power, explanatory depth, external consistency, empirical adequacy* and *fertility*.

In terms of its weaknesses, perhaps the most significant problem relates to the fact that all the evidence supporting it is post hoc; it has not as yet been subject to empirical testing. It would be helpful if the model could be used to explain why an individual committed a sexual offence and used to predict what his subsequent vulnerability factors are, how treatment should proceed, and what contextual variables will increase or decrease his chances of committing future offences. It would also be a good idea to investigate the association between sexual offenders' offence-related dispositions and acute dynamic (state) factors. According to the model they should be strongly related. This problem in the model points to its lack of *empirical adequacy*.

A further weakness arises from the model's dependence on the Ward and Siegert aetiological theory (Chapter 5), itself untested at this point in time. While the theory may prove to be a robust explanation of sexual offending, this remains to be seen. This weakness may indicate a lack of *coherence* and also reflects on its *empirical adequacy*.

CLINICAL UTILITY OF THE MODEL

Despite these problems we believe that the model has considerable potential therapeutic value and is capable of resulting in advances in the treatment of sexual offenders. Although this model is very new, feedback from clinicians has suggested the following. In terms of structuring assessments, it provides assistance in three ways. First, it acts as a framework for looking at historical issues such as abuse or trauma, and makes some connections between those issues and the development of psychological traits. The model pushes clinicians to look at the possible implications of life history, rather than allowing them to report it without making comment. Second, it provides a way of understanding—via the traits or psychological dispositions—the manifest distortions of individual offenders. Clinicians sometimes report confusion concerning whether cognitive distortions drive the offending, or whether they are used as post hoc rationalisations for it. Here the model offers a constructive way of looking at that debate, and directs clinicians toward looking at underlying traits rather than their manifestations. Third, it draws attention to research evidence for some widely assumed and 'known' connections, like childhood abuse and psychosocial problems, attachment and adult functioning, and so on. Connections between these features and their aetiological explanations have been reported as being of use.

CONCLUSIONS

In this chapter we have described a number of concepts in risk assessment and the current utility of a risk assessment model where static, stable and acute dynamic risk factors are considered. We have outlined an aetiological model of risk, attempting to draw all the current elements of risk assessment together in a clear aetiological framework. The major purpose in constructing the model is to link empirical, clinical and theoretical ideas together in order to further the risk–needs assessment field. A contribution of the model is the redefinition of stable and acute dynamic risk factors. We suggest that the usual definitions do not make psychological sense and argue for their replacement by the *trait/stable dynamic* (i.e. dispositional), *state/acute dynamic* and *contextual* risk factor distinctions. State and trait are terms that have a strong grounding in general psychological theory, while the dispositional and contextual constructs are well established in the general risk assessment literature. With this reformulation, the process by which psychological dispositions become acute risk factors when triggered by contextual risk events becomes rather straightforward.

In the model we have also attempted to show how the causal mechanisms and pathways identified in the pathways model of sexual abuse (Ward & Siegert, 2002b; see Chapter 5) can be mapped onto dynamic risk factors. The usefulness of this approach is that it suggests that risk assessment schedules should be more specifically related to the psychological dispositions of the offenders in question. Hopefully, the model also clarifies that the level of risk posed by an offender is a function of a specific array of causes, and the context in which these vulnerability factors are activated.

PART IV
LEVEL III THEORIES
(DESCRIPTIVE MODELS)

Chapter 14

THE RELAPSE PREVENTION
AND SELF-REGULATION MODELS

Level III theories differ from higher level theorising in their exclusive focus on the temporal components of the offence process, combined with a heavier emphasis on proximal rather than distal aetiological factors. By contrast, as we have seen, level I and II theories usually are more concerned with distal factors, with the development of a predisposition to offend, and with the person-based side of the person–situation interaction.

Level III theories are related to other traditions, such as event-based models in criminology (e.g. burglary; Cornish & Clarke, 1986) but most are aetiologically richer because of their explicit or implicit inclusion not just of cognitive elements—such as decision making—but also of behavioural, volitional and affective factors. Those covered in this chapter share with level II models the specification of mechanisms, not just a descriptive focus.

Distinct strands can be discerned among level III theories. These distinctions centre on the methods used to construct the models, and on the emphasis each model gives to the relationship between other theoretical bases and offence-based data. So, some have been explicitly constructed from highly detailed offence descriptions, using systematic and rigorous analysis processes, usually the qualitative research approach to theory building known as grounded theory. These may be densely descriptive models. Others derive more loosely from practice; practitioner-theorists have developed cyclic models, often as tools for use with offenders in treatment. These are also primarily descriptive, and both of these types are covered in the next chapter. A third type is a more complex mix of top-down and bottom-up processes; data derived from descriptive models are integrated with theory as it is in the self-regulation model. These theories then are *not* primarily descriptive. They do not simply explain *how* offending occurs, but also—with variable degrees of success, as we shall see—*why* offenders may do what they do when committing an offence.

Consequently these theories, which are the focus of this chapter, are also in a sense more typical of higher level theorising because they have greater explanatory depth and draw on theoretical constructs and mechanisms. In this chapter, we focus on relapse prevention (RP), and its newer conceptual revision, the self-regulation (S-R) model. We discuss Marlatt's original relapse model first, then Pithers and colleagues' adaptation for sexual offending, before turning finally to Ward and Hudson's self-regulation model. The following chapter examines offence process and offence cycle models.

RELAPSE PREVENTION MODELS OF RELAPSE

Marlatt's Relapse Model

The origins of RP are in the substance abuse literature, where maintenance of cessation behaviour following treatment is also a challenging problem. In the early 1980s, Alan Marlatt and others began to disseminate research into the determinants of relapse, particularly for alcoholics. Nineteen eighty-five saw the publication of Marlatt and Gordon's seminal book on cognitive-behavioural approaches to the maintenance of treatment change. In an area where clients could achieve initial behavioural change but few could maintain it, practitioners eagerly embraced an approach that offered optimism about dealing with setbacks, along with a structured set of strategies for therapists to use. Consequently, RP interventions—the teaching of coping skills to support and maintain change—have become ubiquitous in clinical treatment.

RP can be conceptualised theoretically in two distinct ways (Polaschek, 2003c). It is probably most often thought of as a treatment theory, but it also contains a theory of the offence process. Contributors to Marlatt and Gordon's (1985) book proposed interventions for implementation at distinct points on the pathway to relapse. Therefore, embedded in the RP treatment approach was a new theoretical model of how drinkers relapsed. Marlatt (1985b) described this model as based on qualitative research with relapsing alcoholics. Marlatt's substance-abuse-based relapse model (the Marlatt RM) introduced a new nomenclature, including *high-risk situation, abstinence violation effect, apparently irrelevant decisions* and the *problem of immediate gratification* (Marlatt, 1985b).

The Marlatt RM proposes that an excess of obligations, hassles and negative life events over pleasant events in the background lifestyle of a substance user creates stress and provides the motivational momentum to indulge in the prohibited substance, leading to urges and cravings, and anticipation of substance use (Marlatt & Gordon, 1985). A series of *apparently irrelevant decisions* (AIDs) may follow; superficially trivial decisions outside of overt awareness that nevertheless undermine perceived self-control by collectively increasing perceived risk of relapse.

Besides the covert (AIDs) route to *high-risk situations* (HRSs), there are two other routes in Marlatt's model: (i) accidental, where events outside the user's control unexpectedly put him at risk, and (ii) a direct route where excessive stress leads to negative affect, which eventually may lead to a resumption in substance use as an ingrained method of affect regulation (i.e. the HRS is affective, not physical).

In the absence of effective self-management, HRSs threaten an individual's cessation self-efficacy, enhance positive perceptions about engaging in the prohibited behaviour, and lead to a *lapse*, defined as a single occurrence of the undesirable behaviour (e.g. a first alcoholic beverage). Indulging in the prohibited substance triggers the *abstinence violation effect* (AVE), a complex interaction of negative cognitions and affect that precipitates further lapse behaviour—and ultimately—*relapse*: the return to a full pattern of dysfunctional substance use (Laws, 1999; Marlatt, 1985b).

Evaluation of Marlatt's Relapse Model

In the past decade, Marlatt's RM has undergone both empirical and conceptual appraisal. Witkiewitz and Marlatt (2004) recently reviewed this work and proposed a reformulation with greater emphasis on dynamic situational factors. This new model has more potential to accommodate heterogeneity in interactions between distal and proximal, static and dynamic risk factors. For example, it incorporates feedback loops that recognise reciprocal causal relationships between factors.

Here, we limit ourselves to some general comments about the strengths of the Marlatt RM, and then provide a brief summary of Ward and colleagues' evaluations of its problems, because this is the appraisal work that has most influenced subsequent level III theorising for sexual offenders. Ward has critiqued both the original Marlatt model and the sex offender adaptation (see below).

Prior to RP, the prevailing view of the relapse process in addiction was based on the disease model, which assumed that any ingestion of the prohibited substance constituted a full relapse. Thus one of the most outstanding theoretical and clinical practice contributions of Marlatt's RM is in distinguishing levels of 'failure severity', and even in reframing early signs of backsliding as predictable, constructive learning opportunities rather than the entry points onto the hydroslide to complete self-destruction (Brownell, Marlatt, Lichtenstein & Wilson, 1986). As conceptualised first by Marlatt and colleagues, relapse is a process composed of distinct identifiable steps. Carrying out early steps can indicate changes in the risk of relapse for a particular individual.

When first proposed, the importance and innovation of this model was striking. Cognitive-behavioural approaches to clinical programmes were still new. Many of the theoretical constructs were also relatively new (e.g. self-efficacy and attributional theory) and the model showed a promising level of *unifying power* in bringing them together, and potential *explanatory depth* as a result. The systematic empirical examination of why people seemed to succeed initially but eventually to fail in behavioural change was also just beginning. RP appeared to have enormous *heuristic* value, especially in its application to treatment. However, from the outset it also had a number of epistemic difficulties, which are summarised below from more detailed original sources (Laws, Hudson & Ward, 2000a; Ward & Hudson, 1996).

Marlatt's RM descriptions imply a linear, non-recursive model of relapse. By contrast, empirical evidence suggests that people trying to overcome substance use problems may move both forward and backward through the proposed relapse pathway—and more than once—before finally relapsing (e.g. Saunders & Allsop, 1987). This is a problem of *empirical adequacy* and *scope*. A similar problem is with his explanation of why people sometimes fail to use coping skills they clearly have in their repertoire, in that they have used them before in similar situations (Saunders & Allsop, 1987). Marlatt's assertion that such failures in HRSs were due to the lack of such skills is clearly not sufficient.

Ward and Hudson (1996) also were concerned about the conceptual confusion resulting from the heterogeneity of definition of HRSs. They suggested redefining HRSs simply as actual, environmental situations containing stimuli that were formerly associated with substance use. This idea would solve several problems. First, no additional steps would be needed to explain how a person experiencing low affect deliberately leaves a safe place (e.g. her house) to go and buy a packet of cigarettes, even when she has no car and it is pouring with rain. Second, the original phenomenological definition means that if a relapsing alcoholic does not recognise the degree of risk he is in, he isn't, even if history suggests otherwise. On the other hand, if he believes that his control over abstinence is undermined in a non-threatening situation, the anxiety that results may actually precipitate a lapse where otherwise there was little risk. Ward and Hudson's proposal removes variation in when the HRS occurs that was introduced by this dependence on the accuracy of individuals' risk appraisals.

Marlatt's theory has some problems with *external consistency* also. He has argued that classically conditioned stimuli in the HRS elicit urges and cravings that motivate indulgence. However, important behavioural theories of relapse (see Niaura et al., 1988, for a review) postulate that craving can occur without the presence of such cues. And if a conditioning model is the best way to explain this aspect of the transition to lapse, then his proposal—that conditioning processes are subservient to cognitive processes such as low coping efficacy expectations, or high positive expectancies about use—is redundant, and, according to Ward and Hudson (1996), empirically unconvincing.

The model compromises *internal coherence* because of the lack of clear explanation of the relationships between key components: in some cases the lack of clear definitions, multiple conflicting mechanisms or no mechanisms. For example, when does lapse behaviour become relapse? And by what mechanism does the covert route to HRSs function? Essentially, Marlatt (1985a) described this route as a form of unconscious (i.e. covert) planning. Effectively, he proposed that when highly stressed and thus cognitively compromised, often an individual would engage in apparently elaborate planning. Furthermore, if the plan *is* covert, then logically so is the goal of relapse itself, and perhaps the desire to indulge that generates it. Otherwise how can we explain why the individual is not aware of the link between her desires and actions, Ward and Hudson (1996) have argued? There are current theoretical mechanisms that can manage these problems; Marlatt's model would gain depth and coherence from including them.

Ward and Hudson (1996) noted that Marlatt (1985b) had five proposed mechanisms for the transition between lapse and relapse. They are: lack of coping skills, passive failure to deploy coping skills, active pursuit of substance-based coping to escape negative affect either from lifestyle imbalance (HRS precursors) or from failure to avoid HRSs, and active pursuit of substance use because of an exclusive focus on short-term rewards of use. Aside from threatening the *internal coherence*, the theory thus also lacks *simplicity*.

Another cluster of problems centres around the lapse–relapse transition. Ward and colleagues conducted empirical research (with sex offenders) and subsequently theoretically reformulated the AVE. Interestingly, although their own research with sex offenders (Ward, Hudson & Marshall, 1994) suggests theoretical problems with the AVE, research on the AVE with alcohol and drug users has been somewhat more supportive (Wheeler, George & Marlatt, in press),

Marlatt drew on diverse theoretical sources (*unifying power*), including self-awareness, cognitive dissonance, self-efficacy, drive and attribution theories (Hudson, Ward & Marshall, 1992), for this part of the model (i.e. the lapse–relapse transition). Predictably, the result is again overly complex, but at the same time, constrains *scope* by relying on Weiner's (1972) attribution theory, which itself construed attributions in quite a narrow, rigid and categorical manner. Another example of the lack of *simplicity* is found in the way that both attributional and attribution-independent pathways are proposed to create negative affect.

The effect of the older, more limited definition of attributions is to confuse types of causal inference and their respective dimensions, a problem that is easily overcome by reformulating the AVE using the 1986 version of Weiner's attribution theory. This reformulation—using the dimensions of locus (internal/external), stability, globality and controllability—allows for elegant predictions about the effects of particular types of attributions on subsequent emotions, and on the risk of subsequent relapse. For example, if a person attributes a lapse to chronic lack of ability (a stable, internal, uncontrollable factor) he is likely to experience shame and hopelessness and make no effort to avoid relapse. In contrast, attributing a lapse to lack of effort (an internal, but controllable, factor) may result in feelings of guilt, renewed effort and relapse avoidance (Ward & Hudson, 1996).

There is one other important source of *internal incoherence* at the lapse–relapse transition. The AVE is thought primarily to generate negative affect but, in contrast, a lapse should produce positive affect through what is known as the *biphasic effect* of drug use: a lapse involves substance ingestion, which typically induces initial euphoria followed later by lowering mood. Does this mean that the AVE is a delayed response, in effect the second (dysphoric) phase of the biphasic response? If not, then at the lapse point the hapless person is experiencing both excitement and a sense of well-being, *and* dysphoria and guilt. But if the AVE is delayed, then there is a conflict regarding the nature of the mechanisms generating the dysphoria: the negative affect of the AVE is hypothesised to be generated by an attributional (cognitive) component; the biphasic response is thought to be biologically based, at least for alcohol.

In conclusion, Marlatt's (1985a, b) RM was both a theoretically and clinically *fertile* innovation. Substantial conceptual critiques of the original Marlatt model of RP during the 1990s set the stage for better recognition of the heterogeneity of pathways and mechanisms involved in relapse, whether it be in the substance use or sexual offending domains. We have concentrated here on critiques that set the stage for revisions in the sex offender domain, the most notable of which is the self-regulation model. However, before we examine this model, we turn specifically to the adaptation of Marlatt's RM for sexual offenders.

The Pithers–Marques Relapse Model of Sexual Offending

Pithers, Marques, Gibat and Marlatt (1983) formally recognised the potential of the RP model for sexual offending treatment. Pithers in particular has written a number of articles on RP for sex offenders over the years (e.g. Pithers, 1990; Pithers, Kashima, Cumming & Beal, 1988), but in contrast to Marlatt's original work, his emphasis has always been on using the model in treatment. Therefore, both the theoretical underpinnings of RP and the scientific validity of the embedded RM have received much less attention than in the substance use domain.

Although RP has been influential in the treatment of drug and alcohol disorders, this influence pales into insignificance when contrasted with its domination of sex offender treatment. A decade ago, surveys of north American programmes suggested that almost all reported using RP (Freemann-Longo, Bird, Stevenson & Fiske, 1994), and examination of the published programmes of other Western nations confirms this pattern (Polaschek, 2003c).

What accounts for its appeal? Marlatt's RM came to attention at a time when the predominant learning-oriented model for the treatment of sex offenders was beginning its transition from behavioural to cognitive-behavioural. At that time, when these therapists wanted to develop an understanding of the offence process of their sex offender clients, they did so by conducting a functional analysis of antecedents, behaviours and consequences (Knopp, 1984). Pithers et al.'s (1983) adaptation of RP for sex offenders put together into a simple and elegant graphical depiction Marlatt's work on the precipitants of relapse and the antecedents to HRSs. Here was a ready-made template of the cognitive, affective and behavioural phenomena that underpinned potential treatment failure and provided an optimistic plan for helping clients avoid it (Polaschek, 2003c). So what exactly was that template?

Pithers and colleagues have described their RM in several different articles. Below, we describe the model mainly from the first published account (Pithers et al., 1983; see Figure 14.1). The RM begins with an offender who has a growing sense of self-control resulting from an offence-free lifestyle. His self-confidence continues to strengthen until he encounters an HRS, defined as it was by Marlatt, as a situation in which this sense of self-control is threatened. Pithers et al. noted that HRSs can arise without warning, but offenders can also systematically place themselves into HRSs without apparent awareness. As with Marlatt, these covert planning steps are called AIDs, and are supported by 'the well-known cognitive processes of rationalisation and denial' (Pithers et al., 1983, p. 219).

Once in the HRS, if a restraining offender then fails to perform an effective coping response, he begins to feel helpless and discouraged about preventing

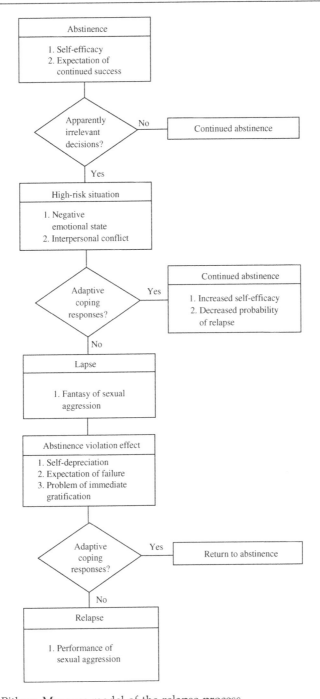

Figure 14.1 Pithers–Marques model of the relapse process
Source: Pithers, W. D., Marques, J. K., Gibat, C. C. & Marlatt, G. A. (1983). Relapse prevention with sexual aggressives: a self-control model of treatment and maintenance of change. In J. G. Greer & I. R. Stuart (Eds), *The sexual aggressor: Current perspectives on treatment* (p. 217). New York: Van Nostrand Reinhold.

future offending. If at the same time he is in the presence of cues that were previously associated with offending, and he anticipates that offending will be an immediately positive experience, then his risk of reoffending is now much increased.

Up to this point the Pithers–Marques RM followed closely the original Marlatt model. However, at the lapse stage, the adaptation encountered an important ethical obstacle. For Marlatt, a lapse was the first occurrence of a prohibited behaviour. If this was translated as the first occurrence of a sexually offensive behaviour, therapy would be seen potentially to condone victim harm as a 'learning experience' for the perpetrator. In order to retain the idea that a lapse was a positive opportunity to learn—and a point at which self-control could, and should, still be exerted—the term *lapse* had to be redefined as an immediately proximal precursor to any form of abusive behaviour. Thus in the 1983 Pithers–Marques model, the lapse became a covert pre-offence event: a sexual fantasy. Later versions included other, sometimes behavioural, precursors (e.g. buying pornography; Pithers, 1990).

At the point of lapse, the offender's experience of an AVE heightens further the likelihood of full relapse. Pithers et al. (1983) defined the AVE in two ways: (i) cognitive dissonance: conflict between abstaining self-image and relapse-related behaviour, which he resolves by deciding that he is still an active sex offender; and (ii) his attribution of the lapse to stable personal deficiencies, so increasing the expectation that he will not be able to prevent the slide into relapse. The problem of immediate gratification (PIG) is not specifically mentioned in the 1983 text, because it is incorporated into the AVE. Therefore a third contributor to the AVE apparently is anticipation of positive experiences in the form of sexual offending.

As with Marlatt, the stage following lapse is *relapse*, defined by Pithers and Marques as the single occurrence of a sexual offence. By contrast, Marlatt's original definition assumed the complete return to the problematic lifestyle associated with the prohibited behaviour (e.g. sustained excessive alcohol consumption). Figure 14.2 summarises the most important differences between the Marlatt and Pithers–Marques RMs.

Evaluation of the Pithers–Marques Relapse Model

Marques and Pithers' recognition of the *fertility* of Marlatt's RM for sexual offending was a defining act in the history of behavioural and cognitive-behavioural treatment of sexual offending (Marshall & Laws, 2003), resulting in an extensive treatment literature, and a small body of research. However, adoption of any model from the substance use domain brought with it certain risks.

The first of these is to do with *scope*. How complete is an addictions-based model as an account of sexual offending? The extent to which it is helpful to view sexually problematic behaviour as an addiction remains in dispute (Cooper, Scherer, Boies & Gordon, 1999). Marlatt (1985b, p. 4) viewed RP's scope as extending to any 'compulsive habit pattern', characterised by immediately

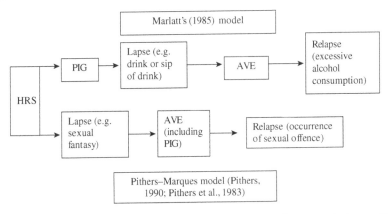

Figure 14.2 Summary of the similarities and differences in the stages between HRS and relapse in the original relapse model and in the adaptation for sexual offenders

positive consequences and longer term negative ones. Laws (1995a) suggested that this definition was consistent with not only 'traditional' addictive behaviours (e.g. of substances) but also other disorders of impulse control (e.g. fetishism, unsafe HIV-related sexual practices, compulsive spending and interpersonal violence). This is a sensible suggestion: that RP offers a range of strategies that should be useful to anyone who keeps repeating a behaviour they wish to stop. However, many sex offenders report no evidence or awareness of a sexually-based impulse control difficulty (Grubin & Gunn, 1990; Polaschek & Gannon, 2004), and in support of their views may be official evidence of only occasional sexual offences many years apart.

Gold and Heffner (1998) found little evidence to support the concept of sexual addiction in general. When applied to sexual offending, there is a variety of problems, including a lack of convincing evidence about the essential phenomena of craving, withdrawal and loss of control over behaviour. Taken together, the shortcomings suggest that the use of other models appears desirable (McGregor & Howells, 1997).

Pithers and colleagues' original research into the precursors of sexual offending (e.g. Pithers, Buell, Kashima, Cumming & Beal, 1987) evidently supported what Hanson (2000, p. 31) has recently termed 'orderly offence cycles'. Pithers et al. (1983) reported a common, even invariant, sequence of offence precursors: negative affect → fantasy → conscious plan → behaviour (see also Pithers, Kashima, Cumming, Beal & Buell, 1988). However, recent research (Polaschek, Hudson, Ward & Siegert, 2001; Ward, Louden, Hudson & Marshall, 1995d) has found much more diversity, suggesting that the RM fails to accommodate pathways to reoffending found in many offenders (*scope*) and, indeed, that only a minority of sex offenders may report an offence process that resembles the RM (Hudson, Ward & McCormack, 1999).

A strength of Marlatt's (1985b) work was the way that it drew together a complex range of theoretical ideas, clinical observations and research findings. As we noted, this very integration brought with it a variety of theoretical difficulties and confusions that were transported into the Marques–Pithers version. However, because of the primarily heuristic, treatment-oriented focus of Pithers' writings on the RM, these replicated theoretical problems are largely invisible.

In addition to the epistemic strengths and weaknesses it shares with the Marlatt RM, the Pithers–Marques RM has unique strengths and problems. A novel strength is that Pithers et al. (1983) increased the *scope* of their model by giving explicit recognition in their text to the possibility that HRSs can occur by chance, or factors outside of the offender's careful control. Note that this route is omitted from their figure (see Figure 14.1). A problem not shared with Marlatt's RM is the apparent lack of a mechanism to explain why an offender begins to work his way away from his confidently abstinent state (*explanatory depth*). Marlatt used the sense of deprivation arising from lifestyle imbalance to provide the momentum for covert planning, but Pithers et al. did not discuss this aspect.

Ward, Hudson and Siegert (1995) identified a series of theoretical and empirical problems arising from redefining the lapse as an offence precursor. The change put both the AVE and the PIG—clearly contradictory mechanisms— between lapse and relapse. The AVE is associated with negative affect and self-attributions of failure, and the PIG with positive affect and appetitive goals (Ward & Hudson, 1996), leading to an implausibly complex cognitive and affective state. This change is an important source of *internal incoherence*, and appears to be *empirically inadequate* as well. Ward et al. (1994) demonstrated this problem with data obtained from pre-treatment child sex offenders; almost 70% experienced an AVE at relapse rather than lapse. By contrast, phenomena more closely resembling the PIG (e.g. positive affect) dominated offenders' experience at lapse. Why? Perhaps offenders do not experience 'lapse' behaviour as defined by the Pithers–Marlatt modification as indicative of personal failure to the extent that the model suggests it should be. Offenders may be unconvinced that a precursor behaviour, such as pornography use or fantasising, really is threatening enough to their self-control to be considered a lapse, in the same way that many people struggle with moderation goals before recognising that abstinence is the only way *they* can manage their alcohol consumption (Rosenberg, 1993). Furthermore, it is hard to identify what should be chosen as the lapse when it is not a discrete well-defined event such as sipping an alcoholic drink. How close to the likely occurrence of an offence should the lapse be? So the clinical utility of the definition may also be a problem.

One final problem is with the definition of relapse. By redefining a relapse as a single criminally sexual act, Pithers and colleagues were forced to undo one of the important gains of Marlatt's RP model, that backsliding was still worth trying to stop as long as things could still get worse. So for an offender in RP treatment based on the Pithers–Marques RM, there appears to be no point in further attempts at restraint once an offence has begun. Ward and Hudson (1996) suggested that this feature should result in the exacerbation of sexually offensive behaviour once commenced. Since most offenders experienced an AVE *after* the relapse rather than the lapse, Ward and Hudson proposed that a single offensive act be renamed *relapse one*, and subsequent offences or more severe acts within the same offence be termed *relapse two*. For most offenders, the AVE occurs in between. Harm reduction advocates (e.g. Laws, 1996) support this idea, and recently have focused theoretical attention on developing a more advanced understanding of this far end of the relapse process, and the implications for treatment (Stoner & George, 2000).

Balanced against the problematic features has been the obvious value of the Pithers–Marques RM as an *heuristic* in intervention design and implementation. However, this strength may have been overstated. The reported dominance of RP appears to be more a result of its intuitive appeal than established scientific validity (Hanson, 2000; Polaschek, 2003c). RP's appeal to treatment providers took three forms:

1. It generated therapist optimism about the opportunities for therapeutic intervention in the presence of backsliding (Hanson, 1996; Hudson & Ward, 2000), in the face of little or no evidence that sex offender treatment was effective (Furby, Weinrott & Blackshaw, 1989).
2. RP packaged up a complex clinical phenomenon in a coherent language with a credible theoretical pedigree: mainstream cognitive-behavioural theory (Eccles & Marshall, 1999; Hanson, 2000).
3. RP reduced therapist anxiety about exactly what to do in treatment.

But RP was originally a unique *post-treatment* maintenance strategy (Laws, 1989). Now, it is not. Most programmes that report using RP describe themselves as having 'an RP framework'. Theoretically, that framework is largely what would be expected of any comprehensive programme based on the cognitive-behavioural approach (Hanson, 2000). Second, empirical evaluations of the effects of RP treatment on subsequent recidivism in sexual offenders also do not distinguish it from other treatments (Marshall & Anderson, 2000). In short, although it is methodologically difficult to examine the effectiveness of any single programme component, there is no compelling evidence that RP is adding unique value to the current treatment enterprise (Polaschek, 2003c).

In summary, Marlatt, Marques, Pithers and colleagues developed and promoted an extremely popular level III model of the offence process, under the umbrella of relapse prevention. A number of shortcomings with these models— conceptual and empirical—now have been identified. Following on from their theoretical critique of RP, and their empirical research into the RM with sexual offenders (discussed more fully in Chapter 15), Ward and colleagues obtained data that showed just how heterogeneous are the offence processes of sexual offenders. Furthermore, their work on the descriptive model of child molesters' offences (Ward et al., 1995d) revealed that their initial view that offender goals, affect and regulatory style would covary also did not appear to be right. Consequently, they began a major conceptual revision of the 'relapse process', replacing RP theory with self-regulation theory.

THE SELF-REGULATION MODEL OF THE RELAPSE PROCESS

Like the RM, the self-regulation model (S-R model; Ward & Hudson, 1998b, 2000a; Ward, Hudson & Keenan, 1998) represents a level III theory that is more informed by existing theory than those in the next chapter. Ward and colleagues have given their offence pathway research a rich theoretical substrate, by integrating it with self-regulation theory (Baumeister & Heatherton, 1996; Carver & Scheier, 1981, 1990).

Having established a clear picture of the strengths and weaknesses of existing models of the relapse process, Ward and Hudson's (1998b) aim was to construct a multiple pathway model with an explicit temporal focus, that could accommodate the dynamically heterogeneous nature of sexual offences, including a range of goals and of emotional states at different points. Within each pathway, the steps to offending as they are understood currently would also be accommodated (e.g. background factors, proximal decisions, offence precursors, the offence itself and post-offence responses). The psychological mechanisms that hold the whole together would also be outlined coherently.

Ward and colleagues chose self-regulation theory because of its focus on how individuals behave in a purposive, goal-directed manner over time and across situations. Self-regulation theory gives to goals a central role in guiding, planning, overseeing and modifying behaviour. Individuals regulate their behaviour and even their emotional states in order to achieve key goals. Regulation can involve doing either more (i.e. enhancing) or less (suppression) of particular actions.

A key distinction in goal types was made by Cochran and Tesser (1996): between *approach* (acquisitive) and *avoidance* (inhibitory) goals. Approach goals focus on obtaining or achieving a particular end. Individuals monitor progress *towards* approach goals against information that indicates they are succeeding, tend to experience setbacks as instigators to strive harder, and feel generally positive about such goals. By contrast, avoidance goals focus on avoiding the occurrence of a prohibited behaviour or situation. There are many ways to fail at such goals (Wegner, 1994), but the only success is when complete suppression is achieved, probably by constant monitoring and effort. Consequently these inhibitory goals are associated with much more distress, and more failure-related perceptions and memories, than are approach goals (Emmons, 1996).

Goals can be activated by environmental cues, resulting in goal-directed behaviour that is automated and executed largely without the involvement of conscious decision-making processes (Bargh & Barndollar, 1996). More often, behavioural self-regulation involves conscious, controlled, effortful cognitive processing (Carver & Scheier, 1990). Individuals actively monitor their behaviour, comparing it against the currently salient or activated goal, and making adjustments when discrepancies are detected. Under these effortful circumstances, reduced self-awareness will tend to impair self-regulation, probably because the importance of the goal is reduced.

Two patterns of dysfunctional self-regulation appear applicable to sexual offending (Baumeister & Heatherton, 1996; Carver & Scheier, 1990). *Under-regulation* occurs when individuals behave in a disinhibited or impulsive manner because they fail to exert adequate control over their feelings or behaviour. Under-regulation can be associated with both approach and avoidance goals, and with positive or negative affective states. *Mis-regulation* involves attempts to exert control through the use of strategies that are ineffective and may ultimately result in the reoccurrence of the very feelings or behaviours that were being avoided. A third pattern described by Ward and Hudson (1998b) as an example of dysfunctional self-regulation occurs when the offender actually achieves valued goals by effective self-regulation strategies, but the goals themselves are socially unacceptable because their achievement inevitably harms others.

Ward and Hudson (1998b) integrated self-regulation theory with the temporal scaffold that both the RM and their own work on the offence process had established. The result was a model with nine phases and four pathways, organised around two constructs: the nature of sexual offence goals (avoidant versus approach) and the nature of the self-regulation strategies employed to achieve those goals.

The S-R model (Ward & Hudson, 1998b, 2000; see Figure 14.3) comprises:

- Phase 1: Life event
- Phase 2: Desire for deviant sex or activity
- Phase 3: Offence-related goals established
- Phase 4: Strategy selected
- Phase 5: High-risk situation entered
- Phase 6: Lapse
- Phase 7: Sexual offence
- Phase 8: Post-offence evaluation
- Phase 9: Attitude toward future offending.

Summarised from Hudson and Ward (2000), the four pathways are:

1. *Avoidant-passive*: resembling a traditional relapse model, on this pathway stressful life events overload coping resources. A desire to 'cope' through deviant sex emerges, which the individual wants to restrain. However, covert planning takes him into an HRS. He feels out of control and gives in to his desires, offends and feels personally defective and ashamed afterwards.
2. *Avoidant-active* begins in the same way as avoidant-passive, but the offender responds to the emergent desire with active but ill-chosen strategies to avoid offending that ultimately backfire, increasing offence risk and perceived loss of control over behaviour. The offender then abandons attempts to restrain, and, as for the first type, experiences an AVE after the offence. This time it is associated with guilt rather than shame.
3. *Approach-automatic*, in which an offender has developed automated behavioural scripts from previous direct experience or extensive fantasising. The offender encounters an HRS opportunistically rather than seeking it out, and it is only then that an already developed template or script for offending becomes activated, with minimal attentional involvement. Such offences appear 'out of the blue' (i.e. there is limited or no evidence of offender planning) and are brief in duration. The offender experiences positive post-offence affect, with negative victim attitudes.
4. *Approach-explicit*, involving conscious, strategic planning, a strong desire to obtain sexual gratification from offending, positive post-offence affect and subsequent refinement of offence-related strategies.

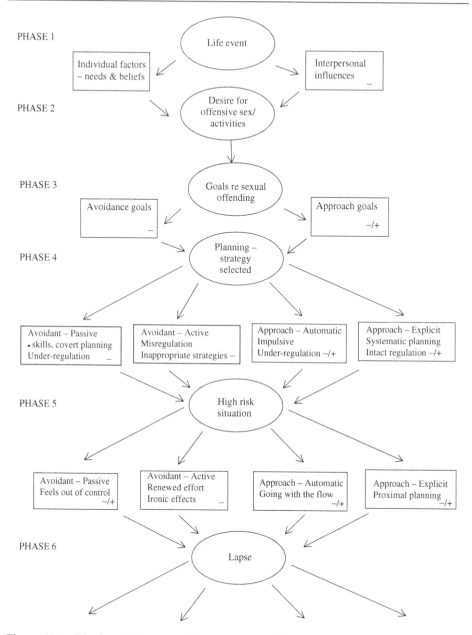

Figure 14.3 Ward and Hudson self-regulation model
Source: Ward, T. & Hudson, S. M. (2000). A self-regulation model or relapse prevention. In D. R. Laws, S. M. Hudson & T. Ward (Eds), *Remaking Relapse Prevention with sex offenders: A sourcebook* (pp. 86–87). Newbury Park, CA: Sage.

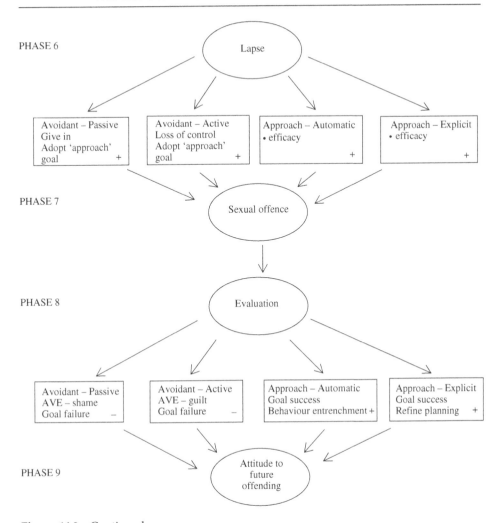

Figure 14.3 Continued

EVALUATION OF THE SELF-REGULATION MODEL

The S-R model represents a major theoretical reconceptualisation of the relapse process in sexual offending. It retains some of the strengths of the RM but resolves a number of the theoretical difficulties identified in our previous critique. Helpfully, it retains some of the RM's names for phases in the process (e.g. HRS, lapse). It has greater *internal coherence* through its primary reliance on a single body of theory from the social cognitive domain. And there are some elegant solutions to vexing RM problems. For example, the S-R model provides a mechanism for covert planning; on the avoidant-passive pathway, offenders relinquish higher level behavioural control by disengaging self-evaluative processes through cognitive deconstruction (see Baumeister, 1990; Ward, Hudson & Marshall, 1995a). Behaviour is consequently regulated by 'a more basic-level feedback system' (Ward & Hudson, 2000a, p. 91), probably operating at the programme level where behaviour is 'more automatic and "mindless" ' (p. 94). In a second example, the difficulties with the PIG and AVE largely have been resolved by (i) shifting the AVE to the post-offence evaluative phase, and (ii) building in a temporary goal shift for avoidant offenders, to accommodate their positive expectations and affect immediately prior to the offence.

Ward and Hudson have made genuine progress on their first aim: proposing a model that provides a more coherent level III theory than RP. The S-R model largely relies on a single theoretical source for its internal mechanisms (*internal coherence*). At the same time, it incorporates the currently understood elements of the offence process established by previous theory and research (*external consistency*).

What of their second aim: to accommodate the diversity of offence pathways? The S-R model is a significant step forward in this respect too. The complexity of the model's pathways (Figure 14.3) compared to the RM clearly displays its dynamic nature and much expanded *scope*. Within the S-R model, Ward and Hudson noted that even more heterogeneity can be accommodated if it is understood that having started down a path, offenders may move back and forth at different phases and even depart the process at any point. The model is rich in *explanatory depth* too. For example it can accommodate the different types of post-offence cognition and affect associated with their own AVE research, as well as non-AVE phenomena they identified (Ward, Hudson & Marshall, 1994).

Another example of its *explanatory depth*—arguably also a demonstration of *unifying power* and *external consistency*—lies in the incorporation of previous research on the paradoxical effects of thought suppression (Johnston, Ward & Hudson, 1997). This work is built into the avoidant-active pathway to explain why some forms of self-regulation backfire, effectively increasing the problems they were chosen to solve.

The *predictive accuracy* and *scope* of the model also are enhanced by Ward and Hudson's explicit attempts to incorporate findings from their own research on offence processes in rapists and child molesters that were unable to be accommodated within the RM. The S-R model builds on both the offence chain model for child molestation (Ward et al., 1995d) and the later rape model (Polaschek et al., 2001), with its focus on goals, strategies and evaluation. The S-R model's specific inclusion of nonsexual motives and goals clearly brings it more in to line with the rape model (see Chapter 15 for more detail).

Four studies provide early support for the *empirical adequacy* of some of the S-R model's central features. Using cluster analysis on data from 44 untreated extrafamilial child molesters in Canada, Proulx, Perreault and Ouimet (1999) derived a two-cluster solution—labelled coercive and non-coercive pathways— that is broadly comparable to the approach/avoidance goal distinction in the S-R model. Interesting, the majority of offences fell into the approach-goal category.

Bickley and Beech (2002) set out to code offences for 87 UK child molesters in a residential treatment clinic. Specific hypotheses were derived from the S-R model and tested using self-report and offence-related demographic information. Working independently, two therapists first allocated each offender to one of the four S-R pathways. Then analyses were conducted for differences in offence demographics and self-report responses on assessment questionnaires. A variety of predicted differences were found across both the avoidant/approach and the passive/active dichotomies. Again, the majority of offenders were classed as having approach goals. An attractive feature of this study was the inclusion of data showing differential patterns of treatment responsiveness (e.g. changes in cognitive distortion measures) for approach versus avoidant offenders. Consistent with S-R predictions, approach-goal offenders were assessed as being at higher risk of reoffending.

Yates, Kingston and Hall (2003) used a mixed sample of 80 imprisoned Canadian sexual offenders to examine the validity of the S-R model and its relationship to dynamic and static risk factors. They made pathway allocations for the entire sample, based on file review only. Of their 19 rapists, just one did not follow an approach pathway. Most were approach-automatic. Most child molesters in this study also appear to have had approach goals.

Webster (in press) examined the relationship of the S-R model to post-treatment recidivism in 25 British child molesters and rapists. Offenders were interviewed post-reconviction using an interview guide structured to align with the S-R model phases. Data for pre- and post-treatment offences were transcribed and coded into the model. Webster then set out to allocate a pathway type to each of the 50 offences, and was able to do so for almost two-thirds of them. The majority were approach-explicit, consistent with Hudson and Ward's (2000) suggestion that treatment is least effective with these men at present. An important observation was that pathways were consistent across both offences for the 11 men who had two classifiable pathways. Treatment then, did not result in change, as it should have for at least the approach-goal offenders. Although Webster concludes that he found strong support for the model, nevertheless a third of offences could not be coded, chiefly because some men's offences followed several pathways simultaneously through the model.

Finally, we see the S-R as having good *fertility*; it opens up numerous possibilities for productive future research, as the four studies above attest, and its value in generating new approaches to intervention also appears notable. However, it is a new and complex theory. Although some suggestions have been made about how aspects of the model may inform treatment (e.g. Mann, 2000), the development work needed to translate it fully into a treatment approach that clinicians can readily use is only now under way (Ward et al., 2004a).

There are several areas in which the S-R theory may have problems that suggest the need for further development or clarification. We make suggestions about these below; broadly they are also in the domains of *scope, simplicity* and *explanatory depth*.

Hudson and Ward (2000) noted that there had been some criticism of whether the RM applies to untreated offenders; indeed, whether pre-treatment offences can even be viewed as 'relapses'. Their stance on this issue is that it is most fruitful to build models that accommodate both pre-treatment and post-treatment offending in their scope. They also note that a commitment to avoid reoffending at the outset of an offence process may not be predictive of treatment involvement and success, and indeed is not a dichotomous construct anyway. We certainly agree that whether men are committed in their day to day lives to abstaining from future offending is not a function of treatment. Many sex offenders presumably not only establish their own abstinence goals, but achieve them as well without the 'benefit' of treatment (Hanson, 2000).

Why, then, does the S-R model limit its scope to explaining the behaviour of men who are initially committed to non-offending (i.e. only to offenders who at the time of their previous offence were in the contemplation, action or maintenance phases of the transtheoretical model of change; Prochaska, DiClemente & Norcross, 1992)? The authors did not explain why it was important to incorporate this restriction, particularly when the inclusion of approach goals—for example—allows for the encompassing of more antisocial individuals who are quite unmotivated to recognise their behaviour as problematic at any point. Thus it appears that the model sets out to exclude unnecessarily some offence processes, and consequently to limit its *heuristic value*. Effectively this feature implies that regardless of their current motivation to change, the S-R model has no contribution to make to treatment endeavours with offenders who were unmotivated to abstain from offending at the time of their offence: a problem it shares with the RM.

The perpetuation of the term *relapse process* as the focus of the model also serves to reinforce that the model is intended only to explain the behaviour of initially restraining men (Hudson & Ward, 2000). Yet elsewhere, the authors' laudable aim is to have us view sexual offending as a *problem behaviour process* regardless of where the offender is up to in his rehabilitation or attitude to it. Using this more neutral language that has less of an association with illness and disease would also be necessary if scope was to be widened to considering all offence processes in self-regulatory terms.

Within the proposed four pathways, Ward and Hudson have striven to incorporate a wide range of offence patterns in the S-R model. This is an exceptionally difficult task, which they achieve with uneven success. For example, the model seeks to recognise offenders for whom the trigger for the desire to offend arises from serendipitous contact with a potential victim, who may be assaulted just minutes later. Alongside this pattern are the more traditional avoidant paths, where loss- and stress-related negative life events start a slide towards a sexual assault, that may last weeks before an offence. Furthermore, the S-R model attempts to recognise that the early motivation to offend may not be sexual, but that in line with research on rapists (Polaschek & Hudson, 2004; Polaschek et al., 2001), initial goals may be aggressively nonsexual. But they term these nonsexual motives the desire for 'maladaptive activity' (Ward & Hudson, 1998b, p. 709), a label that is unsatisfactorily vague, in that it still may require us to invoke unconscious cognitive processes in the offender, a criticism the authors levelled at the RM. For example, imagine an offender who goes around to his estranged wife's house uninvited. He sets out intending to coerce her into sorting out custody arrangements of their children so that he can see them, and hopes that maybe they can begin to patch things up (approach goals). When he gains entry to her house, he begins to discuss the custody issue, she becomes hostile and angry with him and he realises that he is not going to make progress. Meanwhile he has been noticing how attractive she is. When it becomes clear that there is also no likelihood that they will reconcile in the foreseeable future, he decides he will have sex with her one last time, and rapes her. This type of offence was quite common in the sample used to construct the rape model (Polaschek et al., 2001), and the S-R model should therefore be able to accommodate it. A key feature here is the overt desire to achieve a reasonably adaptive approach goal (e.g. sort out custody, seek reconciliation), using ineffective or antisocial strategies to achieve it. The alternative argument is that this individual has a covert goal to rape his wife and plans it implicitly. So either the *desire for maladaptive activity* box needs clarification or modification, or the S-R model needs implicit planning mechanisms for approach as well as avoidance pathways.

The concerns above likely reflect variation in the *internal coherence* of the model. The left-hand (avoidant) side of the model clearly is much more developed than the approach side. This observation would be expected given the relationship of the avoidant pathways to the RP model and the consequent detailed work Ward and colleagues have done on critiquing and reformulating these aspects. Recognising the relevance of approach pathways is a relatively recent innovation in this area, and their inclusion here represents a very important advance over the RM. The recognition of the approach-automatic pathway is particularly interesting. Theory and research on automatised goal setting and behaviour are used to provide a mechanism for this path.

However, the approach-explicit pathway presently has limited *explanatory depth*. This problem is a direct result of Ward and Hudson's (1998b) observation that approach-explicit offences do not reveal self-regulatory skill problems. Recall that here socially harmful goals are pursued by individuals with effective self-regulation skills. Arguably then, it follows that a self-regulation model that does not explain both *why* and *how* offenders choose socially harmful goals may have little to offer to understanding these types of offences. The same argument may extend to the approach-automatic pathway. Here Ward and Hudson suggested that offences triggered by situational events unfold in a relatively automated way by following established offender scripts. Automated behaviour always appears under-regulated in that the advantage of automation is that such behaviour can occur efficiently, without taking up cognitive resources. Consider driving as an example. Experienced drivers often drive for long periods with little conscious awareness of either the mechanics of operating the car, or the process of navigating well-known routes while obeying road rules and dealing with other drivers' behaviour. However, when something unusual, challenging or dangerous occurs, such drivers commonly experience a sudden return to conscious control of behaviour, because now goal achievement (i.e. getting from A to B safely and smoothly) may be threatened or disrupted. Therefore, commonly automatised driving behaviour would tend only to be classified as under-regulated if a driver could not stop herself driving from A to B when she should not, or, if, when something goes wrong on the trip, she cannot disrupt her own processes and resume conscious control. Applying this example to offending: why would an offender direct attention toward disrupting well-rehearsed behaviour when it is serving a desired goal? Surely this behaviour is only evidence of under-regulation if the goal was to do something else, or if, having recognised that he is not achieving the goal, he is *unable*—rather than unwilling—to stop.

The rape model (RM; Chapter 15) also demonstrated the diversity of approach goals. Some differences within approach goals may have important theoretical and practical implications that would make it worthwhile unpacking the category a little further. For example, desiring to have sex and desiring to harm someone are both approach goals. However, in the first, the offender's attentional focus is often exclusively on himself, while in the other, it is largely on the victim and the impact of his behaviour on him or her.

Relatedly, Ward and Hudson continue to combine anger with other less energising negative emotions such as low mood. This practice creates a confused affective picture particularly in conjunction with approach goals, where the only 'negative' emotion is typically anger. Anger gives much more forward momentum to behaviour than low mood, and offenders report that anger—if not frankly pleasurable—is often what might be termed 'righteous': they anticipate satisfaction from achieving their plans to punish the victim. Some offenders openly describe anger as pleasurable. In contrast, despondency, loneliness and despair are seldom described in these quasi-positive, energising terms, and are commonly associated with avoidance goals. The affective picture for approach goals would be clearer if a distinction was made between anger—an emotion that if not actually positively experienced is at least associated with a positive expectation—and other negative emotions was made clearer.

Having made these points, we reiterate that overall the S-R model is an exciting conceptual innovation that, along with its level I sibling, the pathways model (Ward & Siegert, 2002b; and see Chapter 5), looks likely to capture significant research and therapeutic resources over the next decade.

CLINICAL UTILITY OF THE SELF-REGULATION MODEL

Many practitioners may see debate about exactly which mechanisms mediate the transition to lapse, or to relapse, and at what point a lapse is defined as a relapse as so much preoccupation with minor technical matters. What difference does the resolution of these issues make to practice? In some cases, perhaps not too much. However, our view is that although level III theories do not provide a complete basis on which to develop a formulation of a client and an intervention plan, the adequacy of these models is crucial to assessment and treatment effectiveness.

Before we consider these matters, though, we note that no level III theory can provide a complete basis on which to establish the criminogenic needs of sexual offenders and how these needs interact with each other. In particular, level III theories do not unpack the background vulnerabilities that create risk: these are left in a kind of 'black box' at the top of these models, and this work is done largely by level I and II theories. Nor do level III theories indicate clearly where such important factors as cognitive distortions, victim empathy and sexual dysfunction fit into the treatment plan. These are not functions of a level III theory but such factors may be important to treat, and will be overlooked if RP or any other level III theory (e.g. an offence process model) is used exclusively to structure treatment.

We now turn specifically to the clinical implications of the RM. Our review has established that it poorly represents key features of the offence process. Its use to guide assessment of offences should be terminated. It is not simply that there are problems of theoretical coherence. The RM cannot accommodate many sexual offences—perhaps most—if the preponderance of approach-goal offences in recent research is representative. This is no trivial matter. If the template does not fit what an offender already knows about his offending, or pushes an offender to see his offending in ways that do not make sense, surely the credibility of the programme and the staff is compromised. The offender is less likely to engage and begin to make difficult personal changes as a result. Alternatively, pressure to make his offence 'fit the model' may lead the offender and therapists to subtly alter parts of the offence so that key aspects and risk mechanisms are obscured. Intervention then is directed at an inaccurate for-mulation.

Of course, it follows that if the RM is inadequate, therapists who rely on it will struggle to make adequate therapeutic responses to the treatment needs of myriad offenders with other offence process patterns (see Chapter 15). The problems uncovered with the scope of the RM suggest the need to rethink the interventions that spin off the various phases of it. For example, avoidant-active offenders arguably do not need the degree of help in learning to identify with HRSs that avoidant-passive (RM-type) offenders need. Instead they need to be convinced that their chosen strategies are not as effective as they originally intuited.

Put simply, the RM assumes that men recognise that their offending is wrong, and are at least in the preparation stage in respect of their motivation to change, that they plan covertly, are generally restraining themselves from offending, and fail due to a lack of alternative coping skills. Such assumptions may be true only for a minority of offenders. Yet RP interventions are based on them, so what do we offer to the rest?

Although it is in a very early stage of clinical development and evaluation, the S-R model's utility in assessment and treatment planning has been drawn out by Hudson and Ward (2000). The model looks to have the ability not only to accommodate a wider range of offence goals and strategies, but to make distinctive predictions about the types of treatment needs associated with each. Recently a manual has been published for S-R model-based assessment (Ward et al., 2004a) and a treatment manual is under development.

The S-R model underlines the point that RP has directed too much attention to offender strategies, when the goals themselves may be the problem. Offenders with approach goals are not offending as a maladaptive form of coping with negative events, and they may not be deficient in the skills we currently seek to teach, merely disinclined to use them because of the distorted goal structures that they deploy to meet fundamental needs. The intriguing finding that the majority of sex offenders in early S-R research have approach goals emphasises the need to make sure that new treatments target goal selection itself. The several studies of the S-R model suggest that sex offenders, even those entering treatment programmes, are—at least at the time—apparently much more comfortable with their offensive sexual behaviour than their therapists are. In this sense they are more like other serious offenders than we often recognise. This observation may create discomfort for therapists, who have come into this arena from more traditional mental health domains, where patients less often set out to hurt people in the knowledge that they will, but it must be accepted if we are to optimise treatment impact.

Embracing the RM also enabled us to ignore other evidence of the wider antisociality of our client group, including high rates of violent and general offending, especially in rapists (Polaschek & King, 2002) but also in child sexual offenders (Smallbone & Wortley, 2004b). The challenge to programme designers now is to respond to this evidence of more 'egosyntonic antisociality', especially in the right-hand pathways of the S-R model, by developing approaches to deal with the wider range of dynamic risk factors implicit in the model, including those that overlap with other serious offending. Some of these components may already be available in the criminal rehabilitation literature. Approach-goal offenders may benefit from cognitive skills training such as that provided to nonsexual offenders. Such a benefit has already been demonstrated once with sex offenders (Robinson, 1995). The S-R model makes it easier to extend the range of criminogenic or offending-related treatment needs beyond the narrow scope of relapse prevention. Thoughtful innovation may enable us to develop an effective treatment for rapists (Polaschek & King, 2002).

Unfortunately, the S-R model shares with RP a lack of direct applicability to the issue of creating and maintaining a commitment to avoiding reoffending. How can treatment develop a commitment to abstinence? Essentially with men entering treatment, this is equivalent to the problem of maintaining motivation to change. Without more work in this area, offenders encounter programmes at odds with their current motivational stage. Such an experience may entrench their risk by increasing resistance to change. Many therapists have noted that motivational considerations make a much better basis on which to select and structure treatment components than the order in which component problems appear in the RM. As a starting place, Mann and Thornton (2000) make a number of excellent practical suggestions about how to engage clients better in RP-type treatment. These suggestions include allowing clients to choose personally meaningful treatment goals, encouraging them to develop a learning, not achievement, orientation, developing client self-efficacy for new goals, and managing over-optimism (Mann and Thornton, 2000). They also suggest warning signs for offenders who may not benefit from RP: (i) lack of an abstinence goal regarding sexual offending, (ii) failure to accept that RP is an appropriate model for their risk of subsequent offending, or (iii) failure to accept the kinds of tasks that are required of them to prevent further offending.

In a shift away from the inherent limitations of the RM and RP, both Mann (2000) and Fernandez and Marshall (2000) describe refocusing offenders' treatment objectives away from avoidance to approach goals, because of the research demonstrating that avoidant goals are more difficult to achieve. However, there may be hidden risks to such reframing, especially for high-risk offenders. Approach goals are associated with a focus on the achievement of the desired end (e.g. a healthy, offence-free lifestyle). Setbacks are seen as less serious and may simply serve to spur the person on (Ward & Hudson, 1998b). The focus of attention is relatively narrowly restricted to indicators of success. We do not know yet whether the associated lack of vigilance is actually equally enhancing, or even safe for *all* offenders, but it is time to investigate the issue.

The task, then, is to develop and implement the S-R model in treatment, since both theoretically and empirically it is already superior to the RM, and then establish which aspects of RP are worth keeping and where new interventions are needed to cater for all sex offenders with equal attentiveness.

CONCLUSIONS

This chapter reviewed the RM—the theoretical scaffold for sexual offence processes for more than two decades—before examining a reformulation, the S-R model, which is in the early stages of implementation. The pervasiveness of the RM in sex offender treatment stands as a strong example of the folly of ignoring the importance of research in determining the validity of theory. Despite its attractiveness and plausibility, as a theory of the offence process, the RM has substantial flaws. The worst of these flaws is its lack of scope and theoretical incoherence. For these reasons alone, it should no longer be used in the assessment and treatment of sex offenders. The S-R model corrects a number of its problems, but is young and likely to need further refinement, particularly to its most novel aspects, before its potential is fully realised. At present, it remains largely untried in a practical sense. Conceptually, it is clearly superior.

Chapter 15

OFFENCE CHAINS, OFFENCE CYCLES AND OFFENCE PROCESS MODELS

Level III theories are micro-models of how—rather than why—sexual offences unfold. They are explicitly temporal, but vary in how descriptive they are. The two level III theories reviewed in the previous chapter—the relapse prevention (RP) and self-regulation (S-R) models—are more abstract and contain more explanatory depth (i.e. they also provide some answers to questions about *why* particular things happen in the offence process) than the models that are the focus of this chapter. The models in both chapters are richly endowed with cognitive, behavioural, affective, volitional and contextual factors, but in this chapter they are also more explicitly connected to the grist of clinical practice with sex offenders; the accounts offenders give for how their offences occurred. These are better thought of primarily as *descriptive* models but this descriptive emphasis does not mean they avoid any theoretical substrate. Often, implicit in the way that they are built is the developer's own model of the clinical world (e.g. cognitive-behavioural), and so they are in a sense collective, integrated versions of offence chain functional analyses or individual case formulations by practitioners trained in a particular tradition (see Polaschek, 2003a).

An early example of an offence chain approach in the context of cognitive-behavioural treatment of sexual offenders was the cognitive-behavioural chain, an addition to RP treatment outlined by Nelson and Jackson (1989), and intended to assist offenders in identifying high-risk situations and learning alternative ways to manage them. In this approach, as their name suggests, the content of these chains was limited to what the offender and others actually did, and his interpretations of these actions.

With the advent of behavioural and then cognitive-behavioural models, the offence process was brought to prominence by the shift towards offence-focused intervention. This new focus made models of the offence chain a vital treatment tool. In this chapter we briefly describe and critique in turn offence cycle models put forward by Wolf (1984), Freeman-Longo and Pithers (1992), Carich (1994), Lane (1991, 1997) and Salter (1995), and finally, our own models of the offence process in rapists and child molesters. We conclude with treatment implications.

WOLF'S ADDICTION CYCLE

Description of the Model

Wolf (1984, 1985) developed a 10-step model of the cycle of sexual offending based on his clinical experience and research at Northwest Treatment Associates in Seattle (see Figure 15.1). It is not clear by what method he derived it. He referred to it as an *addiction cycle*. It begins with an offender's negative perception of himself, which Wolf attributed to a chronically dysphoric response to life stressors. This negative self-image creates expectations of rejection by others, leading to social avoidance and isolation, a passive, unassertive coping style that perpetuates the low self-image, and negative affect. To compensate for his isolation and sense of deprivation, the offender engages in 'need-fulfilment fantasies' (Wolf, 1985, p. 368): usually *sexual* fantasies that enhance his sense of control and efficacy. They are sexual because offenders in this cycle have learned to use sex as an escape from negative circumstances. Fantasies also allow for

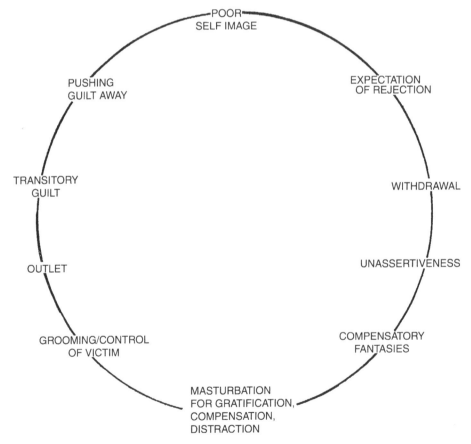

Figure 15.1 Wolf's cycle of sexual offending
Source: Wolf, S. C. (1985). A multifactor model of deviant sexuality. *Victimology*, 10, 368.

offence rehearsal and serve to increase the attractiveness of particular acts or victims. They are subsequently paired with masturbation.

Cognitive distortions develop to reduce guilt and to facilitate emergent planning and grooming of a potential victim. The actual offending behaviour is characterised by an exclusive focus on the offender's own, primarily sexual, needs and goals. Any feelings of guilt that may follow are alleviated by minimisation or justification and may function to facilitate further offending. However, Wolf suggested that awareness at some level of the wrongness of the act may further lower the offender's self-esteem and help to perpetuate the cycle.

Evaluation

This model has the virtue of providing a fine-grained description of offending behaviour and its associated processes, particularly prior to the offence itself. It is relatively simple and coherent.

However, its *scope* is seriously limited. Essentially it proposes a single pathway with an exclusive focus on pre-offence negative affect and the offender's ineffective attempts to manage this state. It has in common with a number of these models that the primary mechanism proposed for sexual assault is a maladaptive coping/compensatory one. Offenders are assumed to overuse sex as a learned strategy for coping with negative life events and dysphoria. This mechanism has apparent *predictive accuracy*: the coping aspect of the mechanism has obtained some recent empirical support in that it may have a high base-rate in sex offenders (Cortoni & Marshall, 2001). However the model needs to explain how 'sexual addiction' gets translated into illegal sex, is targeted at children, is aggressive and so on: why it is that offenders do not just have many consenting sexual partners instead.

The compensatory mechanism itself has little *explanatory depth*. Effectively, what is being proposed is a form of self-regulation, where sexual fantasy and offending both alleviate negative affect (in behavioural terms, a negative reinforcement mechanism) and create their own positive affect because sex is inherently enjoyable (i.e. positive reinforcement). So this is a mechanism which has the potential to accommodate offending that occurs both as an approach and avoidant strategy in the terms of Ward and Hudson's (1998b) self-regulation (S-R) model as outlined in the previous chapter.

Additionally, Wolf's model assumes that offenders are concerned exclusively with meeting their own needs. Yet there is some preliminary evidence that offenders can have different foci during the offence: they may be focusing on their own, the victim's, or mutual needs (Ward, Louden, Hudson & Marshall, 1995d), suggesting *external inconsistency* and lack of *scope*.

The model is vague and lacking *internal coherence* in that there is little or no information about the processes going on in the immediate offence build-up or the offence itself. It emphasises mainly internal psychological processes in the distal build-up at the expense of understanding more proximal and external events.

FREEMAN-LONGO'S FOUR-STAGE MODEL

Description of the Model

Freeman-Longo's model of the assault cycle consists of four stages: build-up, acting out, justification and pretend normal (Bays & Freeman-Longo, 1990; Freeman-Longo & Pithers, 1992). In the *build-up* stage, the offender becomes preoccupied with sexual fantasies, and their associated pleasure or excitement, and decides to commit a sexual offence. His deviant sexual interests escalate and he develops a clearly defined plan. During this first phase offenders usually experience negative emotions; they may feel particularly anxious, fearful or angry. The second stage, *acting out*, involves the actual sexually offensive behaviour. Following the occurrence of a sexual assault the offender enters the third, *justification*, phase, where he evaluates his behaviour and may feel guilty or concerned about getting caught. In order to manage these feelings he develops a number of rationalisations and excuses, and may resolve never to engage in deviant sexual activity again. In the final stage, *pretend normal*, the offender returns to his normal routine and sets about portraying himself as a normal person. He may resume the activities and behaviours that previously led to the build-up phase, or attempt to 'turn over a new leaf'. This phase signals the beginning of the cycle for offenders once they have carried out their first offence.

Evaluation

The four-stage model is overly simplistic. Although it captures some of the important features of the offence process, it has the appearance of a template intended for use directly with offenders in treatment rather than as a level III theory for practitioners. It lacks any real *explanatory depth*; it fails to account for both the complexity of the processes involved, and the different offending pathways. Again, it primarily focuses on a negative affect pathway with post-offence guilt and resolve not to offend further, and so its *scope* is constrained. However, it is vague concerning the actual processes involved. Instead, assorted bundles of processes are attributed to each of the phases except for the offence phase itself. For example, implicit planning, high risk factors and situations, and maladaptive coping responses are all part of the build-up phase (Carich, 1994). Do they apply to all offenders? How do they interact with each other?

The sexual assault phase itself is not unpacked at all (*internal coherence*). Again, it is not clear how the model was constructed, but the implication is that it evolved from extensive clinical practice rather than a specific research methodology. Compared to actual data on the offence process (Hudson, Ward & McCormack, 1999; Proulx, Perreault & Ouimet, 1999), it therefore lacks *empirical adequacy*.

Lastly, because this model appears to have developed out of treatment intuition with no clear theoretical basis, rather than from processes that allow for the confirmation and disconfirmation of beliefs, it has no significant *fertility*, either for research or intervention.

CARICH'S SIX-STAGE MODEL

Description of the Model

Carich and his colleagues have developed a comprehensive treatment framework for sex offenders that is based on relapse prevention (Carich & Stone, 1995). Their overarching relapse intervention approach includes a six-stage model of the sexual assault cycle, developed to enable more detailed identification of the phases of offence processes (see also Carich, 1994). The six stages are: *initial (triggering) stage, pre-search, search, set-up, offending/relapse* and *post-offending aftermath* (Carich, 1994).

The first stage starts with a triggering event that activates underlying needs and habitual coping strategies. These triggers can be internal—cognitive, affective or physiological—or external, and may differ in the degree of risk they pose for the individual. As a consequence of the triggering event, the offender develops the motivation to commit a sexual offence. This motivation may result from the re-emergence of long-standing conflicts concerning control, identity or self-esteem. He then starts to develop a plan and begins the search for a potential victim. This planning can be explicit and conscious, or unconscious, depending on whether the offender has a pre-existing commitment to remain offence-free. Once a possible victim is identified the grooming process is initiated and the offender creates an opportunity to engage in sexually deviant behaviour. The next step involves the actual offence, followed by the offender's reaction to this event. A temporary feeling of satisfaction may be followed by guilt or shame, and subsequent cognitive distortions to reduce this negative affect and the threat associated appraisals pose to self-esteem. The whole cycle may be repeated if not interrupted by the offender or an external agent.

Evaluation

A particular strength of Carich's model is his emphasis on cognitive distortions or defences throughout the offence process, and the recognition that adverse developmental experiences contribute to the formation of distorted attitudes and motives. The existence of both conscious and unconscious planning is also a strength and allows for different types of planning, and subsequent offending pathways. Both of these observations expand its *scope* considerably, compared to Freeman-Longo's four-stage model.

However, this model does have a number of limitations. The initial triggering events or processes are viewed as constituting challenges to individuals, implying that they have a negative impact on the offender. Therefore, the major affective pathway is arguably once again negative, leading to disinhibition or counterproductive regulation of behaviour. The loss of control over internal states, or the deliberate use of maladaptive strategies to reduce negative mood, ultimately results in a sexual offence.

Once again, it is not clear how it was constructed, but like Freeman-Longo's model, it has limited *fertility* or *heuristic value* because it lacks novelty and *empirical adequacy* in that it does not fit with existing offence chain research (Hudson et al., 1999).

LANE'S SEXUAL ABUSE CYCLE MODEL

Description of the Model

Lane (1991, 1997) has formulated a richly complex representation of the sexual abuse cycle for juvenile sexual offenders. There are three major phases of Lane's abuse cycle that collectively integrate the various contextual, cognitive, affective and behavioural factors into an overall conceptual model: the *precipitating, compensatory* and *integration* phases.

Precipitating phase

In the *precipitating* phase, an offender experiences a negatively construed event in a habitual manner, resulting in feelings of passivity, helplessness and abandonment. Exposure to negative life events in childhood results in the development of this habit of responding, which comprises negative feelings and their associated cognitions (e.g. 'I should get what I want', 'I should know what to do'; Lane, 1997, p. 93) Once established, it can be triggered by a negatively construed event, which leads into several specific types of distorted cognition that Lane has built into her model. The *personalisation distortion* refers to the tendency to over-personalise negative events. According to Lane, the pattern is complex. The youth may see malevolent intent in another's actions, feel overly responsible himself for some negative event, or believe that commonly occurring negative events indicate that he is getting a raw deal in life. The affective consequences are invariably negative and, with time, begin to generalise (Lane, 1997).

  Negative anticipation is the next part. Here, the young person develops the expectation that the future will be just as bad as the past and begins to experience generalised feelings of anxiety, dread and hopelessness. The *hopelessness distortion* becomes prominent: he feels increasingly unable to cope with the situation, instead resorting to *avoidance* of anticipated negative outcomes (e.g. by excessive sleeping, drug abuse and solitary activities such as gaming, reading or listening to music; Lane, 1997).

Compensatory phase

In the compensatory response stage, the offender attempts to improve his self-image and restore his sense of power and control by manipulating or sexually abusing others. He engages first in the *externalising distortion*, where he blames others for his perceived misfortune and as a consequence of this defence becomes increasingly angry with the world. He moves on to *power and control* strategies: attempts to dominate others through nonsexual behaviour, fuelled by beliefs that he has been unfairly treated and is justified in making others pay. These behaviours are the first point at which the compensatory nature of this phase becomes externally observable. Initially these strategies appear to work; he experiences feelings of authority or superiority, but the effects are short-lived, and result in the *increased need distortion*. Now the offender briefly either (i) experiences rising anxiety because of the temporary nature of his success, or (ii) enjoys the sense of controlling others enough to want more of it. Consequently his need for control increases, ultimately leading to the emergence of *fantasy*. Here, Lane (1997) describes a progressive sequence starting with nonsexual fantasies of unlimited power or invincibility, which can appear innocuous (e.g. wanting to be a star) or offensive (e.g. wanting to torture or kill someone). At some point the fantasies develop an explicitly sexual nature. They again may appear non-abusive but contain strong elements of dominance and control (e.g. being irresistible to others, having a partner who complies with his every sexual whim). The youth begins to appear sexually preoccupied and sexualises others around him. However, 'the compensatory effects of the fantasy begin to diminish' (Lane, 1997, p. 105) and the youth searches for new sources of gratification.

In the final part of this phase, the offender sets up and commits an offence. In *offence set-up*, the youth begins to plan a sexual offence. He selects a victim, evaluates his likelihood of success, rationalises and justifies his behaviour, looks for or creates an opportunity to offend, and decides to act. Finally, he carries out the *sexual abuse*. Lane described a range of offences with a variety of affect and cognition during the offence.

Integration phase

This third phase begins with a *reinforcing distortion*: the young offender (re)interprets his offending as demonstrating his mastery and control over the victim. He congratulates himself at first. Then he moves into *fugitive thinking*, a stage where he begins to experience anxiety and concern about getting caught. He may regret committing the offence but usually shows little concern for the impact on his victim or the moral wrongness of his behaviour. After often only a few days, he moves on to the *control distortion*: he believes his victim will not disclose his behaviour and that he is still in control of her. However, these cognitive manoeuvres are only partially successful and he starts to experience ambivalence about himself, alternating between self-doubt and self-affirmation. This is *reframing*. Finally, the youth moves on to the *suppression distortion*. This last cognitive error serves to minimise his anxiety by suppressing any concerns about whether he is a weird or nasty person, whether he has a problem and so on. He becomes more defensively self-protective but experiences a lurking sense of inadequacy, low self-esteem and powerlessness all the same. These feelings are obviously similar to those that started the cycle. The compensatory gratification that the offending provided maintains the deviant sexual abuse cycle.

Evaluation

Lane's model represents a creative integration of existing clinical and research information concerning the offence process. It is best suited to highly recursive offending behaviour, and can accommodate the different phases of sexually deviant behaviour. It accommodates explicitly different levels of offender experience with sexual offending and there are a number of points at which it has clear *heuristic value* for treatment provision. The distal background elements of the precipitating phase are particularly well elucidated in this model; Lane recognises a wide range of events that can contribute to the development of a 'victim stance', and predispose individuals to exploit others.

It has research-related *fertility* too. For example Lane suggested that prior to sexual offending, a young offender will be seen to engage in a variety of nonsexual forms of control and dominance, some of which should be quite observable. This prediction is different from that of most models of sexual offending in adults, where the pre-offence behaviour is often more subtle and socialised (e.g. grooming).

However, Lane's model shares with earlier models the view that offending results from maladaptive coping and loss of behavioural control (i.e. disinhibition). So it lacks the *scope* to account for offenders who plan their offending without concern for whether others disapprove, experience no sense of defectiveness, feel positive throughout and believe that their actions are beneficial for both them and their victims.

This is primarily a psychodynamic model, with its emphasis on underlying (often unconscious) inadequacy and compensatory behaviour. Thus its central theoretical mechanism is not directly examinable because it is theorised to be unconscious. The model gives a prominent role to different types of cognitive distortions, and is unusually replete with examples of each type. Yet inexplicably, Lane sacrificed *external consistency* by largely eschewing the substantial literature on cognitive distortions in sex offenders. Instead she drew on Yochelson and Samenow's (1977) phenomenological work. A strength of this choice is that she connected young offenders' cognitive processes with those of criminals in general. However, by intent, Yochelson's and Samenow's work was atheoretical, and their categories often do not even refer to purely cognitive phenomena (e.g. 'lack of effort'; 'fear of being put down'; Lane, 1997, p. 88). Hence these parts of the model (e.g. 'poor me victim stance' and 'super-optimism') may be useful for offenders to grasp but have no clear *explanatory depth* in themselves.

SALTER'S DEVIANT CYCLE MODEL

Description of the Model

Salter (1995; see Figure 15.2) described a detailed offence process for rapists and child molesters. The cycle is initiated by the experience of (i) a negative affective state, (ii) deviant sexual arousal or (iii) a more generally antisocial belief that an offender has the right to use anyone for his own sexual gratification.

The offender then engages in covert or explicit planning to create high-risk situations, and therefore the opportunity to commit an offence. Covert planning (i.e. *seemingly unimportant decisions*[1]) indicates that the offender is consciously

---

[1] Seemingly unimportant decisions (SUDs) is an equivalent term for apparently irrelevant decisions (AIDS) in the sex offender relapse prevention model (Pithers, Marques, Gibat & Marlatt, 1983).

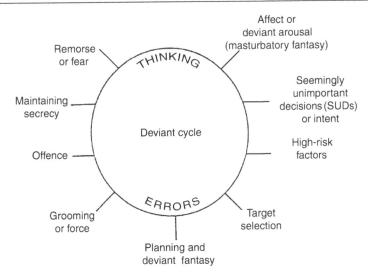

Figure 15.2 Salter's deviant cycle
Source: Salter, A. C. (1995) *Transforming trauma: A guide to understanding and treating adult survivors of child sexual abuse* (p. 45). Thousand Oaks, CA: Sage.

attempting to control his behaviour while at the same time unconsciously planning to offend. Overt *intent* to offend is indicated by explicit planning. Interestingly, Salter suggested that rapists mainly report conscious intent rather than implicit planning, and their decision-making and planning is simpler than for child molesters because legitimate access to children is more difficult to set up.

Such plans bring an offender into the *high-risk factors* portion of the model. Salter did not clearly define a high-risk situation, but it appears that it is a physical situation or role in which 'he has access to and power over potential victims' (1995, p. 52). Offenders usually gain access by the strategic use of a vocation or hobby, developing relationships with adults who themselves have access to children (e.g. a solo mother), physical proximity (spending time in parks or cruising the streets at night), or emotional proximity (e.g. befriending the victim). The intended relationship between high-risk situations and high-risk factors is unclear, but the latter includes both actual proximity to a victim and other less tangible risks that may be idiosyncratic to particular offenders (e.g. alcohol and drug use, taking photos, using pornography or access to a car; Salter, 1995). So *high-risk factors* include diverse factors that increase the likelihood of an offender committing a sexual assault, but unlike Pithers et al. (1983), Salter did not specifically include mood states as high-risk factors.

High-risk factors create access to potential victims, so now the offender begins the process of *target selection*. According to Salter (1995), victims are selected both for their attractiveness and for their apparent vulnerability to successful victimisation (e.g. degree of loneliness, distress, extent of supervision, absence of bystanders).

The next stage is *planning and deviant fantasy*. Here, Salter noted that when an offender admits early explicit intent to offend, he may also report using masturbatory fantasy (e.g. of previous victims) prior to forming that intent, and may have started planning the offence at that point. However, if he denies explicit awareness early in the offence cycle (i.e. he engaged in SUDs and implicit planning), then he is more likely to report sexual fantasy only during or after target selection.

Salter (1995) also described two kinds of planning at this point: active and passive. Passive planning refers to planning that the offender still describes in covert terms. In other words, the offender is clearly moving in on the victim but still describes his actions as having a non-offending purpose (e.g. befriending a woman or child).

Having identified a potential victim, the offender attempts by *grooming*, *force* or some combination to direct her toward sexual activity. Following the setting up of the right conditions he commits the actual sexual *offence*. Salter did not describe any within-offence patterns but discussed instead the issue of between-offence changes in repetitive offenders (e.g. escalation).

After offending, in order to minimise the chances of being apprehended sex offenders engage victims in strategies intended to *maintain secrecy*: to ensure the victim's silence by threatening or bribing her. However, Salter (1995) noted that some offenders make no active effort to protect disclosure; they assume that they have adequate control of the victim through his or her trust of them. Still others take their own precautions such as moving away from the area.

Finally, as a consequence of their offending behaviour some individuals experience *remorse or fear*. Salter (1995) suggested that offenders' reactions to disclosure most often took the form of self-centred anxiety and distress. Much more rarely, offenders experience genuine contrition or guilt for their behaviour. However, a typical response to these emotions is to restructure their thinking to avoid further self-recrimination or a resolution to avoid future offending situations. Thus guilt seldom results in reduced risk, though it is helpful in motivating treatment participation.

Salter also drew on Yochelson and Samenow's (1977) thinking error research to provide a substrate for the cognitive elements of her sexual offending cycle. She noted that thinking errors occurred throughout the offence process. She drew a distinction between process and content errors but noted that they all function to justify and minimise offending behaviour.

Evaluation

Salter's model has some similarities to the offence process of the Pithers et al. (1983) relapse prevention model (Chapter 14) but represents an important advance over this earlier work in several ways. Salter made plentiful use of case examples in describing her model, and so it is clear that it is intended to accommodate much more heterogeneity than the RM, and so has more *scope* and more *fertility*, from a treatment design perspective. For example, she acknowledged the role of deviant sexual arousal and positive affect, as well as casual sexual exploitation by generally antisocial individuals, in initiating an offence sequence. She also recognised the possibility of explicit fantasy and planning preceding victim selection, as well as implicit planning and denial of fantasy until after target selection. However, she still did not allow for the possibility of individuals unexpectedly finding themselves in high-risk situations or encountering by chance an opportunity to offend.

Taken together, these differences imply an important strength—that Salter recognised the need for a multiple-pathway model—but this potential is not fully developed and the pictorial depiction of the model (see Figure 15.2) is limited to a single, linear progression. Further, in describing these variations, Salter implied that the pathway portrayed in the figure applied to child molesters, while rapists followed the alternative: including positive or angry affect, explicit intent to offend, explicit planning, force rather than grooming immediately prior to the offence, and so on. This is an overly simplistic view of the differences and similarities between rape and child molestation and has turned out to be *empirically inaccurate* (see Hudson et al., 1999, discussed more fully below).

Salter recognised that some offenders might be committed to avoiding offending at the start of the cycle, but did not follow this aspect through to the post-offence phase, where logically offenders should show distinctive cognitive and affective responses depending on their pre-offence stance (*internal coherence*). In the RM, this is the phenomenon of the abstinence violation effect (*external consistency*), and data from offenders support its importance (*empirical accuracy*).

Implicit planning features prominently in Salter's model, but as with other aspects of the model, the concept lacks *explanatory depth*, or indeed any coherent theoretical substrate. Salter stated that both the intent and the actual planning were unconscious in some cases. However, she described the mechanism associated with this phenomenon as 'internal subterfuge', and as 'an internal lie—an attempt by an offender to convince himself that the action he is taking... has nothing to do with sexual aggression' (1995, p. 52). There is no question that implicit planning is very difficult to explain in a theoretically adequate manner (Ward & Hudson, 2000b). However, Salter's discussion leaves confusion about whether offenders are seen as (i) resorting to the use of psychodynamic defence mechanisms postulated to create genuine loss of conscious awareness of goals and plans; (ii) providing an account of how they consciously ignored the less palatable aspects of their functioning; or (iii) transparently seeking to avoid audience opprobrium by engaging in post-hoc face-saving lies.

Lastly, Salter recognised that cognitive processes and content are important throughout the offence chain. However, the inclusion of this component has no particular explanatory value, because there is no *internally coherent* focus on examining whether particular cognitions are important at particular stages. A rich source of information about sex offender cognition would come from a more systematic examination of the phases between target selection and the end of the offence. *Explanatory depth* is also hampered because, like several earlier models, Salter relied on Yochelson and Samenow's work as the main resource for cognitive distortions. As we noted earlier, their cognitive error work is very interesting from an ethnographic perspective but has no explicit theoretical framework. Consequently, it is a difficult jumble of implicitly psychoanalytic and lay concepts, and the phenomena it labels 'cognitive' are a mishmash of multicomponent cognitive skill deficits, psychological processes and folk ideas. Hence Salter cited 'I can't' as an example of a cognitive processing error, and gave as an example of a content error *palliative comparison*: the social-cognitive process of reducing culpability by drawing attention to ostensibly more severely abusive behaviour in others (Bandura, Barbaranelli, Caprara & Pastorelli, 1996; Murphy, 1990).

To this point we have reviewed five examples of offence process models. All have in common that they view offending as cyclical, that they were designed by treatment providers, and that the process of their development appears to have been clinically intuitive rather than scientific. The two models that follow are derived from a slightly different approach.

DESCRIPTIVE MODELLING OF OFFENCE PROCESSES USING GROUNDED THEORY

Grounded Theory (GT; Glaser & Strauss, 1967; Strauss & Corbin, 1990) is a methodology for use with qualitative data that allows for theory to be built by inductive analysis of the data about a particular phenomenon. Qualitative approaches are particularly helpful 'where existing theory is incomplete, inappropriate or entirely absent' (Henwood & Pidgeon, 1992, p. 102).

In GT studies, data often, though not always, take the form of narrative descriptions gained from interviews. Descriptions are broken into small units—often a clause—and coded into provisional categories that over time, are collapsed and combined into new and more abstract categories as they assimilate more data. The key process for researchers is that of *constant comparison*, whereby they move back and forth between the data themselves and the gradually emerging categories and subcategories. The process stops when saturation occurs; where new data protocols no longer generate new categories, but can be subsumed in the existing model. Saturation is best achieved and the model has more depth and clarity if the processes of data collection and analysis are conducted simultaneously. In this way, the interview process is directed to clarifying new patterns that may be emerging in the data analysis. Researchers document their growing understanding of the analysis as they conduct it, noting ideas about the data, the categories and their theoretical implications. This memo process increases the rigour of the method because it can make the researcher's own assumptions explicit and can expose them to scrutiny by others.

From the perspective of scientific psychology, with its preoccupation with the hypothetico-deductive method and quantitative analysis techniques, approaches like GT are viewed with some suspicion. Concern is often expressed about generalisability given the small sample sizes, and the implicit subjectivity of the analytic method. However, for clinicians, the strengths of GT include its ability to accommodate the subtle nuances and complexities of clinical data, which often seem to get lost in quantitative research, and to summarise them in meaningful ways. When successful, the resulting model helps to reduce that complexity to manageable proportions, but is still recognisably related to the grist of clinical practice. The GT approach was used to develop two offence process models during the 1990s, explicitly because existing offence models did not appear to have sufficient scope to accommodate the range of phenomena evident in clinical practice.

THE WARD ET AL. CHILD MOLESTER OFFENCE CHAIN MODEL

Description of the Model

Ward et al. (1995d) collated descriptions of their offence chains written by 26 incarcerated child sex offenders as they were assessed for a prison treatment programme. They applied GT analysis techniques to these descriptions, and by the processes documented above, developed the model summarised in Figure 15.3. The first nine offence descriptions were analysed independently by two researchers and reliability of coding was checked. The model was fully saturated with 16 descriptions. Final refinement resulted in a nine-stage model, which describes the cognitive, affective and behavioural sequence of events up to and following the commission of a sexual offence against a child.

Stage 1 focuses on the offender's perception of his lifestyle and circumstances, including current work and leisure activities, general mood state and self-image, and relevant current vulnerabilities arising from adverse childhood experiences. Offenders associated this stage with primarily negative or positive affect. Stage 2 comprises early planning for contact with a potential victim. Covert or implicit planning (i.e. planning not acknowledged by the offender at the time) usually occurred in conjunction with a negative affective state. Alternatively, some planning was overt or explicit and associated with positive affect. A third alternative, chance contact with a victim, obviated the need for distal planning. Here particular circumstances—victim vulnerability or offender intoxication, for example—had a contributing role alongside cognitive distortions, which were found to be especially influential at this stage. Sexual arousal also influenced distal planning, particularly in conjunction with positive affect.

In the third stage, offenders reported initiating nonsexual contact with their victim. Stage 4 involved consciously or unconsciously evaluating or restructuring both the events that had transpired so far and the current situation. Sexual arousal and cognitive distortions were again significant influences at this point. Such evaluations typically produced an affective state that was either negative or positive. When feeling negative, offenders tended to report low perceived self-control, attempts to deny feelings and high sexual arousal. Where positive affect was present, their evaluations were typically developed further through the use of explicit sexual fantasy, in which the victim was viewed as the initiator of sexual contact, or at least a willing partner.

In stage 5, immediately before beginning sexual contact with the victim, offenders engaged in proximal planning, influenced by their sexual arousal and cognitive distortions. The actual characteristics of the offence-related behaviour were determined in part by differences in offender foci at this point. Self-focused offences were brief, intrusive (i.e. more likely to be penetrative and

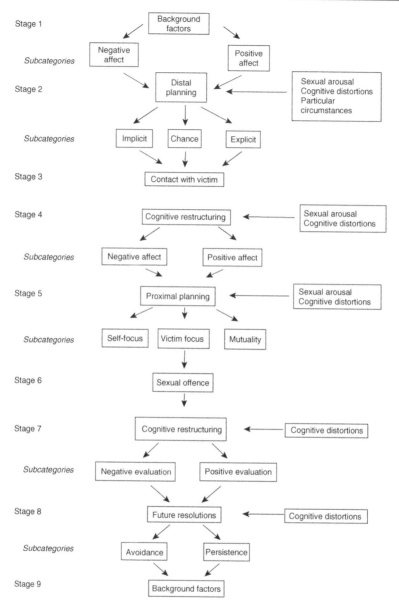

Figure 15.3 Descriptive model of child sexual offenders' offence process
Source: Ward, T., Louden, K., Hudson, S. M. & Marshall, W. L. (1995d). A descriptive model of the offence chain for child molesters. *Journal of Interpersonal Violence*, 10, 458.

severe) and involved offence planning associated with gratifying the offender's own needs without regard for the victim. They were accompanied by high levels of sexual arousal and cognitive distortions regarding ownership of the victim, or viewing the victim as an object. A victim focus was associated with claims that the victim's needs were paramount. Associated cognitive distortions emphasised victim initiation of contact, willingness and gratification. Sexual arousal was reported to be low. Duration of offence varied but intrusiveness was lower. Offenders with a mutual focus declared that they sought to meet both their own and the victim's perceived needs. They viewed the relationship as featuring the reciprocity of a mutual friendship or of lovers. They experienced high levels of sexual arousal and inferred that the victim did too. Their offences lasted longer and were less intrusive.

Stage 7—immediately following the offence—involved another period of evaluation or restructuring. For men who did not reach orgasm during the offence but masturbated afterwards, sexual arousal was still prominent, but for others, it now had minimal influence. Some offenders evaluated their behaviour negatively, and felt guilty and disgusted. Others restructured the situation by distorting or minimising it, or blaming the victim so that a positive evaluation of their own behaviour could be made. This restructuring process was especially prevalent in offenders who had experienced positive affect throughout the chain.

In stage 8 offenders made future resolutions, which were determined by the affective tone of the preceding evaluation. Where it was negative and accompanied by perceptions that the victim was unwilling to participate in, or had been harmed by the offence, offenders resolved to avoid reoffending. Positive evaluations accompanied by perceptions that the victim enjoyed or benefited from the offending led to an expectation of persistent offending and refinement of future plans.

Evaluation

A major strength of the Ward et al. (1995d) child molester (CM) model is its novelty of approach in adopting an explicitly empirical method of level III theory generation. The result is a rigorously conducted summary and integration of a series of cognitive-affective-behavioural chains typical of those developed for individual offenders in treatment programmes. This model is *externally consistent* with significant existing models, such as the relapse prevention model, but confirms Ward and colleagues' claims of inadequate scope in that model. In particular, the CM draws attention to (i) offences committed primarily in states of positive affect, and not triggered by building stress, (ii) the importance of both chance factors and explicit planning in setting up victim contact, and (iii) differences in the offender's focus as he goes into the offence, and in how he views the outcome. The clearly multiple pathway layout of the model (Figure 15.3) accommodates different types of offending through the construction of different pathways down—and if necessary across—the model. Ward et al. (1995d) discussed how the model could accommodate common patterns, and in Study 2, found that of 12 new offence descriptions, approximately half followed the left-hand (negative affect) side of the model, and the other half, the right-hand side. This tentative indication of its *fertility* with respect to offence classification was investigated more fully by Hudson et al. (1999), who classified the pathways taken through the model by 86 new offences, including 72 from the same programme as the original study, and 14 untreated rapists. They found evidence of eight distinct pathways, but almost three-quarters of the offences were captured by just three patterns. A third of all offences followed a pathway completely omitted from the RM, characterised by positive distal affect, explicit offence planning, positive pre-offence affect, a perception of mutuality with the victim during the offence and a resolve to continue offending. Thus there is early evidence that the model has *empirical adequacy*, at least with the population on which it was constructed.

Like Salter (1995), Ward et al. (1995d) noted the importance of cognitive distortions throughout the offence process, but unlike Salter, they were able to give examples of the form and prominence of such distortions at different points, and to link them to affect and behaviour at these points, suggesting greater *explanatory depth*, and also drawing attention to the importance of assessing offenders' cognitive distortions across the full offence process; they may only emerge at specific stages (*fertility*).

The model readily generates testable research questions (also *fertility*). For example, one might imagine that a self-focused offender is much less likely to notice victim distress than a victim-focused offender. The latter may therefore be more likely to take more time with grooming so that the victim is unable to express that distress, whereas the self-focused offender may use more force. Offence focus is also likely to be important in tailoring cognitive distortion interventions with different offenders.

There are a variety of limitations to the CM model. It lacks any explicit volitional component: what drives the offending? Are offenders trying to avoid offending or moving toward it with enthusiasm? Are all of these offences sexually motivated from the outset? This is an area that needs more clarity.

Although the model has a greatly improved ability to accommodate offender heterogeneity, its *scope* may still have been limited by its reliance on data from offenders who had volunteered for treatment. Use with an independent sample of untreated child molesters would help establish that it is saturated for child molesters, and the small number of rapists in the Hudson et al. sample suggests replication with more rapists is important too. The reliance on offenders' written descriptions, a lack of follow-up questioning regarding what offenders wrote and the relative brevity of these descriptions may also have constrained the model's depth. Most people who have worked to obtain good descriptions of their offences from offenders would agree that without follow-up probes, offenders often give inadequate and superficial accounts of their behaviour. Lack of literacy may have caused a selection bias too. Finally, there was no analysis of offender behaviour during the offence itself, and the influence of victim behaviour on offenders is also omitted. This is surprising given the importance of victim behaviour and offender perceptions of it in the next model.

THE POLASCHEK ET AL. RAPE MODEL

Description of the Model

The impetus to develop the rape model came from recognition of the value of the CM model in providing a clearer picture of the offence process in child sexual assault, but also a continued concern that existing research sometimes obscured the ability of researchers to detect the extent to which rape was similar and different to child sexual assault. Those who work with men who have committed sexual offences observe that there are similarities and differences between those who sexually abuse children, and those who rape adults (Pithers, 1993). There is a range of broad, multivariate aetiological theories for rape. However, at the more specific levels of theorising, rapists have often been collapsed together with child sex offenders, and the nature of the actual mechanisms involved in their offending have been poorly specified (Polaschek, Ward & Hudson, 1997). Moreover, empirical research has not yet established any effective treatment for rapists (Polaschek & King, 2002), so specific attention to these offenders appears warranted.

Polaschek, Hudson, Ward and Siegert (2001) used a modified method to collect the raw data for the rape model. Participants were 24 European New Zealand men currently incarcerated for sexual violation offences against adults. Instead of obtaining written descriptions from offenders, Polaschek et al. interviewed each offender, recording his narrative onto a portable computer, and actively questioning him throughout to gain detail and clarity about his affect, goals and behaviour, as well as his perceptions about the victim and her behaviour, and his other cognitions. Interviews lasted from 3 to 10 hours.

From these data, Polaschek et al. developed a model containing 21 main categories and 43 subcategories, divided into 6 phases containing between 3 and 5 main categories each. These six phases were I Background, II Goal formation, III Approach, IV Preparation, V Offence, and VI Post-offence (see Figure 15.4).

In Phase I Background, offenders described their *background factors* (i.e. their lifestyle and circumstances prior to offending) either in generally positive or generally negative terms, which they dealt with by using a characteristic *management (coping style)*: either problem-focused or emotion-focused. The emotion-focused style predominantly relied on strategies that temporarily ameliorate negative affect without solving the associated problem. This coping style was seen to have a bearing on the development of his *proximal mood*, which was generally positive, depressed or angry.

In Phase II Goal formation, the *establishment of dominant goals* in conjunction with *proximal mood* guided *distal goal-related planning*; planning explicitly concerned with achieving this dominant goal. Phase II goals were either to seek sexual gratification (to *enhance existing positive mood* or to *escape existing negative mood*) or to *redress perceived harm to self* (either by *harming the victim* or *solving a pre-existing problem* with her).

In Phase III Approach, offenders had *encountered the victim*, to whom they *communicated intent* explicitly related to their dominant goal, in a variety of ways. *Victim response* refers to the offenders' perceptions of the victims' reactions to their behaviour. Offenders *evaluated progress towards their goal* using information from the victim response, and other factors. Such evaluations were always consistent with the victim's perceived response (i.e. positive if she was perceived as compliant and negative if she was thought to be resisting). For about one-third of the sample the establishment of a secondary goal followed the evaluation. Such proximal goals either replaced or supplemented the (distal) dominant goal.

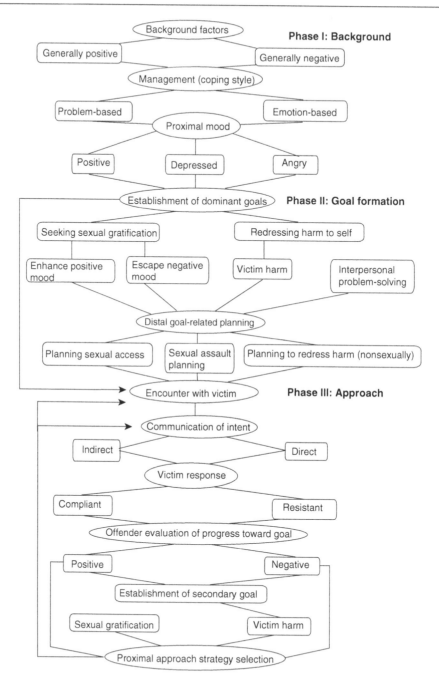

Figure 15.4 Descriptive model of rape
Source: Reprinted by permission of Taylor & Francis from Polaschek, D. L. L. & Hudson, S. M. (2004). Pathways to rape: preliminary examination of patterns in the offence processes of rapists and their rehabilitation implications. *Journal of Sexual Aggression*, 10, 9–10. http://www.tandf.co.uk/journals.

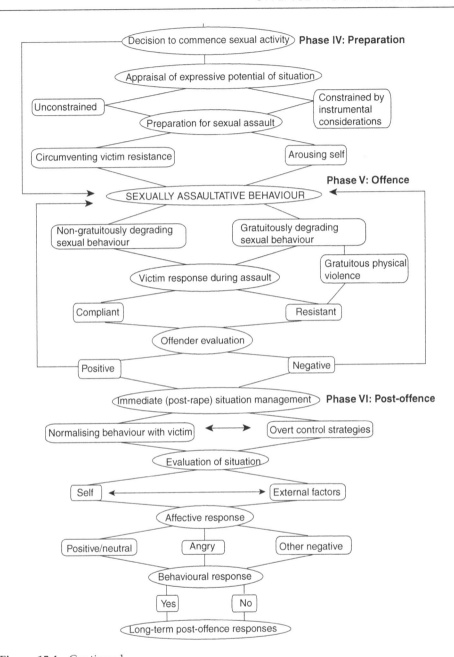

Figure 15.4 Continued

Finally, whether they formed a secondary goal or not, offenders completed their *approach* when they selected a *proximal approach strategy*; this decision either led back into another cycle of approach behaviour or, more commonly, into deciding to have sex or commit a sexual assault.

With the *decision to commence sexual activity*, Phase IV Preparation, commences. In the next stage, *appraising expressive potential of situation*, offenders decided whether they could do whatever they liked, or were constrained by the circumstances (e.g. time, risk of detection). From here offenders moved into *preparation for sexual assault*. The left-hand-side arrow shows that some offenders omitted preparation altogether.

Phase V Offence commences with *sexually assaultative behaviour*. There were two broad types, *non-gratuitously degrading sexual behaviour*, where the offender did not primarily focus his sexual behaviour on degrading the victim, and *gratuitously degrading sexual behaviour*, where the offender made a concerted effort to humiliate the victim. This phase also includes offenders' perceptions of the *victim response during assault*, and their *evaluation* of the interaction between themselves and the victim.

Once the sexual assault has been completed, Phase VI Post-offence commences with *immediate (post-rape) situation management*, where the offender is concerned with practical issues of managing the circumstances he now finds himself in. *Evaluation of the situation* then occurs; this is a broader evaluation related to the original dominant goals rather than just the immediate quality of the sexual interaction with the victim. This evaluation generates an *affective response* that ranges from neutral or positive to angry or other negative feeling, and is followed by an *immediate behavioural response*, the selection and implementation of a behaviour for ending the interaction, such as leaving the site and going home. Finally *long-term post-offence responses* refer to offenders' reactions to having committed a serious sexual assault and being convicted of it.

Evaluation

The rape model is a very detailed description of rapists' offence behaviours, and the volitional, affective and cognitive elements that go along with them. Although still clearly cognitive-behavioural in approach, it differs somewhat from the CM model in taking a more descriptive, offender-centred approach, more typical of research in ethnographic criminology (e.g. Cromwell, Olson & Avary, 1991). This distinction is particularly important when considering the goals of rape. Few previous descriptive models have given the exact nature of goals specific attention. One reason for this omission may be that most models assume that the offender's dominant goal throughout the offence process is to commit a sexual assault—usually for sexual gratification—and thus that all behaviour is in the service of this goal (e.g. Carich, 1994; Salter, 1995; Ward & Hudson, 1998b). This assumption immediately requires another: that from early in the offence process, all offenders are *planning* to commit a sexual assault. When the inteviewer fails to uncover overt evidence of sexual assault planning, implicit or covert planning must be assumed. Variations in the types of goals and the strategies for achieving them may also have been often ignored because most offence cycle models in this chapter have focused primarily on sexual offending against children; the main goals suggested for child sexual abuse are assumed to be sexual or intimacy-related (Knight & Prentky, 1990).

The authors of the rape model (Polaschek et al., 2001) decided to build it around offenders' explicit rather than inferred goals for several reasons. First, a wider range of goals have been implicated in sexual aggression towards adults, including more enduring interest in sexual gratification, antisocial opportunism, intimacy and victim harm goals (see Knight, Rosenberg & Schneider, 1985; Pithers, 1993). Second, there are many legitimate reasons for men to spend time alone with adult women, obviating the need for the extended planning that can be required to gain suitable access to children. In fact Polaschek et al. argued that many kinds of rape require little or no planning, and minimal skill. So on balance, if there was no actual evidence that distal goals were sexual in nature, Polaschek et al. decided to assume that they were not. Although opening researchers to accusations of serious gullibility, taking goals at face value does avoid the problem of suggesting that researchers have privileged access to offenders' mental processes.

The RM's *fertility* as a potential classification tool and in suggesting distinct treatment implications was recently examined by Polaschek and Hudson (2004), who found three distinct pathways through the model that show promise in disentangling the issue of how to best provide for rapists' diverse treatment needs (Polaschek & King, 2002). One pathway closely resembled the RM, while another was more like those associated with physically violent offences (Polaschek & Murdoch, unpublished data) and suggested that such men might be successfully treated in programmes equipped to deal with violent offenders. A third was associated with positive affect, a preference for frequent sexual contacts with interpersonally insignificant partners, and the exploitation of situations in which it is difficult for victims to decline consent (e.g. assaulting intoxicated or sleeping victims).

The model broadly is consistent with existing level I theories of rape (*external consistency*). However, the right-hand track through the model comprised an initial goal of redressing harm to self, the use of coercive and aggressive tactics to achieve this goal, and then later sexual assault either as victim punishment or as a response to the situation of having control of a potential sexual partner. These forms of offence are not particularly well captured in current multivariate theories, other than perhaps Malamuth's (see Chapter 6). More consideration of this pathway may stimulate treatment innovation with rapists (*fertility*).

The rape model has various limitations. First, the focus on a more overtly descriptive model shares with some of the other models a corresponding reduction in *explanatory* depth. Its complexity makes it difficult to grasp and use, and may hide problems with *internal coherence*. Further collapsing of the categories may increase its attractiveness and heuristic value, and make the underlying mechanisms clearer. Some categories appear redundant, in that they do not separate offences from each other: self- and external evaluation in the post-offence phase is one example. And it is likely that some categories are much more important than others in distinguishing between offence pathways. Polaschek and Hudson (2004) found that when pathways were organised around offence goals, some categories systematically co-varied with those goals, but others showed no pattern. These concerns suggest that the model may not be fully saturated, an observation that is supported by Polaschek (1999), who noted that the sample contained few very violent offences, no overt sadists, no offenders who committed their rapes in the context of a stranger burglary, just two offences against male victims, and although a lot of victims were acquaintances and current and ex-partners, none were dates. However, recent analysis that included new offences suggested no clear evidence of a need to extend the model (Polaschek & Gannon, 2004).

TREATMENT IMPLICATIONS

Offence process models have a key role in theory development, in ensuring that higher level theorising recognises fully the phenomenon it seeks to explain. However, most offence process models—including those in the previous chapter— were developed to meet the needs of therapists. As a result, there is some confusion about their appropriate use. We attempt to clarify these issues below.

Offence process models can be thought of as models of an *event*: in this case a sexual assault. As such, they can do a good job of highlighting important stages in the path to carrying out an offence, but they are not a substitute for models and theories that describe how a propensity for sexual offending develops in the first place (i.e. aetiological models), and how it is maintained in a particular offending career.

For example, an offender may experience chronic loneliness, and conflict in adult relationships, along with depression, underemployment and financial troubles, which he mismanages by getting drunk. Or he may fraternise with pro-offending friends, taking drugs and behaving in a hostile manner towards women as a vehicle for chronic anger derived from childhood abuse and neglect. However, in his current offence although these issues will show up in the very early stages of the offence process, offence process models do not assist therapists in unpacking the relevance of these issues to current offending risk. In part they do not do this because that is what aetiological models do (see Chapter 5 for an example).

Are these issues important for treatment? Actually they are probably *more* important than such matters as planning and victim-approach behaviours in reducing risk. As we noted in Chapter 13, Hanson and Harris (2000a) distinguished between *acute* and *stable* dynamic risk factors. Acute factors are those that occur in the minutes, hours and days before an offence. Stable factors are those that are changeable, but without personal effort may endure for months or even years. Hanson and Harris state that 'acute dynamic factors are related to the timing of re-offending but they may have little relationship to long-term risk potential' (2000a, p. 7). As such, they suggest that intervention must target stable, not acute, dynamic factors (e.g. alcohol intoxication, anger, access to victim) to create the greatest possibility for reduced risk.

By contrast, acute factors on the path to offending are much harder to control, and we have no real idea whether offenders actually can pull themselves back once they have started to move towards an offence. Thus the most important function of the offence process in treatment is to provide information that will be used for acute risk management once the offender has completed treatment. Offence process models are not intended to serve as some kind of template for the treatment structure itself. They are not and never will be theoretically adequate for this task.

Surely this is an obvious point? Polaschek (2003c) noted that many programmes describe themselves as following the 'relapse prevention model', but often provide little detail about how. One possibility is that programmes are using the Pithers–Marques relapse model (see Chapter 14) as a structure from which all treatment targets emerge. Eccles and Marshall's (1999) critique of the Ward et al. (1995d) CM model is certainly consistent with this view. Eccles and Marshall note that stage 1 of the CM model contains all of the relevant current issues and childhood factors, and gives them little attention. In fact, they go on to say that 'Ward et al., by collapsing so many factors into stage 1, fail to emphasise the importance of each of them, so there is a risk that important predisposing factors will receive only brief consideration in treatment' (p. 135). Marshall and Eccles clearly express concern that this is how such models are used by some therapists, even though they should not be.

So this is the first point: offence process models, when used in treatment, are not intended to provide an adequate basis on which to design an individual intervention. However, they are very useful in helping offenders to (i) develop personal motivation to undertake pertinent treatment elements by identifying their own idiosyncratic habits, and (ii) develop plans for subverting those habits before they reinstate themselves fully.

A second point is that offence process models are not intended for direct use with offender clients, in modules that focus on identifying each person's offence process. Some of the models reviewed here, with their simple descriptive terms (e.g. Freeman-Longo's model: build-up → acting out → justification → pretend normal), appear to be serving to 'inform' both offenders and therapists. This is a concern. How can such a theoretically impoverished model provide enough of a substrate for effective therapist guidance?

The descriptive models covered in the last part of this chapter are intended to help treatment agents in recognising the diversity of offence processes, goals and strategies: how various components of cognition, affect and behaviour interact to create these offences. Other than Salter's cycle, which is vague but appears to allow for multiple pathways, all of the earlier models, and the relapse model itself, have inadequate scope; they simply omit common offence pathways and emphasise a single, not-so-common one. If presented in treatment as a template for offender use, offenders have to force their offences to conform in ways that may cause them to feel alienated from the treatment process ('they don't understand me; I really didn't plan how to rape my victim, I was already living with her'). Second, if offenders learn the wrong sequence of offence components in order to manage reoffending risk, they may fail to recognise the actual sequence when it happens.

Adequate offence process models can certainly shed light on treatment needs. For example, different pathways through the rape model highlight the importance of education around the concept of consent versus non-consent for some rapists. For others attitudes to violence will be more important because they already understand that they did not have consent. However, many treatment targets will also come from careful unpacking of the predisposition to offend in each offender. The availability and utility of offence process models does not substitute for these assessment processes. Clearly the best of such models also guide therapists through offender assessment. Offenders need their own models, usually simple templates to help shape their offence disclosures. For example, for this purpose we often have used a circle divided into four segments: background, build-up, offence, post-offence.

CONCLUSIONS

In contrast to the previous chapter, this one has presented a series of offence cycles and process models with a predominantly descriptive focus. These models vary from simple cyclical rubrics for use with offender clients who are disclosing their own offence chains, through to elaborate multiple-pathway models based on rigorous analysis of transcript data. The majority of these models appear to be clinical practice-derived modifications of the relapse prevention model (Pithers et al., 1983). And they share its pitfalls; in particular, their preoccupation with a negative affect-initiated single pathway to relapse suggests that they are not valid for sole use with sex offenders, now that there is substantial empirical evidence of the need for multiple pathways in such models. We argued in the previous chapter that, theoretically, the relapse model was internally incoherent in some aspects. However, these offspring have little or no obvious theoretical basis. Instead, some appear primarily phenomenological, and so it is hard to judge what were the developers' objectives in departing from the relapse model.

Others do a more comprehensive job of accommodating accurately the clinical realities of sexual offending. Salter's (1995) deviant cycle, and both the child molester and the rape descriptive models are examples of richer, denser models.

Offence process models have an important role in sex offender intervention. Their most appropriate use is in identifying risk management issues and strategies, and helping motivate offenders to take control of their destinies through understanding their own habitual patterns. Offence process analysis mainly reveals *acute dynamic* risk factors. But *stable dynamic* risk factors should be the main focus of sex offender treatment aimed at long-term behavioural change. Analysis of the upper portion of an offence process *can* provide evidence of stable dynamic risk factors but a complete formulation of these issues requires detailed unpacking of an offender's predisposition to commit sexual offences. Offender predisposition is only obliquely reflected in the offence process itself.

To use the offence chain to determine the content of treatment, the length of time spent on each component and even the ordering of the elements is to misunderstand its contribution to theory and treatment. Offence process research has come a long way in the past decade, but we hope that this book makes it evident that all three levels of theory are necessary to inform fully the treatment endeavour.

PART V

TREATMENT THEORIES

Chapter 16
THE RISK–NEED TREATMENT MODEL

The treatment of sexual and general offenders is a potential public relations disaster. The general public is more concerned with reducing their chances of being robbed, and assaulted, or with being the target of some other kind of crime than in the welfare of individuals who inflict these harms on others (Garland, 2001). In fact, what the public wants when they hear of a serious crime is punishment for the offender because of the misconception that this will stop recidivism (Ogloff & Davis, 2004). Treatment is only tolerated if it is effective in lowering recidivism rates and saving the community money and suffering. Public attitudes toward serious offenders are even more punitive and they are frequently regarded as intrinsically bad or flawed individuals who by virtue of their antisocial actions have forfeited any rights to be considered part of the community (Kekes, 1990). In other words, the implicit idea is that criminal actions are committed by bad people whose ongoing welfare and happiness should not be the concern of any law-abiding citizen.

An important implication of these attitudes toward crime and the treatment of offenders is that correctional policy is typically formulated in terms of harm reduction, or lowered recidivism rates. The aim of intervening with offenders is primarily to prevent future harm to innocent people: in other words, to reduce the risk to the community. Rehabilitation initiatives based on the promotion of offender happiness are unlikely to be adopted and, in fact, are rarely sighted in the current correctional landscape (Ogloff & Davis, 2004).

The problem for clinicians and policy makers desperate to reduce reoffending rates is how to work within the constraints imposed by negative views of treatment and to avoid a simplistic punishment-based treatment model. According to the deterrence perspective, simply inflicting punishments on offenders will be enough to modify their future behaviour and therefore to lower the crime rate. Unfortunately, there is precious little evidence that such a strategy is effective, and it has been argued by some researchers that punishment or deterrence approaches to the problem of crime may in fact increase recidivism rates (Andrews & Bonta, 1998; Hollin, 1999; McGuire, 2000). Thus, those individuals interested in helping offenders to modify their behaviour are caught on the horns of a dilemma. If treatment is offered to offenders then therapists and correctional policy makers are accused of being soft on crime and may find that their funding dries up. On the other hand, simply punishing those who commit criminal acts is unlikely to promote prosocial behaviour.

The solution to this dilemma is to base interventions on the principles of risk and need, and therefore to focus therapy on individual and social risk factors that are likely to reduce crime rates if suitably modified. In our view this insight has resulted in the development of a suite of empirically derived and effective treatments for a range of crimes, including sexual offending, and has constituted a revolution in the way criminal conduct is managed in Canada, the UK, Europe, Australia and New Zealand. The principal architects of the risk–need (RN) model of offender rehabilitation are the Canadian researchers James Bonta, Don Andrews and Paul Gendreau (e.g. Andrews & Bonta, 1998; Gendreau & Andrews, 1990).

In this chapter we outline the theoretical assumptions underlying the RN model, then we critically evaluate this model, and finally, we discuss the clinical utility of this model for the treatment of sex offenders. It is important to note that the RN model was developed to guide the treatment of offenders in general and not just sexual offenders. However, its general principles underlie much of relapse prevention and the current emphasis of the field on risk management.

THE RISK–NEED MODEL

A good theory of rehabilitation should specify the aims of therapy, provide an aetiological justification of these aims, identify clinical targets, and outline how treatment should proceed in the light of these assumptions and goals. Aetiological theories and practice models are conceptually linked by an overarching theory of rehabilitation, which functions as a bridging theory. The bridge is between factors that are thought to cause offending and the way treatment strategies are actually implemented. The RN model is an example of a rehabilitation theory, and as such has a number of assumptions about the causes of crime and the aim of treatment. First, it assumes that the best way to reduce recidivism rates is to identify and reduce or eliminate an individual's array of dynamic risk factors (these are the aims and aetiological assumption). Second, the concern (a values-based commitment) is to reduce harm to the community through the management of dynamic risk factors (e.g. antisocial attitudes and deviant sexual arousal). Third, these factors constitute clinical needs or problems that should be explicitly targeted (identification of clinical treatment targets). Fourth, according to the RN model, risk assessment should drive the treatment process and offenders' assessed levels of risk should determine the intensity and duration of treatment. It is assumed that focusing rehabilitation on dynamic risk factors (or criminogenic needs; see below) will result in better outcomes. This is achieved through the reduction or management of psychological and social characteristics found to be associated with criminal acts and increased offending rates (treatment style). In sexual offending treatment the RN model is translated into a relapse prevention approach where the implementation of treatment revolves around teaching individuals how to recognise and cope with risk factors.

The Psychology of Criminal Conduct (PCC)

The PCC (Andrews & Bonta, 1998) is a complex theory of criminal behaviour based on a number of cognitive, behavioural, biological and situational factors. It provides the conceptual base for the RN model although this is rarely acknowledged by its proponents (Ward & Stewart, 2003a). A key assumption of the PCC is that criminal behaviour is acquired and maintained through a combination of operant and classical conditioning, and observational learning (Andrews & Bonta, 1998). The theory also utilises ideas from differential association theory (Sutherland, 1939), claiming that individuals can adopt antisocial attitudes, goals and behaviours though their association with people who already fail to inhibit antisocial behaviour (not necessarily offenders). If antisocial behaviour is reinforced through rewards or escape from painful stimuli, it is likely to be strengthened and become part of a person's general repertoire in the future. In addition to direct experience, individuals also learn from *observing* other people and noticing whether their actions are punished or reinforced. A good example of social learning in a criminal context is when a young man watches his father 'solve' interpersonal conflicts through the use of violence, resulting in him using the same tactics as an adult. The PCC argues that personality dispositions such as impulsivity, lack of social skills and antisocial attitudes can predispose some people to commit an offence in certain circumstances; they are essentially vulnerability factors. What this means in practice is that offenders will behave in antisocial ways for varying reasons and therefore exhibit different profiles of risk factors. Treatment providers need to take these individual differences into account. Otherwise an intervention programme is likely to be ineffective. Thus the main assumption of the PCC is that people behave antisocially for various reasons, and as a consequence of these differences will exhibit varying levels of risk.

Principles of the Risk–Need Model

The emphasis of the PCC on dynamic risk factors and its stress on taking individual risk profiles into account when planning treatment has resulted in the formulation of a number of principles of effective rehabilitation: the risk, need, responsivity and professional discretion principles (Andrews & Bonta, 1998). The first two principles are to be used to select treatment targets, and the whole set used to guide the way practice is actually implemented.

First, the *risk* principle is concerned with the match between individuals' levels of risk for reoffending and the amount of treatment they should receive. The assumption is that risk is a rough indicator of clinical need and therefore according to this principle, high-risk individuals should receive the most treatment, typically at least 100 hours of cognitive-behavioural interventions

(Hollin, 1999). Those offenders displaying moderate levels of risk should receive a lesser dose of treatment, while those designated as low risk warrant little, if any, intervention. Risk can be divided into static and dynamic risk factors (see Chapter 13). Static risk factors are variables that cannot be changed; for example, historical markers of recidivism such as number of past offences or gender. Dynamic risk factors are attributes of the individual or of his or her situation that are able to be modified in some important respects; for example, impulsiveness or deviant sexual preferences. Furthermore, an important assumption is that the severity of risk (i.e. whether low, medium or high) is likely to co-vary with the intensity and depth of the criminogenic needs present.

Second, according to the *need* principle, treatment programmes for offenders should primarily focus on changing criminogenic needs; that is, dynamic offender characteristics that, when changed, are associated with reduced recidivism rates. These include pro-offending attitudes, aspects of antisocial personality (e.g. impulsiveness), poor problem solving, substance abuse, high hostility and anger, and criminal associates (Andrews & Bonta, 1998). Criminogenic needs are identified in at least three different ways: though the statistical examination of large data sets (the major means of identification), theoretically, and through clinical observation. Therefore they may vary for different types of crimes. They are primarily empirically derived and according to Andrews and Bonta, the process of detecting them is value-free. Examples of criminogenic needs for sexual offenders are deviant sexual arousal, intimacy deficits and loneliness, and problems with emotional regulation (Hanson & Harris, 2000a). Criminogenic needs are contrasted with non-criminogenic needs, which according to the RN model are aspects of the individual or his or her circumstances that if changed may not have a direct impact on recidivism rates. Examples of non-criminogenic needs are clinical phenomena such as low self-esteem and mental health problems such as depression or unresolved grief. While clinicians may sometimes decide to treat non-criminogenic needs in therapy, they should not expect their efforts to result in lower recidivism rates. For example, setting out to enhance an offender's self-esteem may leave him feeling better about himself, but according to Andrews and Bonta will not on its own reduce reoffending rates. In fact, according to some research, targeting such variables may in fact increase an individual's chances of reoffending (Ogloff & Davis, 2004).

It is important to note that both criminogenic and non-criminogenic needs are not to be equated with primary human needs (see below and Chapter 18) but are best viewed as problems. Primary human needs are propensities for engaging in certain activities that are essential for human well-being, for example, hunger, thirst, security, relatedness, autonomy and competence (Deci & Ryan, 2000). Secondary needs—also called instrumental needs—are ways of achieving or meeting primary needs, such as types of relationships or accommodation. In the Level of Service Inventory—Revised (LSI-R) designed by Andrews and Bonta (1995) to enable clinicians to identify offender problems, they include items such as accommodation or financial problems, which are in effect instrumental or secondary needs. They also include some items that point to primary human needs (e.g. companions) but do not explicitly consider the relationship between human needs and risk factors (see below).

Third, the *responsivity* principle is used to refer to the use of a style and mode of intervention that engages the interest of the client group and takes into account their relevant characteristics, such as cognitive ability, learning style and values (Andrews & Bonta, 1998). In other words, responsivity is concerned with how the individual interacts with the treatment environment, and covers a range of factors and situations. Responsivity can be divided further into internal and external responsivity (Andrews, 2001). Attention to internal responsivity factors requires therapists to match the content and pace of sessions to specific client attributes such as personality and cognitive maturity. External responsivity refers to a range of general and specific issues, such as the use of active and participatory methods. External responsivity can be divided further into staff and setting characteristics (Kennedy, 2001; Serin & Kennedy, 1997). Within the broad responsivity principle resides an invitation to attend to an offender's motivation to engage in therapy and to commit to change. Responsivity as usually understood in the rehabilitation literature is primarily concerned with therapist and therapy features and is, therefore, essentially concerned with adjusting treatment delivery in a way that maximises learning.

Finally, the principle of *professional discretion* states that clinical judgement should override the above principles if circumstances warrant it. This principle allows for treatment flexibility and innovation under certain circumstances. For example, if a man is extremely distressed after hearing that his wife has left him, it may be sensible to spend some time listening to his worries and dealing with the practical issues this event entails rather than simply moving on to the next scheduled phase of treatment. According to Andrews and Bonta, it is critical that the principle of professional discretion is not applied in an overly liberal manner, otherwise the principles of risk and need may be violated.

The implications of the RN model for assessment and treatment of offenders are quite significant. First, an adequate assessment should be comprehensive and should cover the variables research has determined predict reoffending. To help in this process, Andrews and Bonta (1995) developed the LSI-R, a 54-item measure that addresses a wide range of static and dynamic variables associated with criminal conduct. The domains covered by the LSI-R instrument include offending history, education, employment, family and marital relationships, accommodation, friendships, the use of alcohol and drugs, emotional problems and attitudes toward offending (Andrews & Bonta, 1995). Instruments such as the LSI-R and measures of risk are used to allocate offenders to treatment programmes and to determine the necessary intensity or 'dose' of treatment.

Second, in conjunction with empirical validation, Andrews and Bonta (1998) stressed that there are six main principles needed for effective rehabilitation. They argue that treatment programmes should be: (i) cognitive-behavioural in orientation, (ii) highly structured, specifying the aims and tasks to be covered in each session, (iii) implemented by trained, qualified and appropriately super-vised staff, (iv) delivered in the correct manner to ensure treatment integrity, (v) manual based and (vi) housed within institutions with personnel committed to the ideals of rehabilitation (Andrews & Bonta, 1998; Hollin, 1999; McGuire, 2002; McGuire & Priestly, 1995; Ogloff & Davis, 2004). According to the proponents of the RN model, we now have considerable knowledge and technology to aid in the reduction of reoffending rates, and this implies that the debate over whether or not it is possible to rehabilitate offenders is at an end. From this perspective, arguably it is simply a question of continuing to refine treatment strategies and increase our understanding of the variables that contribute towards criminal actions.

Finally, researchers and theorists are continuing to strengthen the RN model, and one area of current interest is that of responsivity, including the problem of offender motivation. In particular, Ogloff and Davis (2004) have made some valuable suggestions for improving treatment outcome by addressing *responsivity impediments* such as acute mental illness and lack of motivation. They suggest that these problems can adversely affect offenders' ability to behave autonomously and therefore should be dealt with before embarking on treatment targeting criminogenic needs. Furthermore, Ogloff and Davis recommend that following sufficient progress in reducing criminogenic needs, efforts can be made to enhance offenders' well-being and therefore help them to adopt ways of living that will prove more satisfying than a criminal lifestyle.

EVALUATION OF THE RISK–NEED MODEL

The RN model of offender rehabilitation is a wonderful achievement that has helped to reduce reoffending rates in correctional populations. The provision of the four principles in conjunction with the PCC, which provides the underlying explanatory theory for the RN model, gives clinicians a clear structure for the assessment and treatment of offenders. It could be argued that the RN model is a complex suite of ideas and theories that collectively constitute a powerful rehabilitation approach. The component ideas are social learning theory (SLT), the PCC and the four principles outlined above. Certainly, this is the view of eminent researchers and theorists (e.g. C. R. Hollin, personal communication, February 2005). If one accepts this view, then any evaluation should take into account the complete suite of ideas rather than focus simply on one or more of them. While we accept that this is a plausible argument, it is our experience that the RN model is often operationalised only in terms of the four rehabilitation principles. We would also like to suggest that despite Andrews and Bonta's, and others, claims, the complete theory (i.e. the PCC, the four principles and SLT) has not been consistently presented as *the RN model*. Therefore, in this chapter we will focus primarily on the four principles and only make the occasional comments about the other two components.

In the sexual offending field, the shift to a risk management perspective and the focus of therapeutic efforts on the modification of acute and stable dynamic risk factors (see Chapter 13) means that the RN model is essentially the premier rehabilitation theory. This feature speaks to the *fertility* (clinical utility) of the RN model. A second strength is the fact that the theory is underpinned by a strong empirical base, and therefore assessment and treatment strategies are carefully evaluated and tested to ensure their validity and reliability (McGuire, 2002). This feature of the theory reflects its *empirical scope* and *adequacy*. Third, the claim that crime is a multifaceted phenomena and the incorporation in the PCC of a wide range of variables and learning principles attest to the RN model's potential *unifying* power.

Alongside these strengths, in our opinion, are a number of weaknesses. We have written extensively on these problems in a number of publications (see Ward & Stewart, 2003a, b), and in this chapter will deal only with some of the most pressing issues raised in these critiques. However, we will still examine the theory in considerable depth because of its importance in the sexual offending field.

Risk and Treatment

Our first point concerns the clinical utility of using estimated risk levels to make decisions about the type and extent of treatment offenders receive. Of course, there is some evidence supporting this procedure, but we would advise against relying routinely on this strategy. One reason for this is because we believe that treating sexual offenders also involves taking into consideration human welfare issues, as well as recidivism issues. This is because offenders are much more likely to respond to treatment initiatives if they feel the therapists are genuinely interested in them as people and also if they are likely to have better lives as a consequence of giving up crime.

Individuals who are assessed as low risk may exhibit a number of significant problems that adversely impact on their functioning, for example, low mood or relationship conflict. While such problems may not be criminogenic needs, individuals could still benefit from therapeutic attention and the untreated problems may have a downstream effect on their chances of being effectively rehabilitated. As an example, a man who is feeling depressed or anxious may fail to apply for a potentially valuable vocational programme because he sees it as irrelevant to his current problems. It is also possible that the psychological consequences of not being treated for non-criminogenic needs could later result in increased offending and subsequent elevated risk level. For example, feelings of resentment and deprivation arising from refusal of treatment could cause violent behaviour in prison and the development of antisocial tendencies. It is important to note that this point is based on clinical observation and not supported currently by research evidence. The RN model argues that it is not necessary to focus on these type of problems.

A complicating factor is that many of the risk assessment instruments used by psychologists to determine a person's overall level of risk for reoffending rely on static factors (e.g. Static-99; see Chapter 13). Criminogenic needs frequently are not assessed systematically at all and only factored into a case formulation in an ad hoc manner. The failure explicitly to measure dynamic risk factors might result in an inability to detect individuals who could be low risk on a static measure but high risk (need) once dynamic factors are considered. It is also possible to encounter offenders who are assessed as high risk but appear to have relatively low needs, at least in some respect. Such individuals could have quite circumscribed problems that may put them at risk for reoffending, but do not display a *wide range* of problems. For example, a high functioning sexual offender may possess some problems in establishing intimate relationship with adults but possess excellent self-regulation, emotional and general social skills (Ward & Siegert, 2002b). Such an individual might need intensive schema-related work to modify his deeply rooted fears about intimacy, but very little else. The danger is that by designating him as high risk the assumption will be that he also has significant clinical needs and he will be subjected to hours of needless therapy. What this example illustrates is the dependence of the risk principle on a comprehensive measure of criminogenic needs that allows for a determination of the number and severity of a person's problems and their causal relationship to his offence. This means going beyond simple psychometric assessment to the explicit construction of a case formulation (McGuire, 2000). Thus, the relationship between level of risk (an estimate or prediction) and level of clinical need is a complex one and not exhausted by the symmetry *implied* in the risk–need principle (i.e. high risk equates to greater number of needs). It must be noted that in our opinion this is implicit in the RN model and not explicitly stated. This concern indicates a possible lack of *coherence* in the theory.

Risk Management

A second point is that basing treatment on *risk management* assumes that the major aim of rehabilitation is to reduce the chances of harm to a community and that this is best achieved by managing risk. There are two problems with this assumption. First, it is unclear how an approach focused on the prevention of harmful consequences to others can encourage offenders to change their own behaviour in fundamental ways. This is really an issue of how best to motivate offenders to engage in therapy (see Chapter 18). Second, while the RN model is concerned with meeting secondary needs such as accommodation, it does not explicitly consider the role of primary human needs (e.g. relatedness, autonomy and their attendant goods). In our view, focusing on secondary needs in the absence of primary needs does not make much (theoretical) sense although it has a direct effect in reducing offending. The difficulty is that in the absence of a theoretical analysis we do not know why.

The first problem here is that while reduction of risk to the community is an excellent social aim, it does not translate well into clinical aims when working with individual offenders. What is required at this level is some attention to helping offenders build better lives through the attainment of primary human goods, in ways that are personally meaningful and satisfying, and socially acceptable. Second, concentrating on criminogenic needs is arguably not that helpful to clinicians (and offenders) because it encourages them to focus largely on the elimination or modification of offender problems rather than on what factors to promote or enhance (see Chapter 18). Furthermore, because the RN model is silent on the issue of how human needs are related to criminogenic needs, it does not give clinicians much guidance in formulating a more constructive approach. Avoidance goals (e.g., the elimination of risk factors) are extremely difficult to achieve, because they do not specify what should be sought but merely what should be avoided or escaped from (Mann, Webster, Schofield & Marshall, 2004). Therefore, any therapeutic approach based on a risk management model needs to be supplemented by additional theories that specify what goods or goals are to be sought and how this can happen (see Chapter 18). For example, a treatment goal that focuses on the acquisition of relationship skills is more useful than one that simply aims to reduce intimacy deficits. The RN model can easily accommodate approach goals, but in our experience it is often implemented in a simple minded way, and clinicians can forget this important point. Motivational concepts like that of need, which concern specific goals and valued outcomes, provide exactly this type of guidance.

Status as a Theory

The RN model is not a comprehensive theory of rehabilitation at all: it is essentially a set of principles that are related loosely. It is important for a rehabilitation theory to function as a bridge between aetiological assumptions and the implementation of treatment. The trouble is that there is simply not enough substance to the RN model to do this adequately. Furthermore, the RN model does not provide an integrated abstract or theoretical account of how the different criminogenic needs interact to produce criminal conduct. As stated earlier, it is arguable that the RN model involves the PCC and social learning theory, but in our experience this fact is often forgotten, and the four principles are regarded as the core or basis of this approach to rehabilitation. Because of the way Andrews and Bonta (1998) conceptualised risk (see below), criminogenic needs are derived statistically from large data sets and examined individually for their ability to predict reoffending. Thus in our view, according to the RN model each risk factor has its own (statistical) relationship to reoffending and functions somewhat in isolation from the others. In addition, the PCC is really only a theoretical framework describing how developmental, early learning, family relations, school experiences and so on could converge to produce crime-supportive appraisals. It does not go beneath the surface to propose in detail exactly how these variables interact to create different aetiological pathways to offending. Therefore, the RN model is an *incomplete* rehabilitation theory, and the PCC, which is supposed to provide an explanation of how criminogenic needs are created, is not a well developed supporting aetiological theory. These features indicate that the RN model lacks *scope* and *explanatory depth*.

Criminogenic Needs as Range Riders

For the most part, criminogenic needs are little more than range riders: they simply inform therapists that a problem exists in some domain but do not specify how it is to be resolved. For this, substantive theories about the need in question (e.g. impulsiveness or deviant sexual preferences) are required. Such a theory should spell out how to effect change in the relevant mechanisms that cause impulsiveness and also explain how it relates to other criminogenic needs. It should also explain how the particular criminogenic need in question is generated and what mechanisms are currently contributing to its maintenance. This is clinically useful because different aetiological pathways to offending require distinct intervention plans (see Chapter 1). A policy that states simply that criminogenic needs should be primary treatment targets without invoking additional theory and clinical models will not result in effective treatment. While Andrews and Bonta have recognised this and tried to construct a broad psychological theory of criminal conduct, their theory is essentially a framework and does not provide clear descriptions of the relevant causal mechanisms that generate criminogenic needs. This problem points to a lack of *fertility* with respect to treatment guidance.

The Conceptualisation of Risk

It is clear that the concept of risk plays a pivotal role in the RN model, but strangely enough there is no attempt by Andrews and Bonta (1998) to articulate the conceptual basis for this concept in their theory. This is a problem because in the correctional domain risk has been construed in at least two quite different ways: *fluid risk* and *categorical risk* (Brown, 2000). Fluid risk is viewed as consisting of discrete individual characteristics associated with offending behaviour, and thus risk is thought to exist on an identifiable underlying behavioural continuum ranging from low to high. The core idea is that individuals are basically a bundle or cluster of properties that are in principle observable and measurable. The methods used to assess risk are analytic and reductionist, enabling clinicians to examine the relationship of specific characteristics to criminal behaviour. Risk factors are thought to be susceptible to manipulation and management and therefore rehabilitation programmes set out to target identified risk factors and to teach the offender new, pro-social ways of thinking and acting. The idea is to give individuals the skills necessary to cope with problems in socially acceptable ways. In a theoretical analysis Brown states that it is this fluid risk model that underlies psychological and psychiatric estimates of risk.

According to the categorical model (Brown, 2000), risk reflects aspects of human character (e.g. virtue) and therefore it is categorical rather than continuous in nature. Individuals are arguably best viewed as autonomous agents who act upon the world in such a manner that expresses aspects of their character. It is this expression of character that enables perceptive observers to estimate whether or not offenders constitute an ongoing risk to themselves or the community. Thus, risk markers in the categorical view of risk are carefully considered features of human individuality rather than disembodied and atomised 'factors' (as in the fluid risk assessment). A good example of a character-based characteristic relevant to risk assessment is remorse. For risk evaluators relying on the categorical model, remorse is viewed as a virtue indicating that a person truly understands the harm he has done. In addition, the presence of remorse reveals a determination to accept responsibility for his criminal conduct and a desire to change his or her antisocial inclinations. Therefore, from the perspective of the categorical model, risk cannot be 'measured' in a quantitative manner but can be assessed only through systematic and careful judgement: a holistic and partly intuitive process. The preferred intervention approach is not the packaged cognitive or skills approach characteristic of most contemporary psychological treatment programmes but rather assistance in personal development that would allow the individual concerned to reform his or her character, and to experience the appropriate moral emotions. According to Brown the categorical risk model frequently underlies the assessments of judicial decision makers and other criminal justice practitioners, who reject the quantitative model of risk assessment.

The difficulty is that correctional professionals such as psychologists, correctional officers, policy analysts and judges rarely acknowledge that they work with contrasting models of risk, and therefore often talk at cross-purposes when discussing risk assessment with each other. It is clear to us that the RN model assumes the validity of the fluid conception of risk and therefore is most concerned with issues of management, and disinterested in questions of value or character, unless the latter are viewed as sources of antisocial behaviour that can be measured. Both models have their basis in broader conceptualisations of the world and of the nature of people. In our view, it would be helpful to openly debate the issue of risk conceptualisation and to deepen our understanding of this complex topic. We do not assume that one model is more valid than the other, but would simply like to point out that each has its domain of application and should be a focus of critical inquiry. Failure to consider alternative ways of understanding risk and rehabilitation is likely to hinder the effective treatment of offenders rather than facilitate the process. This feature of the risk–need model indicates its lack of *unifying power* and *external consistency*.

The Relationship between Human Needs and Criminogenic Needs

Despite utilising the concept of need (i.e. in the formulation of *criminogenic* needs) in the formulation of the RN model, the concept is not systematically discussed or its relationship to criminogenic needs analysed. In our view this is a real pity because there is potentially a fruitful relationship between human needs and criminogenic needs that could help to resolve certain problems in offender treatment. For one thing, human needs and their attendant human goods are inherently motivating and, second, it is arguable that offenders are seeking to meet their needs (or to obtain certain primary goods) through their criminal conduct.

But, what is a human need? Deci and Ryan (2000) usefully define human needs as 'innate psychological nutriments that are essential for ongoing psychological growth, integrity, and well-being' (p. 229). Thus, human needs outline the conditions essential for psychological well-being, which must be met in an appropriate manner for individuals to experience deep satisfaction and happiness. If basic physical, social or psychological (i.e. primary) human needs are not met then a person is likely to be harmed in some manner: for example, suffer physical ill health or lowered levels of psychological well-being. Basic needs require external and internal conditions for their fulfilment: for example, adequate parenting, opportunities to learn and make independent decisions, and the possession of skills necessary to establish intimate relationships. There is not much point in having a need for relationships if an individual lacks the social skills required to communicate effectively with another person, or simply does not have the opportunity to interact with others. The various goods or valued activities that typically comprise a satisfying life (e.g. health, knowledge, creativity and friendship) are only possible if basic human needs are being met (Braybrooke, 1987; Thomson, 1987).

In our view criminogenic needs are not primary human needs. To have a *need* indicates a deficiency of some kind, a lack of a valued good. Needs are concerned with the attainment of objective goods that sustain or enhance an individual's life; their absence will likely result in some kind of harm, or increase the chances of harm occurring in the future. It does not make much sense to say that a criminogenic need such as impulsivity is designed to achieve an objective good, or, alternatively, to speak of a need to behave impulsively. Therefore, criminogenic needs are not basic or primary human needs (Wiggins, 1991).

Perhaps it is possible to view criminogenic needs as instrumental (i.e. secondary) needs? Recall that secondary needs are ways of achieving primary needs. Under this interpretation, impulsivity would be instrumentally related to criminal actions and therefore would provide a means to the goals associated with a particular crime. The claim that a criminogenic need such as impulsivity is instrumentally related to further offending suggests that individuals choose to act in an impulsive manner in order to achieve the further goal of offending. (Of course Andrews and Bonta would not claim this to be the case.) It is confusing to view what is essentially a loss of behavioural control as an intentional action; individuals do not choose to behave impulsively, they fail to inhibit problematic impulses or desires. In our view the same point applies for all the other criminogenic needs such as antisocial attitudes, deviant sexual interests and antisocial peers.

Perhaps a more accurate way of understanding the relationship between criminogenic needs and offending behaviour is to say that they are necessary conditions for offending to occur. In other words, criminogenic needs could be seen as distortions or omissions in the conditions necessary for basic human needs to be meet. Thus they are not needs in an instrumental or categorical sense, but rather obstacles to need fulfilment (see Chapter 18). This weakness in the RN model points to a lack of *explanatory depth* and also some degree of *incoherency*.

Agency and Personal Identity

The RN model (and the PCC) does not address the role of personal identity in the change process and therefore suffers from a lack of *explanatory depth* and *external consistency*. It is important to note that this is not part of the model; our point is simply that any comprehensive model of offender rehabilitation should incorporate this important concept. There is evidence from research on the change process in offenders generally, and also from recent therapeutic initiatives in the treatment of intellectually disabled sex offenders, that the formation of a pro-social identity is a facilitative condition for desisting from reoffending. The first piece of evidence comes from Shadd Maruna's (2001) research on the self narratives of offenders who desist from committing further offences. Maruna (2001) found that in order to be rehabilitated effectively, individuals needed to establish an alternative coherent and pro-social identity. This required the construction of a narrative that made sense of their earlier crimes and experiences of adversity and created a bridge between their undesirable lives and new ways of living. Desisting offenders appeared to live their lives according to a *redemption script*, where negative past experiences were reinterpreted as providing a pathway or conduit to the forging of a new identity and more authentic ways of living.

Second, in the sexual offending field, Haaven and Coleman (2000) developed a model for the treatment of developmentally disabled sex offenders based on the construction of a new personal identity. In this model, treatment is based around the distinction between a 'new me' and an 'old me'. The 'old me' constitutes the individual who committed sexual offences, and encompasses values, goals, beliefs and ways of living that directly generate offending behaviour (i.e. risk factors). The construction of a 'new me' involves the endorsement of a new set of goals that specify a 'good' life for an individual: that is, a life in which important primary goods are achieved in ways that are socially acceptable and personally fulfilling. The RN model's lack of attention to the role of personal identity in the change process indicates that it cannot provide adequate guidance to therapists. In other words, it suffers from a lack of *fertility* in this respect and a lack of *explanatory depth*.

Relatedly, we argue that the RN model could be strengthened significantly by also focusing on the issue of personal agency rather than exclusively on factors such as criminogenic needs (i.e. dynamic risk factors). The capacity of individuals to seek meaning and to direct their actions in the light of reasons and values constitutes an essential aspect of human functioning according to research on well-being and self-regulation (Cummins, 1996; Deci & Ryan, 2000; Emmons, 1996, 1999). The presence of conflicting goals and a reduced sense of autonomy are likely to result in a lower level of well-being and higher incidence of psychopathology (Emmons, 1999). The capabilities underpinning the capacity for autonomous functioning—along with other basic human needs and goods—should arguably be instilled in therapy. The conditions and skills constituting autonomy would allow offenders to exercise personal choice in the shaping of their lives, and the various components collectively constituting such lives (e.g. relationships, work, play, mastery experiences). The fact that the RN model is silent concerning these factors indicates a lack of *explanatory depth* and *external consistency*.

Non-criminogenic Needs and Therapist Factors

Andrews and Bonta (1998) acknowledged the importance of non-criminogenic needs but stated that priority should be given to targeting criminogenic needs because of their positive impact on recidivism rates. However, we suggest that some non-criminogenic needs like anxiety, low self-esteem and psychological distress may impede the establishment of a therapeutic alliance with offenders (Marshall et al., 2003a). Therefore, arguably they should be targeted in order to facilitate the learning of new skills or competencies. In other words, before persons are capable of acquiring, for example, pro-social attitudes, they need to be motivated to participate in the whole process of therapy. Recent developments in sexual offender research are pointing towards the crucial role of non-criminogenic needs in determining treatment outcome. This includes work demonstrating that (i) increasing sexual offenders' self-esteem has a facilitating effect on most of the primary targets of sexual offender therapy (Marshall, Cripps, Anderson & Cortoni, 1999b); (ii) working collaboratively with offenders in developing treatment goals results in a stronger therapeutic alliance (Mann & Shingler, 2001); and (iii) therapist features such as displays of empathy and warmth, and encouragement and rewards for progress facilitate the change process in sex offenders (Marshall et al., 2003a). So it seems that both therapist and process factors act as facilitators of therapy change. The creation of a safe, supportive environment where the offender feels understood and at ease is likely to enable him to learn more effectively. In addition, some process variables function as mediators and so directly contribute to changes in an offender's cognition, emotions and behaviours. In other words, they represent causal mechanisms that act on the offender to produce desirable changes in his functioning. For example, a warm and supportive therapist who sets clear boundaries with a fearful and somewhat suspicious sex offender is likely to disconfirm his belief that the world is a dangerous place and most adults are intent on hurting or rejecting him. The change in beliefs is arguably a direct consequence of the therapist's behaviour. Therefore, non-criminogenic needs (anxiety, fear etc.), and therapist responses to these variables, may play a moderating or mediating role in the production of good therapeutic outcomes. The weakness highlighted by this criticism indicates that the RN model lacks sufficient resources to guide therapists effectively: a lack of *fertility* and also poor *external consistency* with the important literature on process variables in the psychotherapy field. In our view a rehabilitation model or theory should have something to say on these issues.

Values and the Risk–Need Model

Another criticism concerns the relationship of criminogenic needs to values or normative issues. Andrews and Bonta describe their approach to offender rehabilitation as a value-free enterprise. By this, they presumably mean that it is strictly empirical in nature and therefore totally reliant on the discovery of certain facts. These facts are the dynamic characteristics of offenders and their situations that if modified are associated with decreased recidivism rates. There are two problems with this argument. First, because criminogenic needs (i.e. dynamic risk factors) increase the likelihood that an offender will engage in *harmful* behaviour in the future, they are value-laden terms. The assumption is that if criminogenic needs are targeted in treatment less harm, and greater good, will accrue to society. The difficulty is that 'harm' and 'good' are value-laden terms and therefore the RN model does presuppose normative judgements concerning what is beneficial to the community and to the offender. In other words, the very notion of risk itself is conceptually tied to the ideas of harms and benefits; value-laden terms. Second, the underlying assumption of the RN model appears to be that values are nothing more than subjective preferences of individuals, much as taste is. Just as one person might like ice cream while another could dislike it, human values reflect subjective preferences. However, there is a robust and developing literature that argues that there are certain conditions that reliably increase individuals' level of well-being and reduce their chances of experiencing harm (e.g. Arnhart, 1998; Aspinwall & Staudinger, 2003; Braybrooke, 1987; Deci & Ryan, 2000; Emmons, 1999; Keyes & Haidt, 2003; Murphy, 2001; Nussbaum; 2000; Thomson, 1987). Basic human needs are examples of motives that incline individuals to seek certain experiences and objects: outcomes that objectively result in greater physical health and well-being. They are objective and based on human beings' natural inclinations and needs. Thus criminogenic needs are partially defined in terms of their relationship to harmful and beneficial outcomes (e.g. reduction of crime or increased security), which indicates they are not simply factual constructs. This feature of the RN model threatens its *coherence* in that its claims to be value free are in fact incorrect.

'Tick and Flick' Approach to Treatment

The fact that the RN model prescribes offender treatment upon the basis of risk and criminogenic needs has been translated in correctional services into a rather mechanistic approach to rehabilitation. Our point is while the RN model does not recommend such an approach, in our experience it is frequently implemented in this manner. Offenders are screened for risk level and criminogenic needs and then allocated to intervention streams according to their assessment results. Programmes are selected on the basis of their demonstrated ability to ameliorate dynamic risk factors and are typically manualised and delivered in a group format. One concern is that there is often a lack of appreciation that generic programmes like this may fail to address important preferences and circumstances pertaining to individual offenders. In our view, there are strong grounds for arguing that human beings are embedded in local social and cultural contexts and any treatment plan should focus on the skills and resources required to function in the particular contexts they are likely to be released into (Ward & Stewart, 2003b). The trouble with most manual-based programmes is that they tend to have built into them generic conceptions concerning what kinds of goods or goals should be achieved rather than taking into account individual offenders' capabilities, preferences and likely living circumstances. For example, intimacy training is routinely given to all sex offenders undertaking standard cognitive-behavioural treatment (Marshall, 1999), teaching skills that are designed to enable individuals to develop deeply satisfying, intimate relationships with other adults. What we advocate is that the type of intimacy training given should correspond to offenders' expressed preferences concerning the significance of intimate relationships in their lives. Individuals legitimately vary in terms of how they rank the importance of close relationships in their overall life plan. For some it is the most valued aspect of their lives while for others work or even leisure pursuits may be more important. Therefore, it makes sense to adjust the depth and type of relationship training given to offenders in light of their overall plan for living. And this requires an awareness of both their goals and the environment into which they are likely to be released. Factors such as opportunities and resources constrain what is possible to achieve and should be factored into any therapeutic programme. Unfortunately, the RN model is not equipped to allow for such adjustments easily because of its focus on risk factors rather than persons who live in local communities. What we are arguing is that it lacks ecological validity and in this respect suffers from lack of *explanatory depth* and also therapeutic *fertility*.

THE CLINICAL UTILITY OF THE RISK–NEED MODEL

In a sense, we have already touched upon the clinical utility of the RN model earlier in the chapter. The fact that treatment targets and interventions are empirically derived means that outcomes are likely to be positive. The utilisation of structured assessment and structured treatment strategies is also a useful feature of this rehabilitation theory. However, the fact that it has some weaknesses means that it makes sense to augment the theory with additional models and interventions.

In the sexual offending area this means paying more attention to therapist and process variables and seeking to establish a sound therapeutic relationship prior to employing the technical aspects of therapy. It is also important to understand the problematic internal and external conditions that are associated with, or in fact constitute, the offender's criminogenic needs and to build therapy around their implementation. *We* find it useful to view criminogenic needs as red flags that signal there is a problem in the way offenders are seeking important personal goals (of course, this is not the way the RN views it!). Once they have been detected it is necessary to ascertain exactly what the problems are. It may be that individuals lack the necessary conditions to make autonomous decisions and therefore frequently behave in an impulsive manner. Alternatively the trouble could lie in their tendency to mix with antisocial individuals. Furthermore, we recommend ensuring that a treatment plan based on criminogenic needs is presented to offenders in the form of both approach and avoidant goals rather than exclusively in terms of risk management. Finally, we caution against using the RN model and the PCC as explanatory theories for the purposes of assessment and case formulation. In particular, the former is not designed to perform that task satisfactorily and a case formulation based on criminogenic needs is likely to be incomplete and consist of an unconnected list of problem areas.

On a final note, it is important to acknowledge that our critique of the RN model has been hotly contested. In a recent commentary on the original paper by Ward and Stewart (2003b) concerning the relationship between criminogenic needs and human needs, Bonta and Andrews argued that the model presented in that paper simply constituted a reworking of old discredited ideas and that there is little evidence for the utility of more strength-based approaches in the treatment of offenders (see Bonta & Andrews, 2003; Ward & Stewart, 2003c). They also pointed out that the evidence for the efficacy of the RN is extremely strong and were concerned that Ward and Stewart' (2003a) emphasis on goods promotion alongside risk management (see Chapter 18) might result in a return to a simple welfare model and a subsequent reduction in the efficacy of rehabilitation efforts. In their reply, Ward and Stewart (2003c) stated that their aim was simply to explore the relationship between human needs and dynamic risk factors and not to reject totally the RN perspective. We certainly would like to acknowledge the value of the RN model and accept that at this point the RN is the rehabilitation model of choice when working with offenders, although it is important to state that it does contain some conceptual weaknesses (see above) that limit its value as a *theory* of rehabilitation.

CONCLUSIONS

The RN model of offender rehabilitation represents a considerable achievement and is a useful treatment resource in the sexual offending area. The requirement that treatment should ensure dynamic risk factors are eliminated, reduced or managed is sensible and likely to resonate with politicians and the general public: an important virtue in any offender treatment model. However, the problems noted in our evaluation of the theory indicate that it suffers from a lack of explanatory depth, poor external consistency, and also, somewhat surprisingly, a lack of fertility with respect to certain aspects of treatment. In our view, a major concern is that the relatively simple and straightforward nature of the theory may lead people to think in a simplistic and cursory manner about offender treatment (although it should be emphasised that Andrews and Bonta are not guilty of this error). Furthermore, such difficulties may, together with the unfortunate focus on range-rider type factors, account for the modest impacts of correctional interventions. While a 10% reduction in reoffending is a promising start (Hollin, 1999; Marshall & McGuire, 2003), there is still some room for improvement. We are not convinced that it is simply a question of fine-tuning existing assessment and treatment strategies and, in fact, argue that it might be time to rethink the whole approach to offender rehabilitation (see Chapter 18). To foreshadow the ideas covered in that chapter, we argue that correctional treatment should have twin foci: promoting offender goods and reducing risk. Both are necessary ingredients of treatment.

Chapter 17

CLASSIFICATION AND TREATMENT

Everitt and Dunn (2001) have observed that, 'an important component of virtually all scientific research is the classification of the phenomena being studied' (p. 125). They also note that in the behavioural sciences such classification could be by an individual's personal characteristics or patterns of behaviour, with the investigator being interested in finding taxonomies in which items of interest are sorted into a small number of homogeneous groups or clusters. Knight and Prentky (1990) emphasise that understanding the taxometric structure of a deviant population is the 'keystone of theory building and the cornerstone of intervention' (p. 23). Sexual offenders, however, have been found to be an extremely diverse group in terms of personal characteristics, life experiences and criminal histories. Therefore, it has been suggested by Marshall (1997) that a priority for future research should be to reduce this heterogeneity to manageable proportions (i.e. to move towards identifying different types of sexual offenders using typological or taxometric approaches).

In this chapter, we will describe how researchers have classified sexual offenders to gain an understanding of sexual offending behaviour. In some cases, classifications are derived from theory, while other approaches are reliant upon empirical research or clinical judgement, although they still draw upon theoretical ideas to some degree. Whatever the perspective taken, all approaches enrich the theoretical ideas that we have outlined earlier, and all have been seen by their proponents to inform treatment. The chapter is not an all-embracing approach to this topic, which would need a book in its own right, but is meant to inform the reader of ideas that have led to classificatory approaches, commonly known or employed by those in the field of sexual molestation to classify child molesters. We restrict our descriptions of classificatory approaches to child molesters given that these are, at the present, probably better worked out than systems that have been applied to other types of sexual offender (e.g. rapists, exhibitionists or sexual murderers). Because space precludes such an all-embracing overview of the topic we will also give only the most common exemplars to illustrate the different approaches.

APPROACHES TO CLASSIFICATION

In the general offender literature (Blackburn, 1993), and in the sexual offending literature (Bickley & Beech, 2001), four main ways of classifying offenders have been identified. In brief, these classifications may be based upon: (i) identifying attributes of central concern to a particular theory and distinguishing types of offenders based on these; (ii) clinical descriptions, which represent the proto-typical features of group members; (iii) pragmatically examining the offence demographics in an individual's history to generate useful demographic clusters; and (iv) using multivariate statistical techniques to generate psychometric profiles that determine group membership. Blackburn also suggested a way of illustrating to the reader where these approaches come from, and which of the 'Psy' disciplines (i.e. psychiatry, psychology, social work or those who work in the criminal justice system) are likely to apply such systems. We should also note that Polaschek (2003a) has pointed out that classification systems can only be evaluated meaningfully in terms of their intended purpose. Therefore it is important to bear in mind the purposes they serve and their theoretical rigour.

In this chapter we will outline classification systems that illustrate Blackburn's observations. For the first description, identifying attributes of central concern to a particular theory (or *theory-led* classification), we will describe classification systems derived from psychodynamic theory. For the second method, classifica-tion by clinical description, which represents the prototypical features of the group members, we will describe the psychiatric classification of child sexual abuse. Here, we observe that this medical model is rooted in the theoretically older Platonic tradition of the possibility of discovering *ideal types* and hence is informed implicitly by theory. For the third method, pragmatically examining an individual's offence demographics, we will outline current risk assessment systems that arrive at classification. Finally, we will illustrate the fourth method using classification based on psychometric instruments to assess the level of functioning in sex offenders to gauge level of treatment need.

Bickley and Beech (2001) note that classification systems should also be assessed in terms of their reliability, consistency and ease of usage, pertinence to the population assessed, valid distinction between types, and relevance to treatment in order to assess their efficacy and validity. We will deal with these issues by providing a critique and a guide to the clinical utility of each of the approaches.

THEORY-LED CLASSIFICATION

Chapter 5 of this book outlines the pathways model of sexual offending (Ward & Siegert, 2002b), a theory-led classification system that draws upon the best parts of the theories outlined in Chapters 2–4. However, because the pathways description of child sexual abuse is relatively new and empirically untested, it has not yet had a major influence in the classification of either risk or treatment need of child molesters. However, in our view the idea that there are multiple pathways to child sexual offending is an important insight and should be capitalised on in any future research work.

A number of classification systems of child molesters have been informed by psychodynamic theory. A good example of these is Cohen, Seghorn and Calmas's (1969) classification system, which expanded upon Freud's (1953) notion of sexual fixation and regression, and outlines how these attributes may distinguish types of child molesters. Clearly, this approach illustrates how the central concepts of a particular theory can be used to distinguish *types* of sexual offender. Cohen et al. described three types of paedophilic child molesters in terms of their propensity to abuse sexually. The *paedophile-fixated* type was described as having arrested psychosocial/psychosexual development, such that the individual is characterised by an inability to sustain long-term relationships with adults and has an exclusive preference for children both socially and sexually. The *paedophile-regressed* type will probably be able to engage in stable adult relationships, but may regress to sexual activity with children in times of stress. For the third type of paedophilic offender, the *paedophile-aggressive* type, the offender is hypothesised to have *fused* together the concepts of sex and aggression. Because of this, he is driven to commit sadistically violent offences in order to obtain sexual satisfaction. The Cohen et al. approach is useful because it highlights the potentially different needs and levels of risk of different classes of child molester. In brief, the fixated type is regarded as the most likely to recidivate but is seen as the least likely to cause serious physical harm to his victims. The regressed type's risk of recidivism is seen as depending upon his ability to cope with life stresses. The aggressive type is obviously seen as the most likely to cause serious physical harm or kill his victims in the course of his sexual assaults.

Knight and Prentky (1990) have attempted to develop a reliable and valid taxonomic system (the Massachusetts Treatment Center Child Molester Typology, Version 3; MTC: CM3) for child molesters, both from theory (i.e. applying existing theoretical ideas from Cohen et al., 1969) and from data-driven cluster analytic strategies (which we will outline in detail later in this chapter). Knight and Prentky reported that the system was operationalised in the following way. First, variables were selected for the analysis based upon their relevance to Cohen et al.'s theoretical ideas and from these the basic MTC: CM3 typology was derived. This basic typology was then refined further using empirical data and statistical techniques. The revisions consisted of a reconceptualisation of the notions of fixation and regression, the separation of the offender's relationship with his victim(s) and intensity of paedophilic interest.

Therefore, the revised version, MTC: CM3 (see Figure 17.1), consists of two main axes: fixation/regression (Axis 1) and amount of contact with victim (Axis 2). *Axis 1* (fixation/regression) is used to separate child molesters into those who have an enduring sexual interest in children and those without such an interest. Knight and Prentky suggested that each of these two groups can be separated into those with a high level of social competence and those with a low level of social competence. Thus, four different types of offender can be derived from Axis 1 (Type 0, high fixation/low social competence; Type 1, high fixation/high

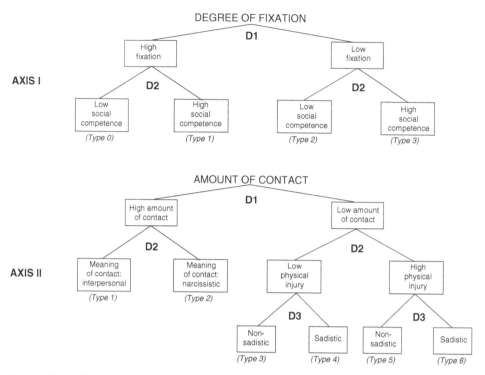

Figure 17.1 Knight and Prentky's MTC: CM3
Source: Knight, R. A. & Prentky, R. A. (1990). Classifying sexual offenders: the development and corroboration of taxonomic models. In W. L. Marshall, D. R. Laws & H. E. Barbaree (Eds), *Handbook of sexual assault: Issues, theories, and treatment of the offender* (p. 31). New York: Plenum Press.

social competence; Type 2, low fixation/low social competence; Type 3, low fixation/high social competence).

Axis 2 is employed to understand the meaning for the offender of the contact with the victim. Six types of offender are derived on the basis of a series of hierarchical bifurcatory decisions. The first decision is about the amount of contact an individual has had with his victim(s). For those where the amount of contact is high, Knight and Prentky suggested that the meaning of this contact should be considered. If the offender's motivation is socio-emotional/sexual in that he perceives that he has engaged in a loving relationship with his victim(s) then he is described as a *Type 1: interpersonal offender*. When the offender's primary motive is to achieve self-gratification so that victims are regarded as little more than masturbatory objects, the offender is described as a *Type 2: narcissistic offender*. If the amount of contact is low, the amount of physical injury caused to the victim and the presence or absence of sadistic fantasies and/or behaviours is considered. A series of two further bifurcatory decisions based on these parameters yields another four types in this system. If the offender is described as committing generally impulsive acts, where there is relatively little injury to the victim, where immediate sexual gratification is likely to be the main aim, and there is no evidence of sadistic thoughts and behaviours then the offender is a *Type 3: exploitative offender*. Where there is evidence of offence planning, but relatively little evidence of injury to the victim, coupled with evidence suggesting that the offender had deviant/sadistic fantasies, this suggests a *Type 4: muted sadistic offender*. Evidence of a high degree of physical injury to victims, and impulsive behaviours in the offence process, but no evidence that anger was eroticised, suggests a *Type 5: aggressive offender*. Finally, where there is evidence of a high degree of planning in the offences, and where the perpetrator is viewed as being highly aroused by frightening victims or subjecting them to painful, humiliating and/or degrading acts, this indicates a *Type 6: overt sadistic offender*.

EVALUATION OF THE MTC: CM3

Although a number of theories have described the aetiology and maintenance of specific types of sexual deviancy, the proportion of these that has actually led to any well-known classification system is rather small. Probably the best-known classification system derived from theoretical ideas is the MTC: CM3 classification. Because of the status of this system, compared to other approaches, we will restrict our comments in this section to this classificatory system.

The MTC: CM3 is a sophisticated and impressive system for categorising child molesters (and the rapist version is also impressive: see Knight & Prentky, 1990). It appears to have good construct validity and as such captures important clinical and aetiological aspects of child molesters' functioning. This indicates the system has good *explanatory depth*. Of course, classification systems are not strictly speaking explanatory theories. Yet they are based on aetiological and typological assumptions concerning the best way to categorise sexual offenders. In the case of the MTC: CM3 these assumptions appear to be well founded. A second strength is its usefulness for empirical research and the fact that it is consistent with aetiological theories and incorporates the best aspects of other types of classification systems (e.g. Cohen et al., 1969). This reveals the system's *external consistency* and *potential unifying power*.

Given these undoubted strengths, the MTC: CM3 also suffers from a number of weaknesses. First, from Figure 17.1 it can be seen that it is theoretically possible to distinguish 24 different types of extrafamilial offender. On the face of it, this seems to suggest a large degree of *empirical scope*. However, 11 of the 24 possible types of offender were not well represented in their sample (i.e. they found 3 or fewer cases, i.e. less than 2% of the total sample of 177 cases). This finding suggests that somehow they have not carved the domain accurately, implying a lack of *explanatory depth*. In addition, incest-only offenders were excluded completely when developing the MTC: CM3 because there were too few of them. These problems result in a typology which gives either little or no detail for certain types of child abusers. This lack of coverage greatly reduces its usefulness to the practising clinician and illustrates a lack of *empirical scope* and *fertility (clinical utility)* in its present form.

Second, Fisher and Mair (1998) argue that the detailed information required to assign offenders accurately in the MTC: CM3 is often not available to the clinician. This makes its utility somewhat limited and may force therapists to use more intuitive and less valid classifications systems. In addition, Bickley and Beech (2001) note that it is possible that such a level of complexity in the system renders its practical application somewhat limited. Both these issues indicate that the Prentky and Knight system lacks *fertility* (clinical).

Therefore, we would suggest that further examinations are required to establish the generalisability of the system to a broader sample of child molesters; as yet it remains to be seen whether this typology will lead to reliable predictions about offending patterns and risk of reoffending. We will now consider the clinical utility of the system.

CLINICAL UTILITY OF MTC: CM3

Despite our critical comments, it does seem that the MTC: CM3 has some clinical utility. First, the focus on fixation and amount of contact with the victim would appear to have some relevance to risk assessment. Prentky, Knight and Lee (1997) reported that in a sample of 111 offenders discharged from prison, fixation was found to be significantly related to recidivism, and therefore must be viewed as an important factor to consider in any assessment of risk. Interestingly, amount of contact was reported by Prentky et al. to be related to nonsexual recidivism. We are not currently aware of any treatment programmes that specifically use this system to inform treatment. The Axis 1 fixation concept, and the splitting of Axis 2 into a number of types where the meaning of the relationship between the offender and victim ranges from interpersonal to sadistic, could clearly be something that should be explored in any functional analysis. The results of such an analysis, if informed by the Knight and Prentky system, could help therapists determine the underlying motives, meaning and functions of an individual's offending behaviour.

THE CLINICAL APPROACH TO CLASSIFICATION

The clinical description of sexual offenders is best illustrated by the psychiatric approach to classification. This approach is intended to serve a number of purposes, including the identification of individuals who have common symptoms (Polaschek, 2003a). Polaschek notes that the psychiatric approach also allows for communication between clinicians, treatment planning, and the enhanced understanding of the genesis of such problems. This method of classification is an example of the use of clinical descriptions or ideal types (Blackburn, 1993). In other words, the diagnosis is based upon the subjective impression of the clinician detecting the apparent co-variation of the relevant attributes outlined in the diagnostic criteria (Bickley & Beech, 2001). Polaschek (2003a) suggests that in both child abuse and rape, it is possible to define sets of characteristics that co-occur as a syndrome.

The medical classification of unusual, and sometimes illegal, sexual behaviours is probably most clearly illustrated in the *Diagnostic and Statistical Manual of*

Mental Disorders—Version IV (DSM-IV-TR; American Psychiatric Association, 2000). Here, a mental disorder is defined as 'a clinically significant behavioral or psychological syndrome or pattern that occurs in an individual and that is associated with present distress' (p. xxi). In terms of the presentation of a particular disorder, DSM-IV-TR ducks the notion of aetiology of mental disorder by observing, '[that] whatever its original cause, it must currently be considered a manifestation of a behavioral, psychological or biological dysfunction in the individual' (pp. xxi–xxii). The DSM-IV-TR provides a classification for a number of identified paraphilias, in particular paedophilia.[1] Here paedophilia is placed under the heading of 'Sexuality and gender identity disorders' and refers to an individual's sexual preference for children rather than age-appropriate adults. The main criterion of paedophilia in DSM-IV-TR is that:

> The offender has experienced, for at least six months, recurrent and intense sexually arousing fantasies, sexual urges, or behaviors involving sexual activity with a prepubescent child or children (generally aged 13 years or younger); these fantasies, sexual urges, or behaviors cause clinically significant distress or impairment in social, occupational, or other important areas of functioning to the offender; and that the offender is at least age 16 years and that the perpetrator is at least five years older than his/her victim/s. (p. 528).

We will now critically examine this approach to classification.

EVALUATION OF THE DSM-IV

Polaschek (2003a) observes that there are a number of reasons why diagnostic classification can be of pragmatic value, including an understanding of aetiology, risk, treatment planning, or at the very least, providing a systematic way of identifying the syndrome in question. She notes that for sexual offending, the DSM-IV-TR fails to achieve any of these aims. Specifically, she argues that there is no evidence that those with diagnosed paraphilias are more or less risky, more or less treatable, or for that matter require different treatment interventions. In terms of identification of paraphilic syndromes, both Polaschek and Marshall (1997) propose that these criteria have no special status in either understanding or managing sexually coercive behaviour (lack of *fertility*). Polaschek also observes that dynamic risk variables such as cognitive distortions (see Chapter 8), intimacy deficits (see Chapter 12) and self-regulation problems (see Chapter 15) must be worthy of inclusion in order for a serious psychiatric diagnosis of paraphilias to evolve. In other words, this classification system fails to take into account the range of factors that has been found to be related to child molesting. This problem highlights a lack of *explanatory depth* and *unifying power*, and poor *external consistency*. Other criticisms that have been made about DSM diagnosis include problems in inter-rater reliability for specific paraphilias (O'Donohue,

---

[1] The other paraphilias identified in DSM-IV are exhibitionism, fetishism, frotteurism, sexual sadism, sexual masochism, tranvestic fetishism, voyeurism, and paraphilia not otherwise specified. Polaschek (2003a) notes that rape is omitted from this scheme unless it fits the diagnostic criteria for sexual sadism.

Regev & Hagstrom, 2000) and that there were no field trials for any of the DSM-IV paraphilia criteria.

In terms of more specific criticisms of the clinical diagnosis of child abuse, Bickley and Beech (2001) note that despite revisions, the DSM-IV-TR still has some major limitations as a classification system. First, insisting that evidence is required that an individual has had recurrent and intense sexual urges, fantasies or behaviours involving children for at least six months significantly hinders the reliability of the DSM-IV-TR diagnosis. This is because the majority of men identified as having sexually molested a child will deny and minimise their deviancy (Fisher & Mair, 1998; Marshall, 1997; Salter, 1988). It is often quite hard to find this evidence unless an offender admits it. Therefore, the differing skills of clinicians in overcoming this denial, or the implications of disclosure to the individual (e.g. incarceration), may determine the diagnostic conclusion reached, threatening the *fertility* or clinical usefulness of this typology. Second, in addition to this problem, most of the descriptions outlined in the DSM-IV-TR criteria, for example 'recurrent and intense' and 'clinically significant distress or impairment' (p. 528) lack rigour and are, therefore, open to the subjective interpretation of the clinician. Therefore, subjective bias is likely to undermine further both the process and reliability of this approach to classification. This issue threatens the *internal coherence* of the system.

Third, the DSM-IV-TR classification of paedophilia, according to Marshall (1997), probably only applies to about 25–40% of paedophiles and therefore excludes the majority of this type of offender. Therefore by employing only a single categorical diagnosis for those who engage in sexual activity with children, the DSM-IV-TR criteria fail to distinguish between types of child molester (Bickley & Beech, 2001). For example, the fantasies and behaviours described in the criteria are unlikely to cause clinical distress to a fixated paedophile who sees nothing wrong with sexually abusing children. Consequently this would exclude such individuals from the diagnosis and illustrates a lack of *empirical scope*.

Thus in summary, the DSM-IV-TR diagnosis of paedophilia has little relevance in the mainstream treatment of child sexual abuse, and for that matter does not advance our understanding of the aetiology or maintenance of child abuse, or of the offence process itself (Bickley & Beech, 2001). Because it essentially precludes well over half of those who have committed sexual offences against children, it cannot be said to theoretically advance our understanding of child sexual abuse.

CLINICAL UTILITY OF THE DSM-IV

The psychiatric classification of paedophilia is strongly linked to the disease model of mental disorders and as such tends to suggest a medical mode of treatment, including the use of prescription drugs. Bradford (1990) noted that anti-androgens are one of the organic treatments for sexual offenders, the others being stereotaxic neurosurgery and surgical castration. Hence, drug treatment is often called *chemical castration*. In North America, the two most commonly used drug treatments are medroxyprogesterone acetate (MPA) and cyproterone acetate (CPA; Adi et al., 2002). The effects of MPA and CPA are accomplished through the reduction of serum testosterone levels. MPA does this through accelerating the metabolism of testosterone in the liver. CPA is considered to be more of a true 'anti-androgen' in that its mode of action is the disruption of androgen receptor sites, blocking, among other things, intracellular testosterone uptake. Testosterone is the most important of the sex hormones in the human male. The relationship of testosterone and this type of offending has been extensively researched and a link has been reported, in a number of studies, between plasma testosterone levels and sexually aggressive behaviour (e.g. Monti, Brown & Corriveau, 1977; Rada, Laws & Kellner, 1976). Decreases in reoffending are probably due to several of the effects of anti-androgens: decreases in erotic fantasy, decreased frequency of erections and orgasms, reduction in sexual drive and activity, and reductions in irritability and aggression (Bradford, 1990). But as Adi et al. (2002) note, there are potential side effects of this medication that make it an undesirable option. When given to males, CPA inhibits spermatogenesis, reduces the volume of ejaculate, causes temporary infertility, and permanent enlargement of the mammary glands may occur. There have also been reports of hepatitis, jaundice and hepatic failure, sometimes fatal, developing during anti-androgenic therapy. Poor compliance is a major problem in prescribing anti-androgens because of the adverse effects.

THE PRAGMATIC APPROACH TO CLASSIFICATION

The third method of classification described by Blackburn (1993) is the pragmatic combination of variables of immediate interest (e.g. previous offence history) to predict an offender's risk and need for treatment. The specific use of past behaviour to predict future behaviour is an example of the *actuarial* method of prediction (Hall, 1996), where individuals are categorised in terms of level of risk (e.g. low, medium, high). Most actuarial risk predictors rely almost exclusively on historical factors (i.e. those factors that cannot change). The most commonly accepted factors in the prediction of future risk are offending history, deviant sexual arousal patterns and previous convictions (Hanson & Bussière, 1998; Prentky et al., 1997; Quinsey, Rice & Harris, 1995). Constructors of such risk prediction instruments have typically devised ways of coding the presence of these factors to arrive at a score for an individual, which gives a probability of reconviction for a sexual offence over some specified follow-up period.[2] This approach to classification involves the comparison of an individual's offence history with the demographic information collected on a large sample of offenders whose reconviction history is known. Therefore, in much the same way that car insurance policies are calculated, an individual's risk is determined by the behaviour of similar individuals.

At the present time actuarial risk prediction is the most accurate method of risk prediction available for sexual offenders, commonly outperforming clinical judgement of risk (Hanson, Morton & Harris, 2004). Therefore the current

---

[2] See Prentky and Burgess (2000, pp. 267–292) for a description and the scoring protocols of a number of the better known risk assessment instruments currently available.

importance of such an approach to classification cannot be overemphasised because an offender's assessed risk for recidivism can have a marked influence on his management within the criminal justice system (Hanson & Thornton, 1999). That is, an offender who is assessed as high risk will often receive greater restrictions on his liberty, such as an indeterminate sentence, post-sentence detention and long-term community supervision.

The following is a brief description of some of the most well-known actuarial risk predictors developed for adult male offenders in the UK and North America.

Structured Anchored Clinical Judgement (SACJ)

This scale was developed by David Thornton based on data from HM Prison Service in the UK (see Grubin, 1998; Hanson & Thornton, 2000). SACJ assesses risk of sexual and violent recidivism. It has two stages; the first stage involves five items, which cover current and past criminal history and grade the offender into a risk category (low, medium or high). The second stage has eight items, which are referred to as 'aggravating factors'. The presence of two or more of these raises the risk category by one level.

Rapid Risk Assessment for Sexual Offence Recidivism (RRASOR)

This scale was developed in Canada using predominantly North American samples but has since been validated in England and Wales using a prison sample (see Hanson, 1997a). It is intended to assess risk of sexual recidivism. RRASOR contains four items. Each of these has been found by Hanson to be related to sexual reconviction. These items are past sexual offences, young age at commencement of offending, extrafamilial victims, and the abuse of males.

Static-99

Hanson and Thornton (2000) decided to combine the data from SACJ and RRASOR and developed the Static-99, which, as its name implies, is based solely on static factors. It consists of 10 items: prior sex offences, prior sentencing occasions, convictions for non-contact sex offences, index non-sexual violence, prior non-sexual violence, unrelated victims, stranger victims, male victims, lack of a long-term intimate relationship, and whether the offender will be aged under 25 on release (or is now under 25, if in the community).

Risk Matrix 2000 (RM2000)

This scale was developed as a revision of the SACJ, and has separate indicators for risk of sexual recidivism, non-sexual assault, and overall violence (see Thornton et al., 2003). The Prison, Probation and Police Services in England and Wales have adopted the scale nationally. The first stage involves three static items: age at commencement of risk (i.e. when the offender next has the opportunity to offend), sexual offending-related court appearances and total criminal appearances. Points are awarded and the offender is placed in one of four categories (low, medium, high, or very high). The second stage of RM2000 contains four aggravating factors: male victim, stranger victim, non-contact sexual offences and lack of a long-term intimate relationship. If two aggravating factors are present the risk category is raised one level and if all four are present the risk is raised two levels.

Sex Offence Risk Appraisal Guide (SORAG)

The SORAG was developed in Canada (Quinsey, Harris, Rice & Cormier, 1998). It was designed to predict violence committed by sexual offenders. SORAG has 14 items, which cover living with both biological parents until age 16, school maladjustment, alcohol problems, evidence of a sustained intimate relationship, non-violent criminality, violent criminality, previous sexual contact convictions, convictions against girls under 14 only, failure on prior conditional release, age at index offence, evidence of personality disorder, schizophrenia, evidence of deviant sexual preferences, and psychopathy (as defined by the Psychopathy Checklist—Revised, Hare 1991).

EVALUATION OF THE ACTUARIAL (PRAGMATIC) APPROACH

As noted above, statistical prediction commonly outperforms intuitive or clinical judgement; in other words, it has better predictive accuracy. This is a clear strength (*empirical adequacy*). However, it is important to note that this approach has its own inherent problems. Reducing heterogeneity by pragmatic distinctions on the basis of implicit dimensions of offending has limited utility unless tied to a specific theory (Bickley & Beech, 2001). Therefore, these instruments have little theoretical relevance in themselves to the understanding of the offence process. Bickley and Beech also note that sexual offending is not simply due to the combination of such statistically identified offence-specific variables, and it is possible that these variables have little value until their meaning to the individual offender is considered. Beech, Fisher and Thornton (2003) also note that the risk assessment approach has at least four specific limitations.

First, actuarial instruments are by their very nature empirically derived. Therefore they are essentially atheoretical in character; they provide no guidance on which psychological risk factors underlie risk and hence no indication of how risk can be reduced or when such a reduction in risk has taken place, say through successful treatment (see Chapter 13 for a thorough discussion of these issues).

Second, an actuarial approach yields a probability, not a certainty, of future recidivism. For example, suppose that the Static-99 suggests that there is a 45% chance that a high-risk sexual offender will recidivate within 10 years. However, this does not mean that a specific offender has a 45% chance of committing or being reconvicted for a sexual, or sexually related, offence. Rather, it means that 45 out of 100 men with the same characteristics as the offender in question are likely to recidivate. At first glance this may seem helpful until one realises that this statistic means that 55 out of 100 men with such a profile are predicted not to recidivate. Therefore, although actuarial methods may statistically identify a group of men who are at 'higher' risk of recidivism, they often tell us little about an individual offender. This problem highlights the system's lack of *fertility*.

Third, since actuarial instruments have been developed around official recidivism events (i.e. reconviction rates), the probabilities associated with each risk category inevitably underestimate true offending rates. Thus, an individual with a low actuarial risk classification may nevertheless sometimes be highly likely to reoffend in particular high-risk situations (e.g. a male incest offender having continuing unsupervised access to his past victim). This problem threatens validity and therefore leads to a lack of *explanatory depth.*

Finally, actuarial estimates of risk may be misleading for unusual individuals with characteristics that were not well represented in the samples used to construct or test the actuarial instruments. For example, it would be totally misleading to apply the risk assessment instruments briefly outlined above, which have been developed for the prediction of risk in male adult sexual offenders, to adolescent sexual offenders. Again, this weakness indicates the actuarial approach to classification has a lack of *empirical scope* and *fertility.*

CLINICAL UTILITY OF THE ACTUARIAL APPROACH

Despite the limitations of this approach, actuarial assessment presently represents the most cost-effective method of classification for informing decisions about custodial requirements, intensity of supervision, or the allocation of treatment resources. Beech et al. (2003) have noted that initial decisions about the intensity of supervision and monitoring, or of appropriate treatment services, can be cost-effectively assessed using relatively straightforward instruments such as Static-99 or RM 2000. This is because they use items that can be obtained largely from police records and because the evidence base for the static actuarial scales is large. These tools are also appropriate when the offender is unwilling to cooperate with a more fine-grained assessment process or when major costs to the offender depend on the result (e.g. US civil commitment trials).

Where concern is with tailoring treatment to the needs of the offender, Beech et al. (2003) propose that actuarial assessment should be combined with offence chain analysis (as described in Chapter 15; see also Polaschek, 2003a), and the assessment of stable dynamic risk factors (as described in the next section of this chapter). Therefore a number of assessment procedures can be sensibly combined, so that the initial results from actuarial assessments can guide decisions about the use of later procedures. For example, if an offender is identified as high or medium-high risk actuarially, then it is important that there is a careful assessment of dynamic/changeable factors in order to inform treatment provision and to measure whether risk is being reduced in treatment.

Beech et al. (2003) also note that if the offender is under supervision in the community, then routine monitoring of acute risk factors (see Chapter 13) is essential at all levels of actuarial risk (low, medium or high). Where intensive treatment is involved for a population that may contain individuals with multiple diagnoses (e.g. substance dependence, personality disorder, multiple paraphilias), then a more comprehensive instrument like the SORAG will have advantages in that it was developed from a population of sexual offenders with these sorts of problem.

THE STATISTICAL PROFILING APPROACH

There is a growing body of research on the final method: using standardised psychological tests to profile sexual offenders. These tests are typically employed as part of risk assessment or assessment of treatment need. The use of such tests has led to the emergence of a number of classification systems based on the statistical analysis of these data, using various techniques such as cluster analysis. This is a mathematical technique in which individuals are compared to each other on a number of scales in an effort to identify groups of individuals with similar characteristics. The aim of such analysis applied to sex offenders is to find the best fit of individuals to cluster membership and, as we noted earlier, to reduce to manageable proportions the heterogeneity commonly observed in this group (Marshall, 1997). The use of such statistical techniques is, of course, completely atheoretical but obviously the derived clusters represent classification of the material which has been chosen by the investigator. Here, it would be expected that the choice of data gathered would be theoretically informed—that is to say, that most investigators would have an *a priori* idea of which areas of behaviour, cognitions or affect are problematic for sexual offenders.

Recently attempts have been made to use statistical analysis to assess an individual's need for treatment and a second phase of dynamic risk assessment (see Chapter 13 for more detail). An example of this approach, with child molesters, is the work of Beech (1998), who conducted a cluster analysis on a range of measures designed to assess pro-offending attitudes and socio-affective problems in sexual offenders (see Beech, Fisher & Beckett, 1999 for a fuller description of these measures). Based on pre-treatment profiles of a sample of untreated child molesters, he reported that child molesters essentially could be divided into two main groups on the basis of cluster analytic techniques. These two main types he termed 'high deviancy' and 'low deviancy' on the basis of their level of deviation on the psychosexual and socio-affective measures employed from non-offenders' normative data.

The *high deviancy* type of child molester was described as having a chronic level of socio-affective difficulties, and an entrenched belief system containing implicit theories that children are sexual beings and that little harm can come to them from having sex with adults. An individual with this type of profile typically reports chronic emotional loneliness, and is also likely to report that his emotional needs can be met better by children than adults. Such an offender will typically be rated as *high risk* on actuarial assessments because he has a number of previous convictions for sexual offences, has abused a large number of victims, has committed extrafamilial offences, or both intra- and extrafamilial offences, and has committed offences against boys, or both boys and girls. This type of offender could also be regarded as an 'approach goal' offender as described in Chapter 14.

In comparison, the psychological profile of a *low deviancy* man suggests a very different type of sexual offender. Here, the offender does not regard children in general as sexual beings but he does have significant distorted attitudes about his own victims, and a sense of entitlement to sex, whatever the cost. These attitudes are coupled with a low level of emotional identification, which makes it easier for the individual to offend against his victim(s) as again he is either switched off or is denying any form of empathic relationship with his victim. This type of offender is much more likely to have offended against girls within his family (e.g. daughters or stepdaughters) and have one or two victims that he has abused over a considerable period of time. Low deviancy offenders are typically less likely to have previous convictions for a sexual offence than high deviancy men, and tend to have a lower score on any of the actuarial measures of risk outlined above.

At one level, it could be said that high deviancy men fit the profile of the fixated, approach goal, preferential offender who sexually abuses a number of young boys who are strangers, while the low deviancy offender appears more likely to fit the profile of an incestuous child molester who offends against his daughter(s). However, it should be noted that nearly a third of the men who would be identified as incestuous or low risk offenders were found to be classified as high deviancy in this system, and hence could be regarded as the 'lazy paedophile' (Salter, 1988), in that they would offend again if the opportunity arose within, say, their home situation, but are unlikely to offend against those that they do not know. An example of this type of offender is a man who has offended against his own daughter for a number of years and then offends or attempts to offend against nieces or granddaughters. This suggests that the consideration of psychological profiles is an important component of risk assessment and may provide a better indication of treatment need than actuarial assessment or clinical judgement alone.

The psychometric profile approach has been useful in moving both risk assessment and the assessment of treatment need forward. We will now consider the relative strengths and weaknesses of using a psychological profile approach in the risk and treatment areas.

EVALUATION OF THE STATISTICAL PROFILING APPROACH

The use of psychometric data to generate clinically relevant ways of classifying sexual offenders represents a significant advance in the development of more sophisticated risk assessment protocols. In the most in-depth analysis so far, Thornton and Beech (2002) and Beech et al. (2003) report data on 174 child sexual offenders in order to tease out the relative contribution of actuarial assessment (using the Static-99) and psychological profile (deviance) to prediction of subsequent recidivism. Static-99 was found to be effective in identifying those who are unlikely to be sexually reconvicted over a relatively short period (the longest follow-up in these samples was six years). If psychological deviance was considered there was a marked improvement in risk prediction over actuarial assessment alone. This research attests to the predictive accuracy of this approach (*empirical adequacy*). In addition, its identification of sexual offenders with high levels of clinical need is extremely useful and helps therapists to focus their efforts on the most problematic groups of offenders.

In addition to its positive features, the statistical profiling approach exhibits a number of difficulties. First, a problem with this approach is that the group differences described are not linked or tied to a specific theory. Without this aetiological link, classifications are unlikely to further the scientific understanding of the domain, or to inform any proposed intervention. This indicates a lack of *explanatory depth* and *fertility*. Further evidence of these problems is apparent when one notes the distinction between statistical and clinical significance. That is, although providing some useful information about group differences, the practical use of psychological profiles remains uncertain both in terms of risk assessment and treatment. For example, just how many factors need to be present for somebody to be deemed high risk, and to what extent for the classification to be made? Also, to what extent can such a psychological profile be relied upon to guide treatment intervention for individuals to be treated in the way that their psychological profile suggests?

Other, more minor, problems include the fact that offenders can fake their response on self-report measures, making the resultant profiles invalid. Furthermore, this approach assumes that the obtained data are stable, generalisable and readily accessible. These assumptions are somewhat questionable and need to be explicitly argued for (Ward, Hudson, Johnston & Marshall, 1997). There are some techniques for attempting to detect response bias (i.e. faking); for example, by employing social desirability measures to detect for faking and adjusting scores on this basis (see Saunders, 1991, for a description of such techniques). However, these systems cannot be regarded as infallible, and hence caution should be used when assessing an individual's profile, especially when this is indicative that the individual does not appear to have any marked problems. In terms of future directions in the assessment of psychological profiles less fakeable tasks are now being described in the literature: for example, computer-based tasks to assess sexual interest (Abel, Huffman, Warberg & Holland, 1998) and socio-affective problems (Smith & Waterman, 2004). These minor problems reveal that statistical profiling approaches may have limited validity on occasions, pointing to a lack of *explanatory depth*.

CLINICAL UTILITY OF THE STATISTICAL PROFILING APPROACH

In the UK, psychometric profiles using the deviance classification have had an influence in the development of both probation and prison programmes, due to the finding that those with a high deviancy psychological profile require twice as many hours of treatment as those with a low deviancy profile if they are to show change in treatment (Beech et al., 1999). Such a finding obviously has implications for treatment, as it is important not to waste resources by providing offenders either with more input than they probably need, or ineffective treatment that does not provide adequate coverage of the offender's problems. In current UK programmes for sex offenders in the Probation services, high deviancy offenders are always allocated to the longest period of treatment currently available, while low deviancy men are given shorter treatment. Similarly, in the UK Prison Service it has been found that around 80 hours of treatment worked well in treating low deviancy/low risk offenders. As a result, a rolling programme of treatment has been introduced for the low deviancy men. This is typically around

100 hours of group-based cognitive-behavioural treatment. Men with an identified high deviancy profile would typically get around 300 or more hours of treatment (Beech & Mann, 2002). In our view, as long as the limitations outlined above are taken into account, the statistical profiling approach can be clinically useful.

CONCLUSIONS

In this chapter we have described different approaches to classification that are derived either from theory, clinical observation or empirical research. The four different approaches are broadly illustrative of the different ways that classification has been achieved. We stated at the beginning of the chapter that each approach should be assessed in terms of its reliability, consistency and ease of usage, pertinence to the population assessed, validity in distinguishing between types, and relevance to treatment in order to assess its efficacy and validity. We note that some systems are better than others in many of these respects. The shortcomings noted in the systems include the limitations of the classification procedures themselves, the small samples that the classifications have been derived from, and the validity and coverage of some of the systems. Consequently, no one standardised method is universally applied in the classification of child molesters and, therefore, comparisons between the various approaches remain problematic.

Perhaps the most significant shortcoming of the research into the classification of child molesters is its lack of impact on the development of appropriate methods of intervention for these individuals. Given the considerable financial constraints faced by many treatment facilities, a major aim of an effective classification system should be to inform the targeting of interventions to make the best use of limited funds. The ability to tailor treatment to the specific needs of distinct groups of offenders would certainly ensure the most effective use of clinical resources. It can only be hoped that more adequate targeting of resources on this basis can be achieved in the not too distant future.

Chapter 18
STRENGTH-BASED TREATMENT THEORIES

In Chapter 16 we critically examined the risk–need theory of offender rehabilitation and contrasted it with positive treatment approaches that are based on promoting the well-being of offenders. The aim of positive treatment approaches is to enhance individuals' capacity to live meaningful, constructive and ultimately happy lives so that they can desist from further criminal actions. Key assumptions of strength-based or positive psychological theories is that all human beings are naturally inclined to seek certain types of experiences or human goods, and that they experience high levels of well-being if these goods are obtained. Criminal actions are thought to arise when individuals lack the capabilities to effectively realise their goals in pro-social ways. In other words, crime is hypothesised to be a direct consequence of maladaptive attempts to meet human needs (Ward & Stewart, 2003a). The therapeutic implications of positive psychology are clear: offenders should be given the knowledge, skills, opportunities and resources to live a 'good' life, which takes into account their particular preferences, interests and values. In short, treatment should provide them with a chance to be better people with better lives.

In this chapter we describe the good lives model (GLM) of offender rehabilitation, a strength-based approach to the treatment of sexual offenders developed by Ward and his colleagues (Ward & Stewart, 2003b). First, we discuss the basic assumptions of positive psychology and their relevance for forensic psychology. Next, the GLM is outlined and critically evaluated. Finally, we examine the clinical utility of this perspective.

It is important to note that the GLM was not influenced by the principles of positive psychology during the seminal period of theory construction. It is only 'after the fact' that it has become clear that the GLM shares many of the core assumptions of positive psychology. This is quite remarkable and in our view points to the *explanatory depth* and *unifying power* of this approach to understanding human behaviour.

WHAT IS A STRENGTH-BASED APPROACH?

Positive psychology is an example of a strength-based approach to the study of human behaviour; it focuses on promoting human welfare and instilling strengths in individuals rather than simply emphasising psychological deficits (Aspinwall & Staudinger, 2003). Positive psychology has ancient roots and is evident in Aristotle's view that human beings are naturally oriented toward seeking fulfilment of their potentialities, and furthermore, that a fulfilling or flourishing life is only possible if these potentialities are realised (Jorgensen & Nafstad, 2004). It is the perfection of essential human qualities that yields happiness in the sense of psychological well-being or fulfilment. According to Aristotle, human flourishing, or *eudaimonia*, is not the same thing as subjective happiness. He argued that a person could be happy in the sense that they tend to experience pleasant states but be essentially unfulfilled. In other words, these individuals are choosing to live in ways that deny important aspects of their character and needs; they are not striving toward realising their potential as human beings. For example, a hedonist could live a life of pleasure seeking and neglect his needs for personal growth, autonomy, relatedness, mastery and creativity. It is possible to trace the Aristotelian view of happiness or well-being through a line of philosophers, scholars and psychologists from the middle ages and the Enlightenment, to modern theorists such as Werner, Maslow, Lewin, Rogers, MacIntyre, Seligman and Csikszentmihalyi (Jorgensen & Nafstad, 2004). The stress on human nature and human flourishing indicates the strong humanistic strand in positive psychology.

Positive psychology operates on a number of assumptions about human nature. First, positive psychology views human beings as *naturally predisposed* to seek a number of primary goods that, if achieved, are likely to result in high levels of psychological well-being. We will now describe the concept of human goods in more detail before examining the other assumptions inherent in positive psychology.

Human goods are viewed as objective and tied to certain ways of living that, if pursued, involve the actualisation of potentialities that are distinctively human. These goods all contribute to a happy or fulfilling life but are intrinsically valuable in themselves (e.g. relatedness, creativity, physical health and mastery). Thus, positive psychology adopts a pluralist view concerning the values that people should, and do, seek if they are to be happy. Primary goods emerge out of basic needs while instrumental or secondary goods provide concrete ways of securing primary goods: for example, certain types of work, relationships or language ability. The nature of the primary goods sought by individuals and their weightings are formed in specific cultural contexts and represent individuals' interpretations of interpersonal and social events. This knowledge is clearly influenced by culturally derived beliefs, values and norms (D'Andrade, 1995). The underlying metaphor is that of a complex, dynamic system where the way individuals seek specific human goods impacts on the other goods sought, the environment and, ultimately, the quality of their lives and subsequent levels of well-being.

A critical issue concerns the range and type of goods sought by human beings and what, if any, research evidence there is for these phenomena. Taking into account the findings from a number of disciplines, including anthropology, social science, social policy, psychology, evolutionary theory, practical ethics and philosophical anthropology, we propose that there are at least ten types of primary human goods (see Arnhart, 1998; Aspinwall & Staudinger, 2003; Cummins, 1996; Emmons, 1999; Linley & Joseph, 2004; Murphy, 2001; Nussbaum, 2000; Rescher, 1990). In no particular order they are: life (including healthy living and functioning), knowledge, excellence in play and work (including mastery experiences), excellence in agency (i.e. autonomy and self-directedness), inner peace (i.e. freedom from emotional turmoil and stress), friendship (including intimate, romantic and family relationships), community, spirituality (in the broad sense of finding meaning and purpose in life), happiness, and creativity. Although this list is comprehensive it is not meant to be exhaustive. It is also possible to divide the primary goods into related but more fine-grained categories. For example, the good of inner peace could be broken down into a number of related goods, such as the eight sets of emotional competency skills described in Chapter 5 of this volume (Saarni, 1999). The eight emotional competency skills include awareness of one's emotional state, the capacity to identify other people's emotions, the ability to use the emotional vocabulary of one's culture, possessing the capacity to respond empathically to other people, and the ability to adjust one's emotional presentation depending on circumstances. Furthermore, the high degree of consensus concerning these primary goods among researchers working with diverse research methods and in distinct disciplines provides strong evidence for their validity.

The second assumption made by the positive psychology viewpoint is that individuals should be understood in a holistic, integrated manner rather than through the pursuit of reductionistic research programmes. A particularly important feature of humans beings is that of personal identity and the subsequent attempts by individuals to construct accounts of their lives that give them purpose and value. Third, the aim of treatment initiatives guided by positive psychology is to give people the necessary capabilities to live more fulfilling lives rather than simply seek to reduce risk factors or focus on the amelioration of psychological deficits (see Chapter 16). People are viewed as psychological agents who flourish when able to make their own decisions concerning the direction of their lives, provided they possess the necessary skills, capabilities and resources to do so. Human well-being is a self-directed activity and therefore springs from each individual's own choices and effort; it cannot be a result of factors beyond the control of the person in question. Furthermore, the existence of strengths can act as a buffer against the development of psychological problems and disorders. For example, optimism might reduce the chances of a person becoming depressed or the presence of good social skills may protect someone from developing schizophrenia (Seligman & Peterson, 2003). Fourth, people are viewed as contextually embedded organisms who depend on each other for the provision of the resources, skills and opportunities to lead worthwhile and satisfying lives. Any attempt to explain or remedy individuals' problems needs to take into account the environment in which they live. Fifth, there is no such thing as the ideal or perfect human life.

Individuals vary legitimately in the weightings they give to particular sets of primary goods and in the way these goods are translated into specific activities and experiences (e.g. types of mastery experiences, kind of relationships). The emphasis given to the primary kinds and the different ways they are realised will depend on a person's abilities, preferences and life circumstances. Thus the basic goods that comprise human nature cannot be read off like some kind of recipe and combined in the same way for all individuals. Seligman and Csikszentmihalyi have provided a nice description of positive psychology that captures most of the elements described above:

> The field of positive psychology at the subjective level is about valued subjective experiences: well-being, contentment, and satisfaction (in the past); hope and optimism (for the future); and flow and happiness (in the present). At the individual level, it is about positive individual traits: the capacity for love and vocation, courage, interpersonal skill, aesthetic sensibility, perseverance, forgiveness, originality, future mindedness, spirituality, high talent, and wisdom. At the group level, it is about the civic virtues and the institutions that move individuals toward better citizenship: responsibility, nurturance, altruism, civility, moderation, tolerance, and work ethic (Seligman & Csikszentmihalyi, 2000, p. 5).

The emphasis on three levels of application of positive psychological ideas is useful and reminds researchers and clinicians that clients' degree of well-being is strongly affected by their environments. It also highlights the crucial role of psychological traits and capabilities in producing the mental states constituting well-being: for example satisfaction and happiness. An important part of positive psychology is its insistence that human fulfilment emerges from certain types of activities rather than simply the attainment of material goods or social status. The significant activities are those associated with the attainment of primary human goods such as relatedness and creativity. The process of pursuing a vision of a good life is clearly a dynamic and ongoing one: it never ends. A positive psychological approach to understanding human behaviour will always take the dynamic character of human well-being into account and therefore focus on the interaction between subjective experience, character traits, and the social, cultural and personal environment of the participants concerned.

Applied Positive Psychology

The application of positive psychology to the explanation and reduction of human problems is called *applied positive psychology* (Linley & Joseph, 2004). Practitioners and researchers applying this perspective to human problems work to 'promote optimal functioning across the full range of human functioning, from disorder and distress to health and fulfilment' (Linley & Joseph, 2004, p. 4). According to Linley and Joseph, the aim is to help people to achieve their personal goals rather than to dictate how they should live their lives. The criterion for any intervention is always to facilitate optimal functioning, viewed essentially as the achievement of primary human goods in ways individuals find meaningful and relevant to their lives and circumstances. This initiative will require the instillation of positive individual traits such as empathy and respect for others, wisdom, a capacity for autonomy, and the ability to establish close and intimate relationships with other people. In particular, the desired outcome for practitioners is psychological well-being in their clients rather than simply subjective happiness or pleasure. To recap, objective well-being emerges from a person successfully implementing a good lives plan that is consonant with his or her profile of values, capacities and personal circumstances.

Applied positive psychology is not content to remove a person's symptoms or risk factors; the aim is always to move clients to optimal ways of functioning: in other words, to promote human goods alongside risk management (Linley & Joseph, 2004). Therefore, there are twin foci in treatment: enhancing welfare and reducing harm. In Chapter 16, we suggested that a useful way of understanding the relationship between goods promotion and risk management treatment initiatives is to view risk factors as internal or external obstacles that frustrate or block the acquisition of human goods. We will revisit this idea later in the chapter and for now will simply acknowledge the importance of goods promotion in any rehabilitation theory. Thus from the perspective of a positive psychological model, treatment should focus first on identifying the various obstacles preventing clients from living a balanced and fulfilling life, and then seek to equip them with the skills, beliefs, values and supports needed to counteract their influence. A final point made by Linley and Joseph (2004) is that positive psychology is not really a new specialty within professional psychology but rather is a way of capturing the common interests and views of practitioners seeking to promote psychological well-being in their clients.

Despite the ancient roots of positive psychology, research into aspects of psychopathology and human problems using this approach is relatively new. We do not have the space exhaustively to review this research in this chapter. We will only briefly summarise some of the more recent work.

Research indicates that patients diagnosed with mood and anxiety disorders display significantly lower levels of well-being compared to control groups (Runi & Fava, 2004). Furthermore, work on personal goal strivings and happiness by Emmons and his colleagues has revealed that failure to achieve important personal goals and goal conflict are associated with psychological and physical ill-being (e.g. Emmons, 1999). In therapy outcome research, Fava, Rafenelli, Grandi, Conti and Belluardo (1998) found that adding a well-being component to a CBT package for recurrent depression was instrumental in reducing the relapse rate at a six-year follow-up (40% compared to 90%). A number of other therapeutic initiatives based on positive psychology are currently being undertaken in the applied psychology field (e.g. in patients suffering from post-traumatic disorders, existential psychotherapy, fostering resilience in high-risk environments, with aging adults, public health interventions, and the facilitation of forgiveness; Linley & Joseph, 2004).

POSITIVE PSYCHOLOGY AND SEXUAL OFFENDING

In recent years the treatment of sexual offenders has been dominated by relapse prevention, a risk management approach (Chapter 14, this volume; Laws, Hudson & Ward, 2000b). Relapse prevention seeks to ensure that individuals acquire coping skills to manage high-risk situations in an adaptive manner and therefore lessen their chances of reoffending. The phases of lifestyle imbalance, offence precursors, high-risk situations, lapse and relapse constitute offence-related anchor points for therapy and post-release follow-up. Despite the emphasis on risk management inherent in the field, a number of clinical theorists and researchers have consistently stressed the need for humanistic values when working with sexual offenders and have warned about the possible consequences of focusing too narrowly on reducing dynamic risk factors (e.g. Ellerby, Bedard & Chartrand, 2000; Freeman-Longo, 2001; Haaven & Coleman, 2000; Marshall, 1999). Marshall, in particular, has eloquently argued that viewing sexual offending as an unacceptable expression of basic human needs enables therapists to construct more useful case formulations and leads to better treatment plans. The focus of treatment then becomes equipping individuals with the knowledge, skills and values to meet their primary needs in socially more acceptable, and personally more fulfilling, ways.

A number of researchers have also made valuable contributions to working more positively with sexual offenders. Ellerby et al. (2000) developed a holistic model for aboriginal Canadian sexual offenders that emphasises the systemic nature of intrapersonal functioning, and also the deep interdependency between individuals and their family, communities and the natural world. According to the model, it is important that an individual's mental, physical, emotional and spiritual needs are explicitly considered, and that ways of satisfactorily meeting them are incorporated into a wellness plan. This strongly humanistic and integrated approach to treatment appreciates offenders' strengths and weaknesses, and seeks to equip them with the competencies to meet their needs in pro-social ways. The overall focus is on promoting wellness alongside reducing risk and the aim is to help the person to lead a balanced, and ultimately more fulfilling, life. Freeman-Longo (2001) adapted aspects of this model to non-aboriginal sexual offenders. Again, the focus is on enhancing wellness and helping offenders establish a new identity revolving around personally meaningful ways of meeting their human needs and pursuing their interests.

James Haaven and his colleagues have been pioneering the use of positive psychological principles with intellectually disabled sexual offenders for a number of years (Haaven & Coleman, 2000). In this 'old me, new me' theory, treatment is based around the distinction between dysfunctional ways of behaving (i.e. 'old me'), and the adoption of a new identity and offence-free lifestyle ('new me'). The 'old me' represents the person who committed the sexual offences and is associated with attitudes, feelings and ways of behaving that support sexually abusive behaviour. The 'new me' involves the endorsement of a set of positive and growth oriented goals that specify a different and better kind of life for the individual concerned. In this new life, important needs and aspirations are realised in ways that are likely to bring about greater happiness for the offender and also reduce his chances of committing further offences. The setting of new goals and ways of living highlights the internal (i.e. skills, beliefs, attitudes) and the external (i.e. access to resources, opportunities, social supports) conditions necessary to achieve them. Therapy, then, is based on instilling the competencies required to meet the goals, instituting the conditions, and structuring the environment in ways consistent with living a more fulfilling life.

The treatment theories outlined above are exciting additions to the sexual offending field and certainly reflect positive psychological principles. They stress the importance of helping offenders to function in more balanced and integrated ways and to work towards establishing a constructive and positive view of how their lives could be different. These features of the theories indicate their therapeutic *fertility* and *external consistency*. In addition, the Haaven theory also demonstrates the virtue of *simplicity* and elegance.

Despite these strengths, the theories share some significant weaknesses. A first problem is the lack of research support for the theoretical assumptions underpinning the therapeutic practices, indicating poor *empirical adequacy*. Furthermore, the theories do not really justify their treatment suggestions with argument or an appeal to aetiological assumptions. In Chapter 16 we argued that any theory of rehabilitation needs to make some aetiological assumptions, otherwise it is not clear why therapists should implement the treatment techniques or, if they are effective, why this is so. This aspect of the theories points to their lack of *explanatory depth*.

GOOD LIVES MODEL OF OFFENDER REHABILITATION

In this section we outline the good lives model of offender rehabilitation and its relevance for sexual offending. We argue that the GLM is able to clarify the underlying theoretical basis of wellness (i.e. well-being) and personal identity, and also directly address the contextual nature of human functioning. In a sense, it provides the theoretical underpinning for the treatment theories outlined above.

The Basic Theoretical Assumptions of the Good Lives Model

The GLM is an example of a positive psychological approach to the treatment of sexual offenders and shares a number of the core assumptions of this perspective. First, it assumes that as human beings, sexual offenders are goal-directed organisms who are predisposed to seek a number of primary goods. Primary goods are states of affairs, states of mind, personal characteristics, activities or experiences that are sought for their own sake and are likely to increase psychological well-being if achieved. Instrumental or secondary goods provide concrete ways (i.e. are means) of securing these goods: for example, certain types of work, relationships or language ability. It is assumed that sexual offending reflects socially unacceptable and often personally frustrating attempts to pursue primary human goods. Second, rehabilitation is a value-laden process and involves a variety of different types of values, including prudential values (what is in the best interests of sexual offenders), ethical values (what is in the best interests of the community), and epistemic or knowledge-related values (what are our best practice models and methods).

Third, in the GLM there is an important emphasis on the construct of personal identity and its relationship to sexual offenders' understanding of what constitutes a good life. In our view, individuals' conceptions of themselves directly arise from their basic value commitments (human goods), which are expressed in their daily activities and lifestyle. People acquire a sense of who they are and what really matters from what they do; their actions are suffused with values. What this means for therapists is that it is not enough simply to equip individuals with skills to control or manage their risk factors; it is imperative that they are also given the opportunity to fashion a more adaptive personal identity, one that bestows a sense of meaning and fulfilment.

Fourth, in our view the concept of psychological well-being (i.e. good lives) should play a major role in determining the form and content of rehabilitation programmes, alongside that of risk management. Thus, a treatment plan needs to incorporate the various primary goods (e.g. relatedness, health, autonomy, creativity, knowledge) and aim to provide the internal and external conditions necessary to secure these goods. This necessitates obtaining a holistic account of an offender's lifestyle leading up to his offending and the use of this knowledge to help him develop a more viable and explicit good lives plan. Fifth, the GLM assumes that human beings are contextually dependent organisms and ,as such, a rehabilitation plan should always take into account the match between the characteristics of the offender and the likely environments he will be released into. Thus, we argue that the notion of adaptive or coping skills should always be linked to the contexts in which offenders are embedded.

Finally, according to the GLM, a treatment plan should be *explicitly* constructed in the form of a good lives conceptualisation. In other words it should take into account offenders' strengths, primary goods and relevant environments, and it should specify exactly what competencies and resources are required to achieve these goods. An important aspect of this process is respecting the offender's capacity to make certain decisions himself, and in this sense, accepting his status as an autonomous individual. In the context of sexual offending treatment such decisions are likely to revolve around the weightings of the primary goods (see the following subsection) and also the specific types of activities utilised to translate the primary goods into an offender's daily routine; for example, the kind of work, education and further training, and types of relationships identified and selected.

The Good Lives Model

The GLM theory of sexual offender rehabilitation is a strength-based approach that embodies a number of the positive psychological principles outlined above. The primary aim of treatment is to instil in offenders the knowledge, skills and competencies to implement a meaningful and viable good lives plan in the type of environment they are likely to be released into. The focus is, therefore, on the core ideas of agency, psychological well-being, and the opportunity to live a different type of life: one that is likely to provide a viable alternative to a criminal lifestyle (Kekes, 1989; Rapp, 1998; Ward & Stewart, 2003b).

We will now outline these ideas in more detail. The possibility of constructing and translating conceptions of good lives into actions and concrete ways of living depends crucially on the possession of internal (skills and capabilities) and external (opportunities and supports) conditions. The specific form that a conception will take depends on the actual abilities, interests and opportunities of each individual and the weightings he or she gives to specific primary goods. The weightings or priority allocated to specific primary goods is constitutive of an offender's *personal identity* and spells out the kind of life sought and, relatedly, the kind of person he or she would like to be. For example, an offender who places greater weight on relationships than other primary human goods might seek to work as a community volunteer (of course, this should only occur in situations where the risk of reoffending is deemed low). The importance of this primary good would be reflected in his self-conception and give his life a sense of dignity and meaning. However, because human beings naturally seek a range of primary goods or desired states, it is important that all the classes of primary goods are addressed in a conception of good lives; they should be ordered and coherently related to each other. For example, for the offender who decides to pursue a life characterised by service to the community, a core aspect of his identity will revolve around the primary goods of relatedness and social life. The offender's sense of mastery, self-esteem, perception of autonomy and control will all reflect this overarching good and its associated sub-clusters of goods (e.g. intimacy, caring, honesty). The resulting good lives conceptions should be organised in ways that ensure each primary good has a role to play and can be secured or experienced by the individual concerned. The basic idea is that primary goods function like essential cooking ingredients, and all need to be present in some form if a person is to experience high levels of well-being. A conception that is fragmented and lacks coherency is likely to lead to frustration and harm to the individual concerned, as well as a life lacking an overall sense of purpose and meaning (Emmons, 1996). Additionally, a conception of good lives is always *context dependent*; there is no such thing as the right kind of life for an individual across every conceivable setting.

Earlier in the chapter we mentioned the importance of adopting twin foci for the treatment of sexual offenders: goods promotion and risk management. But is it really possible to integrate these two seemingly contrasting approaches to offender rehabilitation? We argue that it is, and in the section that follows we outline how risk can be related to the GLM so that offenders can receive both goods promotion and good risk management.

In the GLM, criminogenic needs or dynamic risk factors are internal or external obstacles that frustrate or block the acquisition of primary human goods. What this means is that the individual concerned lacks the ability to obtain important outcomes (i.e. goods) in his life and, in addition, frequently is unable to think about his life in a reflective manner. That is, an offender's GLM is likely to be implicit and therefore not within his conscious awareness. All the person is aware of is wanting certain experiences, situations or characteristics, and feeling frustrated and unhappy if things do not turn out as he had hoped. In this situation, a sexual offender does not have a consciously constructed plan for organising his values and formulating strategies to realise them in a systematic and efficient manner. Internal conditions pertain to factors within a person such as beliefs, values, skills and desires. In a collective sense they are usefully referred to as capabilities (Nussbaum, 2000). The fact that offenders may not possess the capabilities to achieve human goods in a socially adaptive manner reflects the influence of external factors such as impoverished learning environments, physical or sexual abuse, poor nutrition, brain injury and so on. The end result is the kind of deficits outlined in earlier chapters: intimacy deficits, impulsivity, poor planning ability, emotional incompetence, antisocial attitudes and deviant sexual preferences. This analysis helps us to understand why criminogenic needs predict reoffending. Effectively they signal that a person's ability to secure human goods in socially acceptable and personally fulfilling ways is impaired (i.e. was never present) or compromised (i.e. was present, but is not now). Therefore, criminogenic needs function as *markers* that there is a problem in the way that an individual is seeking primary human goods, a problem that is directly related to his or her acting in an antisocial way. The different types of risk factors are likely to be related to distinct clusters of primary human goods. For example, the presence of deviant sexual interests indicates that some of the necessary internal and external conditions required for healthy sexuality and relationships are missing or distorted in some way. These might include knowledge about appropriate sexual practices, dysfunctional sexual scripts or fears concerning intimacy. The precise nature of the obstacles will depend on the particular set of causes generating an individual's sexually abusive behaviour (Thornton, 2002).

It is also useful to think more globally about the relationship between risk and human goods and to this end we suggest that there are four major types of difficulties often evident in offenders' GLM. In our view, these types of problems are overlapping but conceptually distinct. It is also important to note that the real problem resides in the secondary goods rather than the primary ones. In other words, it is the activities or strategies used to obtain certain primary goods that create problems, not the primary goods themselves. So, some individuals seek primary goods through inappropriate *means*, and may inadvertently create situations where the way they seek certain goods actually lessens their chances of achieving them. For example, a sexual offender might seek the good of relatedness by attempting to dominate and control his partner. This is likely to result in relationships characterised by intense interpersonal conflict or a lack of equality and therefore intimacy. An offender's GLM might also reveal lack of *scope* with a number of important goods left out of his plan for living. For example, the good of *work-related competence* might be missing, leaving the offender with chronic feelings of inadequacy and frustration. Some offenders may also have *conflict* (and a lack of coherence) among the goods being sought and therefore experience acute psychological stress and unhappiness (Emmons, 1999). An example of conflict in a GLM is where the pursuit of *autonomy* through attempting to control or dominate a partner makes it less likely that the goods related to intimacy will be achieved. A final problem evident in an offender's GLM is when he lacks the *capabilities* (e.g. knowledge, skills) to form or implement a GLM in the environment in which he lives, or to adjust a GLM to changing circumstances (e.g. impulsive decision making). This problem has both internal and external dimensions. The internal dimension refers to factors such as skill deficits while the external dimension points to a lack of environmental opportunities, resources and supports.

According to the GLM, the identification of risk factors simply alerts clinicians to problems (obstacles) in the way offenders are seeking to achieve valued or personally satisfying outcomes. Therefore, the identification of risk elements is a critical part of assessment because they flag the existence of problems in the way individuals seek primary human goods. Different categories of risk factors point to problems in the pursuit of different types of human goods. For example, impulsivity indicates problems in behaving autonomously. Hopefully, we have demonstrated how dynamic risk factors (criminogenic needs) and the GLM can be conceptually related. On the basis of this analysis we argue that a treatment plan should be *explicitly* constructed in the form of a good lives conceptualisation, that takes into account offenders' preferences, strengths, primary goods and relevant environments, and specifies exactly what competencies and resources are required to achieve these goods. The process should be explicit, specific, individualised and based around the constructs of personal identity, primary goods and ways of living.

Steps Involved in Assessing and Treating Sexual Offenders using the GLM

The first step is to construct a case formulation that details the clinical phenomena associated with an individual's offending and their relationship to primary human goods. This includes an estimate of risk and identification of criminogenic needs and their location in offender vulnerabilities and lifestyles. The criminogenic needs are used to indicate problems in an offender's (typically implicit) GLM.

The second step is to ascertain what goods are associated with an individual's sexual offending. Possibilities include the pursuit of emotional equilibrium, intimacy, personal control, grievance, sexual pleasure (goods of health and the body) or play (i.e. to get a thrill). This enables therapists to understand why individuals might choose to commit offences and how the pursuit of primary human goods could underpin abusive actions. In other words, focusing on the reasons or goals that ground the actions of offenders makes their behaviour intelligible and can also provide a more effective means of motivating them to enter treatment. The problem does not reside in the primary human goods that underlie offending, but in the way individuals seek these goods. Once this is clear, the therapist should find out what kinds of problems exist in the internal and external conditions required to achieve the relevant goods in a socially acceptable and personally fulfilling manner. An analysis of the offender's GLM in terms of the four types of structural flaws described above is a useful way of doing this. For example, assessment of a sexual offender might indicate that he has problems establishing intimate relationships with adults, experiences frequent periods of low mood and is sexually aroused by children: all criminogenic needs. An analysis of his GLM may reveal that he lacks the capabilities to develop satisfactory relationships with adults, is isolated and therefore does not really have much opportunity to make social contact anyway, and is overly aggressive in dealing with others when his mood is low (inappropriate means and GLM conflict).

The third step is the identification of the core or overarching primary good(s) endorsed by the sexual offender. This is important as research indicates that people vary in terms of the weightings they give to their set of primary goods (e.g. Emmons, 1999). The overarching or core good is likely to be intimately related to an individual's personal identity and therefore provides valuable insight into what kind of new identity should be formed and the values that should underpin it. While all goods should be built into a offender's GLM, the overarching good is the pivot around which the others revolve: they need to support and be coherently related to it. For example, a sexual offender might have real problem-solving strengths and enjoy working out how machines function, and also acquiring new skills. Therefore, the primary goods associated with work (e.g. mastery, knowledge) would be selected as the core or super-ordinate good and used to construct the other aspects of his treatment plan. In this example, he might enrol in a night course on practical mechanics (knowledge), join a car club (relatedness) and eventually train as a car mechanic (mastery at work).

The fourth step involves the selection of secondary goods or values that specify how the primary goods will be translated into an offender's lifestyle and daily routines. This is particularly important as a poor choice may result in an offender losing interest in treatment and disengaging from the change process. In making this decision it is necessary to think explicitly about individuals' interests, skills and abilities, and preferences. This is necessary as some basic abilities are unlikely to be modified in treatment and should function as constraints when considering treatment options (e.g. intelligence, and excellence in certain subjects such as mathematics). For example, a sexual offender might value work above all else and enjoy the sense of mastery that comes from solving a difficult problem and pride from doing a good job. In this case, the overarching value is that of excellence in work and its associated goods, such as doing a good job, solving problems and knowing how things function. The secondary goods required to instil this core good for a person with an interest in, and aptitude in working with, computers could be working as a computer operator or engineer, doing night classes at a technical college, joining a club, making friends with like-minded people, or planning to train as an IT specialist. These activities are concrete ways of realising the more abstract primary good. The kind of work chosen should reflect offenders' abilities and interests.

In the fifth step, the therapist should discover the contexts or environments the offender is likely to be living in once he is released from prison or completes the treatment programme. Consistent with the assumptions of positive psychology and the GLM, we think it is a mistake to equip offenders with generic skills derived from manual-based programmes. In our experience, therapists can make a mistake by applying therapy programmes rigidly and not attempting to tailor them to individual offenders' particular problems or their probable living environment. This is essentially an issue of ecological validity and we suggest that individuals' release environments, in conjunction with their preferences, interests and values, should strongly influence the type of treatment programme they receive. Thus, it is necessary to consider carefully the likely contexts a given individual will be released into, keeping in mind short-, medium- and long-term possibilities. This will require information concerning opportunities for work, social supports, culture of the likely community and neighbourhood(s), and possible living arrangements.

For example, a sexual offender might be reluctant to return to his previous neighbourhood and may be keen to live in a small rural town where he hopes he can make a fresh start. This could cause problems in that there are very few educational facilities in such places, which would make it difficult for him to continue his training as a computer programmer. In view of the importance of work to the offender in question, his therapist investigates the possibilities of beginning training while in prison and completing the remainder of his course by a distance programme when he is released. Furthermore, in view of the individual's reluctance to establish deeply intimate relationships with other people, it is decided to focus treatment on core social and problem-solving skills. Such skills will enable him to meet his basic needs for relatedness through the development of friendships and allow him time and space to develop more intensive relationships in the future.

The key issue in this phase of treatment planning is to take into account each person's internal and external constraints and not to expect them to respond optimally to treatment initiatives that do not reflect their profile of values and goals. Of course it is critical that destructive or maladaptive inclinations are not reinforced and therapists are in the difficult position of having to balance therapeutic priorities (e.g. risk reduction and efficiency) with offenders' unique needs and interests. Despite this, in our experience tailoring interventions to individuals in the ways outlined above is likely to help motivate offenders and also ensure that therapeutic resources are used in more efficient ways. There seems little point in attempting to get offenders to develop skills they are not committed to and have no intention of using when they are released. And as long as the treatment plan is based on the steps outlined above, there is no real danger of collusion or enhancing risk.

The final step is to design an individual GLM treatment plan based on an offender's identified problems, his level of risk, the relationship between his pursuit of human goods and his offence, detection of the problems in his implicit GLM, identification of secondary goods, and the awareness of his probable release environment. The aim is to equip the individual concerned with the capabilities he requires to have a reasonable chance of putting the plan into action once he leaves the programme. A plan is then developed that effectively links the good lives conception with treatment interventions. This plan dictates what kind of treatment interventions the offender actually receives and how they should be delivered. One aspect of the GLM approach that applies to all sexual offenders is that they play an active role in shaping the therapeutic plan. This is an issue of respect for their status as psychological agents and also functions to motivate them to work hard during the change process. It is important to stress that another set of skills operates more at the meta-level: those associated with relapse prevention. Here the aim is to help the offender become more reflective about his life and needs, enabling him to understand the relationship between risk factors, human goods and sexual offending.

Once treatment is initiated, it is expected that the therapist will consistently return to the GLM plan, to ensure that the offender understands the significance of each phase in light of his case formulation. The focus is on the kind of person he is becoming and the new life that is possible at the end of therapy. A particularly helpful feature of this type of approach is that it is much easier to manage issues related to self-esteem and efficacy. If an offender is able to discriminate clearly between the person he was and the person he is in the process of becoming, it is easier to teach him to learn from his past abusive behaviour without denying it.

It is clear that the GLM operates at all three levels of positive psychology. The first or personal level is attended to by virtue of the offender experiencing greater levels of well-being and satisfaction. What he is learning in therapy is how to obtain valued experiences and activities in ways that are more fulfilling and less destructive to himself and others. Because the GLM addresses a wide range of human goods, this also ensures that offenders feel therapists are interested in them as people and not just in their offending. The second level of the positive psychological approach refers to the development of psychological traits: this is the instillation of the internal conditions (i.e. capabilities) to facilitate the achievement of important human goods. The third level is concerned with the individual's relationship to the broader community. This is addressed in the GLM by its ecological focus and its stress on helping offenders achieve the good of community relatedness.

EVALUATION OF THE GLM

The GLM is a new theory of offender rehabilitation and in our view is quite promising. The fact that it is based strongly on the principles of positive psychology and is also able to find a place for the key ideas of the risk–need theory indicates its *external consistency* and *unifying power*. In addition, the clear articulation of a set of theoretical assumptions underpinning the practice aspects of the theory is a real strength. This aspect of the GLM points to its potential *explanatory depth*. It is interesting to note that the GLM is able to ground or provide a theoretical base for the three other positive treatment models described earlier in the chapter. The focus on human needs, the holistic orientation and the cultivation of new personal identities are all consistent with the GLM's theoretical tenets. This feature suggests that the GLM has a high degree of *external consistency*. Finally, the fact that the primary goods postulated by the GLM converge with those identified by quite different discipline and research programmes (e.g. personal strivings, quality of life research, well-being research, evolutionary psychology, anthropology, social policy and so on) highlights its *external consistency*.

In our view the GLM also has a number of weaknesses. First, the definition of primary human goods is a little problematic because it actually contains two somewhat contrasting interpretations of this idea. On the one hand, primary goods are defined as activities, experiences and so on, that are sought for their own sake, linking their status with a tendency to intrinsically motivate offenders. However, on the other hand, primary goods are also viewed as experiences that are beneficial to human beings and that increase their welfare. The problem is that these two ways of defining primary goods are not necessarily coupled and it is possible that a person may find some type of experience or activity intrinsically motivating though it is harmful. This issue points to a possible lack of *internal coherence* in the theory.

A second problem is that it is not really clear that the GLM is of additional value to the risk management approach already well entrenched in sexual offender treatment programmes. It could be argued that in view of the evidence that interventions based on the risk–need model can reduce reoffending by at least 10%, there is nothing to be gained by adopting the GLM. This problem raises the issue of theory *simplicity*, and suggests that there is no real point in complicating treatment by adding unnecessary components. A possible rejoinder to this criticism is that the GLM can add additional value by virtue of its capacity to account for the importance of non-criminogenic needs in treatment, the fact that it integrates risk management and goods promotion in treatment, and because it deals more effectively with the issue of offender motivation. However, this is clearly an unresolved issue that requires empirical attention.

A third, related criticism revolves around the issue of empirical support. The evidence for the theoretical assumptions of the GLM is slowly accumulating and is now the focus of sustained effort because of the rapid rise of the positive psychology movement. However, there is no or little evidence for the assessment and treatment aspects of the theory other than the rationally based reasons outlined above. This weakness reveals that the theory lacks *empirical adequacy*. Clearly, we have no idea what value the GLM will have for the risk management approach already being implemented and we await with anticipation future research using the GLM.

CLINICAL UTILITY OF STRENGTH-BASED APPROACHES

Since we have already described the clinical implications of the GLM in some detail earlier in the chapter, at this point we will articulate only the most crucial implications for clinical practice.

First, the GLM enables us to understand why individuals might choose to commit sexual offences and how the pursuit of primary human goods might underpin sexually abusive actions. In other words, focusing on the reasons or goals that ground the actions of sexual offenders makes their behaviour intelligible and can also provide a more effective means of motivating them to enter treatment. If offenders understand that the primary goods associated with their sexual offending are legitimate objectives it is much easier to persuade them to think about alternate ways of managing life problems. This is particularly the case with the core or overarching goods, which are closely linked to individuals' personal identities and basic values. For example, a sexual offender may abuse a child because he is keen to 'help' others and show 'love' to vulnerable individuals. The goods of community service and helping others could be decoupled from sexual offending and alternative means of achieving these goods selected (e.g. working with adult drug addicts).

Second, the GLM explains why attending to non-criminogenic needs and process factors in therapy is helpful. A key assumption is that the offender is a psychological agent whose autonomy ought to be respected. This means actually working hard to establish an effective dialogue with the offender and to take his treatment-related suggestions seriously. Furthermore, the GLM hypothesises that individuals commit criminal and destructive actions because they are seeking human goods in ways that are inappropriate, possibly due to the fact they lack the necessary internal and external conditions. Such an attitude toward offenders makes it easier to treat them with respect and to avoid fruitless negative exchanges based on dislike and suspicion (e.g. 'they are inherently evil').

Finally, in our view the GLM is very helpful in creating a more constructive atmosphere in sexual offender treatment and therefore helps to reduce levels of denial and cognitive distortions. Therapists are able to utilise all of the treatment strategies currently endorsed by outcome research, but in a way that saves resources (i.e. takes individual preferences and constraints seriously) and is focused on approach goals. Research indicates that the substitution of avoidance or negative goals with approach goals is clinically effective and also creates a more positive therapeutic environment (Mann, Webster, Schofield & Marshall, 2004).

CONCLUSIONS

In this chapter, we examined a number of strength-based treatment models for sexual offenders and considered their relationship to the principles of positive psychology. We focused on the GLM rehabilitation theory in considerable depth, as in our opinion, it is the most theoretically developed of the four positively oriented sexual offending treatment theories. The GLM suggests that the most effective way to rehabilitate offenders is to ensure that they possess the competencies, values, opportunities and resources to live good lives in the particular contexts in which they are to function in society. A helpful way of explaining the major difference in orientation between the risk–need theory and the GLM is that while the former focuses on deficits in the conditions necessary to achieve human goods (i.e. what is lacking and problematic), the latter is concerned with providing the conditions to obtain them. In this sense, it has twin foci of goods promotion and capability building.

We suspect that positive psychological theories and principles will continue to grow and exert more influence in the domain of forensic clinical psychology. Whether or not this development will prove to be therapeutically useful depends considerably on the quality of the theories underpinning positive practice, and also the degree to which such interventions are rigorously evaluated. It is our hope that this chapter will serve to stimulate the growth of strength-based treatment initiatives and their empirical evaluation. One thing is clear, we have not reached the end of the road as far as effective treatment for sexual offending is concerned. It may be time to lift our eyes to other psychological horizons; positive psychology appears to have a lot to offer sexual offender treatment.

Chapter 19
THEORIES OF TREATMENT RESPONSIVITY

Treatment for sexual offenders has become a big industry in both North America and the UK in the past 10 years. Treatment for sexual offenders aims to reduce sexual arousal to deviant material, enhance social and empathy skills, restructure offence-supportive attitudes and enhance self-management. These approaches to therapy are informed by theoretical ideas and practical techniques that have been discussed in previous chapters of this book (specifically in Part III). However, despite the wealth of knowledge and theorising about the reasons why someone commits a sexual offence (i.e. the aetiology of sexual offending; see Part II) and how sexually motivated offences are actually committed (see Part IV), various studies have shown that treatment is not as effective as we would hope given our current knowledge of the field (e.g. Friendship, Mann & Beech, 2003; Hanson et al., 2002). Therefore, facilitation of the change process and theoretical ideas around 'treatment responsivity' must be considered a hot topic in the area. Ward, Day, Howells and Birgden (2004b) have suggested a framework for considering offender change and how it can be maximised; they argue that change should be addressed at the *individual* level, the *process* level and the context (*system*) level.

A key factor in treatment effectiveness is that of responsivity. This idea, according to Gendreau (1996), holds that treatment programmes for offenders should be delivered in a way that facilitates the acquisition of anti-offending, pro-social skills. They should also invite the offender to be motivated to engage in therapy and to commit to change. Gendreau also noted that the responsivity principle is one of fitting offenders to treatment as well as the importance of therapist style in treatment effectiveness. Gendreau stated that there can be 'a potent interaction between the characteristics of individuals and their settings or situations' (p. 122), which could be either positive or negative. More specifically, this means that responsivity refers to the extent to which offenders are able to absorb the content of a treatment programme and how this can subsequently change the behaviour of an offender. Ward et al. (2004b) note that the *responsivity* principle is used to refer to a style and mode of intervention that engages the interest of the client and takes into account relevant character-istics such as his cognitive ability, learning style and values. Responsivity as usually understood in the rehabilitation literature is primarily concerned with therapist and therapy features and is, therefore, essentially concerned with adjusting treatment delivery in a way that maximises learning (Ward et al., 2004b).

In this chapter, we examine three main approaches to treatment change. First, we will outline the core elements of the 'what works' approach, which has had a major influence on the thinking around the *system level* and the *individual level* for sexual and general offender treatment over the past ten years. This work has addressed important issues about how treatment can be maximised, so that appropriate treatment decisions are made (i.e. they are appropriate according to ethical, humanitarian and clinical standards). We will then describe more recent work related to therapist style and its effect upon *process* issues in treatment, as well as the process issues that have been extensively described in the general psychotherapy literature. Finally, we will look at 'up-to-date' thinking on processes of change at an *individual level*. Specifically, we examine Ward et al.'s (2004b) notion of readiness to change. As we shall see, this incorporates a much wider notion of how people are prepared to change compared to the responsivity concept and the motivation to change literature.

THE 'WHAT WORKS' APPROACH TO TREATMENT

A major influence on the current treatment of sexual offenders is the 'what works' (WW) literature, which is derived from the wider criminological literature (e.g. Andrews & Bonta, 1998; McGuire, 1995). This approach has had a major influence in moving the whole idea of rehabilitation from the idea that 'nothing works' (Martinson, 1974) to the notion that treatment can work if it follows a number of rigorous principles, identified from research, that are related to treatment efficacy. Gendreau (1996) noted that those involved in WW initiatives have investigated 'the black box of treatment programs' (p. 118) with the aim of identifying the principles that distinguish effective programmes from less effective or ineffective programmes. In this literature, the following principles have been identified as being important in the effective treatment of offenders (Andrews & Bonta, 2003).

The Use of Effective Therapies in Treatment

The WW approach argues that styles and modes of treatment should be employed that are capable of reducing the influence of criminogenic needs (i.e. dynamic risk factors). The treatment approaches suggested in the WW literature are skills oriented, cognitive-behavioural and social learning methods, as these have been found to be the most effective in producing change in offenders, rather than non-directive, relationship-oriented, or psychodynamic, insight-orientated therapy (Andrews & Bonta, 2003). Further to these ideas Gendreau and others (Gendreau, 1981; Gendreau & Ross, 1979) have advocated the use of multi-modal techniques in order to match treatment to the offender rather than viewing all offenders as being the same (i.e. they all have identical personality traits, attitudes and beliefs). What this means in practice is ensuring that offenders receive therapy in a form that engages their interest and is consistent with their learning styles and values; for example, utilising action or behavioural techniques with individuals who have poor verbal skills and find it difficult to process information in a verbal format.

The Targeting of High-Risk Cases for Treatment

It is argued in the WW approach that intensive treatment services should be delivered towards higher, as opposed to lower, risk cases.[1] The argument for targeting treatment at high-risk cases is influenced by the results of a number of meta-analyses that have investigated treatment outcome (e.g. Andrews et al., 1990). It is noted that when higher risk cases are considered, then larger treatment effects are found in terms of reductions in recidivism compared to lower risk cases. Such targeting is of course essential if resources are scarce because high-risk individuals, if untreated, are much more likely to recidivate than lower risk cases. Further to this, it has been found that providing intensive resources to lower risk cases rarely produces reductions in recidivism rates (Bonta, 1996).

Identifying Treatment Needs

The WW literature argues that 'criminogenic needs' (e.g. pro-criminal attitudes) should be specifically targeted in treatment (see Chapter 16). These criminogenic factors are also called 'dynamic risk' factors because there is the possibility that these can change in treatment. The reason to identify such treatment targets is probably best exemplified by Dowden (1998), who reported that targeting criminogenic needs was more likely to reduce recidivism compared to targeting non-criminogenic needs. Promising targets for change were identified by Dowden as changing antisocial attitudes, changing antisocial feelings, reducing antisocial peer associations, promoting identification and association with anti-criminal role models, increasing self-control, self-management and problem solving skills, reducing chemical dependency, and changing other attributes that have been identified with criminal conduct. Less promising targets were identified, by Dowden, as increasing self-esteem without simultaneous reductions in antisocial thinking, increasing positive emotions, pro-social peer associations, focusing on vague emotional complaints that have not been linked with criminal conduct, increasing the cohesiveness of antisocial peer groups without changing antisocial attitudes, showing respect for antisocial thinking on the grounds that the values of one culture are as valid as the values of another

---

[1] Typically, high-risk cases are those that have a long history of known offending. Such individuals are regarded as being at high 'static' risk (i.e. they score highly on historical, non-changeable risk factors that have been shown to predict future risk, as opposed to dynamic or changeable risk factors).

culture, and attempting to turn the client into a better person when the standards of being a better person do not link with recidivism.

Taking Account of Responsivity Issues

Gendreau (1996) noted that three components of responsivity have been identified in the WW literature. These are: (i) matching the treatment approach with the learning style and personality of the offender; (ii) matching the characteristics of the offender with those of the therapist; and (iii) matching the skills of the therapist with the type of programme being delivered. Responsivity has more recently been divided into the consideration of *internal responsivity* issues around matching the content and delivery of treatment to specific client attributes such as personality and cognitive maturity (Andrews, 2001), and *external responsivity* issues, including a range of general and specific issues, such as the use of active and participatory methods of therapy, and staff and environmental characteristics (Andrews, 2001).

EVALUATION OF THE 'WHAT WORKS' APPROACH TO TREATMENT

The WW literature provides a clear treatment framework for clinicians so that responsivity in the criminal justice field can be maximised. In summary, it has set out a number of principles that need to be addressed in treatment (see Chapter 16): (i) treatment should be derived from Cognitive Behavioural Therapy (CBT) theory, behavioural theory and social learning theory because this type of package has a track record of being effective with offenders; (ii) treatment should focus on high-risk cases; (iii) treatment should target criminogenic needs; and (iv) offenders should be matched to treatment type. These core principles illustrate the *fertility* (clinical utility) of the WW approach. One of the main reasons clinicians are guided by this approach is because it has been informed largely by empirical research. In other words, the WW approach has *empirical adequacy* and provides clear, testable hypotheses in relation to treatment evaluation. For example, CBT will be more effective than less offence-focused therapy, treatment will be more effective for higher risk cases than lower risk cases, targeting specific criminogenic needs will be more effective in reducing recidivism rates in offenders than treating non-criminogenic needs, and treatment will be more effective if matched to an offender's learning style. The fact that the WW approach incorporates principles relating to a number of the theories reported in previous chapters of this book speaks to its *unifying power* and *external consistency*.

Although the WW approach has considerable strengths, we do, however, hold some concerns about the ubiquitous application of the WW principles.

First, we argue that a blanket approach of WW principles could threaten the theory's *clinical utility* or *fertility value*. For example, although it is important to target high-risk individuals in treatment, this takes the focus away from treating others deemed to be at lower risk. We argue that these individuals may be high risk in particular situations. An example would be an incest offender who may typically be seen as low risk because he does not have a large number of victims in his offence history. This type of sexual offender may have abused the same victim over a period of years and would do so again if an opportunity arose; in other words, this offender may be at high risk if he has access to that victim.

A further drawback of the WW approach is that heavy application of the principles has led to a manualised approach to treatment in the UK, restricting the notion of flexibility. Although, we would not advocate, as do Serran, Fernandez, Marshall and Mann (2003), that adopting a manualised approach to treatment is a 'mistake' (p. 371), we do argue that sticking rigidly to manuals may leave little room for manoeuvre if other issues come up that are not addressed in the treatment manual for the particular programme. For example, a client's receptiveness to working on a particular area of problems in that particular session may be low because of recent life events or crises, so that session goals need to be reprioritised.

One problem with the WW approach is that it focuses mainly on the *system:* it assumes that treatment will be effective given the systematic application of such principles in therapy. It does not say anything about the quality of the client–therapist relationship, the processes that are unleashed in therapy, or the change process within the individual; this highlights some potential problems with *explanatory depth.* Further problems with explanatory depth are associated with the relative lack of attention paid to the underlying constructs. There is no real explanation of how the different processes and structures impacting on responsivity are interrelated. Therefore, there has been a failure to realise that the ability to capitalise on therapeutic opportunities also involves the dynamic interaction between person, therapy and contextual factors (Ward et al., 2004b).

CLINICAL UTILITY OF THE 'WHAT WORKS' APPROACH TO SEXUAL OFFENDER TREATMENT

Generally, the innovative work of Canadian, British and American researchers from the WW approach has led to the refinement of rehabilitation theory and the formulation of explicit practice guidelines (e.g. Andrews & Bonta, 1998; Layton-MacKenzie, 2000; McGuire, 2001). This work has been guided empirically, and indeed, the determination to discern what actually works in the correctional domain has been a striking and welcome change (Ward et al., 2004b). Ward et al. also note that the call to utilise empirically supported therapies and strategies has increasingly been accepted. At the same time, the emergence of a risk management perspective and its attendant risk–need model of offender rehabilitation has provided the offender rehabilitation field with an organisational framework to guide service providers, policy makers and correctional administrators. Therefore, Ward et al. argue that evidence-based offender treatments have become an established part of efforts to reduce crime, and prison, probation and forensic mental health services all now offer such treatments.

Current methods of treatment used by both the prison and probation services in the UK and North America for sexual offenders have been heavily influenced by the WW literature. All offender treatment programmes in England and Wales have to be accredited by the Correctional Services Panel formerly the Joint Prison and Probation Services Accreditation Panel for England and Wales (Rex, Lieb, Bottoms & Wilson, 2003). This Panel is made up of international experts and their task is to accredit treatment programmes that reach a suitable standard. Programmes are judged on a range of criteria based on WW principles, such as the targeting of high-risk cases for treatment, the careful targeting of dynamic risk factors[2] (Thornton, 2002) and addressing responsivity issues, such as matching treatment to the learning style and personality of the offender. The way that this has been addressed in current sexual offender treatment programmes in the UK, in the broadest sense, means that programmes should be designed specifically for offenders who have learning difficulties, offenders from different cultural backgrounds, and personality disordered offenders (Beech & Mann, 2002). The Adapted Sex Offender Treatment Programme is an example of a programme devised for borderline learning-disabled offenders in the UK. Programmes for the treatment of personality disordered offenders based on WW principles are also currently under development.

However, in terms of matching the skills of the therapist with that of the programme, Beech and Mann (2002) note that comparitively little has been written about the qualities that should be present in an effective sexual offender therapist and even less about how therapists acquire therapeutic skills. We will now consider how therapist style has been investigated in relation to responsivity in psychotherapeutic settings and, more specifically, sexual offender interventions.

THERAPIST STYLE, PROCESS ISSUES AND RESPONSIVITY IN TREATMENT

As we have already noted, there have been a number of recently reported studies that have demonstrated the effectiveness of cognitive-behavioural group-based treatment for sexual offenders (Friendship et al., 2003; Hanson et al., 2002). However, as Marshall et al. (2003a) observe, far more offenders who have been through treatment reoffend than is desirable. They also note that treatment effects vary considerably across programmes, in that some programmes are more effective than others, which they suggest 'may also be due to the differing styles of the therapists or in the therapists' abilities to create those conditions that maximise the full and effective participation of the clients' (p. 207). The aim of this section is to consider some of the therapist attributes and process issues described in the general psychotherapy literature, where a considerable amount has been written about engaging clients in treatment and hence increasing responsivity. Such processes in therapy include the ability of therapists to create an appropriate alliance with the client, inculcate that there is possibility for change, ensure that the client will benefit positively from such changes, provide

---

[2] That is, sexual interests (see Chapter 10), pro-offending attitudes (see Chapter 8), socio-affective problems (see Chapter 12) and self-management problems (see Chapters 16 and 17).

the client with an opportunity to learn from therapy, and to engage the client emotionally in treatment.

Therapist Features

Marshall et al. (2003a) argue that cognitive approaches that are supportive rather than confrontational are the most effective in producing change. They suggest that a number of attributes are needed by therapists in order to produce responsivity on the part of the client. These are empathy, genuineness, warmth, resourcefulness, supportiveness, self-disclosure, an ability to ask open-ended questions, to be directive yet flexible, to encourage participation in therapy, to be rewarding, to use appropriate humour, to be attentive, confident, emotionally responsive, and trustworthy, and to instil positive expectations on the part of the client. In contrast, they note a number of features of therapists that may impede change. These are the use of aggressive confrontation in therapy, rejection, manipulation, low interest, excessive criticism, sarcasm, hostility, discomfort with silences, unresponsiveness, dishonesty, being judgmental, authoritarian, defensive, needing to be liked, nervousness, having boundary problems, rigidity and emotional coldness. The most damaging treatment style is thought to be the 'aggressive stimulator' (Marshall et al., 2003a, p. 215), in which there are harsh confrontational challenges of group members.

Marshall et al. (2003a) state that in general psychotherapeutic treatment the quality of the relationship between therapists and client (therapeutic alliance)[3] can account for 25% of the variance in treatment effectiveness; a similar finding has been reported by Marziali and Alexander (1991) for treatment outcome in CBT. In contrast, Marziali and Alexander, and Marshall et al. (2003a), conclude that a poor quality of therapeutic alliance between client and therapist predicts treatment dropout, and obviously there is little treatment responsivity in those no longer undertaking treatment.

Until comparatively recently, therapist style has either been ignored (Serran et al., 2003), or when it has been described in relation to treatment for sexual offenders, therapists have generally emphasised the importance of the aggressive stimulator (e.g. Salter, 1988; Wyre, 1989). However, a number in the field have begun to question the validity of this approach (e.g. Beech & Mann, 2002; Marshall et al., 1999a) and it is now generally recognised that direct, confrontational approaches to the treatment of sexual offenders will be likely to lead to increased resistance as opposed to change (Beech & Fordham, 1997; Kear-Colwell & Pollack, 1997). Respect, support, confidence, emotional responsivity, self-disclosure, open-ended questioning, flexibility, positive reinforcement, and the use of appropriate humour have been linked to group participation, improved

---

[3] The therapeutic alliance is defined in the psychotherapy literature as the implicit cooperative compact between therapist and patient, where the psychotherapist offers therapy and the patient agrees to obey the fundamental rules of therapy.

perspective taking, coping skills, taking responsibility and accepting future risk (Marshall et al., 2003b). In other words, these positive characteristics are likely to increase responsivity.

Mann (2001) lists four essential qualities for an effective sexual offender therapist, based on experience of training and supervising sexual offender treatment providers. These are positive attitudes towards sexual offenders, a self-evaluating approach, an inquiring mind, and a warm interpersonal style. Marshall et al. (2003b) report some tentative evidence indicating the potential importance of consideration of therapist variables and treatment responsivity. Here, they found that the positive therapist qualities (see Marshall et al., 2003a) of empathy, warmth, rewardingness, and directive, non-confrontational therapy were related to an increase in the level of coping skills on the part of the offender who has undertaken treatment. In addition, the therapist qualities of encouraging participation and dealing effectively with problems were discovered to be related to an increase in perspective-taking abilities on the part of the offenders in therapy. Finally, appropriate body language on the part of the therapist was found to be related to helping offenders deal with relationship difficulties.

Process Features

But how does therapist style relate to the process of therapy itself? Treatment for sexual offenders is typically delivered via group-based CBT. Group therapy, it has been argued (Yalom, 1985), facilitates a number of therapeutic processes. Beech and Fordham (1997) outlined the benefits of being in a group and group work as the following: groups provide an environment that can offer both support and challenge to the individual; group work provides the opportunity for discussion with peers, and provides opportunities for increasing self-esteem and empathic responding; and groups also offer a forum for support and sharing of problems, which may be a completely new experience for many sexual offenders, particularly child sexual abusers, who are generally isolated individuals, often with interpersonal deficits and feelings of inadequacy. Having the experience of being valued, being able to help others, practising social skills, and getting to know others in detail can greatly improve an individual's self-esteem and interpersonal functioning. Given that feelings of inadequacy and lack of appropriate relationships may be important vulnerability factors for many child sexual abusers (Thornton, Beech & Marshall, 2004), improvement in these areas is an important element in reducing reoffending.

Beech and Fordham (1997) reported one of the few studies that attempted to identify the effect of group process—which is strongly influenced by therapist style—on treatment change. They found that the most effective changes occurred in men experiencing a group treatment programme that was cohesive, well organised and well led, encouraged the open expression of feelings, produced a sense of group responsibility and instilled a sense of hope in members. By contrast, it appeared that over-controlling, over-directive, confrontational leaders had a detrimental effect upon group climate. This is consistent with evidence from the psychotherapy literature on group processes (e.g. Belfer & Levendusky, 1985; Yalom, 1985). In terms of the relationship between therapeutic style and group processes, many authors emphasise the importance of leadership in producing cohesiveness, appropriate group norms and the instillation of hope for the future, as these are of particular importance in running effective groups and inculcating responsivity in group members (Belfer & Levendusky, 1985; Yalom, 1985).

More recently Beech and Hamilton-Giachritsis (2005) report that men who have undertaken treatment in sexual offender groups that were cohesive, and where the members showed involvement and commitment to the group, as well as the members showing concern and friendship for each other, were more likely to change in therapy than groups where this was not the case.

EVALUATION OF THERAPIST STYLES AND PROCESS ISSUES

Marshall et al. (2003a) note that 'there can be little doubt that the empirical attitude of the early behavior therapists paved the way for rapid and significant advances in the treatment of a variety of disorders... but the neglect of research attention to process variables appears to have been an error' (p. 206). It is certainly the case in the sexual offender field that few studies have examined therapist and process issues in the treatment of sexual offenders. However, this does appear to be a fertile area for future research and may have important implications for treatment (potential *fertility*). What little work has been carried out suggests that change is not only affected at the system and individual levels but may also be promoted at the *process* level of treatment. For example, Beech and Fordham (1997) found that a confrontational approach by therapists in treatment produced less positive changes in therapy than a more supportive, warm approach to therapy. The argument we would suggest as to why such groups are more likely to inculcate change is due to the following. In a highly cohesive group, appropriate challenges by other members of the group would be carried out in an atmosphere where members felt supported rather than 'got at'. Therefore, they are likely to be more willing to take on board the messages about their offending behaviour than they would in less cohesive groups. This is particularly important in engaging sexual offenders in assessment and treatment, given the differences in comparison to general psychotherapy clients (see below).

It is probably too early to judge the theoretical value of this approach. Certainly the concentration on process issues has *external consistency* in that it is consistent with the psychotherapy literature and would appear to have *internal coherence*. But we cannot at the moment really comment upon this approach's *empirical adequacy* and *scope*. The major problem is that at the present time there are few, if any, theories explaining why process variables are important determinants of treatment outcome. Furthermore, there is a paucity of theoretical work on the mechanisms that actually generate the factors discovered to mediate good therapeutic outcomes.

CLINICAL UTILITY OF CONSIDERING THERAPIST AND PROCESS ISSUES

Beech and Mann (2002) have pointed out that in many ways sexual offenders are qualitatively different from general psychotherapy clients, so the need for a high level of therapists' skills is paramount. Sexual offenders generally enter treatment because they are mandated to do so, not through free choice, so the level of engagement may be less than one would hope. Furthermore, whereas general psychotherapy clients are usually motivated to change due to being distressed by their psychological state, sexual offenders often enjoy their offending and are not motivated to change (Beech & Mann, 2002). Plus, the stigma and vilification experienced by sexual offenders is unparalleled, so that in treatment they may be extremely sensitive to indications of labelling, hostility or lack of empathy by therapists (Beech & Mann, 2002). If therapists fail to take these dynamics into account, the value of treatment effects may be reduced, no matter at what level the WW principles have been addressed. It can be argued that all of the attributes of good therapists outlined above are even more necessary in sexual offender treatment, especially in the early stages of treatment where the major task is to positively engage individuals in therapy. Here, Marshall et al. (2003a) note that the relationship between therapist and client is of particular importance in the early stages of therapy, as clients generally have difficulties in confidence in early sessions of treatment and this will potentially restrict their willingness to be open and honest about their problems.

Therapists need to be well trained to deliver treatment effectively. In English and Welsh prisons, comprehensive introductory training is provided when introducing trainee therapists to a structured sexual offender programme based on WW principles (Mann & Thornton, 1998) even if the trainees have previous experience working with sexual offenders. Beech and Mann (2002) note that potential tutors are assessed on a range of competencies. These include understanding of CBT theory and concepts, application of CBT techniques, warmth and empathy, impartiality, clear use of language, flexibility of style, discussion leading and presentation skills, team working, agenda skills, skills for giving feedback, questioning skills, maintenance of boundaries, tenacity, professionalism, preparation, participation and open coping style, and openness to feedback (Sacre, 1995).

In the last section of this chapter we will examine a new approach to the description of treatment change. Ward et al. (2004b) have attempted to take a wider perspective on treatment change in describing a multifactor readiness to change model. Ward et al. (2004b) suggest that the constructs of responsivity and motivation are not sufficiently rich to provide the guidance required to build a sound alliance with offenders, whereas the construct of readiness for treatment can do so. This approach has not yet been specifically applied to sexual offender work, but we argue that it will be a useful approach to take in the field.

READINESS TO CHANGE

Ward et al. (2004b) argue that there has been little attempt in the extant literature on the subject to distinguish between responsivity, treatment motivation and readiness in terms of change at the individual level. We will now briefly examine these concepts. *Responsivity*, as we have noted earlier in this chapter, refers to the extent to which offenders are able to absorb the content of treatment and subsequently change their behaviour. *Motivation* (to change) involves assessing whether or not someone really wants to enter treatment and therefore is willing to change his or her offending behaviour. *Readiness*, according to Ward et al. (2004b), is defined as the presence of characteristics (states or dispositions) within either the client or the therapeutic situation, which are likely to promote engagement in therapy and which, thereby, are likely to enhance therapeutic change. To be ready for treatment means that the person is motivated to change, is able to respond appropriately, finds it relevant and meaningful, and has the capacities to successfully enter the treatment programme. Ascertaining whether an offender is motivated to enter treatment involves assessing their volitional state (i.e. whether they genuinely want and intend to enter treatment).

The major assumptions underlying this approach, according to Ward et al. (2004b), are that the treatment readiness of offenders is a function of both internal (person) and external (context) factors. *Person* factors are cognitive (beliefs, cognitive strategies), affective (emotions), volitional (goals, wants or desires), behavioural (skills and competencies) and identity (personal and social). *Contextual* factors are circumstances (mandated versus voluntary, offender type), location (prison, community), opportunities (availability of therapy and programmes), resources (quality of programme, availability of trained and qualified therapist, appropriate culture), interpersonal supports (availability of individuals who wish the offender well and would like to see him or her succeed in overcoming their problems) and programme characteristics (e.g. programme type and timing of treatment).

The readiness model suggests that an offender will be ready to change dependent upon to the extent that he or she possesses certain cognitive, emotional, volitional and behavioural properties and lives in an environment where such changes are possible and supported. More specifically, the offender needs to possess the capacities and inclination to change his behaviour in general, solve a particular problem, accept a particular intervention, and to do all this at a particular time (now versus some future date). From the perspective of the readiness model, it is hypothesised that the subject and contextual factors combine to increase the likelihood a person is ready to engage in treatment. The model incorporates whether or not a person is ready to change his or her behaviour (in the general sense), to eliminate a specific problem, to eliminate a specific problem by virtue of a specific method (e.g. CBT) and finally to eliminate a specific problem by virtue of a specific method at a specific time. The idea is that readiness will increase the degree to which a person moves from the first treatment target to the final one. In our view this aspect of the model maps rather well onto the stages of change model (Prochaska, DiClemente & Norcross, 1992).

EVALUATION OF THE READINESS APPROACH

In current practice it is widely accepted that offender motivation constitutes an important requirement for selection into rehabilitation programmes, and therapists are expected to have the skills to initiate, enhance and sustain motivation in reluctant individuals as discussed in the previous section of this chapter. However, despite a large body of literature on motivational interviewing and related interventions, Ward et al. (2004b) note that there has been comparatively little attention paid to clarifying the relevant underlying mechanisms or consideration of the relationship between motivational states and other aspects of treatment preparedness in the general offender literature. It is too early to say how Ward et al.'s ideas will impact upon sexual offender treatment in the future but this approach may address the suggested deficiencies of a simple motivational or responsivity approach. Such an approach would clearly appear to have *internal coherence* and *external consistency* with a number of ideas in the field. Again, as noted above, it is too early to make comments upon the predictive and empirical adequacy of this approach. However, as an explanation of volition to change it would appear to have wider scope than the early WW responsivity approach.

CLINICAL UTILITY OF THE READINESS APPROACH

Most sexual offenders are likely to have entered treatment with an ambivalent attitude towards changing their offending behaviour (Beech & Fisher, 2002). Many will have enjoyed the offence but not the negative consequences for themselves. Others may be reluctant to change because they have little else in their lives. Some may be unmotivated because they do not believe they have the ability to change and may be very fearful of what change will involve. By demonstrating that change is possible, and that there are alternatives to offending, and by understanding that an abuse-free life will ultimately be more rewarding than continuing to offend, it is possible to develop a readiness to change in offenders. The delivery style of group facilitators will be a key element in this and they will need to be supportive, encouraging, praising and respectful. As noted earlier, Beech and Fordham (1997) reported that an important component of group-based treatment is the instillation of hope in group members (i.e. indicating to abusers that they have the ability to change).

In the readiness model, Ward et al. (2004b) argue that low efficacy is as much a feature of the therapy context and setting as it is of the internal characteristics of the client (e.g. motivation and locus of control), and that to increase the chances that an intervention will engage an offender it is necessary to keep in mind the importance of cognitive factors such as treatment expectations and appraisals, motivation, external supports and an appropriate institutional culture (Howells & Day, 2003). Although the model has not been applied specifically to sexual offenders, many of these factors are particularly relevant to the circumstances facing such offenders.

According to the readiness model, it is possible to intervene therapeutically to increase offenders' readiness for treatment: that is, to facilitate their entry into a therapy programme. In brief, it is possible to (i) *modify the client* by using motivational interventions or instilling basic readiness skills depending on the problems or obstacles concerned (e.g. impaired cognitive skills); (ii) *modify the therapy* by amending the treatment methods in order to match the offender's particular cognitive, affective and behavioural skill set (e.g. taking into account literacy or ethnicity), or by altering the structural components of treatment (e.g. treatment intensity); and finally (iii) *modify the setting*, for example by changing the prison culture to be more supportive of rehabilitation (e.g. by staff training), or by shifting prisons or units, or giving offenders leave to attend community-based programmes.

CONCLUSIONS

In this chapter we have argued that it is important to consider the issues of responsively as it is only if we can effectively change offenders' behaviour so that they no longer offend sexually that we can properly reintegrate such individuals into society. Hence, we have examined the notions of treatment change at a number of levels. First we have examined the WW approach, which has had a strong influence on the delivery of treatment for sexual offenders. Although WW authors have noted the importance of responsivity factors, we would note that there has been an underspecification of issues related to the process of change in treatment and the readiness or volitional issues. We have also reviewed some of the recent work that has examined therapist and process issues in sexual offender work and, finally, examined a recent model of offender readiness. Here, we would observe that it is probably too early to comment upon what influence some of this work will have upon therapy for sexual offenders in the future. We propose, however, that even greater responsivity might occur when programmes are able to be responsive to individual needs. Here, we have argued that the level of fit between the client and the treatment is increasingly acknowledged as a critical factor in effective treatment programmes (Ward et al., 2004a). Therefore the effectiveness of treatment programmes is likely to be a result of both the availability of high quality and responsive treatments and efforts to encourage individuals to enter and stay in treatment.

PART VI
CONCLUSIONS

Chapter 20

TOWARD A UNIFIED THEORY OF SEXUAL OFFENDING

We have come to the end of a fascinating and, at times, complicated journey. Theories pertaining to all aspects of sexual offending have been described, evaluated and applied to clinical practice. We have examined comprehensive explanations of sexual abuse, single factors associated with sexual abuse (e.g. intimacy, empathy and cognitive distortions), offence process models and, finally, prominent theories of how best to treat sexual offenders. It has been an exhilarating experience, and confirmed in our minds that the field should be proud of its theoretical achievements. They are indeed considerable, and in conjunction with a number of excellent research programmes, advance our understanding of the causes of sexual offending and the best ways to eradicate this serious social problem.

But where do we go from here? What more is there to do? It could be argued that we should continue to refine and evaluate the different theories in a piecemeal way. However, we think that it is possible to attempt something much more ambitious than this: a global explanation of all aspects of sexual offending using our current knowledge of the surface facts. Throughout this book, we have shown that there is still much to learn at a descriptive level about all aspects of sexual offending. For example, the kinds of questions that require answers include what sort of intimacy, empathy, cognitive, social, sexual and emotional problems are evident in sexual offenders, and how are they correlated with offender type? Are there indeed different offence and relapse processes and how do they relate to the psychological deficits noted above (e.g. empathy, cognitive distortions)? What treatments models are most effective? Is it advisable to tailor treatment to suit individual offenders or should we continue to embrace a 'one size fits all' strategy? And what is the best way to measure risk? We recognise that there are numerous other unresolved issues that require research attention over the next few years. However, we think that it would be seriously neglectful for us to narrow our focus on developing research at the expense of theory construction. In our view, both tasks need to be pursued to ensure future fruitful research and further theory development. It is not wise or possible to separate out the tasks of theory construction, development and evaluation from those integral to empirical research. As is evident from this book, good theories help to create conceptual space for problems to be identified and investigated. For example, the conceptual analysis and reformulation of Marshall's attachment theory of sexual offending facilitated the discovery of different attachment styles in sexual offenders and their relationship to offence characteristics (Chapter 12). There are many other examples of how theory critique and construction has helped the field to discover more about the nature of sexual crimes and develop new therapeutic interventions. But it is also important not to get too carried away by the euphoria of creating new ideas and neglect the painstaking empirical work needed to test these theories. Each set of tasks is equally important.

We think it is timely to outline a theoretical framework for unifying our knowledge of sexual offending, one that we hope will help to set the agenda for future research programmes. In this final chapter, we draw together the wide range of theories described in this book to outline a preliminary theory of sexual offending: a unified theory. First, we describe the roots of this theory, and outline its fundamental tenets. Then, we critically evaluate its usefulness as it currently stands.

A UNIFIED THEORY OF SEXUAL OFFENDING

If there is one thing we have been reminded of repeatedly as we reviewed the different types of theories in this book, it is that human beings are multifaceted, integrated organisms. Because of this, we believe that any new theory of sexual crimes should reflect this complexity. The unified theory represents our attempt to acknowledge these features of human nature and human functioning. It is intended simply as a promissory note, and we are currently working on a fully fleshed theory (Ward & Beech, in press).

In brief, the unified theory (see Figure 20.1) is intended to stimulate research and further theory development by explicitly linking sets of causal factors in order to explain why sexual offenders exhibit the symptom or problem clusters they do, which in turn may lead to sexual offending. Drawing from the theories and the empirical research discussed in this book, we argue that there are a number of types of causes frequently invoked to explain sexual crimes. They include early developmental experiences (e.g. sexual and physical abuse), genetic predispositions, social and cultural structures and processes, contextual factors (e.g. intoxication, severe stress) and psychological dispositions or trait factors (e.g. empathy deficits, cognitive distortions, deviant sexual preferences, emotional skill deficits and interpersonal incompetence). We have reduced this multiplicity of causal elements to three sets of factors which interact continuously. They are biological factors (genetic and brain development), the offender's proximal and distal ecology (social, cultural and personal circumstances), and three neuropsychological systems (motivational/emotional, action selection and control, and perception and memory systems). In the unified theory, these three sets of causal factors combine to generate the clinical problems evident in offenders, and their sexually abusive actions. The consequences of sexually

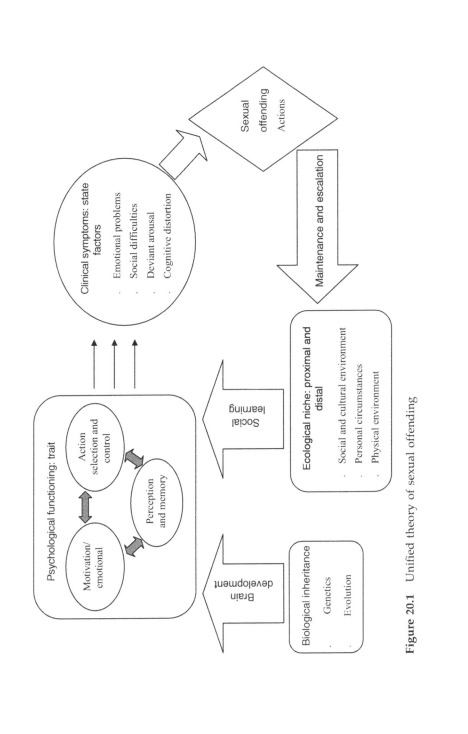

Figure 20.1 Unified theory of sexual offending

abusive behaviour, in turn, function to maintain or entrench the offender's vulnerabilities through their impact on the environment, and psychological functioning. According to the unified theory, sexual offending occurs through the ongoing confluence of distal and proximal factors that interact in a dynamic way. Genetic predispositions and social learning have a significant impact on individuals' developing brains and result in the establishment of three interlocking neuropsychological systems. So, genetic predispositions and social learning interact to establish individuals' psychological functioning, and this functioning may be compromised in some way by poor genetic inheritance, biological insults or developmental adversity to make it difficult for the individual concerned to function in an adaptive manner. The resultant vulnerabilities may lead to antisocial behaviour under certain circumstances. Our unified theory of sexual offending draws strongly upon the work of Bruce Pennington (2002), who has provided a developmental account of psychopathology involving four main levels of analysis. We outline his main ideas before fleshing out the unified theory in more detail.

Levels of Analysis

We accept Pennington's suggestion that a neuroscientific account of human psychopathology requires considering four levels of analysis: aetiology, brain mechanisms, neuropsychology, and symptom levels. The *aetiological level* is broadly concerned with the influence of genetic and environmental factors in causing psychopathology. For example, a genetic vulnerability to developing schizophrenia in conjunction with severe early stressors might adversely affect the proliferation and density of neurotransmitter receptors and ultimately increase the chances of an individual developing the disorder. The level of *brain mechanisms* is concerned with the effect of the aetiological factors on the development of the brain and its subsequent functioning. Severe and prolonged abuse or neglect might cause structural and functional changes to the brain that adversely affect individuals' chances of adjusting to social challenges and problems. For example, prolonged chronic stress, such as that induced by sexual or physical abuse, is associated with changes in the neurobiology of the person concerned (e.g. hippocampal atrophy; Sapolsky 1997). The level of *neuropsychological functioning* is concerned with the brain-based psychological systems generating human behaviour, for example, spatial perception and language production. At this level, there is a careful attempt to ensure that the construction of theories concerning psychological systems is consistent with what we know about brain circuitry and architecture. Finally, the *symptom or surface* level is concerned with the clinical phenomena thought to characterise the various forms of psychopathology (e.g. mood, sleep, appetite disturbances in depression). In sexual offenders, the symptom level is constituted by the four clusters of problems noted above and in Chapter 5: emotional problems, social difficulties, deviant sexual arousal and cognitive distortions. Pennington argues that all four levels are required in order to develop an adequate neuroscientific explanation of psychopathology. All four levels are mutually constraining and theories at the different levels need to be consistent with each other. In effect, this means that researchers should seek to construct multidimensional aetiological theories of the symptoms exhibited by sexual offenders and work alongside their colleagues in other fields: for example, behavioural genetics and neuropsychology. It is important to note that seeking to explain sexual offending by reference to these four levels of analysis does not entail biological reductionism. Our view is that the level of personal agency and meaning-seeking is a crucial feature of human functioning and ought to be safeguarded in any explanation of sexual offending. However, genetic factors and brain development and functioning subserve or underpin psychological functioning and should figure in aetiological theory building. In other words, the ability of human beings to form intentions and decide on a course of action crucially depends on the integrity and functioning of their brains.

Psychological Functional Systems

The four levels of analysis described above are necessary for the development of a comprehensive scientific theory of sexual offending. A critical element as far as understanding the psychological vulnerabilities of sexual offenders is concerned is the neuropsychological level. It is this level of analysis that directly informs researchers of the mechanisms generating offenders' psychological symptoms and problems. We will now briefly discuss the functional systems associated with this level of analysis.

Pennington follows Luria in hypothesising that it is possible to divide the human central nervous system into three functional systems, each associated with distinct psychological functions and brain structures.[1] The first of these systems is the *motivational/emotional system*, which is associated with the cortical, limbic and brainstem brain structures. According to Pennington, a major function of this system is 'to allow goals and values to influence both perception and action selection rapidly and to adjust motivational state to fit changing environmental circumstances' (2002, p. 79). This system interacts with the *action selection and control system*, which is associated with the frontal cortex, the basal ganglia and parts of the thalamus. A major function of this system is to help the organism to plan, implement and evaluate action plans, and to control behaviour, thoughts and emotions in the service of higher goals. Finally, the *perception/memory system* is associated primarily with the hippocampal formation and the posterior neocortex. A major function of this system is to process incoming sensory information and to construct representations of objects and events, and make them available to the other two systems. The three functional systems interact to produce all psychological processes and phenomena. Pennington argues that because each system is associated with distinct brain systems and psychological functions, it is also likely to generate unique types of mental disorders if compromised in some way. For example, he hypothesises that depression is a disorder of the motivation/emotional system, conduct disorder of the action selection and control system, and developmental language disorders are caused by impairments in the perception and memory system (Pennington, 2002).

---

[1] We have changed the labels for these systems slightly in the descriptions that follow.

The Unified Theory of Sexual Offending

Like Pennington (2002), we see both genetic and environmental factors as playing a strong and interactive role in the development of brain functioning. In our theory, there are three forms of developmental resources responsible for providing the psychological and social competencies necessary for human beings to function in the world. These three systems are genetic/evolutionary resources, social/cultural resources and individuals' life circumstances. An individual is hypothesised to enter the world with various genetic advantages and disadvantages (e.g. an overly anxious temperament), that in conjunction with environmental factors (e.g. relationship conflict) may create offence-related vulnerabilities. Some of these genetically based predispositions might be linked to the sex of the individual, and in this sense, create gender-linked vulnerabilities: for example, the tendency for males to engage in impersonal sex (see Chapters 6 and 7). However, the cultural and social context in which a person develops can also create problems, ultimately increasing his chances of behaving in a sexually aggressive manner (see Chapters 3 and 11). For example, being exposed at an early age to parental violence and abuse can both adversely affect an individual's brain development, and undermine the integrity of the three primary psychological systems. The impairment of these systems will compromise a person's adaptive functioning in any number of ways, depending on the specific damage inflicted (e.g. make it harder for him to effectively regulate his mood: *action selection and control*). Exposure to antisocial models also is likely to teach individuals maladaptive ways of solving personal and interpersonal problems and result in problematic values and attitudes: the *perception and memory system*. Furthermore, an individual's unique circumstances are hypothesised to influence his psychological and social development by virtue of their influence on the core functional systems (see Chapters 2–6, 9 and 12). For example, the loss of a parent at an early age may result in the formation of the dangerous world implicit theory, making it hard for the person concerned to trust other people and to establish robust relationship skills (see Chapter 8). As a result of this, these individuals may display social difficulties as their clinical symptoms.

We have used the term 'ecology' to refer to the set of cultural, social and personal circumstances confronting each person as he or she develops throughout life. According to Steiner, 'Ecology is, by definition, the reciprocal relationship among all organisms and their biological and physical environments' (2002, p. 2). The *habitat* is the actual locality in which a person resides and the *niche*, the role(s) occupied by that person in an ecological community (Steiner, 2002). In our view, thinking of the cultural, social and personal circumstances as ecological components helps to keep in mind the fact that human beings are animals who purposively interact with their environment and develop in a dynamic and interactive manner (see Chapter 7). Sexual offending emerges from a network of relationships between individuals and their local habitats and niches, and is not simply the consequence of individual psychopathology.

Throughout development, it is hypothesised that the three types of developmental resources (genetic, social/cultural and individuals' circumstances) combine and interact to shape an individual's unique psychological functioning.

More specifically, the motivational/emotional, perception and memory, and action selection and control functional systems emerge in ways that are relatively adaptive or problematic. These systems *interact* with each other to produce all actions, and play a critical role in generating psychological and social phenomena. Although the systems may be differentially compromised in some ways, it is likely that problems in any of the systems will adversely affect the others in some respects.

The *motivational/emotional system* may be associated with a number of defects relating to offenders' genetic inheritance, cultural upbringing or individual experiences. For example, someone who was brought up in an emotionally impoverished environment might find it difficult to identify his emotions in an accurate manner and also become confused when confronted with emotionally charged interpersonal situations. Such an individual might become angry and act in an antisocial manner on occasions (see Chapters 3, 5 and 9). Another type of problem could be related to the range of primary goods or goals sought by a person. Poor early learning could lead to an individual lacking the skills necessary (internal conditions) to establish strong interpersonal relationships, resulting in social isolation and further psychological and social deficits (see Chapter 18). The other types of problems evident in individuals' good lives plans could have their origin in biological, cultural or individual circumstances.

Problems in the *perceptual and memory system* leading to sexually abusive behaviour might have their origins in maladaptive beliefs, attitudes and subsequent interpretation of social encounters. One source of difficulty could reside in dysfunctional implicit theories such as the dangerous world or entitlement theories (see Chapter 8). The presence of implicit theories that are chronically activated (i.e. frequently available to guide information processing) is likely to cause the subsequent activation of problematic goals and emotions, which in turn make it difficult for a person to effectively control his sexual behaviour. We hypothesise that these cognitive structures can function as pre-attentive filters, biasing the processing of social information and resulting in a variety of personal and social difficulties.

It is an interesting feature of the unified theory that phenomena grouped together at the level of symptom manifestation may in fact have quite different causes and be generated by distinct psychological systems. For example, we suggest that rationalisations, excuses, minimisation and so on are primarily a function of social and intrapersonal impression management. The person has conflicting goals and uses these types of negative distortions to reduce his feelings of guilt or to deflect other people's disapproval of him (the motivation/emotional, and action selection and control system). By way of contrast, implicit theories or offence-supportive beliefs are likely to have been formed during an offender's early life and therefore exert their effects through the filtering of perceptual information. In other words, they are located in the memory system rather than the motivation/emotional and action selection and control systems. Of course, it is possible that cognitive distortions initially utilised to deflect social and personal criticism (i.e. associated with motivational concerns) could end up as stable, maladaptive beliefs stored in long-term memory (see Chapter 8).

The *action selection and control system* is concerned with the formation and implementation of action plans designed to achieve individuals' goals. It draws heavily upon the motivational/emotional system for the goals that effectively energise behaviour and the perception and memory system for procedural and declarative knowledge (i.e. knowledge about how to do certain things, and relevant facts and information pertaining to a given situation). Problems that might arise from malfunctions in the action control and selection system essentially span the full range of self-regulation problems noted in this book. They include impulsivity, failure to inhibit negative emotions and replace them with more adaptive ones, inability to adjust plans to changing circumstances, poor problem solving skills, and a lack of social competence (see Chapters 3, 5, 14, 15 and 18).

The three functional systems are hypothesised always to interact to cause a sexual offence but the motives and particular issues related to a person's offence pathway will vary depending on the specific types of problems with these systems. For example, for one individual, the primary causal factor might be his emotional incompetence (motivational/emotional system) while for another it could be his high degree of impulsivity (action selection and control system). In addition, there are numerous types of problems that can occur *within* the three systems that might result in different clinical presentations and treatment needs. For example, impairment of the motivational/emotional system could be due to goal selection or poor emotional recognition.

A primary source for offence-related vulnerability factors is early developmental experiences and the three groups of factors described earlier: genetic, social/cultural and individual circumstances. These vulnerabilities are thought to function as a diathesis, making it more probable that an individual will struggle to meet effectively specific environmental challenges, and therefore will commit a sexual offence. This is a distal dimension. The person's current ecology is also an important contributor to the aetiology of sexual offending through making available potential victims, and by creating the specific circumstances that trigger the psychological deficits involved. This is a proximal dimension. A second source of offence-related vulnerabilities is the ecological niche (social and cultural roles of the offender) and habitat (environment in which the person lives) itself, which in certain circumstances may cause a person to commit a sexual offence in the absence of any significant psychological deficits or vulnerabilities. For example, the experience of fighting in a war, being subject to social circumstances such as the erosion of one culture by another, or the death of a partner may sometimes lead to individuals deciding to commit a sexual offence. In other words, sometimes the major causal factors resulting in sexual offending reside in the ecological niche, not within the person. The offending may be quite opportunistic, or the consequence of circumstances that effectively erode an individual's capacity to behave in an ethical (and typical) manner.

According to the unified theory, psychological functioning—in conjunction with the offender's ecology—creates the clinical phenomena typically noted in sexual offenders: emotional problems, social difficulties, deviant arousal and cognitive distortions. The clinical phenomena are usefully viewed as state factors or acute dynamic risk factors, while the psychological deficits are trait factors or stable dynamic risk factors (see Chapter 13). Once these clinical phenomena are expressed in a state form they are likely to lead the individual concerned to commit a sexual offence, depending of course on the availability and accessibility of a potential victim (an ecological variable). It is expected that the consequences of sexual offending will function to maintain or escalate sexually deviant actions. This is hypothesised to occur through the modification of environmental factors and the reduction or enhancement of the individual's psychological functioning (e.g. mood, sexual arousal and satisfaction, feelings of powerlessness and so on). For example, reducing negative mood states is likely to negatively reinforce the maladaptive emotional regulation strategies utilised, while an improvement in mood will function as a positive reinforcer. According to the unified theory, there are likely to be multiple aetiological pathways leading to the onset of sexual offending (see Chapters 5, 14 and 15). The fact that the three functional systems can individually or collectively create offence-related vulnerabilities means that different types of deficits in these systems will be associated with different offence variables. That is, individuals are hypothesised to commit sexual crimes for quite different reasons and therefore present with diverse clinical problems. Treatment plans should take this into account and a 'one size fits all' approach is unlikely to prove satisfactory from the perspective of the unified theory.

FUTURE DIRECTIONS

All we have been able to do in this final chapter is to sketch out a possible framework for integrating many of the factors identified in the book as important determinants of sexual offending. Although it is clearly premature to systematically evaluate the unified theory, in our view it does have certain strengths. First, as its name suggests, the unified theory shows considerable potential for bringing together theories from all three levels of theory scope (strong *unifying power*). It incorporates the insight from the comprehensive aetiological theories that there are multiple trajectories to sexual offending. It also provides a useful way of incorporating single-factor theories in terms of the three psychological systems outlined earlier. Individually and collectively, the three systems can be utilised to explain specific problems evident in sexual offenders, such as emotional loneliness or deviant sexual arousal. It is also possible to create a unified or integrated account such as the one sketched out in this chapter. Finally, theories of the offence and relapse process are easily accommodated by virtue of the unified theory's stress on self-regulatory capacities and the role of ecological factors in facilitating sexual crime. Cultural factors are considered to be both a developmental resource and also part of the offender's current ecology.

Second, according to the unified theory, biological, cultural, social, individual learning and psychological traits are all implicated in the commission of a sexual offence. In other words, the theory unifies a range of sexual offending theories that are currently accepted (*unifying power* and *external consistency*) and draws upon the empirical research findings outlined throughout this book (*empirical adequacy* and *scope*). Because of this, it has the potential to provide well-grounded guidance to researchers working on different facets of sexual offending, and remind those operating purely with psychological or social models that it is ultimately necessary to cash them out in biological and neuroscientific terms. All of the four levels of analysis are important if we are to satisfactorily explain and manage the complex problem of sexual abuse. Clinicians need to think about their clients in biological as well as cultural, social and psychological terms. As we have seen throughout this book, treatment approaches typically lack this biological perspective at present.

Third, the theory has the capacity to change the way we think about the surface clinical phenomena evident in sexual offenders (*heuristic value* or *fertility*). Rather than inferring that each class of problems has a common cause, it is arguable that they sometimes have unique causes, located in different functional systems. For example, an offender may articulate offence-supportive statements which appear to stem from offence-supportive implicit theories (the perception and motivation system), but which are actually the function of impression management strategies instead (motivation/emotional and action selection and control systems). This is really a point about the utility of our current classification systems for sexual offending (see Chapter 17). It may make more sense to allocate individuals to groups based on the type of functional systems compromised rather than upon the basis of their surface symptoms (Pennington, 2002). Our prediction is that future diagnostic systems are likely to be based on explanatory theories comprised of Pennington's four levels of analysis. A major implication is that future aetiological theories of sexual offending will be solidly grounded in neurobiological constructs. Our current theories will increasingly be seen as simply examples of sophisticated folk psychology with little explanatory power.

Finally, the unified theory is really an abstract framework for thinking systematically about sexual offending and its constituent causal variables. It is necessary for researchers to unpack its assumptions in greater detail and apply it to different types of sexual crimes: for example, rape, exhibitionism or child molestation (i.e. to achieve greater explanatory depth, and to improve upon existing heuristic value).

FINAL THOUGHTS

Coming to the end of the book leaves us feeling a combination of relief, frustration and excitement. Relief, because the process of writing has been long and difficult; theories are slippery things, hard to pin down and write about. Frustration, because we are painfully aware of how much more there is to say with only limited space to do this in. Finally, excitement because of the sense we have that the field is developing rapidly and in productive ways. Thought and action are both essential elements of effective practice. We hope the journey has been worthwhile for readers and that they are left with a useful range of cognitive tools that will enable them to improve their practice, and perhaps engage in a little bit of theory construction themselves!

REFERENCES

Abel, G. G., Becker, J. V. & Cunningham-Rathner, J. (1984). Complications, consent, and cognitions in sex between children and adults. *International Journal of Law and Psychiatry*, **7**, 89–103.

Abel, G. G., Becker, J. V., Cunningham-Rathner, J., Mittelman, M. S., Murphy, W. D. & Rouleau, J. L. (1987a). Self-reported sex crimes of nonincarcerated paraphiliacs. *Journal of Interpersonal Violence*, **2**, 3–25.

Abel, G. G., Becker, J. V. & Skinner, L. J. (1987b). Behavioral approaches to treatment of the violent sex offender. In L. H. Roth (Ed.), *Clinical treatment of the violent person* (pp. 95–118). New York: Guilford Press.

Abel, G. G., Gore, D. K., Holland, C. L., Camp, N., Becker, J. & Rathner, J. (1989). The measurement of the cognitive distortions of child molesters. *Annals of Sex Research*, **2**, 135–153.

Abel, G. G., Huffman, J., Warberg, B. & Holland, C. L. (1998). Visual reaction time plethysmography as measures of sexual interest in child molesters. *Sexual Abuse: A Journal of Research and Treatment*, **10**, 81–95.

Abel, G. G., Mittelman, M. S. & Becker, J. V. (1985). Sexual offenders: results of assessment and recommendations for treatment. In M. H. Ben-Aron, S. J. Hucker & C. D. Webster (Eds), *Clinical criminology: Current concepts* (pp. 191–205). Toronto: M&M Graphics.

Abel, G. G., Rouleau, J. L. & Cunningham-Rathner, B. A. (1986). Sexually aggressive behavior. In W. J. Curran, A. L. McGarry & S. A. Shah (Eds), *Forensic psychiatry and psychology* (pp. 289–314). Philadelphia, PA: Davis.

Adi, Y., Ashcroft, D., Browne, K., Beech, A., Fry-Smith, A. & Hyde, C. (2002). Clinical effectiveness and cost-consequences of selective serotonin reuptake inhibitors in the treatment of sex offenders. *Health Technology Assessment*, **6**, 1–66.

Ainsworth, M. D. S. (1979). Infant–mother attachment. *American Psychologist*, **34**, 932–937.

Ainsworth, M. D. S. (1989). Attachments beyond infancy. *American Psychologist*, **44**, 709–716.

Ainsworth, M. D. S., Blehar, M. C., Waters, E. & Wall, S. (1978). *Patterns of attachment: A psychological study of the strange situation*. Hillsdale, NJ: Lawrence Erlbaum Associates.

Alexander, R. D. (1979). *Darwinism and human affairs*. Seattle, WA: University of Washington Press.

Alford, B. A. & Beck, A. T. (1997). *The integrative power of cognitive therapy*. New York: Guildford Press.

American Psychiatric Association (2000). *Diagnostic and Statistical Manual of Mental Disorders* (4th edn). Washington, DC: APA.

Anderson, C. A., Anderson, K. B. & Deuser, W. E. (1996). Examining an affective aggression framework: weapon and temperature effects on aggressive thoughts, affect, and attitudes. *Personality and Social Psychology Bulletin*, **22**, 366–376.

Anderson, C. A. & Bushman, B. J. (2002). Human aggression. *Annual Review of Psychology*, **53**, 27–51.

Andrews, D. A. (2001). Principles of effective correctional programs. In L. L. Motiuk & R. C. Serin (Eds), *Compendium 2000 on effective correctional programming* (vol. 1). Ottawa, Canada: Ministry of Supply Services.

Andrews, D. A. & Bonta, J. (1995). *The Level of Service Inventory—Revised*. Toronto: Multi-Health Systems.

Andrews, D. A. & Bonta, J. (1998). *The psychology of criminal conduct* (2nd edn). Cincinnati, OH: Anderson.

Andrews, D. A. & Bonta, J. (2003). *The psychology of criminal conduct* (3rd edn). Cincinnati, OH: Anderson.

Andrews, D. A., Bonta, J. & Hoge, R. D. (1990). Classification for effective rehabilitation: rediscovering psychology. *Criminal Justice and Behavior*, **17**, 19–52.

Andrews, D., Zinger, I., Hoge, R., Bonta, J., Gendreau, P. & Cullen, F. (1990). Does correctional treatment work? A clinically-relevant and psychologically-informed meta-analysis. *Criminology*, **28**, 368–404.

Araji, S. K. (1997). *Sexually aggressive children: Coming to understand them*. Thousand Oaks, CA: Sage.

Araji, S. K. & Finkelhor, D. (1985). Explanations of pedophilia: review of empirical research. *Bulletin of the American Academy of Psychiatry and the Law*, **13**, 17–37.

Arnhart, L. (1998). *Darwinian natural right: The biological ethics of human nature*. Albany, NY: State University of New York Press.

Aspinwall, L. G. & Staudinger, U. M. (Eds) (2003). *A psychology of human strengths: Fundamental questions and future directions for a positive psychology*. Washington, DC: American Psychological Association.

Avital, E. & Jablonka, E. (2000). *Animal traditions: Behavioural inheritance in evolution*. Cambridge: Cambridge University Press.

Awad, G. A., Saunders, E. & Levene, J. (1984). A clinical study of male adolescent sexual offenders. *International Journal of Offender Therapy and Comparative Criminology*, **28**, 105–155.

Baker, E. & Beech, A. R. (2004). Dissociation and variability of adult attachment dimensions and early maladaptive schemas in sexual and violent offenders *Journal of Interpersonal Violence*, **119**, 1119–1135.

Bandura, A. (1973). *Aggression: A social learning analysis*. Englewood Cliffs, NJ: Prentice Hall.

Bandura, A. (1977). *Social learning theory*. Englewood Cliffs, NJ: Prentice Hall.

Bandura, A. (1986). *Social foundations of thought and action: A social cognitive theory*. Englewood Cliffs, NJ: Prentice Hall.

Bandura, A. (1997). *Self-efficacy: The exercise of control*. New York: W. H. Freeman.

Bandura, A., Barbaranelli, C., Caprara, G. V. & Pastorelli, C. (1996). Mechanisms of moral disengagement in the exercise of moral agency. *Journal of Personality and Social Psychology*, **71**, 364–374.

Barbaree, H. E., Marshall, W. L. & Lanthier, R. D. (1979). Deviant sexual arousal in rapists. *Behaviour Research and Therapy*, **17**, 215–222.

Barbaree, H. E. & Seto, M. C. (1997). Pedophilia: assessment and treatment. In W. O'Donohue (Ed.), *Sexual deviance: Theory, assessment and treatment* (pp. 175–193). New York: Guilford Press.

Bard, L. A., Carter, D. L., Cerce, D. D., Knight, R. A., Rosenberg, R. & Schneider, B. (1987). A descriptive study of rapists and child molesters: developmental, clinical, and criminal characteristics. *Behavioral Sciences and the Law*, **5**, 203–220.

Bargh, J. A. & Barndollar, K. (1996). Automaticity in action: the unconscious as repository of chronic goals and motives. In P. M. Gollwitzer & J. A. Bargh (Eds), *The psychology of action: Linking cognition and motivation to behavior* (pp. 457–481). New York: Guilford Press.

Bartholomew, K. & Horowitz, L. M. (1991). Attachment styles among young adults: a test of a four-category model. *Journal of Personality and Social Psychology*, **61**, 226–244.

Baumeister, R. F. (1990). *Escaping the self*. New York: Basic Books.

Baumeister, R. F. (1996). Self-regulation and ego threat: motivated cognition, self-deception, and destructive goal setting. In P. M. Gollwitzer & J. A. Bargh (Eds), *The psychology of action: Linking cognition and motivation to behaviors* (pp. 27–47). New York: Guilford Press.

Baumeister, R. F., Bushman, B. J. & Campbell, W. K. (2000). Self-esteem, narcissism, and aggression: does violence result from low self-esteem or from threatened egotism? *Current Directions in Psychological Science*, **9**, 26–29.

Baumeister, R. F. & Heatherton, T. F. (1996). Self-regulation failure: an overview. *Psychological Inquiry*, **7**, 1–15.

Baumeister, R. F, Smart, L. & Boden, J. M. (1996). Relationship of threatened egotism to violence and aggression: the dark side of high self-esteem. *Psychological Review*, **103**, 5–33.

Bays, L. & Freeman-Longo, R. (1990). *Why did I do it again? Understanding my cycle of problem behaviours*. Orwell, VT: Safer Society Press.

Beck, A. T. (1976). *Cognitive therapy and the emotional disorders*. New York: International Universities Press.

Becker, J. V. (1998). What we know about the characteristics and treatment of adolescents who have committed sexual offences. *Child Maltreatment*, **3**, 317–329.

Beckett, R., Beech, A., Fisher, D. & Fordham, A. S. (1994). *Community-based treatment for sex offenders. An evaluation of seven treatment programmes*. London: Home Office.

Beech, A. R. (1998). A psychometric typology of child abusers. *International Journal of Offender Therapy and Comparative Criminology*, **42**, 319–339.

Beech, A. R. (2001). Case material and interview. In C. Hollin (Ed.), *Handbook of offender assessment and treatment* (pp. 123–138). Chichester: John Wiley & Sons.

Beech, A. R. & Fisher, D. D. (2002). The rehabilitation of child sex offenders. *Australian Psychologist*, **37**, 206–214.

Beech, A. R., Fisher, D. & Beckett, R. C. (1999). *STEP 3: An evaluation of the prison sex offender treatment programme*. London: HMSO. Available at: www.homeoffice.gov.uk/rds/pdfs/occ-step3.pdf.

Beech, A. R., Fisher, D. D. & Thornton, D. (2003). Risk assessment of sex offenders. *Professional Psychology: Research and Practice*, **34**, 339–352.

Beech, A. R., Fisher, D. & Ward, T. (in press). Sexual murderers' implicit theories. *Journal of Interpersonal Violence*.

Beech, A. R. & Fordham, A. S. (1997). Therapeutic climate of sex offender treatment programs. *Sexual Abuse: A Journal of Research and Treatment*, **9**, 219–237.

Beech, A. R. & Hamilton-Giachritsis, C. E. (2005). Relationship between therapeutic climate and treatment outcome in group-based sexual offender treatment programs. *Sexual Abuse: A Journal of Research and Treatment*, **17**, 127–140.

Beech, A. R. & Mann, R. E. (2002). Recent developments in the treatment of sexual offenders. In J. McGuire (Ed), *Offender rehabilitation: Effective programmes and policies to reduce reoffending* (pp. 259–288). Chichester: John Wiley & Sons.

Beech, A. R. & Mitchell, I. J. (2005). A neurobiological perspective on attachment problems in sexual offenders and the role of selective serotonin re-uptake inhibitors in the treatment of such problems. *Clinical Psychology Review*, **25**, 153–182.

Beech, A. R. & Ward, T. (2004). The integration of etiology and risk in sexual offenders: a theoretical framework. *Aggression and Violent Behavior*, **10**, 31–63.

Beitchman, J., Zucker, K., Hood, J., DaCosta, G., Akman, D. & Cassavia, E. (1992). A review of the long-term effects of child sexual abuse. *Child Abuse and Neglect*, **16**, 101–118.

Belfer, P. L. & Levendusky, L. (1985). Long-term behavioral group psychotherapy: an integrative model. In D. Upper and S. M. Ross (Eds), *Handbook of Behavioral Group Therapy* (pp. 119–144). New York: Plenum Press.

Berkowitz, L. (1993). Towards a general theory of anger and emotional aggression: implications of the cognitive–neoassociational perspective for the analysis of anger and other emotions. In R. S. Wyer & T. K. Srull (Eds), *Perspectives on anger and emotion: Advances in social cognition* (vol. VI, pp. 1–46). Hillsdale, NJ: Lawrence Erlbaum Associates.

Bickley, J. A. & Beech, A. R. (2001). Classifying child abusers: its relevance to theory and clinical practice. *International Journal of Offender Therapy and Comparitive Criminology*, **45**, 51–69.

Bickley, J. & Beech, A. R. (2002). An investigation of the Ward and Hudson pathways model of the sexual offence process with child abusers. *Journal of Interpersonal Violence*, **17**, 371–393.

Binet, A. (1888). *Le fetichisme dans l'amour*. Paris: La Bibliothèque des introuvables sur la psychoanalyse.

Blackburn, R. (1993). *The psychology of criminal conduct: Theory, research and practice*. Chichester: John Wiley & Sons.

Blaicher, W., Gruber, D., Bieglmayer, C., Blaicher, A. M., Knogler, W. & Huber, J. C. (1999). The role of oxytocin in relation to female sexual arousal. *Gynecologic and Obstetric Investigation*, **47**, 125–126.

Boer, D. P., Hart, S. D., Kropp, P. R. & Webster, C. D. (1997). *Manual for the Sexual Violence Scale Risk-20*. Obtainable from the Mental Health, Law, and Policy Institute, Simon Fraser University, Burnaby, British Columbia, Canada, V5 1S6. www.sfu.ca/psychology/groups/mhlpi.

Bonta, J. (1996). Risk–needs assessment. In A. T. Harland (Ed.), *Choosing correctional options that work: Defining the demand and evaluating the supply* (pp. 293–335). London: Sage.

Bonta, J. & Andrews, D. A. (2003). A commentary on Ward and Stewart's model of human needs. *Psychology, Crime and Law*, **9**, 215–218.

Bradford, J. M. W. (1990). The antiandrogen and hormonal treatment of sex offenders. In W. L. Marshall, D. R. Laws & H. E. Barbaree (Eds), *Handbook of sexual assault: Issues, theories and treatment of the offender* (pp. 297–310). New York: Plenum Press.

Bradford, J. M. W. (1995). *An open pilot study of Sertraline in the treatment of outpatients with paedophilia*. Paper presented at the Annual American Psychiatric Association Congress, Miami, Florida, 24 May 1995.

Bradford, J. M. W. (1999). The paraphilias, obsessive-compulsive spectrum disorder, and the treatment of sexually deviant behavior. *Psychiatric Quarterly*, **70**, 209–219.

Bradford, J. M. W., Boulet, J. & Pawlak, A. (1992). The paraphilias: a multiplicity of deviant behaviors. *Canadian Journal of Psychiatry*, **37**, 104–108.

Braybrooke, D. (1987). *Meeting needs*. Princeton, NJ: Princeton University Press.

Breckenridge, J. (1992). An exotic phenomenon? Incest and child rape. In J. Breckenridge & M. Carmody (Eds), *Crimes of violence: Australian responses to rape and child sexual assault* (pp. 18–37). Sydney: Allen & Unwin.

Bremner, J. D., Licinio, J., Darnell, A., Krystal, J. H., Owens, M. J., Southwick, S. M., Nemeroff, C. B. & Charney, D. S. (1997). Elevated corticotropin-releasing factor concentrations in posttraumatic stress disorder. *American Journal of Psychiatry*, **154**, 624–629.

Bremner, J. D., Randall, P., Scott, T. M., Bronen, R. A., Seibyl, J. P., Southwick, S. M., Delaney, R. C., Mccarthy, G., Charney, D. S. & Innis, R. B. (1995). MRI-based measurement of hippocampal volume in patients with combat-related posttraumatic stress disorder. *American Journal of Psychiatry*, **152**, 973–981.

Brennan, K. A. & Shaver, P. R. (1995). Dimensions of adult attachment: an integrative overview. In J. A. Simpson & W. S. Rholes (Eds), *Attachment theory and close relationships* (pp. 46–76). New York: Guilford Press.

Brewin, C. R. (1988). *Cognitive foundations of clinical psychology*. Hove, Lawrence Erlbaum Associates.

Briere, J. & Smiljanich, K. (1993). *Childhood sexual abuse and subsequent sexual aggression against adult women*. Paper presented at the 101st annual convention of the American Psychological Association, Toronto, Ontario.

Brown, M. (2000). Calculations of risk in contemporary penal practice. In M. Brown & J. Pratt (Eds) *Dangerous offenders: Punishment and social order* (pp. 94–108). London: Routledge.

Browne, K. D. & Herbert, M. (1997). *Preventing family violence*. Chichester: John Wiley & Sons.

Brownell, K. D., Marlatt, G. A., Lichtenstein, E. & Wilson, G. T. (1986). Understanding and preventing relapse. *American Psychologist*, **41**, 765–782.

Brownmiller, S. (1975). *Against our will: Men, women, and rape*. New York: Simon & Schuster.

Buller, D. J. & Hardcastle, V. G. (2000). Evolutionary psychology meets developmental neurobiology: against promiscuous modularity. *Brain and Mind*, **1**, 307–325.

Bumby, K. M. (1996). Assessing the cognitive distortions of child molesters and rapists: development and validation of the MOLEST and RAPE scales. *Sexual Abuse: A Journal of Research and Treatment*, **8**, 37–54.

Bumby, K. M. (2000). Empathy inhibition, intimacy deficits, and attachment difficulties in sex offenders. In D. R. Laws, S. M. Hudson & T. Ward (Eds), *Remaking relapse prevention with sex offenders: A sourcebook* (pp. 143–166). Thousand Oaks, CA: Sage.

Bumby, K. M. & Hansen, D. J. (1997). Intimacy deficits, fear of intimacy and loneliness among sexual offenders. *Criminal Justice and Behavior*, **24**, 315–331.

Bumby, K. M., Levine, H. & Cunningham, D. (1996). *Empathy deficits, shame, guilt, and self-consciousness*. Paper presented at the 15th annual conference of the Association for the Treatment of Sexual Abusers, Chicago, IL, November.

Bumby, K. M., Marshall, W. L. & Langton, C. M. (1999). A theoretical model of the influences of shame and guilt on sexual offending. In B. K. Schwartz (Ed.), *The sex offender*, vol. 3: *Theoretical advances, treating special populations, and legal developments* (pp. 5-1–5-12). Kingston, NJ: Civic Research Institute.

Burk, L. R. & Burkhart, B. R. (2003). Disorganized attachment as a diathesis for sexual deviance: developmental experience and the motivation for sexual offending. *Aggression and Violent Behavior*, **8**, 487–511.

Burt, M. R. (1980). Cultural myths and supports for rape. *Journal of Personality and Social Psychology*, **38**, 217–230.

Bushman, B. J. & Baumeister, R. F. (1998). Threatened egotism, narcissism, self-esteem, and direct and displaced aggression: does self-love or self-hate lead to violence? *Journal of Personality and Social Psychology*, **75**, 219–229.

Bushman, B. J., Bonacci, A. M., van Dijk, M. & Baumeister, R. F. (2003). Narcissism, sexual refusal, and aggression: testing a narcissistic reactance model of sexual coercion. *Journal of Personality and Social Psychology*, **84**, 1027–1040.

Buss, D. M. (1989). Conflict between the sexes: strategic interference and the evocation of anger and upset. *Journal of Personality and Social Psychology*, **56**, 735–747.

Buss, D. M. (1999). *Evolutionary psychology: The new science of the mind*. Boston, MA: Allyn & Bacon.

Caldwell, J. D. (2002). A sexual arousability model involving steroid effects at the plasma membrane. *Neuroscience and Biobehavioral Reviews*, **26**, 13–30.

Carich, M. S. (1994). The use of RP/RI in sex offender treatment, part III: The significance of assault cycles. *Sex Offender Treatment Project Newsletter*, Dec, 2–8.

Carich, M. S. & Stone, M. (1995). *Sex offender relapse intervention workbook*. Chicago, IL: Adler School of Professional Psychology.

Carter, C. S. (1998). Neuroendocrine perspectives on social attachment and love. *Psycho-neuroendocrinology*, **23**, 779–818.

Carver, C. S. & Scheier, M. F. (1981). *Attention and self-regulation: A control theory approach to human behavior*. New York: Springer-Verlag.

Carver, C. S. & Scheier, M. F. (1990). Principles of self-regulation: action and emotion. In E. T. Higgins & R. M. Sorrentino (Eds), *Handbook of motivation and social behavior* (pp. 3–52). New York: Guilford Press.

Cattell, R. B. & Kline, P. (1977). *The scientific analysis of personality and motivation*. New York: Academic Books.

Chaouloff, F. (2000). Serotonin, stress and corticoids. *Journal of Psychopharmacology*, **14**, 139–151.

Check, J. V. P., Malamuth, N. M., Elias, B. & Barton, S. A. (1985). On hostile ground. *Psychology Today*, **19**, 56–61.

Check, J. V. P., Perlman, D. & Malamuth, N. (1985). Loneliness and aggressive behavior. *Journal of Social and Personal Relationships*, **2**, 243–252.

Clark, A. (2003). *Natural-born cyborgs: Minds, technologies, and the future of human intelligence.* New York: Oxford University Press.

Cochran, W. & Tesser, A. (1996). The 'what the hell' effect: some effects of goal proximity and goal framing on performance. In L. L. Martin & A. Tesser (Eds), *Striving and feeling: Interactions among goals, affect, and self-regulation* (pp. 99–120). Hillsdale, NJ: Lawrence Erlbaum Associates.

Cohen, M. L., Seghorn, T. K. & Calmas, W. (1969). Sociometric study of sex offenders. *Journal of Abnormal Psychology*, **74**, 249–255.

Coleman, E. (1991). Compulsive and sexual behavior: new concepts and treatment. *Journal of Psychology and Human Sexuality*, **4**, 37–52.

Coleman, E., Gratzer, T., Nesvacil, L. & Raymond, N. (2000). Nefazodone and the treatment of nonparaphilic compulsive sexual behavior: a retrospective study. *Journal of Clinical Psychiatry*, **61**, 282–284.

Collins, N. L. & Read, S. J. (1994). Cognitive representations of attachment. The structure and function of working models. In D. Perlman & K. Bartholomew (Eds), *Advances on personal relationships, vol. 5: Attachment processes in adulthood* (pp. 53–90). London: Jessica Kingsley.

Colman, A. M. (2001). *Dictionary of psychology*. Oxford: Oxford University Press.

Cooper, A., Scherer, C. R., Boies, S. C. & Gordon, B. L. (1999). Sexuality on the internet: from sexual exploration to pathological expression. *Professional Psychology: Research and Practice*, **30**, 154–164.

Cornish, D. B. & Clarke, R. V. (1986). Introduction. In D. B. Cornish & R. V. Clarke (Eds), *The reasoning criminal: Rational choice perspectives on offending* (pp. 1–16). New York: Springer-Verlag.

Cortoni, F. & Marshall, W. L. (2001). Sex as a coping strategy and its relationship to juvenile sexual history and intimacy in sexual offenders. *Sexual Abuse: A Journal of Research and Treatment*, **13**, 27–43.

Cosmides, L. & Tooby, J. (2000). Evolutionary psychology: a primer. Available at: http://cogweb.english.ucsb.edu/EP/EP-primer.html.

Cossins, A. (2000). *Masculinities, sexualities and child sexual abuse*. The Hague: Kluwer Law International.

Craissati, J. (2003). *The relationship between developmental variables and risk.* Doctoral thesis, University of Birmingham, UK.

Craissati, J., McClurg, G. & Browne, K. D. (2002). Characteristics of perpetrators of child sexual abuse who have been sexually victimized as children. *Sexual Abuse: A Journal of Research and Treatment*, **14**, 225–240.

Cromwell, P. F., Olsen, J. N. & Avary, D. W. (1991). *Breaking and entering: An ethnographic analysis of burglary.* Newbury Park, CA: Sage.

Cummins, R. A. (1996). The domains of life satisfaction: an attempt to order chaos. *Social Indicators Research*, **38**, 303–328.

Dalley, J. W., Theobald, D. E., Pereira, E. A. C., Li, P. M. M. C. & Robbins, T. W. (2002). Specific abnormalities in serotonin release in the prefrontal cortex of isolation-reared rats measured during behavioral performance of a task assessing visuospatial attention and impulsivity. *Psychopharmacology*, **164**, 329–340.

D'Andrade, R. (1995). *The development of cognitive anthropology.* Cambridge: Cambridge University Press.

Darwin, C. (1859). *The origin of species.* Hertfordshire: Wordsworth.

Davis, M. H. (1980). A multi-dimensional approach to individual differences in empathy. *JSAS Catalogue of Selected Documents in Psychology*, **10**, 85.

Davis, M. H. (1983). Measuring individual differences in empathy: evidence for a multidimensional approach. *Journal of Personality and Social Psychology*, **44**, 113–126.

Davison, G. C., Neale, J. M. & Kring, A. (2003). *Abnormal psychology* (9th edn). New York: John Wiley & Sons.

Dawkins, R. (1976). *The selfish gene.* Oxford: Oxford University Press.

Dean, K. E. & Malamuth, N. M. (1997). Characteristics of men who aggress sexually and of men who imagine aggressing: risk and moderating variables. *Journal of Personality and Social Psychology*, **72**, 449–455.

Deci, E. L. & Ryan, R. M. (2000). The 'what' and 'why' of goal pursuits: human needs and the self-determination of behavior. *Psychological Inquiry*, **11**, 227–268.

Denzin, N. K. (1997). *Interpretive biography*. Newbury Park, CA: Sage.

Dhaliwal, G. K., Gauzas, L., Antonowicz, D. H. & Ross, R. R. (1996). Adult male survivors of childhood sexual abuse: prevalence, sexual characteristics, and long-term effects. *Clinical Psychology Review*, **16**, 619–639.

Doren, D. M. (2002). *Evaluating sex offenders: A manual for civil commitments and beyond*. London: Sage.

Dowden, C. (1998). A meta-analytic examination of the risk, need responsivity principles and their importance within the rehabilitation debate. Doctoral thesis, Psychology Department, Carleton University, Ottawa, Canada.

Drake, C. R., Ward, T., Nathan, P. & Lee, J. K. P. (2001). Challenging the cognitive distortions of child molesters: an implicit theory approach. *Journal of Sexual Aggression*, **7**, 25–40.

Driver, E. & Droisen, A. (Eds) (1989). *Child sexual abuse: Feminist perspectives*. Basingstoke: Macmillan.

Durham, W. H. (1991). *Coevolution: Genes, culture, and human diversity*. Stanford, CA: Standford University Press.

Eccles, A. & Marshall, W. L. (1999). Relapse prevention. In W. L. Marshall & Y. M. Fernandez (Eds), *Cognitive-behavioural treatment of sexual offenders* (pp. 127–146). Chichester: John Wiley & Sons.

Eldridge, H. & Wyre, R. (1998). The Lucy Faithfull Foundation residential program for sexual offenders. In W. L. Marshall, Y. M. Fernandez, S. M. Hudson & T. Ward (Eds), *Sourcebook of treatment programs for sexual offenders* (pp. 79–92). New York: Plenum Press.

Ellerby, L., Bedard, J. & Chartrand, S. (2000). Holism, wellness, and spirituality: moving from relapse prevention to healing. In D. R. Laws, S. M. Hudson & T. Ward (Eds), *Remaking relapse prevention with sex offenders: A sourcebook* (pp. 427–452). Thousand Oaks, CA: Sage.

Ellis, L. (1989). *Theories of rape: Inquiries into the causes of sexual aggression*. New York: Hemisphere.

Ellis, L. (1991). A synthesized (biosocial) theory of rape. *Journal of Consulting and Clinical Psychology*, **59**, 631–642.

Emmons, R. A. (1996). Striving and feeling: personal goals and subjective well-being. In P. M. Gollwitzer & J. A. Bargh (Eds), *The psychology of action: Linking cognition and motivation to behavior* (pp. 313–337). New York: Guilford Press.

Emmons, R. A. (1999). *The psychology of ultimate concerns*. New York: Guilford Press.

Epperson, D. L., Kaul, J. D. & Hesslton, D. (1998). Final report on the development of the Minnesota Sex Offending Screening Tool-Revised (MnSOST-R). St Paul, MN: Minnesota Department of Corrections.

Everitt, B. S. & Dunn, G. (2001). *Applied multivariate data analysis* (2nd edn). London: Arnold.

Eysenck, H. J. (1978). *Sex and personality*. London: Open Books.

Eysenck, M. W. & Eysenck, H. J. (1980). Mischel and the concept of personality. *British Journal of Psychology*, **71**, 191–204.

Fava, G. A, Rafenelli, C., Grandi, S., Conti, S. & Belluardo, P. (1998). Prevention of recurrent depression with cognitive behavioural therapy. *Archives of General Psychiatry*, **55**, 816–820.

Featherstone, B. & Fawcett, B. (1994). Feminism and child abuse: opening up some possibilities? *Critical Social Policy*, **42**, 61–80.

Featherstone, B. & Lancaster, E. (1997). Contemplating the unthinkable: men who sexually abuse children. *Critical Social Policy*, **17**, 51–71.

Feeney, J. A., Noller, P. & Patty, J. (1993). Adolescents' interactions with the opposite sex: influence of attachment style and gender. *Journal of Adolescence*, **16**, 169–186.

Ferguson, J. N., Young, L. J., Hearn, E. F., Matzuk, M. M., Insel, T. R. & Winslow, J. T. (2000). Social amnesia in mice lacking the oxytocin gene. *Nature Genetics*, **25**, 284–288.

Fernandez, Y. M. & Marshall, W. L. (2000). Contextual issues in relapse prevention treatment. In D. R. Laws, S. M. Hudson & T. Ward (Eds), *Remaking relapse prevention with sex offenders: A sourcebook* (pp. 225–234). Newbury Park: CA: Sage.

Fernandez, Y. M. & Marshall, W. L. (2003). Victim empathy, social self-esteem and psychopathy in rapists. *Sexual Abuse: A Journal of Research and Treatment*, **15**, 11–26.

Fernandez, Y. M., Marshall, W. L., Lightbody, S. & O'Sullivan, C. (1999). The Child Molester Empathy Measure: description and examination of its reliability and validity. *Sexual Abuse: A Journal of Research and Treatment*, **11**, 17–31.

Finkelhor, D. (1984). *Child sexual abuse: New theory and research*. New York: Free Press.

Fisher, D. (1994). Adult sex offenders: who are they? Why and how do they do it? In T. Morrison, M. Erooga & R. C. Beckett (Eds), *Sexual offending against children: Assessment and treatment of male abusers* (pp. 1–24). London: Routledge.

Fisher, D., Beech, A. R. & Browne, K. D. (1999). Comparison of sex offenders to non-sex offenders on selected psychological measures. *International Journal of Offender Therapy and Comparative Criminology*, **43**, 473–491.

Fisher, D., Beech, A. R. & Browne, K. D. (2000). The effectiveness of relapse prevention training in a group of incarcerated child molesters. *Crime, Psychology and Law*, **6**, 181–195.

Fisher, D. & Mair, G. (1998). *A review of classification systems for sex offenders*. Edinburgh: Scottish Office. Available at: www.homeoffice.gov.uk/rds/pdfs/r78.pdf.

Fiske, A. P. (2002). Using individualism and collectivism to compare cultures—a critique of the validity and measurement of the constructs: Comment on Oyserman et al. (2002). *Psychological Bulletin*, **128**, 78–88.

Fiske, S. T. & Taylor, S. E. (1991). *Social Cognition II*. New York: McGraw Hill.

Flax, J. (1990). Postmodernism and gender relations in feminist theory. In L. Nicholson (Ed.), *Feminism/Postmodernism* (pp. 39–62). London: Routledge.

Fox, K. J. (1999). Reproducing criminal types: cognitive treatment for violent offenders in prison. *The Sociological Quarterly*, **40**, 435–453.

Freeman-Longo, R. E. (2001). *Paths to wellness: A holistic approach and guide for personal recovery*. Holyoke, MA: NEARI Press.

Freeman-Longo, R. E., Bird, S. L., Stevenson, W. F. & Fiske, J. A. (1994). *1994 Nationwide survey of sexual offender treatment programs and models*. Brandon, VT: Safer Society Press.

Freeman-Longo, R. & Pithers, W. D. (1992). *A structured approach to preventing relapse: A guide for sex offenders*. Orwell, VT: Safer Society Press.

Freud, S. (1953). Three essays on the theory of sexual deviation. In J. Strachey (Ed.), *The complete psychological works of Sigmund Freud*. London: Hogarth.

Friendship, C., Mann R. & Beech, A. (2003). Evaluation of a national prison-based treatment program for sexual offenders in England and Wales. *Journal of Interpersonal Violence*, **18**, 744–759.

Furby, L., Weinrott, M. R. & Blackshaw, L. (1989). Sex offender recidivism: a review. *Psychological Bulletin*, **105**, 3–30.

Gagon, J. H. (1990). The explicit and implicit use of the scripting perspective in sex research. *Annual Review of Sex Research*, **1**, 1–43.

Gannon, T. A. (2002). Cognitive distortions in child sexual offenders: Fact or fiction? Doctoral dissertation, University of Sussex, Brighton, UK.

Gannon, T. A. (in press). Increasing honest responding on cognitive distortions in child molesters: The bogus pipeline procedure. *Journal of Interpersonal Violence*.

Gannon, T. A. & Polaschek, D. L. L. (in press). Cognitive distortions in child molesters: a re-examination of key theories and research.

Gannon, T. A., Polaschek, D. L. L. & Ward, T. (2005). Social cognition and sex offenders. In M. McMurran & J. McGuire (Eds), *Social problem solving and offenders*. Chichester: John Wiley & Sons.

Garland, D. (2001). *The culture of control: Crime and social order in contemporary society*. Chicago, IL: University of Chicago Press.

Garlick, Y., Marshall, W. L. & Thornton, D. (1996). Intimacy deficits and attribution of blame among sexual offenders. *Legal and Criminological Psychology*, **1**, 251–258.

Geer, J. H., Estupinan, L. A. & Manguno-Mire, G. M. (2000). Empathy, social skills and other relevant cognitive processes in rapists and child molesters. *Aggression and Violent Behavior*, **5**, 99–126.

Gendreau, P. (1981). Treatment in correction: Martinson was wrong. *Canadian Psychology*, **22**, 332–338.

Gendreau, P. (1996). The principles of effective interventions with offenders. In A. T. Harland (Ed.), *Choosing correctional options that work* (pp. 117–130). London: Sage.

Gendreau, P. & Andrews, D. A. (1990). Tertiary prevention: what the meta-analyses of the offender treatment literature tell us about what works. *Canadian Journal of Criminology*, **32**, 173–184.

Gendreau, P. & Ross, R. (1979). Effective correctional treatment: bibliography for cynics. *Journal of Research in Crime and Delinquency*, **25**, 463–489.

George, C., Kaplan, N. & Main, M. (1996). *Adult attachment inventory interview protocol* (3rd edn). University of California at Berkeley.

Gil, E. (1995). Foreword. In L. Fontes (Ed.), *Sexual abuse in nine North American cultures: Treatment and prevention* (pp. ix–xiv). Thousand Oaks, CA: Sage.

Gilbert, P. (1998a). Evolutionary psychopathology: why isn't the mind designed better than it is? *British Journal of Medical Psychology*, **71**, 353–373.

Gilbert, P. (1998b). Shame and humiliation in the treatment of complex cases. In N. Tarrier, A. Wells & G. Haddock (Eds), *Treating complex cases: The cognitive behavioural therapy approach* (pp. 241–271). Chichester: John Wiley & Sons.

Gladstein, G. A. (1983). Understanding empathy: integrating counselling, developmental, and social psychology perspectives. *Journal of Counselling Psychology*, **30**, 467–482.

Glaser, B. G. & Strauss, A. L. (1967). *The discovery of grounded theory*. Hawthorne, NY: Aldine.

Gold, S. N. & Heffner, C. L. (1998). Sexual addiction: many conceptions, minimal data. *Clinical Psychology Review*, **18**, 367–381.

Gopnik, A. (1996). Theories and modules; creation myths, developmental realities, and Neurath's boat. In P. Carruthers & P. K. Smith (Eds), *Theories of theories of mind* (pp. 169–183). Cambridge: Cambridge University Press.

Greenberg, D., Bradford, J., Curry, S. & O'Rourke, A. (1996). A comparison of treatment of paraphilias with three serotonin reuptake inhibitors: a retrospective study. *Bulletin of the American Academy of Psychiatry and the Law*, **24**, 525–532.

Greenwald, A. G., McGhee, L. J. & Schwartz, J. L. (1998). Measuring individual difference in implicit cognition: the Implicit Association Test. *Journal of Personality and Social Psychology*, **85**, 197–216.

Griebel, G., Simiand, J., Gal, C. S. L., Wagnon, J., Pascal, M., Scatton, B., Maffrand, J. P. & Soubrie, P. (2002). Anxiolytic- and antidepressant-like effects of the non-peptide vasopressin V-1b receptor antagonist, SSR149415, suggest an innovative approach for the treatment of stress-related disorders. *Proceedings of the National Academy of Sciences of the USA*, **99**, 6370–6375.

Griffiths, P. E. & Stotz, K. (2000). How the mind grows: a developmental perspective on the biology of cognition. *Synthese*, **122**, 29–51.

Groth, A. N., Burgess, A. W. & Holmstrom, L. L. (1977). Rape: power, anger, and sexuality. *American Journal of Psychiatry*, **134**, 1239–1243.

Grubin, D. (1998). Sex offending against children: understanding the risk. Police Research Series, Paper 99. Available from the Research and Statistics Directorate, Home Office, 50 Queen Anne's Gate, London, SW1H 9AT, UK. Available at: www.homeoffice.gov.uk/rds/prgpdfs/fprs99.pdf.

Grubin, D. & Gunn, J. (1990). *The imprisoned rapist and rape*. London: Institute of Psychiatry.

Haaven, J. L. & Coleman, E. M. (2000). Treatment of the developmentally disabled sex offender. In D. R. Laws, S. M. Hudson & T. Ward (Eds), *Remaking relapse prevention with sex offenders: A sourcebook* (pp. 369–388). Thousand Oaks, CA: Sage.

Halford, W. K., Bernoth-Doolan, S. & Eadie, K. (2002). Schemata as moderators of clinical effectiveness of a comprehensive cognitive behavioral program for patients with depression or anxiety disorders. *Behavior Modification*, **26**, 571–593.

Hall, F. S. (1998). Social deprivation of neonatal, adolescent, and adult rats has distinct neurochemical and behavioral consequences. *Critical Reviews in Neurobiology*, **12**, 129–162.

Hall, G. C. N. (1996). *Theory based assessment, treatment, and prevention of sexual aggression.* New York: Oxford University Press.

Hall, G. C. N. & Hirschman, R. (1991). Towards a theory of sexual aggression: a quadripartite model. *Journal of Consulting and Clinical Psychology*, **59**, 662–669.

Hall, G. C. N. & Hirschman, R. (1992). Sexual aggression against children: a conceptual perspective of etiology. *Criminal Justice and Behavior*, **19**, 8–23.

Hall, G. C. N. & Proctor, W. C. (1987). Criminological predictors of recidivism in a sex offender population. *Journal of Consulting and Clinical Psychology*, **55**, 111–112.

Hanson, R. K. (1996). Evaluating the contribution of relapse prevention theory to the treatment of sexual offenders. *Sexual Abuse: A Journal of Research and Treatment*, **8**, 201–208.

Hanson, R. K. (1997a). The development of a brief actuarial risk scale for sexual offence recidivism. User Report 1997-04. Ottawa: Department of the Solicitor General of Canada. Available at: www.sgc.gc.ca/publications/corrections/199704_e.pdf.

Hanson, R. K. (1997b). Invoking sympathy—assessment and treatment of empathy deficits among sexual offenders. In B. K. Schwartz & H. R. Cellini (Eds), *The sex offender: New insights, treatment innovations and legal developments* (vol. 2). Kingston, NJ: Civic Research Institute.

Hanson, R. K. (2000). What is so special about relapse prevention? In D. R. Laws, S. M. Hudson & T. Ward (Eds), *Remaking relapse prevention: A sourcebook* (pp. 27–38). Thousand Oaks, CA: Sage.

Hanson, R. K. (2003). Empathy deficits of sexual offenders: a conceptual model. *Journal of Sexual Aggression*, **9**, 13–23.

Hanson, R. K. & Bussière, M. T. (1998). Predicting relapse: a meta-analysis of sexual offender recidivism studies. *Journal of Consulting and Clinical Psychology*, **66**, 348–362.

Hanson, R. K., Gizzarelli, R. & Scott, H. (1994). The attitudes of incest offenders: sexual entitlement and acceptance of sex with children. *Criminal Justice and Behavior*, **21**, 187–202.

Hanson, R. K., Gordon, A., Harris, A. J. R., Marques, J. K., Murphy, W., Quinsey, V. L. & Seto, M. C. (2002). First report of the collaborative outcome data project on the effectiveness of psychological treatment for sex offenders. *Sexual Abuse: A Journal of Research and Treatment*, **14**, 169–194.

Hanson, R. K. & Harris, A. J. R. (2000a). Where should we intervene? Dynamic predictors of sexual offence recidivism. *Criminal Justice and Behavior*, **27**, 6–35.

Hanson, R. K. & Harris, A. (2000b). The sex offender need assessment rating (SONAR): a method for measuring change in risk levels. Available at: www.sgc.gc.ca/publications/corrections/200001b_e.asp (Please note this is an older version of SONAR and should not be used.)

Hanson, R. K., Morton, K. E. & Harris, A. J. R. (2003). Sexual offender recidivism: what we know and what we need to know. In R. Prentky, E. Janus, M. Seto & A.W. Burgess (Eds), *Understanding and managing sexually coercive behavior. Annals of the New York Academy of Sciences*, **989**, 154–166.

Hanson, R. K. & Scott, H. (1995). Assessing perspective-taking among sexual offenders, nonsexual criminals, and nonoffenders. *Sexual Abuse: A Journal of Research and Treatment*, **7**, 259–277.

Hanson, R. K. & Thornton, D. (1999). Static 99: Improving actuarial risk assessments for sex offenders. User Report 99-02. Ottawa: Department of the Solicitor General of Canada. Available at: www.sgc.gc.ca/publications/corrections/199902_e.pdf.

Hanson, R. K. & Thornton, D. (2000). Improving risk assessments for sex offenders: a comparison of three actuarial scales. *Law and Human Behaviour*, **24**, 119–136.

Happé, F. G. E. & Frith, U. (1996). Theory of mind and social impairment in children with conduct disorder. *British Journal of Developmental Psychology*, **14**, 385–398.

Hare, R. D. (1991). *The hare psychopathy checklist—revised.* Toronto: Multi-Health Systems.

Hart, S. D. & Hare, R. D. (1997). Psychopathy: assessment and association with criminal conduct. In D. M. Stoff, J. Breiling & J. D. Maser (Eds), *Handbook of antisocial behavior* (pp. 22–34). New York: John Wiley & Sons.

Hart, S., Laws, D. R. & Kropp, P. R. (2003). The risk–need model of offender rehabilitation. In T. Ward, D. R. Laws & S. M. Hudson (Eds), *Theoretical issues and controversies in sexual deviance* (pp. 338–354). London: Sage.

Hazan, C. & Shaver, P. R. (1987). Romantic love conceptualized as an attachment process. *Journal of Personality and Social Psychology*, **52**, 511–24.

Hazan, C. & Zeifman, D. (2003). Pair bonds and attachments: evaluating the evidence. In J. Cassady & P. R. Shaver (Eds), *Handbook of attachment theory: Research and clinical applications* (pp. 336–354). New York: Guilford Press.

Henry, J. P. & Wang, S. (1998). Effects of early stress on adult affiliative behavior. *Psychoneuroendocrinology*, **23**, 863–875.

Henwood, K. L. & Pidgeon, N. F. (1992). Qualitative research and psychological theorizing. *British Journal of Psychology*, **83**, 97–111.

Herman, J. L. (1981). *Father–daughter incest*. Cambridge, MA: Harvard University Press.

Herman, J. L. & Hirschmann, L. (1977). Father–daughter incest. *Signs: Journal of Women in Culture and Society*, **2**, 735–756.

Hildebran, D. & Pithers, W. D. (1989). Enhancing offender empathy for sexual-abuse victims. In D. R. Laws (Ed.), *Relapse prevention with sex offenders* (pp. 236–243). New York: Guilford Press.

Hilton, N. Z. (1993). Childhood sexual victimization and lack of empathy in child molesters explanation or excuse? *International Journal of Offender Therapy and Comparative Criminology*, **37**, 287–296.

Hogue, T. E. (1994). Sex offence information questionnaire: assessment of sexual offenders' perceptions of responsibility, empathy and control. *Issues in Criminological and Legal Psychology*, **21**, 68–75.

Hollin, C. R. (1999). Treatment programs for offenders: meta-analysis, 'what works' and beyond. *International Journal of Law and Psychiatry*, **22**, 361–372.

Hollon, S. D. & Kriss, M. R. (1984). Cognitive factors in clinical research and practice. *Clinical Psychology Review*, **4**, 35–76.

Hood, R., Shute, S., Feilzer, M. & Wilcox, A. (2002). Sex offenders emerging from long-term imprisonment. *British Journal of Criminology*, **42**, 371–394.

Hooker, C. A. (1987). *A realistic theory of science*. Albany, NY: State University of New York Press.

Howells, K. (1994). Child sexual abuse: Finkelhor's precondition model revisited. *Psychology, Crime and Law*, **1**, 201–214.

Howells, K. & Day, A. (2003). Readiness for anger management: clinical and theoretical issues. *Clinical Psychology Review*, **23**, 319–337.

Hoyer, D., Clark, D. E. & Fozard, J. R. (1994). International union of pharmacology classification of receptors for 5-hydroxytryptamine (serotonin). *Pharmacology Review*, **46**, 157–203.

Huesmann, L. R. (1988). An information processing model for the development of aggression. *Aggressive Behavior*, **14**, 13–24.

Huesmann, L. R. (1998). The role of social information processing and cognitive schema in the acquisition and maintenance of habitual aggressive behavior. In R. G. Geen & E. Donnerstein (Eds), *Human aggression: Theories, research, and implications for social policy* (pp. 73–109). San Diego, CA: Academic Press.

Hudson, S. M. & Ward, T. (1997). Attachment, anger, and intimacy in sexual offenders. *Journal of Interpersonal Violence*, **12**, 323–339.

Hudson, S. M. & Ward, T. (2000). Relapse prevention: assessment and treatment implications. In D. R. Laws, S. M. Hudson & T. Ward (Eds), *Remaking relapse prevention with sex offenders: A sourcebook* (pp. 102–122). Newbury Park: CA: Sage.

Hudson, S. M., Ward, T. & Marshall, W. L. (1992). The abstinence violation effect in sex offenders: a reformulation. *Behaviour Research and Therapy*, **30**, 435–441.

Hudson, S. M., Ward, T. & McCormack, J. C. (1999). Offence pathways in sexual offenders. *Journal of Interpersonal Violence*, **14**, 779–798.

Ingram, R. E. & Kendall, P. C. (1986). Cognitive clinical psychology: implications of an information processing perspective. In R. E. Ingram (Ed.), *Information processing approaches to clinical psychology* (pp. 4–22). San Diego, CA: Academic Press.

Insel, T. R. & Winslow, J. T. (1991). Central administration of oxytocin modulates the infant rat's response to social isolation. *European Journal of Pharmacology*, **203**, 149–152.

Insel, T. R. & Winslow, J. T. (1998). Serotonin and neuropeptides in affiliative behaviors. *Biological Psychiatry*, **44**, 207–219.

Jamieson, S. & Marshall, W. L. (2000). Attachment styles and violence in child molesters. *Journal of Sexual Aggression*, **5**, 88–98.

Johnston, L., Ward, T. & Hudson, S. M. (1997). Mental control and the treatment of sexual offending. *Journal of Sex Research*, **34**, 121–130.

Jolliffe, D. & Farrington, D. P. (2004). Empathy and offending: a systematic review and meta-analysis. *Aggression and Violent Behavior*, **9**, 441–476.

Jorgensen, I. S. & Nafstad, H. E. (2004). Positive psychology: historical, philosophical, and epistemological perspectives. In P. A. Linley & S. Joseph (Eds), *Positive psychology in practice* (pp. 15–34). Hoboken, NJ: John Wiley & Sons.

Kafka, M. P. (1994). Sertraline pharmacotherapy for paraphilias and paraphilia-related disorders: an open trial. *Annals of Clinical Psychiatry*, **6**, 189–195.

Kafka, M. P. (1997). A monoamine hypothesis for the pathophysiology of paraphilic disorder. *Archives of Sexual Behavior*, **26**, 343–358.

Kafka, M. P. (2003). The monoamine hypothesis for the pathophysiology of paraphilic disorders. In R. Prentky, E. Janus, M. Seto & A. W. Burgess (Eds), *Understanding and managing sexually coercive behavior. Annals of the New York Academy of Sciences*, **989**, 86–94.

Kafka, M. P. & Coleman, E. (1991). Serotonin and paraphilias: the convergence of mood, impulse and compulsive behaviors. *Journal of Clinical Psychopharmacology*, **52**, 60–65.

Kafka, M. P. & Hennen, J. (2000). Psychostimulant augmentation during treatment with selective serotonin reuptake inhibitors in men with paraphilias and paraphilia-related disorders: a case series. *Journal of Clinical Psychiatry*, **61**, 664–670.

Kafka, M. P. & Prentky R. (1992). Fluoxetine treatment of nonparaphilic sexual addictions and paraphilias in men. *Journal of Clinical Psychiatry*, **53**, 351–358.

Kalmar, D. A. & Sternberg, R. J. (1988). Theory knitting: an integrative approach to theory development. *Philosophical Psychology*, **1**, 153–170.

Kalmus, E. & Beech, A.R. (2005). Forensic assessment of sexual interest: a review. *Aggression and Violent Behavior*, **10**, 193–217.

Kear-Colwell, J. & Pollack, P. (1997). Motivation or confrontation: which approach to the child sex offender? *Criminal Justice and Behavior*, **24**, 20–33.

Keenan, T. & Ward, T. (2000). A theory of mind perspective on cognitive, affective, and intimacy deficits in child sexual offenders. *Sexual Abuse: A Journal of Research and Treatment*, **12**, 49–60.

Kekes, J. (1989). *Moral tradition and individuality*. Princeton, NJ: Princeton University Press.

Kekes, J. (1990). *Facing evil*. Princeton, NJ: Princeton University Press.

Kelly, L. (1988). *Surviving sexual violence*. Cambridge: Polity Press.

Kendall, P. C. & Dobson, K. S. (1993). On the nature of cognition and its role in psychopathology. In K. S. Dobson & P. C. Kendall (Eds), *Psychopathology and cognition* (pp. 3–17). San Diego, CA: Academic Press.

Kennedy, S. M. (2001). Treatment responsivity: reducing recidivism by enhancing treatment effectiveness. In L. L. Motiuk & R. C. Serin (Eds), *Compendium 2000 on effective correctional programming* (vol. 1). Ministry of Supply and Services, Canada.

Kerem, E., Fishman, N. & Josselson, R. (2001). The experience of empathy in everyday relationships: cognitive and affective elements. *Journal of Social and Personal Relationships*, **18**, 709–729.

Keyes, C. L. M. & Haidt, J. (Eds) (2003). *Flourishing: Positive psychology and the life well-lived*. Washington, DC: American Psychological Association.

Kinsey, S. C. (1935). *Sexual behavior in the human female*. Philadelphia, PA: Saunders.

Kitayama, S. (2002). Culture and basic psychological processes—toward a system view of culture: Comment on Oyserman et al. (2002). *Psychological Bulletin*, **128**, 89–96.

Kitayama, S. & Markus, H. R. (1999). Yin and yang of the Japanese self: the cultural psychology of personality coherence. In Y. Shoda (Ed.), *The coherence of personality: Social cognitive bases of personality consistency, variability, and organization* (pp. 242–302). New York: Guilford Press.

Kitcher, P. (2001). *Science, truth, and democracy*. New York: Oxford University Press.

Knight, R. A. & Prentky, R. A. (1990). Classifying sexual offenders: the development and corroboration of taxonomic models. In W. L. Marshall, D. R. Laws & H. E. Barbaree (Eds), *Handbook of sexual assault: Issues, theories, and treatment of the offender* (pp. 23–52). New York: Plenum Press.

Knight, R. A., Rosenberg, R. & Schneider, B. A. (1985). Classification of sexual offenders: perspectives, methods, and validation. In A. W. Burgess (Ed.), *Rape and sexual assault: A research handbook* (pp. 222–293). New York: Garland.

Knopp, F. H. (1984). *Retraining adult sex offenders: Methods and models*. Orwell, VT: Safer Society Press.

Knopp, F. H., Freeman-Longo, R. & Stevenson, W. (1992). *Nationwide survey of juvenile and adult sex-offender treatment programs*. Orwell, VT: Safer Society Press.

Knutson, B., Wolkowitz, O. M., Cole, S. W., Chan, T., Moore, E. A., Johnson, R. C., Terpstra, J., Turner, R. A. & Reus, V. I. (1998). Selective alteration of personality and social behavior by serotonergic intervention. *American Journal of Psychiatry*, **155**, 373–379.

Kogan, B. M., Tkachenko, A. A., Drozdov, A. Z. et al. (1995). [Monoamine metabolism in different forms of paraphilia]. *Zhurnal nevropatologii I Pskhiatrii Imeni SS Korsakova*, **95**, 52–56 (in Russian).

Kolb, B. & Whisaw, I. Q. (1995). *Fundamentals of human neuropsychology* (4th edn). New York: W. H. Freeman & Co.

Koss, M. P. & Oros, C. J. (1982). The Sexual Experiences Survey: a research instrument investigating sexual aggression and victimisation. *Journal of Consulting and Clinical Psychology*, **50**, 455–457.

Kosson, D. S., Kelly, J. C. & White, J. W. (1998). Psychopathy-related traits predict self-reported sexual aggression among college men. *Journal of Interpersonal Violence*, **12**, 241–254.

Kraemer, G. W. (1992). A psychobiological theory of attachment. *Behavioral and Brain Sciences*, **15**, 493–541.

Kremsdorf, R. B., Holmen, M. L. & Laws, D. R. (1980). Orgasmic reconditioning without deviant imagery: a case report with a pedophile. *Behaviour Research and Therapy*, **18**, 203–207.

Kuhn, D. (1989). Children and adults as intuitive scientists. *Psychological Bulletin*, **96**, 674–689.

Kukla, A. (2001). *Methods of theoretical psychology*. Cambridge, MA: MIT Press.

Kunda, Z. (1999). *Social cognition: Making sense of people*. Cambridge, MA: MIT Press.

Kuzel, R. (1999). Management of depression. Current trends in primary care. *Postgraduate Medicine*, **185**, 179–180.

Kwon, S.-M. & Oei, T. P S. (1994). The roles of two levels of cognitions in the development, maintenance, and treatment of depression. *Clinical Psychology Review*, **14**, 331–358.

Laland, K. N. & Brown, G. R. (2002). *Sense and nonsense: Evolutionary perspectives on human behaviour*. Oxford: Oxford University Press.

Lalumiere, M. L. & Quinsey, V. L. (1994). The discriminability of rapists from non-sex-offenders using phallometric measures: a meta-analysis. *Criminal Justice and Behavior*, **21**, 150–175.

Lancaster, E. & Lumb, J. (1999). Bridging the gap: feminist theory and practice reality in work with the perpetrators of child sexual abuse. *Child and Family Social Work*, **4**, 119–129.

Lane, S. (1991). The sexual abuse cycle. In G. D. Ryan & S. L. Lane (Eds), *Juvenile sexual offending: Causes, consequences, and correction* (pp. 103–141). Lexington, MA: Lexington Books.

Lane, S. (1997). The sexual abuse cycle. In G. Ryan & S. Lane (Eds), *Juvenile sexual offending: Causes, consequences and correction* (new and rev. edn, pp. 77–121). San Francisco, CA: Jossey-Bass.

Langevin, R. (1991). A note on the problem of response set in measuring cognitive distortions. *Annals of Sex Research*, **4**, 287–292.

Langevin, R., Wright, P. & Handy, L. (1989). Characteristics of sex offenders who were sexually victimized as children. *Annals of Sex Research*, **2**, 227–253.

Lanyon, R. I. (1991). Theories of sex offending. In C. R. Hollin & K. Howells (Eds), *Clinical approaches to sex offenders and their victims* (pp. 35–54). Chichester: John Wiley & Sons.

Laws, D. R. (Ed.) (1989). *Relapse prevention with sex offenders*. New York: Guilford Press.

Laws, D. R. (1995a). A theory of relapse prevention. In W. O'Donohue & L. Krasner (Eds), *Theories of behavior therapy: Exploring behavior change* (pp. 445–473). Washington, DC: American Psychological Association.

Laws, D. R. (1995b). Verbal satiation: notes on procedure, with speculation on its mechanism of effect. *Sexual Abuse: A Journal of Research and Treatment*, **7**, 155–166.

Laws, D. R. (1996). Relapse prevention or harm reduction? *Sexual Abuse: A Journal of Research and Treatment*, **8**, 243–248.

Laws, D. R. (1999). Relapse prevention: the state of the art. *Journal of Interpersonal Violence*, **14**, 285–302.

Laws, D. R. (2003). Sexual offending is a public health problem: are we doing enough? In T. Ward, D. R. Laws & S. H. Hudson (Eds) *Sexual deviance: Issues and controversies* (pp. 297–316). Thousand Oaks, CA: Sage.

Laws, D. R., Hudson, S. M. & Ward, T. (2000a). The original model of relapse prevention with sex offenders: promises unfulfilled. In D. R. Laws, S. M. Hudson & T. Ward (Eds), *Remaking relapse prevention with sex offenders: A sourcebook* (pp. 3–24). Newbury Park: CA: Sage.

Laws, D. R., Hudson, S. M. & Ward, T. (Eds) (2000b). *Remaking relapse prevention with sex offenders: A sourcebook*. Newbury Park, CA: Sage.

Laws D. R. & Marshall, W. L. (1990). A conditioning theory of the etiology and maintenance of deviant sexual preference and behavior. In W. L. Marshall, D. R. Laws & H. E. Barbaree (Eds), *Handbook of sexual assault: Issues, theories, and treatment of the offender* (pp. 209–230). New York: Plenum Press.

Laws, D. R., Meyer, J. & Holmen, M. L. (1978). Reduction of sadistic arousal by olfactory aversion: a case study. *Behaviour Research and Therapy*, **16**, 281–285.

Laws, D. R. & O'Neil, J. A. (1981). Variations on masturbatory reconditioning. *Behavioral Psychotherapy*, **9**, 111–136.

Laws, D. R. & Osborn, C. A. (1983). How to build and operate a behavioral laboratory to evaluate and treat sexual deviance. In J. G. Greer & I. R. Stuart (Eds), *The sexual aggressor* (pp. 293–335). Toronto: Van Nostrand Reinhold.

Layton-MacKenzie, D. (2000). Evidence-based corrections: identifying what works. *Crime and Delinquency*, **46**, 457–471.

Lee, J. A. (1973). *The colors of love: An exploration of ways of loving*. Toronto: New Press.

Lee, K. (1999). *The natural and the artefactual: The implications of deep science and deep technology for environmental philosophy*. New York: Lexington Books.

Legross, J. J. (2001). Inhibitory effect of oxytocin on corticotrope function in humans, are vasopressin and oxytocin ying-yang neurohormones? *Psychoneuroendocrinology*, **26**, 649–655.

Leitenberg, H. & Henning, K. (1995). Sexual fantasy. *Psychological Bulletin*, **117**, 469–491.

Levy, M. B. & Davis, K. E. (1988). Love styles and attachment styles compared: their relations to each other and to various relationship characteristics. *Journal of Social and Personal Relationships*, **5**, 439–471.

Linley, P. A. & Joseph, S. (2004). Applied positive psychology: a new perspective for professional practice. In P. A. Linley & S. Joseph (Eds), *Positive psychology in practice* (pp. 3–12). Hoboken, NJ: John Wiley & Sons.

Lipton, D. N., McDonel, E. C. & McFall, R. M. (1987). Heterosocial perception in rapists. *Journal of Consulting and Clinical Psychology*, **55**, 17–21.

Loeber, R. (1990). Development and risk factors of juvenile antisocial behavior and delinquency. *Clinical Psychology Review*, **10**, 1–41.

Lund, C. A. (2000). Predictors of sexual recidivism: did meta-analysis clarify the role and relevance of denial? *Sexual Abuse: A Journal of Research and Treatment*, **12**, 275–287.

Lyons-Ruth, K. & Jacobvitz, D. (2003). Attachment disorganization: unresolved loss, relational violence, and lapses in behavioral and attentional strategies. In J. Cassady & P. R. Shaver (Eds), *Handbook of attachment theory: Research and clinical applications* (pp. 520–554). New York: Guilford Press.

Maes, M., De Vos, N., Van Hunsel, F., Van West, D., Westenberg, H., Cosyns, P. & Neels, H. (2001). Pedophilia is accompanied by increased plasma concentrations of catecholamines, in particular epinephrine. *Psychiatry Research*, **103**, 43–49.

Mahrer, A. R., Boulet, D. B. & Fairweather, D. R. (1994). Beyond empathy: advances in the clinical theory and methods of empathy. *Clinical Psychology Review*, **14**, 183–198.

Main, M., Kaplan, N. & Cassidy, J. (1985). Security in infancy, childhood and adulthood: a move to the level of representation. In I. Bretherton & E. Waters (Eds), *Growing points of attachment theory and research. Monographs of the Society for Research in Child Development*, **50**, 66–104.

Malamuth, N. M. (1981). Rape proclivity among males. *Journal of Social Issues*, **37**, 138–157.

Malamuth, N. M. (1983). Factors associated with rape as predictors of laboratory aggression against women. *Journal of Personality and Social Psychology*, **45**, 432–442.

Malamuth, N. M. (1986). Predictors of naturalistic sexual aggression. *Journal of Personality and Social Psychology*, **50**, 953–962.

Malamuth, N. M. (1988). Predicting laboratory aggression against female and male targets: implications for sexual aggression. *Journal of Research in Personality*, **22**, 474–495.

Malamuth, N. M. (1996). The confluence model of sexual aggression: feminist and evolutionary perspectives. In D. M. Buss & N. M. Malamuth (Eds), *Sex, power, conflict: Evolutionary and feminist perspectives* (pp. 269–295). New York: Oxford University Press.

Malamuth, N. M. & Brown, L. M. (1994). Sexually aggressive men's perceptions of women's communications: testing three explanations. *Journal of Personality and Social Psychology*, **67**, 699–712.

Malamuth, N. M., Heavey, C. L. & Linz, D. (1993). Predicting men's antisocial behavior against women: the interaction model of sexual aggression. In G. C. N. Hall, R. Hirschman, J. R. Graham & M. S. Zaragoza (Eds), *Sexual aggression: Issues in etiology, assessment, and treatment* (pp. 63–97). Washington, DC: Taylor & Francis.

Malamuth, N. M., Heavey, C. L. & Linz, D. (1996). The confluence model of sexual aggression: combining hostile masculinity and impersonal sex. *Journal of Offender Rehabilitation*, **23**, 13–37.

Malamuth, N. M. & Heilman, M. F. (1998). Evolutionary psychology and sexual aggression. In C. B. Crawford & D. L. Krebs (Eds), *Handbook of evolutionary psychology: Ideas, issues and applications* (pp. 515–542). Mahwah, NJ: Lawrence Erlbaum Associates.

Malamuth, N. M., Linz, D., Heavey, C. L., Barnes, G. & Acker, M. (1995). Using the confluence model of sexual aggression to predict men's conflict with women: a 10-year follow-up study. *Journal of Personality and Social Psychology*, **69**, 353–369.

Malamuth, N. M., Sockloskie, R. J., Koss, M. P. & Tanaka, J. S. (1991). Characteristics of aggressors against women: testing a model using a national sample of college students. *Journal of Consulting and Clinical Psychology*, **59**, 670–681.

Maletsky, B. M. (1980). Assisted covert sensitization. In D. J. Cox & R. J. Daitzman (Eds), *Exhibitionism: Description, assessment and treatment* (pp. 187–251). New York: Garland STPM Press.

Mann, R. E. (2000). Managing resistance and rebellion in relapse prevention intervention. In D. R. Laws, S. M. Hudson & T. Ward (Eds), *Remaking relapse prevention with sex offenders: A sourcebook* (pp. 187–200). Newbury Park: CA: Sage.

Mann, R. E. (2001). Implementing and managing sex offender treatment programmes. Paper presented at the conference of the International Association for Forensic Mental Health, Vancouver, BC, Canada, April.

Mann, R. E. & Beech, A. R. (2003). Cognitive distortions, schemas and implicit theories. In T. Ward, D. R. Laws & S. M. Hudson (Eds), *Sexual deviance: Issues and controversies* (pp. 135–153). Thousand Oaks, CA: Sage.

Mann, R. E., Carter, A., Creamer, M., Hart, C., Schofield, C. & Shingler, J. (2001). *Sex Offender Treatment Programme: Extended programme manual.* For further information contact Offending Behaviour Programmes Unit, Room 725, Abell House, John Islip Street, London, SW1P 4LN, UK.

Mann, R. E. & Hollin, C. R. (2001). Schemas: A model for understanding cognition in sexual offending. Paper presented at the 20th annual conference of the Association for the Treatment of Sexual Abusers, San Antonio, TX, November.

Mann, R. E. & Shingler, J. (2001). Collaborative risk assessment with sexual offenders. Paper presented at the National Organisation for the Treatment of Abusers, Cardiff, UK, September.

Mann, R. E. & Thornton, D. (1998). The evolution of a multisite sexual offender treatment program. In W. L. Marshall, Y. M. Fernandez, S. M. Hudson & T. Ward (Eds), *Sourcebook of treatment programs for sexual offenders* (pp. 47–57). New York: Plenum Press.

Mann, R. & Thornton, D. (2000). An evidence-based relapse prevention program. In D. R. Laws, S. M. Hudson & T. Ward (Eds), *Remaking relapse prevention with sex offenders: A sourcebook* (pp. 341–350). Newbury Park: CA: Sage.

Mann, R. E., Webster, S. D., Schofield, C. & Marshall, W. L. (2004). Approach versus avoidance goals in relapse prevention with sexual offenders. *Sexual Abuse: A Journal of Research and Treatment, 16,* 65–76.

Marcus, G. F. (2003). *The algebraic mind: Integrating connectionism and cognitive science.* Cambridge, MA: Bradford Books.

Marlatt, G. A. (1985a). Relapse prevention: theoretical rationale and overview of the model. In G. A. Marlatt & J. R. Gordon (Eds), *Relapse prevention: Maintenance strategies in the treatment of addictive behaviors* (pp. 3–70). New York: Guilford Press.

Marlatt, G. A. (1985b). Situational determinants of relapse and skill-training interventions. In G. A. Marlatt & J. R. Gordon (Eds), *Relapse prevention: Maintenance strategies in the treatment of addictive behaviors* (pp. 71–127). New York: Guilford Press.

Marlatt, G. A. & Gordon, J. R. (Eds) (1985). *Relapse prevention: Maintenance strategies in the treatment of addictive behaviors.* New York: Guilford Press.

Marquis, J. N. (1970). Orgasmic reconditioning: changing sexual object choice through controlling masturbation fantasies. *Journal of Behavioral Therapy and Experimental Psychiatry, 1,* 263–271.

Marshall, W. L. (1989). Invited essay: Intimacy, loneliness and sexual offenders. *Behaviour Research and Therapy, 27,* 491–503.

Marshall, W. L. (1993a). A revised approach to the treatment of men who sexually assault adult females. In G. C. N. Hall, R. Hirschman, J. R. Graham & M. S. Zaragoza (Eds), *Sexual aggression: Issues in etiology, assessment, and treatment* (pp. 143–165). Washington, DC: Taylor & Francis.

Marshall, W. L. (1993b). The role of attachments in the etiology and maintenance of sexual offending. *Sexual and Marital Therapy, 8,* 109–121.

Marshall, W. L. (1997). Pedophilia: psychopathology and theory. In D. R. Laws & W. T. O'Donahue (Eds), *Sexual deviance: Theory, assessment, and treatment* (pp. 152–174). New York: Guilford Press.

Marshall, W. L. (1999). Current status of North American assessment and treatment programs for sexual offenders. *Journal of Interpersonal Violence, 14,* 221–239.

Marshall, W. L. & Anderson, D. (2000). Do relapse prevention components enhance treatment effectiveness? In D. R. Laws, S. M. Hudson & T. Ward (Eds), *Remaking relapse prevention with sex offenders: A sourcebook* (pp. 39–55). Newbury Park: CA: Sage.

Marshall, W. L., Anderson, D. & Fernandez, Y. (1999a). *Cognitive behavioural treatment of sexual offenders.* New York: John Wiley & Sons.

Marshall, W. L. & Barbaree, H. E. (1990). An integrated theory of the etiology of sexual offending. In W. L. Marshall, D. R. Laws & H. E. Barbaree (Eds), *Handbook of sexual assault: Issues, theories, and treatment of the offender* (pp. 257–275). New York: Plenum Press.

Marshall, W. L., Barbaree, H. E. & Eccles, A. (1991). Early onset and deviant sexuality in child molesters. *Journal of Interpersonal Violence*, **6**, 323–336.

Marshall, W. L., Champagne, F., Brown, C. & Miller, S. (1997). Empathy, intimacy, loneliness, and self-esteem in nonfamilial child molesters: a brief report. *Journal of Child Sexual Abuse*, **6**, 87–98.

Marshall, W. L., Cripps, E., Anderson, D. & Cortoni, F. A. (1999b). Self-esteem and coping strategies in child molesters. *Journal of Interpersonal Violence*, **14**, 955–962.

Marshall, W. L. & Eccles, A. (1991). Issues in clinical practice with sex offenders. *Journal of Interpersonal Violence*, **6**, 68–93.

Marshall, W. L. & Fernandez, Y. M. (2000). Phallometric testing with sexual offenders: limits to its value. *Clinical Psychology Review*, **20**, 807–822.

Marshall, W. L., Fernandez, Y. M., Serran, G., Mulloy, R., Thornton, D., Mann, R. E. & Anderson, D. (2003a). Process variables in the treatment of sexual offenders: a review of the relevant literature. *Aggression and Violent Behavior*, **8**, 205–234.

Marshall, W. L. & Hambley, L. S. (1996). Intimacy and loneliness, and their relationship to rape myth acceptance and hostility towards women among rapists. *Journal of Interpersonal Violence*, **11**, 586–592.

Marshall, W. L., Hamilton, K. & Fernandez, Y. (2001). Empathy deficits and cognitive distortions in child molesters. *Sexual Abuse: A Journal of Research and Treatment*, **13**, 123–130.

Marshall, W. L., Hudson, S. M. & Hodkinson, S. (1993). The importance of attachment bonds in the development of juvenile sex offending. In H. E. Barbaree, W. L. Marshall & S. M. Hudson (Eds), *The juvenile sex offender* (pp. 164–181). New York: Guilford Press.

Marshall, W. L., Hudson, S. M., Jones, R. & Fernandez, Y. M. (1995). Empathy in sex offenders. *Clinical Psychology Review*, **15**, 99–113.

Marshall, W. L. & Laws, D. R. (2003). A brief history of behavioral and cognitive behavioral approaches to sexual offender treatment: Part 2. The modern era. *Sexual Abuse: A Journal of Research and Treatment*, **15**, 93–120.

Marshall, W. L. & Marshall, L. E. (2000). The origins of sexual offending. *Trauma, Violence, and Abuse*, **1**, 250–263.

Marshall, W. L. & McGuire, J. (2003). Effect sizes in the treatment of sexual offenders. *International Journal of Offender Therapy and Comparative Criminology*, **47**, 653–663.

Marshall, W. L. & Moulden, H. (2001). Hostility toward women and victim empathy in rapists. *Sexual Abuse: A Journal of Research and Treatment*, **13**, 249–255.

Marshall, W. L., Serran, G. A. & Cortoni, F. A. (2000). Childhood attachments, sexual abuse, and their relationship to adult coping in child molesters. *Sexual Abuse: A Journal of Research and Treatment*, **12**, 17–26.

Marshall, W. L., Serran, G., Fernandez, Y. M., Mulloy, R., Mann, R. E. & Thornton, D. (2003b). Therapist characteristics in the treatment of sexual offenders: Tentative data on their relationship with indices of behaviour change. *Journal of Sexual Aggression*, **9**, 25–30.

Martinson, R. (1974). What works? Questions and answers about prison reform. *Public Interest*, **35**, 22–54.

Maruna, S. (2001). *Making good: How ex-convicts reform and rebuild their lives*. Washington, DC: American Psychological Association.

Marziali, E. & Alexander, L. (1991). The power of the therapeutic relationship. *American Journal of Orthopsychiatry*, **61**, 383–391.

Marziano, V., Ward, T., Beech, A. R. & Pattison, P. (in press). Identification of five fundamental implicit theories underlying cognitive distortions in child abusers: a preliminary study. *Psychology, Crime and Law*.

Matthews, B. A. & Norris, F. H. (2002). When is believing 'seeing'? Hostile attribution bias as a function of self-reported aggression. *Journal of Applied Social Psychology*, **32**, 1–32.

Matthews, G. & Deary, I. J. (1998). *Personality traits*. Cambridge: Cambridge University Press.

McGregor, G. & Howells, K. (1997). Addiction models of sexual offending. In J. E. Hodge, M. McMurran & C. R. Hollin (Eds), *Addicted to crime?* (pp 107–137). Chichester: John Wiley & Sons.

McGuire, J. (1995). *What works: reducing reoffending—Guidelines from research and practice.* Chichester: John Wiley & Sons.

McGuire, J. (2000). Explanations of criminal behavior. In J. McGuire, T. Mason & A. O'Kane (Eds), *Behavior, crime and legal processes: A guide for legal practitioners* (pp. 135–159). Chichester: John Wiley & Sons.

McGuire, J. (2001). What works in correctional intervention? Evidence and practical implications. In G. A. Bernfield & D. A. Farrington (Eds), *Offender rehabilitation in practice: Implementing and evaluating effective programmes* (pp. 25–43). Chichester: John Wiley & Sons.

McGuire, J. (2002). Criminal sanctions versus psychologically-based interventions with offenders: a comparative empirical analysis. *Psychology, Crime and Law,* **8**, 183–208.

McGuire, J. & Priestly, P. (1995). Reviewing what works: past, present and future. In J. McGuire (ed.), *What works: Reducing offending—Guidelines from research and practice* (pp. 3–34). Chichester: John Wiley & Sons.

McGuire, R. J., Carlisle, J. M. & Young, B. G. (1965). Sexual deviations as conditioned behavior: a hypothesis. *Behavior Research and Therapy,* **2**, 185–190.

McLeod, M. & Saraga, E. (1988). Challenging the orthodoxy: toward a feminist theory and practice. *Feminist Review,* **28**, 16–55.

McMahon, P. M. (2000). The public health approach to the prevention of sexual violence. *Sexual Abuse: A Journal of Research and Treatment,* **12**, 27–36.

Mercy, J. A. (1999). Having new eyes: viewing child sexual abuse as a public health problem. *Sexual Abuse: A Journal of Research and Treatment,* **11**, 317–321.

Merriam-Webster's Collegiate Dictionary (2002). http://www.m-w.com/cgi-bin/dictionary. Accessed 2 July 2004.

Mihailides, S., Devilly, G. J. & Ward, T. (2004). Implicit cognitive distortions and sexual offending. *Sexual Abuse: A Journal of Research and Treatment,* **16**, 333–350.

Money, J. (1986). *Lovemaps: Clinical concepts of sexual/erotic health and pathology, paraphilia, and gender transposition in childhood, adolescence, and maturity.* Buffalo, NY: Prometheus Books.

Monti, P. M., Brown, W. A. & Corriveau, D. D. (1977). Testosterone and components of aggressive and sexual behavior in man. *American Journal of Psychiatry,* **134**, 692–694.

Moore, B. S. (1990). The origins and development of empathy. *Motivation and Emotion,* **14**, 75–80.

Morf, C. C. & Rhodewalt, F. (2001). Unraveling the paradoxes of narcissism: a dynamic self-regulatory processing model. *Psychological Inquiry,* **12**, 177–196.

Morrison, T., Erooga, M. & Beckett, R. C. (1994). *Sexual offending against children: Assessment and treatment of male abusers.* London: Routledge.

Mrazek, P. J. & Haggerty, R. J. (1994). *Reducing risks for mental disorders: Frontiers for preventive intervention.* Washington, DC: National Academy Press.

Muchimapura, S., Mason, R. & Marsden, C. A. (2003). Effect of isolation rearing on pre- and post-synaptic serotonergic function in the rat dorsal hippocampus. *Synapse,* **47**, 209–217.

Murnen, S. K., Wright, C. & Kaluzny, G. (2002). If 'boys will be boys' then girls will be victims? A meta-analytic review of the research that relates masculine ideology to sexual aggression. *Sex Roles,* **46**, 359–375.

Murphy, M. C. (2001). *Natural law and practical rationality.* New York: Cambridge University Press.

Murphy, W. D. (1990). Assessment and modification of cognitive distortions in sex offenders. In W. L. Marshall, D. R. Laws & H. E. Barbaree (Eds), *Handbook of sexual assault: Issues, theories, and treatment of the offender* (pp. 331–342). New York: Plenum Press.

Murphy, W. D. & Barbaree, H. E. (1994). *Assessments of sex offenders by measures of erectile response: Psychometric properties and decision making.* Victoria: Safer Society Press.

Neidigh, L. & Krop, H. (1992). Cognitive distortions among child sexual offenders. *Journal of Sex Education and Therapy,* **18**, 208–215.

Nelson, C. & Jackson, P. (1989). High-risk recognition: the cognitive-behavioral chain. In D. R. Laws (Ed.), *Relapse prevention with sex offenders* (pp. 167–177). New York: Guilford Press.

Nelson, E. E. & Panksepp, J. (1998). Brain substrates of infant–mother attachment, contributions of opioids, oxytocin, and norepinephrine. *Neuroscience and Biobehavioral Reviews*, **22**, 437–452.

Newton-Smith. W. (2002). *A companion to the philosophy of science*. Oxford: Blackwell.

Niaura, R. S., Rohsenow, D. J., Binkoff, J. A., Monti, P. M., Pedraza, M. & Adams, D. B. (1988). Relevance of cue reactivity to understanding smoking relapse. *Journal of Abnormal Psychology*, **97**, 133–152.

Nussbaum, M. C. (2000). *Women and human development: The capabilities approach*. New York: Cambridge University Press.

Odling-Smee, F. J., Laland, K. N. & Feldman, M. W. (2003). *Niche construction: The neglected process in evolution*. Princeton, NJ: Princeton University Press.

O'Donohue, W., Regev, L. G. & Hagstrom, A. (2000). Problems with DSM-IV diagnosis of pedophilia. *Sexual Abuse: A Journal of Research and Treatment*, **12**, 95–105.

Ogloff, J. R. O. & Davies, M. R. (2004). Advances in offender assessment and rehabilitation: contributions of the risk–needs–responsivity approach. *Psychology, Crime, and Law*, **10**, 229–242.

Overholser, C. & Beck, S. (1986). Multimethod assessment of rapists, child molesters, and three control groups on behavioural and psychological measures. *Journal of Consulting and Clinical Psychology*, **53**, 55–63.

Oxford English Dictionary (2002). http://dictionary.oed.com. Accessed 2 July 2004.

Pearson, H. J. (1990). Paraphilias, impulse control, and serotonin. *Journal of Clinical Psychopharmacology*, **10**, 233.

Pennington, B. F. (2002). *The development of psychopathology: Nature and nurture*. New York: Guilford Press.

Perilstein, R., Lipper, S. & Friedman, L. (1991). Three cases of paraphilias responsive to fluoxetine treatment. *Journal of Clinical Psychiatry*, **52**, 169–170.

Perlman, D. & Fehr, B. (1987). The development of intimate relationships. In D. Perlman & S. Duck (Eds), *Intimate relationships: Development, dynamics, and deterioration*. Newbury Park, CA: Sage.

Pithers, W. D. (1990). Relapse prevention with sexual aggressors: a method for maintaining therapeutic gains and enhancing external supervision. In W. L. Marshall, D. R. Laws & H. E. Barbaree (Eds), *Handbook of sexual assault: Issues, theories, and treatment of the offender* (pp. 343–362). New York: Plenum Press.

Pithers, W. D. (1993). Treatment of rapists: reinterpretation of early outcome data and exploratory constructs to enhance therapeutic efficacy. In G. C. N. Hall, R. Hirschman, J. R. Graham & M. S. Zaragoza (Eds), *Sexual aggression: Issues in etiology, assessment, and treatment* (pp. 167–196). Washington, DC: Taylor & Francis.

Pithers, W. D. (1994). Process evaluation of a group therapy component designed to enhance sex offenders' empathy for sexual abuse survivors. *Behaviour Research and Therapy*, **32**, 565–570.

Pithers, W. D. (1999). Empathy: definition, enhancement, and relevance to the treatment of sexual abusers. *Journal of Interpersonal Violence*, **14**, 257–284.

Pithers, W. D., Buell, M. M., Kashima, K. M., Cumming, G. F. & Beal, L. S. (1987). Precursors to sexual offenses. Paper presented at the Association for the Advancement of Behavior Therapy for Sex Abusers, Newport, OR.

Pithers, W. D., Kashima, K. M., Cumming, G. F. & Beal, L. S. (1988). Relapse prevention: a method of enhancing maintenance of change in sexual offenders. In A. Salter (Ed.), *Treating child sex offenders and victims: A practical guide* (pp. 131–170). Newbury Park: CA: Sage.

Pithers, W. D., Kashima, K. M., Cumming, G. F., Beal, L. S. & Buell, M. M. (1988). Relapse prevention of sexual aggression. *Annals of the New York Academy of Sciences*, **528**, 244–260.

Pithers, W. D., Marques, J. K., Gibat, C. C. & Marlatt, G. A. (1983). Relapse prevention with sexual aggressives: a self-control model of treatment and maintenance of change. In J. G. Greer & I. R. Stuart (Eds), *The sexual aggressor: Current perspectives on treatment* (pp. 214–239). New York: Van Nostrand Reinhold.

Polaschek, D. L. L. (1999). A descriptive model of the offence chain for rapists. PhD thesis, Victoria University of Wellington, New Zealand.

Polaschek, D. L. L. (2003a). Classification. In T. Ward, D. R. Laws & S. M. Hudson (Eds), *Sexual deviance: Issues and controversies* (pp. 154–171). Thousand Oaks, CA: Sage.

Polaschek, D. L. L. (2003b). Empathy and victim empathy. In T. Ward, D. R. Laws & S. M. Hudson (Eds), *Sexual deviance: Issues and controversies* (pp. 172–189). Thousand Oaks, CA: Sage.

Polaschek, D. L. L. (2003c). Relapse prevention, offence process models, and the treatment of sexual offenders. *Professional Psychology: Research and Practice, 34*, 361–367.

Polaschek, D. L. L. & Gannon, T. A. (2004). The implicit theories of rapists: what convicted offenders tell us. *Sexual Abuse: A Journal of Research and Treatment, 16*, 299–314.

Polaschek, D. L. L. & Hudson, S. M. (2004). Pathways to rape: preliminary examination of patterns in the offence processes of rapists and their rehabilitation implications. *Journal of Sexual Aggression, 10*, 7–20.

Polaschek, D. L. L., Hudson, S. M., Ward, T. & Siegert, R. J. (2001). Rapists' offence processes: a preliminary descriptive model. *Journal of Interpersonal Violence, 16*, 523–544.

Polaschek, D. L. L. & King, L. L. (2002). Rehabilitating rapists: reconsidering the issues. *Australian Psychologist, 37*, 215–221.

Polaschek, D. L. L. & Ward, T. (2002). The implicit theories of potential rapists: what our questionnaires tell us. *Aggression and Violent Behavior, 7*, 385–406.

Polaschek, D. L. L., Ward, T. & Gannon, T. A. (2006) Violent sex offenders. In C. Hilarski & J. Wodarski (Eds), *Comprehensive mental health practice with sex offenders and their families*. Binghamton, NY: Haworth Press.

Polaschek, D. L. L., Ward, T. & Hudson, S. M. (1997). Rape and rapists: theory and treatment. *Clinical Psychology Review, 17*, 117–144.

Pollock, N. L. & Hashmall, J. M. (1991). The excuses of child molesters. *Behavioral Sciences and the Law, 9*, 53–59.

Porter, R. J., McAllister-Wiliams, R. H., Lunn, B. S. & Young, A. H. (1998). 5-Hydroxy-tryptamine receptor function in humans is reduced by acute administration of hydrocortisone. *Psychopharmacology, 139*, 243–250.

Prentky, R. A. & Burgess, A. W. (2000). *Forensic management of sexual offenders*. New York: Kluwer Academic/Plenum Press.

Prentky, R. A., Knight, R. A. & Lee, A. F. S. (1997). Risk factors associated with recidivism among extrafamilial child molesters. *Journal of Consulting and Clinical Psychology, 65*, 141–149.

Prochaska, J. O., DiClemente, C. C. & Norcross, J. C. (1992). In search of how people change: applications to addictive behavior. *American Psychologist, 47*, 1102–1114.

Proeve, M. & Howells, K. (2002). Shame and guilt in child sexual offenders. *International Journal of Offender and Comparative Criminology, 46*, 657–667.

Proulx, J., McKibben, A. & Lusignan, R. (1996). Relationship between affective components and sexual behaviours in sexual aggressors. *Sexual Abuse: A Journal of Research and Treatment, 8*, 279–289.

Proulx, J., Perreault, C. & Ouimet, M. (1999). Pathways in the offending process of extrafamilial sexual child molesters. *Sexual Abuse: A Journal of Research and Treatment, 11*, 117–129.

Psillos, S. (1999). *Scientific realism: How science tracks truth*. London: Routledge.

Purvis, M. & Ward, T. (in press). The role of culture in understanding child sexual offending: incorporating a feminist perspective. *Aggression and Violent Behaviour*.

Quinsey, V. L. (2002). Evolutionary theory and criminal behaviour. *Legal and Criminological Psychology, 7*, 1–13.

Quinsey, V. L. (2003). The etiology of anomalous sexual preferences in men. In R. Prentky, E. Janus, M. Seto & A. W. Burgess (Eds), *Understanding and managing sexually coercive behavior. Annals of the New York Academy of Sciences*, **989**, 86–94.

Quinsey, V. L., Harris, G. T., Rice, M. E. & Cormier, C. (1998). *Violent offenders: Appraising and managing risk.* Washington, DC: American Psychological Association.

Quinsey, V. L. & Lalumiere, M. L. (1995). Evolutionary perspectives on sexual offending. *Sexual Abuse: A Journal of Research and Treatment*, **7**, 301–315.

Quinsey, V. L., Rice, M. E. & Harris, G. T. (1995). Actuarial prediction of sexual recidivism. *Journal of Interpersonal Violence*, **10**, 85–103.

Rada, R. T., Laws, D. R. & Kellner, R. (1976). Plasma testosterone levels in the rapist. *Psychosomatic Medicine*, **40**, 265–277.

Rademacher, D. J., Anderson, A. P. & Steinpreis R. E. (2002). Acute effects of amperozide and paroxetine on social cohesion in male conspecifics. *Brain Research Bulletin*, **58**, 187–191.

Raleigh, M. J., McGuire, M. T. Brammer, G. L., Pollack, D. B. & Yuwiler, A. (1991). Serotonergic mechanisms promote dominance acquisition in adult male vervet monkeys. *Brain Research*, **559**, 181–190.

Rapp, C. A. (1998). *The strengths model: Case management with people suffering from severe and persistent mental illness.* New York: Oxford University Press.

Rempel, J. & Serafini, T. (1995). Factors influencing the activities that people experience as sexually arousing: a theoretical model. *Canadian Journal of Human Sexuality*, **4**, 3–14.

Rescher, N. (1990). *Human interests: Reflections on philosophical anthropology.* Stanford, CA: Stanford University Press.

Rex, S., Lieb, R., Bottoms, A. & Wilson, L. (2003). Accrediting offender programmes: a process-based evaluation of the Joint Prison/Probation Services Accreditation Panel. Home Office Research Study, 273. London: Home Office Research, Development and Statistics Directorate, Communications and Development Unit. Available at: www.homeoffice.gov.uk/rds/pdfs2/hors273.pdf.

Rice, M. E., Harris, G. T. & Cormier, C. A. (1992). Evaluation of a maximum security therapeutic community for psychopaths and other mentally disordered offenders. *Law and Human Behavior*, **16**, 399–412.

Robinson, D. (1995). The impact of cognitive skills training on post-release recidivism among Canadian federal offenders (R-41, August). Ottawa: Correctional Research and Development, Correctional Service of Canada.

Rosenberg, H. (1993). Prediction of controlled drinking by alcoholics and problem drinkers. *Psychological Bulletin*, **113**, 129–139.

Roys, D. T. (1997). Empirical and theoretical considerations of empathy in sex offenders. *International Journal of Offender Therapy and Comparative Criminology*, **41**, 53–64.

Runi, C. & Fava, G. A. (2004). Clinical applications of well-being therapy. In P. A. Linley & S. Joseph (Eds), *Positive psychology in practice* (pp. 371–387). Hoboken, NJ: John Wiley & Sons.

Rush, F. (1980). *The best kept secret.* New York: McGraw-Hill.

Russell, D. E. H. (1986). *The secret trauma: Incest in the lives of girls and women.* New York: Basic Books.

Russell, D. E. H. (1999). *The secret trauma: Incest in the lives of girls and women.* New York: Basic Books.

Saarni, C. (1999). *The development of emotional competence.* New York: Guilford Press.

Sacre, G. (1995). Analysis of the role of tutor on the National SOTP: a competency based approach. MSc thesis, Birkbeck College, University of London, UK.

Salter, A. C. (1988). *Treating child sex offenders and victims: A practical guide.* Thousand Oaks, CA: Sage.

Salter, A. C. (1995). *Transforming trauma: A guide to understanding and treating adult survivors of child sexual abuse.* Thousand Oaks, CA: Sage.

Sanday, P. R. (2003). Rape-free versus rape-prone: how culture makes a difference. In C. B. Travis (Ed.), *Evolution, gender and rape* (pp. 337–361). Cambridge, MA: MIT Press.

Sapolsky, R. M. (1997). Stress and glucocorticoid response. *Science*, **275**, 1662–1663.

Saunders, D. G. (1991). Procedures for adjusting self-reports of violence for social desirability bias. *Journal of Interpersonal Violence*, **6**, 336–344.

Saunders, W. A. & Allsop, S. (1987). Relapse: a psychological perspective. *British Journal of Addiction*, **82**, 417–429.

Sawle, G. A. & Kear-Colwell, J. (2001). Adult attachment and pedophilia: a developmental perspective. *International Journal of Offender Therapy and Comparative Criminology*, **45**, 32–50.

Schewe, P. A. & O'Donohue, W. (1996). Rape prevention with high-risk males: short-term outcome of two interventions. *Archives of Sexual Behavior*, **25**, 455–471.

Schlenker, B. R., Pontari, B. A. & Christopher, A. N. (2001). Excuses and character: personal and social implications of excuses. *Personality and Social Psychology Review*, **5**, 15–32.

Schwartz, B. K. (1995). Theories of sexual offenses. In B. K. Schwartz & H. R. Cellini (Eds), *The sex offender: Corrections, treatment and legal practice* (pp. 1–32). Kingston, NJ: Civic Research Institute.

Schwartz, B. K. & Canfield, G. M. S. (1998). Treating the 'sexually dangerous person': The Massachusetts Treatment Center. In W. L. Marshall, Y. M. Fernandez, S. M. Hudson & T. Ward (Eds), *Sourcebook of treatment programs for sexual offenders* (pp. 235–245). New York: Plenum Press.

Scully, D. (1990). *Understanding sexual violence: A study of convicted rapists*. Boston, MA: Unwin Hyman.

Seligman, M. E. P. (1970). On the generality of the laws of learning. *Psychological Review*, **77**, 406–418.

Seligman, M. E. P. & Csikszentmihalyi, M. (2000). Positive psychology: an introduction. *American Psychologist*, **55**, 5–14.

Seligman, M. E. P. & Peterson, C. (2003). Positive clinical psychology. In L. G. Aspinwall & U. M. Staudinger (Eds), *A psychology of human strengths: Fundamental questions and future directions for a positive psychology* (pp. 305–317). Washington, DC: American Psychological Association.

Serin, R. & Kennedy, S. (1997). Treatment readiness and responsivity: contributing to effective correctional programming. Research report, Correctional Services Canada.

Serin, R. C., Mailloux, D. L. & Malcolm, P. B. (2001). Psychopathy, deviant sexual arousal, and recidivism among sexual offenders. *Journal of Interpersonal Violence*, **16**, 234–246.

Serran, G., Fernandez, Y., Marshall, W. L. & Mann, R. E. (2003). Process issues in treatment: application to sexual offender programs. *Professional Psychology: Research and Practice*, **34**, 368–374.

Siegert, R. J., McPherson, C. M. & Dean, S. (in press). Theory development and a science of rehabilitation. *Health and Disability*.

Simons, D., Wurtele, S. K. & Heil, P. (2002). Childhood victimization and lack of empathy as predictors of sexual offending against women and children. *Journal of Interpersonal Violence*, **17**, 1291–1307.

Sjogren, B., Widstrom, A. M., Edman, G. & Uvnas-Moberg, K. (2000). Changes in personality pattern during the first pregnancy and lactation. *Journal of Psychosomatic Obstetrics and Gynecology*, **21**, 31–38.

Skinner, B. F. (1976). *About behaviorism*. New York: Vintage Books.

Smallbone, S. W. (2005). Social and psychological factors in the development of delinquency and sexual deviance. In H. E. Barbaree & W. L. Marshall (Eds), *The juvenile sex offender* (2nd edn). New York: Guilford Press.

Smallbone, S. W. & Dadds, M. R. (1998). Childhood attachment and adult attachment in incarcerated adult male sex offenders. *Journal of Interpersonal Violence*, **13**, 555–573.

Smallbone, S. W. & Dadds, M. R. (2000). Attachment and coercive behavior. *Sexual Abuse: Journal of Research and Treatment*, **12**, 3–15.

Smallbone, S. W. & McCabe, B. A. (2003). Childhood attachment, childhood sexual abuse, and onset of masturbation among adult sexual offenders. *Sexual Abuse: A Journal of Research and Treatment*, **51**, 1–10.

Smallbone, S. W., Wheaton, J. & Hourigan, D. (2003). Trait empathy and criminal versatility in sexual offenders. *Sexual Abuse: A Journal of Research and Treatment*, **15**, 49–60.

Smallbone, S. & Wortley, R. K. (2000). *Child sexual abuse in Queensland: Offender characteristics and modus operandi.* Brisbane: Queensland Crime Commission.

Smallbone, S. W. & Wortley, R. K. (2004a). Criminal diversity and paraphilic interests among adult males convicted of sexual offenses against children. *International Journal of Offender and Comparative Criminology*, **48**, 175–188.

Smallbone, S. W. & Wortley, R. K. (2004b). Onset, persistence, and versatility of offending among adult males convicted of sexual offenses against children. *Sexual Abuse: A Journal of Research and Treatment*, **16**, 285–298.

Smith, P. & Waterman, M. (2004). Processing bias for sexual material: the emotional Stroop and sex offenders. *Sexual Abuse: A Journal of Research and Treatment*, **16**, 163–172.

Snyder, C. R. & Higgins. R. L. (1988). Excuses: their effective role in the negotiation of reality. *Psychological Bulletin*, **104**, 23–35.

Snyder, C. R., Higgins, R. L. & Stuky, R. J. (1983). *Excuses: Masquerades in search of grace.* New York: John Wiley & Sons.

Soothhill, K., Francis, B., Sanderson, B. & Ackerley, E. (2000). Sex offenders: specialists, generalists—or both? *British Journal of Criminology*, **40**, 56–67.

Sperling, M. B. & Berman, W. H. (Eds) (1994). *Attachment in adults: Clinical and developmental perspectives.* New York: Guilford Press.

Stein, D. J., Hollander, E., Anthony, D. T., Schneier, F. R., Fallon, B. A., Liebowitz, M. R. & Klein, D. F. (1992). Serotonergic medications for sexual obsessions, sexual addictions, and paraphilias. *Journal of Clinical Psychiatry*, **53**, 267–271.

Steiner, F (2002). *Human ecology: Following nature's lead.* Washington, DC: Island Press.

Sterelny, K. (2003). *Thought in a hostile world: The evolution of human cognition.* Oxford: Blackwell.

Stoner, S. A. & George, W. H. (2000). Relapse prevention and harm reduction: areas of overlap. In D. R. Laws, S. M. Hudson & T. Ward (Eds), *Remaking relapse prevention with sex offenders: A sourcebook* (pp. 56–75). Newbury Park: CA: Sage.

Strauss, A. & Corbin, J. (1990). *Basics of qualitative research: Grounded theory procedures and techniques.* Newbury Park, CA: Sage.

Strongman, K. T. (1996). The *psychology of emotion: Theories of emotion in perspective* (4th edn). Chichester: John Wiley & Sons.

Sullivan, J. & Beech, A. R. (in press). Professional perpetrators. In C. Hilarski & J. Wodarski: (Eds), *Comprehensive mental health practice with sex offenders and their families* (Chapter 5). Binghamton, NY: Haworth Press.

Sutherland, E. (1939). *Principles of criminology* (3rd edn). Philadelphia, PA: Lippincott.

Symons, D. (1979). *The evolution of human sexuality.* New York: Oxford University Press.

Tangney, J. P. (1991). Moral affect: the good, the bad, and the ugly. *Journal of Personality and Social Psychology*, **61**, 598–607.

Tangney, J. P. (1995). Shame and guilt in interpersonal relationships. In J. P. Tangney & K. W. Fischer (Eds), *Self-conscious emotions: Shame, guilt, embarrassment, and pride* (pp. 114–139). New York: Guilford Press.

Tangney, J. P. (1996). Conceptual and methodological issues in the assessment of shame and guilt. *Behaviour Research and Therapy*, **34**, 741–754.

Tangney, J. P., Burggraf, S. A. & Wagner, P. E. (1995). Shame-proneness, guilt-proneness, and psychological symptoms. In J. P. Tangney & K. W. Fischer (Eds), *Self-conscious emotions: Shame, guilt, embarrassment, and pride* (pp. 343–367). New York: Guilford Press.

Tangney, J. P. & Dearing. R. L. (2002). *Shame and guilt.* New York: Guilford Press.

Teasdale, J. D. (1983). Negative thinking in depression: cause, effect or reciprocal relationship? *Advances in Behaviour, Research and Therapy*, **5**, 3–5.

Teasdale, J. D. (1988). Cognitive vulnerability to depression. *Cognition and Emotion*, **2**, 247–274.

Thompson, R. A. (1994). Emotional regulation: a theme in search of definition. In N. A. Fox (Ed.), *The development of emotion regulation: Biological and behavioral consideration* (pp. 25–52). Monographs of the Society for Research in Child Development, vol. 59, serial no. 240.

Thomson, G. (1987). *Needs.* London: Routledge & Kegan Paul.

Thornhill, R. & Palmer, C. T. (2000). *A natural history of rape: Biological bases of sexual coercion.* Boston, MA: MIT Press.

Thornhill, R. & Thornhill, N. W. (1992). The evolutionary psychology of men's coercive sexuality. *Behavioral and Brain Sciences,* **15**, 363–421.

Thornton, D. (2000) Structured risk assessment. Sinclair Seminars Conference on Sex Offender Re-Offence Risk Prediction in Madison, Wisconsin. Videotape available from sinclairseminars.com.

Thornton, D. (2002). Constructing and testing a framework for dynamic risk assessment. *Sexual Abuse: A Journal of Research and Treatment,* **14**, 139–154.

Thornton, D. & Beech, A. R. (2002). Integrating statistical and psychological factors through the structured risk assessment model. Poster presented at the 21st Association for the Treatment of Sexual Abusers Conference, Montreal, Canada, October.

Thornton, D, Beech, A. & Marshall, W. L. (2004). Pretreatment self-esteem and post-treatment sexual recidivism. *International Journal of Offender Therapy and Comparative Criminology,* **48**, 587–599.

Thornton, D., Mann, R., Webster, S., Blud, L., Travers, R, Friendship, C. & Erikson, M. (2003) Distinguishing and combining risks for sexual and violent recidivism. In R. Prentky, E. Janus, M. Seto & A. W. Burgess (Eds), *Understanding and managing sexually coercive behavior. Annals of the New York Academy of Sciences,* **989**, 225–235.

Thornton, D. & Shingler, J. (2001). Impact of schema level work on sexual offenders' cognitive distortions. Paper presented at the 20th annual conference of the Association for the Treatment of Sexual Abusers, San Antonio, TX, November.

Thornton, S., Todd, B. & Thornton, D. (1996). Empathy and recognition of abuse. *Legal and Criminological Psychology,* **1**, 147–153.

Toderov, A. & Bargh, J. A. (2002). Automatic sources of aggression. *Aggression and Violent Behavior,* **7**, 53–68.

Tomasello, M. (1999). *The cultural origins of human cognition.* Cambridge, MA: Harvard University Press.

Tooby, J. & Cosmides, L. (1992). The psychological foundations of culture. In J. H. Barkow, L. Cosmides & J. Tooby (Eds), *The adapted mind: Evolutionary psychology and the generation of culture* (pp. 19–36). New York: Oxford University Press.

Van Ijzendoorn, M. H., Schuengel, C. & Bakermans-Kranenberg, M. J. (1999). Disorganized attachment in early childhood: meta-analysis of precursors, concomitants, and sequelae. *Development and Psychopathology,* **11**, 255–249.

Waldby, C., Clancy, A., Emetchi, J. & Summerfield, C. (1989). Theoretical perspectives on father–daughter incest. In E. Driver & A. Droisen (Eds), *Child sexual abuse: Feminist perspectives* (pp. 88–106). Basingstoke: Macmillan.

Ward, T. (2000). Sexual offenders' cognitive distortions as implicit theories. *Aggression and Violent Behavior,* **5**, 491–507.

Ward, T. (2001). Hall and Hirschman's quadripartite model of child sexual abuse: a critique. *Psychology, Crime and Law,* **7**, 291–307.

Ward, T. (2002). Marshall and Barbaree's integrated theory of child sexual abuse: a critique. *Psychology, Crime and Law,* **8**, 209–228.

Ward, T. & Beech, A. R. (2004). The etiology of risk: a preliminary model. *Sexual Abuse: A Journal of Research and Treatment,* **16**, 271–284.

Ward, T. & Beech, A. R. (in press). An integrated theory of sexual offending. *Aggression and Violent Behavior.*

Ward, T., Bickley, J., Webster, S. D., Fisher, D., Beech, A. & Eldridge, H. (2004a). *The self-regulation model of the offense and relapse process: A manual,* vol. 1: *Assessment.* Victoria, BC: Pacific Psychological Assessment Corporation.

Ward, T., Day, A., Howells, K. & Birgden, A. (2004b). The multifactor offender readiness model. *Aggression and Violent Behavior,* **9**, 645–673.

Ward, T. & Hudson, S. M. (1996). Relapse prevention: a critical analysis. *Sexual Abuse: A Journal of Research and Treatment,* **8**, 177–200.

Ward, T. & Hudson, S. M. (1998a). The construction and development of theory in the sexual offending area: a meta-theoretical framework. *Sexual Abuse: A Journal of Research and Treatment, 10*, 47–63.

Ward, T. & Hudson, S. M. (1998b). A model of the relapse process in sexual offenders. *Journal of Interpersonal Violence, 13*, 700–725.

Ward, T. & Hudson, S. M. (2000a). A self-regulation model of relapse prevention. In D. R. Laws, S. M. Hudson & T. Ward (Eds), *Remaking relapse prevention with sex offenders: A sourcebook* (pp. 79–101). Newbury Park: CA: Sage.

Ward, T. & Hudson, S. M. (2000b). Sexual offenders' implicit planning: a conceptual model. *Sexual Abuse: A Journal of Research and Treatment, 12*, 189–202.

Ward, T. & Hudson, S. M. (2001). A critique of Finkelhor's precondition model of child sexual abuse. *Psychology, Crime and Law, 7*, 333–350.

Ward, T., Hudson, S. M., Johnston, L. & Marshall, W. L. (1997). Cognitive distortions in sex offenders: an integrative review. *Clinical Psychology Review, 17*, 479–507.

Ward, T., Hudson, S. M. & Keenan, T. (1998). A self-regulation model of the sexual offence process. *Sexual Abuse: A Journal of Research and Treatment, 10*, 141–157.

Ward, T., Hudson, S. M. & Marshall, W. L. (1994). The abstinence violation effect in child molesters. *Behaviour Research and Therapy, 32*, 431–437.

Ward, T., Hudson, S. M. & Marshall, W. L. (1995a). Cognitive distortions and affective deficits in sex offenders: a cognitive deconstructionist interpretation. *Sexual Abuse: Research and Treatment, 7*, 67–83.

Ward, T., Hudson, S. M. & Marshall, W. L. (1996). Attachment style in sex offenders: a preliminary study. *Journal of Sex Research, 33*, 17–26.

Ward, T., Hudson, S. M., Marshall, W. L. & Siegert, R. (1995b). Attachment style and intimacy deficits in sex offenders: a theoretical framework. *Sexual Abuse: A Journal of Research and Treatment, 7*, 317–335.

Ward, T., Hudson, S. & McCormack, J. (1997). Attachment style, intimacy deficits and sexual offending. In H. R. Cellini & B. Schwartz (Eds), *The sexual offender: Correctional treatment and legal practice* (pp. 1–14). Kingston, NJ: Civic Research Institute.

Ward, T., Hudson, S. M. & Siegert, R. J. (1995c). A critical comment on Pithers' relapse prevention model. *Sexual Abuse: A Journal of Research and Treatment, 7*, 167–175.

Ward, T. & Keenan, T. (1999). Child molesters' implicit theories. *Journal of Interpersonal Violence, 14*, 821–838.

Ward, T., Keenan, T. & Hudson, S. M. (2000). Understanding cognitive, affective, and intimacy deficits in sex offenders: a developmental perspective. *Aggression and Violent Behavior, 5*, 41–62.

Ward, T., Louden, K., Hudson, S. M. & Marshall, W. L. (1995d). A descriptive model of the offence chain for child molesters. *Journal of Interpersonal Violence, 10*, 452–472.

Ward, T. & Siegert, R. J. (2002a). Rape and evolutionary psychology: a critique of Thornhill and Palmer's theory. *Aggression and Violent Behavior, 7*, 145–168.

Ward, T. & Siegert, R. J. (2002b). Toward a comprehensive theory of child sexual abuse: a theory knitting perspective. *Psychology, Crime and Law, 9*, 319–351.

Ward, T. & Stewart, C. A. (2003a). Criminogenic needs and human needs: a theoretical model. *Psychological, Crime and Law, 9*, 125–143.

Ward, T. & Stewart, C. A. (2003b). The treatment of sex offenders: risk management and good lives. *Professional Psychology: Research and Practice, 34*, 353–360.

Ward, T. & Stewart, C. A. (2003c). The relationship between human needs and criminogenic needs. *Psychology, Crime and Law, 9*, 219–224.

Ward, T., Vertue, F. M. & Haig, B. D. (1999). Abductive reasoning and clinical assessment in practice. *Behavior Change, 16*, 49–63.

Watkins, B. & Bentovim, A. (1992). The sexual abuse of male children and adolescents: a review of current research. *Journal of Child Psychology and Psychiatry, 33*, 197–248.

Webster, S. D. (in press). Pathways to sexual offence recidivism following treatment: an examination of the Ward and Hudson self-regulation model of relapse. *Journal of Interpersonal Violence.*

Weeks, R. & Widom, C. (1998). Self-reports of early childhood victimization among incarcerated adult male felons. *Journal of Interpersonal Violence*, **13**, 346–361.

Wegner, D. M. (1994). Ironic processes of mental control. *Psychological Bulletin*, **101**, 34–52.

Weiner, B. (1972). *Theories of motivation: From mechanism to cognition*. Chicago, IL: Rand McNally.

Weiner, B. (1986). *An attributional theory of motivation and emotion*. New York: Springer-Verlag.

Weiss, R. S. (1974). The provisions of social relationships. In Z. Rubin (Ed.), *Doing unto others*. Englewood Cliffs, NJ: Prentice Hall.

Weiss, R. S. (1982). Attachment in adult life. In C. M. Parkes & J. Stevenson-Hinde (Eds), *The place of attachment in human behavior*. New York: Basic Books.

Wheeler, J. G., George, W. H. & Dahl, B. J. (2002). Sexual aggressive college males: empathy as a moderator in the 'confluence model' of sexual aggression. *Personality and Individual Differences*, **33**, 759–775.

Wheeler, J. G., George, W. H. & Marlatt, G. A. (in press). Relapse prevention for sexual offenders: considerations for the 'abstinence violation effect'. *Sexual Abuse: Journal of Research and Treatment*.

Wiggins, D. (1991). *Needs, values and truth*. Oxford: Blackwell.

Williams, J. M. G., Watts, F. N., MacLeod, C. & Mathews, A. (1997). *Cognitive psychology and emotional disorders* (2nd edn). Chichester: John Wiley & Sons.

Wilson, E. G. (1975). *Sociobiology: The new synthesis*. Cambridge, MA: Harvard University Press.

Winslow, J. T. & Insel, T. R. (1993). Effects of central vasopressin administration to infant rats. *European Journal of Pharmacology*, **233**, 101–107.

Witkiewitz, K. & Marlatt, G. A. (2004). Relapse prevention for alcohol and drug problems: That was Zen, this is Tao. *American Psychologist*, **59**, 224–235.

Wolf, S. C. (1984). A multifactor model of deviant sexuality. Paper presented at the Third International Conference on Victimology, Lisbon, Portugal.

Wolf, S. C. (1985). A multi-factor model of deviant sexuality. *Victimology*, **10**, 359–374.

Wood, J. T. (1994). *Gendered lives: Communication, gender, and culture*. Belmont, CA: Wadsworth.

Wortley, R. & Smallbone, S. (Eds) (in press). *Situational prevention and child sex offending*. New Brunswick, NJ: Rutgers University Press.

Wright, R. C. & Schneider, S. L. (1997). Deviant sexual fantasies as motivated self-deception. In B. K. Schwartz & H. R. Cellini (Eds), *The sex offender: new insights, treatment innovations and legal developments* (pp. 8.1–8.14). Kingston, NJ: Civic Research Institute.

Wyre, R. (1989). Working with the paedophile. In M. Farrell (Ed.), *Understanding the paedophile* (pp. 17–23). London: ISTD/The Portman Clinic.

Yalom, I. D. (1985). *The theory and practice of group psychotherapy* (3rd edn). New York: Basic Books.

Yates, P. M., Kingston, D. & Hall, K. (2003). Pathways to sexual offending: Validity of Ward and Hudson's (1998) self-regulation model and relationship to static and dynamic risk among treated sexual offenders. Paper presented at the 22nd Association for the Treatment of Sexual Abusers Annual Conference, St Louis, MO, October.

Yllö, K. & Finkelhor, D. (1985). Marital rape. In A. W. Burgess (Ed.), *Rape and sexual assault: A research handbook* (pp. 146–158). New York: Garland.

Yochelson, S. & Samenow, S. E. (1977). *The criminal personality, vol. II: The change process*. Northvale, NJ: Jason Aronson.

Young, J. E., Klosko, M. E. & Weishaar, M. E. (2003). *Schema therapy: A practitioner's guide*. New York: Guilford Press.

Zhong, P. Y. & Ciaranello, R. D. (1995). Transcriptional regulation of hippocampal 5-HT1a receptors by corticosteroid hormones. *Molecular Brain Research*, **29**, 23–34.

INDEX

Lightning Source UK Ltd.
Milton Keynes UK
UKOW07f0224130515

9 780470 094815